A WORK OF HOSPITALITY

A WORK OF
hospitality

the Open Door reader
1982–2002

Peter R. Gathje, editor

The Open Door Community ❖ Atlanta

To request additional copies of *A Work of Hospitality*,
phone, fax, or send an order in writing to:

The Open Door Community
910 Ponce de Leon Avenue, N.E.
Atlanta, GA 30306
Phone: (404) 874-9652
Fax: (404) 874-7964
www.opendoorcommunity.org

09 08 07 06 05 04 03 02   5 4 3 2 1

Generous grants toward publication of this volume were provided by Social Justice
Ministries of the National Ministries Division of the Presbyterian Church (USA) and by
the John & Wilhemina D. Harland Foundation of Atlanta. The volume was produced for
the Open Door Community by JZ Editing & Publishing, Decatur, GA; John C. Turnbull,
owner. Printing by Thomson-Shore, Inc., 7300 West Joy Road, Dexter, MI 48130.

To people on the streets and in the prisons in whom we meet the wounded and suffering Christ, and to the past and present members of the Open Door Community from whom I have received so many gifts of the spirit that empower resistance to sin and death and lead to resurrection. In particular to Ed Loring for his prophetic passion; Murphy Davis for her revolutionary insight and music; Ralph Dukes for teaching me about the blues, baseball, and redemption; Ed Potts for seeing the world in a different way; Willie London for quiet welcome; Dick Rustay for his unfailing enthusiasm; Gladys Rustay for her patient tenacity; and Elizabeth Dede for her courage

Contents

Part III
Hospitality to the Imprisoned

Part IV
The Sacraments of Hospitality

Part V
Saints and Martyrs

Part VI
The Theology of Hospitality

When the Human One comes in glory, and all the angels with him, then he will sit on the throne of his glory. All the nations will be gathered before him, and he will separate people one from another as a shepherd separates the sheep from the goats, and he will put the sheep at his right hand and the goats at the left. Then the ruler will say to those at his right hand, "Come, you that are blessed by my Creator, inherit the kingdom prepared for you from the foundation of the world; for I was hungry and you gave me food, I was thirsty and you gave me something to drink, I was a stranger and you welcomed me, I was naked and you gave me clothing, I was sick and you took care of me, I was in prison and you visited me." Then the righteous will answer him, "Lord, when was it that we saw you hungry and gave you food, or thirsty and gave you something to drink? And when was it that we saw you a stranger and welcomed you, or naked and gave you clothing? And when was it that we saw you sick or in prison and visited you?" And the ruler will answer them, "Truly I tell you, just as you did it to one of the least of these who are members of my family, you did it to me."

—Matthew 25:31–40

Introduction, *by Peter R. Gathje*

The Open Door Community has, almost from its beginning, published *Hospitality* as a means to share, with a broader audience, its life with the homeless and imprisoned. The spirituality, ethics, and history of the Open Door Community can be gleaned from the newspaper's pages, as the many contributors have expressed what it means to meet and serve Christ in the guise of persons who are homeless, imprisoned, or on death row. In writing my history of the Open Door Community, *Christ Comes in the Stranger's Guise, Hospitality* was an invaluable resource for tracing the development of the Open Door from four people who started a night shelter at Atlanta's Clifton Presbyterian Church in late 1979 to the present community downtown at 910 Ponce de Leon Avenue. The present group numbers some twenty people and draws upon hundreds of volunteers from the Atlanta area and beyond to help with its many ministries with homeless and imprisoned persons.

As the Open Door celebrates its twentieth anniversary at 910 Ponce de Leon, it is fitting that we listen to the community's reflections on its life and work from the pages of *Hospitality*. Such reflections reveal the vitality and community tensions and offer several different views from within the Open Door. A large number of people from the community, and those from the extended Open Door Community, have written for *Hospitality*. This great variety made selecting articles for this book a rather difficult task. No doubt someone's favorite article will not be found, while others will wonder, "Why is *this* included?" It is a fair question to ask. Here I provide a rationale for the articles selected.

I selected articles that would best represent what I believe to be the Open Door's central faith convictions and its core social-political analysis, which is rooted in that faith. Thus, even in the more historical articles in the first part, one can begin to discern the convictions and analysis that led to the formation of the Open Door and that have continued to sustain its life. As one reads further, a certain repetition in theme becomes evident. This repetition is intended and testifies to the continuity in the community's spirituality, ethical vision, and

I

activism. This emphasis on the heart of the community has also meant that three authors are represented more than others: Murphy Davis, Ed Loring, and Elizabeth Dede. For those who know the history of the community this is no surprise, given that Murphy and Ed were two of the founders and Elizabeth has been a long-term member and partner.

I also selected articles that most directly expressed the Open Door's central ministries. The Open Door has focused on work with homeless people and with people in prison, in particular those on death row. In these ministries the community has sought to meet immediate needs, while also addressing the structural injustices that shape homelessness, the prison system, and the death penalty. The struggle for justice certainly includes other areas, and articles in *Hospitality* have discussed Latin and Central America, the Georgia-based School of the Americas, nuclear weapons, the Persian Gulf War, and, more recently, the war in Kosovo and the war on terrorism. Such articles are not included, however, in order to keep the focus on the work and issues that have been most clearly characteristic of the Open Door.

Finally, I selected articles that I thought would give readers a sense of the passion and vibrancy of the Open Door as it is grounded in a life of faith practiced in solidarity with "the least of these." This is perhaps the most subjective criterion. I hope that what is included is a fair representation of how the Open Door Community, in its life and in its newspaper, has kept solidarity with those crucified in our streets and prisons, while also sharing the liberating fullness of human life pledged by God in the resurrection of Jesus.

The articles are organized into six parts. In Part One, "Settling In," selections address the history of the Open Door and the theological and social-political convictions that undergird its work. Some of these articles also address the sources the Open Door has drawn upon in shaping its life. The most important source is the Bible, but the Open Door has also drawn from a rich tradition of socially transformative Christianity that includes the Social Gospel, liberation theology, the Catholic Worker movement, and the civil rights movement—especially as that was shaped by Martin Luther King Jr. and the Black Church. In drawing from these traditions, the Open Door stands within an emphasis on strong and countercultural Christian community as the context for shaping persons for nonviolent resistance to and transformation of a sinful and unjust society. In the afterword, I address more systematically the relation between the Open Door and the convictions and practices of the Catholic Worker movement.

Especially important in Part One is the interplay among the Open Door's convictions, the structures of community life (leadership, worship, daily organization), and its work with homeless and imprisoned persons. Creative tension among these three elements is evident in all of these selections. The Open Door's theology is formed within the crucible of life with the poor and from the community's conviction, drawn in particular from Matthew 25:31–46, that in meeting the poor we meet Christ. Being the Body of Christ in the world enables the Open Door to live simply, to offer service to the poor, and to engage in efforts for justice for the poor. At the same time, Christ comes to the Open Door as the homeless person, as the person in prison and on death row. How to exist both as the Body of Christ and to receive Christ in the poor is a vital source of tension and hope at the Open Door.

Part Two, "Hospitality to the Homeless," analyzes homelessness from the perspective of the Open Door's theology, which begins with the conviction that Christ speaks to us in the homeless. Understanding homelessness as a Christian thus requires listening—learning from the homeless what it means to be homeless. This listening and learning is done with biblical ears attuned to God's Word, expressed by those who suffer injustice. God's Word as spoken through the experience of those on the streets challenges conventional economic and political thought. The economics of scarcity and the politics of fear—the foundations for injustice and violence—confront the economics of abundant generosity and the politics of mutual responsibility grounded in God's creative and redemptive work in the world. Biblical economics and politics replace hostility toward homeless persons with hospitality. As several articles make clear, one of the most visible manifestations of this struggle has been the Open Door's commitment to public space which is truly public. Attempts by worldly forces to exclude certain persons from community are manifest in battles over the presence of homeless people in parks and other public facilities. In approaching these battles, the Open Door reveals its commitment to a biblical vision of community.

In Part Three, "Hospitality to the Imprisoned," the community's theological analysis again shapes its ministry and its efforts to confront injustices in the criminal justice system—primarily the death penalty. The starting point, as with the homeless, is listening and learning from those in prison and on death row, and from their families. Those who speak from behind prison bars, like those on the streets, incarnate Christ. The warrant for that statement is the biblical text at the heart of the Open Door, Matthew 25:31–46, in which Jesus identifies with the poor, the stranger, and the imprisoned, and makes treatment of these persons the standard for entrance into heaven. These words are hard to hear regarding the homeless poor, but the difficulty increases with people in prison, because they have usually done clear harm to the human family. Articles in this section approach that difficulty with a biblical faith shaped by God's faithfulness to sinful humanity—a faithfulness that never despairs of redemption, and that, through Jesus' cross and resurrection, has definitively overturned the death penalty. This faith also recognizes what we often deny—that our sinfulness, manifested in a system that despises the poor, contributes mightily to the evils that lead people into criminal life. The Open Door's willingness to learn from and to stand in faith with those in prison and on death row makes clear the cost of discipleship and the grace needed to embrace that cost.

Part Four, "The Sacraments of Hospitality," brings further focus to the Open Door's embrace of Christ, who comes to us as the homeless and imprisoned. Those on the streets and in prison are a sacrament of Christ, and in the celebration of the Church's sacraments the community's commitment to receive and serve the wounded and crucified Christ is renewed. The Open Door's worship reflects both traditional Christian practices such as Eucharist and baptism, along with new forms of worship such as foot washing, and liturgies of solidarity and protest conducted in the streets and parks of Atlanta. The public implications of worship are made clear as the Open Door continually connects its worship with its work among the homeless and imprisoned. This is evident, for example, in how the Open Door spends Holy Week on the streets, experiencing the crucifixion of Christ in the homeless. Likewise, in the fall, the Open Door again goes to the streets during its Festival of Shelters, which parallels the Jewish Festival of Booths, recalling the Israelites' desert wanderings before entering the Promised Land.

One of the important themes that emerges in this section on worship is the need to hold together liturgy and justice. As the prophets and Jesus proclaimed, worship that does not shape us in the practice of justice is idolatry. The God of the prophets and of Jesus tells us that God desires mercy, not sacrifice, and that the Sabbath is for human liberation, not human enslavement (Matt. 12:1–14; Mark 2:23–3:6). Worship as practiced by the Open Door offers the grace and challenge to enter into life with the poor, which is life with Christ. This worship stands opposed to therapeutic worship that reduces faith to individual affirmation, or worship as mere entertainment, which offers an escape from moral responsibility. The succor in the Open Door's worship enables service. The respite from the day's tasks that worship creates is for a renewed spirit in the justice struggle.

Part Five, "Saints and Martyrs," contains stories of the community's guides. In other sections, too, there are references to those who have shaped the community's life—see, for example, Murphy Davis's reflections on Jerome Bowden in "Dorothy Day: The Only Solution Is Love," or Elizabeth Dede's article, "Jeannette Lewis: A Debt Which I Can Never Repay"—but in this section there is more fleshing out of certain individuals' importance. The stories here show the complexity of the persons the Open Door Community has embraced and been embraced by over the years. The mystery and dignity of each person and the challenge to reach out to those from different circumstances are prominent themes.

That some of the persons are the community's saints will be readily apparent. But that some of the stories are about martyrs may be less evident. A *mar-*

tyr is a witness; the word has usually referred to persons who have died in witness to a particular cause or ideology. How is a person who dies on the streets or who is executed by the state a martyr? To what are they witnessing? In part they provide a negative witness; they witness against what ought not to be. The death of a homeless person is a witness against our society's inhumanity. For a person to die on the streets of the wealthiest nation in world history gives witness to that nation's spiritual poverty. It gives witness to our refusal to recognize as brother or sister those made vulnerable by our economic system and by their own faults and foibles. Those executed are likewise martyred by our refusal to recognize our responsibility for compassion rather than abandonment. The martyrs' stories in this section concern failure that is both personal and structural. As martyrs' stories ought to do, these stories leave us with the call to conversion, which is to work for structural transformation.

Part Six, "The Theology of Hospitality," contains theological reflections directed outward. These selections focus less on homelessness, the death penalty, or the community's own life, and more on trends in the Church and American society that intersect with the Open Door's life and work. Several articles consider what it means to be "church"; others engage in biblical interpretation; others reflect theologically on American life. This broader view offers a good place to end, for it calls readers to consider how the Open Door's life and work should intersect our lives and work. For some that intersection may mean coming to the Open Door as a resident volunteer, or eventually becoming a partner. For others it may mean becoming (or continuing) as a weekly or monthly volunteer, preparing breakfast, serving soup, or driving families to prison for visits. The intersection could also mean joining the community's acts of solidarity and protest, spending twenty-four hours on the streets, making vigil against the death penalty, or disrupting—in some creative and joyful way—business as usual at the state Capitol or at city council meetings. The intersection may come through worship, either in person at the Open Door or through prayer in one's own community. For some the intersection may mean joining or continuing work at home that is similar to the Open Door's. Whatever form the intersection takes, most important is that we respond to these articles' call for recognizing and listening to Christ as he speaks in the homeless, the imprisoned, and those on death row, and as he calls us to solidarity, service, and the struggle for justice. If we do that, we will be welcomed by Christ as we have welcomed him, and we shall one day hear, "Come, you that are blessed by my Father, inherit the Kingdom prepared for you from the foundation of the world" (Matt. 25:34).

Part I

SETTLING IN

You know, peoples was not made to dog around. Peoples was made to be respected.

—Jerome Bowden

Five Years at 910, *by Murphy Davis*

JANUARY 1987

Looking back, I realize that it was a matter of only a few months; but in the fall of 1981 the wait to move into our new home at 910 Ponce de Leon Avenue seemed interminable. When we spent the first night in the rambling fifty-six-room building, some of the former occupants were still there.

We were just that anxious to get going. We had two years of work with homeless people under our belts, and five years of working with prisoners. So moved was our little community by the overwhelming need, that we had made the painful decision to leave Clifton Presbyterian Church, where Ed and I had been pastors for six years and Open Door cofounders Rob and Carolyn Johnson were members, so that we could broaden our ministry with the homeless.

The old building was ideal. Formerly an apartment building, it felt more like a home than any of the abandoned churches or schoolhouses we had considered. And home was what we sought. Hospitality was the work that called us, and we wanted a place that could become home to us, our children, and the homeless women and men who would come for food, shelter, showers, and a friendly welcome. And home it has been. It has been home for a few of us for five years. For others, one night; for still others, several months or several years.

We moved into 910 on December 16, 1981, with a sense of urgency. It was already good and cold, and Atlanta had precious little shelter available to the homeless. We wanted our new space to be ready as quickly as possible. We set about to get the old building cleaned up.

If we could have seen very far ahead, we never would have had the courage to begin. But God in her mercy never shows us everything at once; and so it is our task just to work along day to day.

It was a major excavation. We battled roaches and grime. When my parents arrived for a Christmas visit, I met them at the back door with a jug of Clorox and a mop. My greeting, "Make yourself at home," had never rolled off my tongue with such specific intent. But make themselves at home they did—with sleeves rolled up and scrub brushes in hand. When they left after Christmas, that guest room was scrubbed clean, liberally doused with boric acid (for the roaches), and made ready to welcome the guests we brought in the next day.

Thereafter we welcomed each guest with the understanding that cleaning a room was part of the deal. Antonio Guillerme, a cheerful Cuban man, was our first guest. His English was so broken that we understood little of what he said, but he scurried all over the house with a mop, doing heroic duty in the war on grime.

Our official opening was Christmas Day. Patrick Burke and Gary Kaupmann, two Atlanta-area chefs, had volunteered to cook an elegant Christmas dinner for one hundred—a touch of class. The turkey and dressing were the finest; the hollandaise on the broccoli was perfect; the pumpkin pie had real whipped cream . . . what a day!

One by one the rooms filled up. We struggled, day by day, to create some level of order and an atmosphere of trust.

On the last Saturday of January (1982) we opened our first regular soup kitchen. Friends from Jubilee Partners came to help, bringing some of the Cambodian refugees who were then living at Jubilee. As our tired and hungry friends filed through the door, the Cambodians stood aghast. "Who are these people?" they asked in shock. "They are poor! Surely they cannot be Americans!"

In April we added Sunday to our regular soup-kitchen schedule. In May we opened seven days a week. Since then, our kitchen has never closed, except for Thanksgiving Day, when lots of other churches open to serve a meal.

In January 1983, we added the Butler Street Breakfast. Ed Loring and Mary Himburg had been spending time in labor pools and were moved by watching so many people leave for a day of hard manual labor on an empty stomach. They started taking coffee and grits to the city labor pool on Coca Cola Place. But a city bureaucrat quickly declared that city property was no place to eat breakfast. We were ushered out—only to meet a friendly welcome from Thomas Brown, the new pastor of the Butler Street CME Church. For four years now the grits, eggs, coffee, and oranges have traveled every morning from the Open Door kitchen to the basement of Butler Street CME. There the breakfast is served by Open Door and Butler Street folks to growing lines of homeless men, women, and children.

The requests for showers came early. So the hot water has run for these five years as a balm to many a dirty, aching body. How different people look as they leave with a clean body in fresh, clean clothes.

Sharing life with the homeless quickly led us to a greater awareness and deeper caring for their needs. We began to move to the streets for liturgy and action. Each fall, we've needed to mark the coming of cold weather and the certainty of death and disease for numbers of the homeless. In the spring, as most of the free shelters have closed, we've needed to join the homeless in an affirmation that shelter is not a seasonal need. It is impossible for us simply to serve soup and provide shelter without crying out that homelessness is a gross injustice and an indictment of a society that has so much and yet will not make available to all persons the basic necessities of food and housing.

All along we have affirmed that our work with the homeless and with prisoners is the same work. The people we meet in prison and those on the streets are people for whom there simply is no room. The common denominators are poverty, unemployment, hunger, poor schooling . . . Our friends on the streets are condemned to death by neglect and exposure as surely as our friends on death row are condemned to death by judicial death penalty.

Not long after we began our work on Ponce de Leon, a soup-kitchen volunteer angrily took me aside and said, "You know, you could get a lot more support for your soup kitchen if you'd drop your work against the death penalty." She was probably right. The death penalty pushes us to the limit. It calls into question our need to judge others and to define the "good" people and the "bad" people. It raises the question whether there is a hope and redemptive power entirely beyond our control.

But the big questions aside, we have stuck with our friends on death row for the same reason we hang in with the homeless: because they have become our friends. I've often heard volunteers say after coming to the soup kitchen, "When I met these folks face to face and shared food with them, they didn't seem like strangers to me anymore. I became less afraid." On death row it's been the same. The frightening thing to learn about people guilty of murder is not how different they are, but how much they are like the rest of us. When we learn that truth, we face the hard task of meeting the murderer within ourselves. We face the need that each of us has for mercy and forgiveness, a new start and fresh hope, reconciliation and healing.

But forgiveness and reconciliation and healing are not on the political agenda of our nation these days. So we have stood with our friends as they have been prepared as ritual sacrifices for our corporate anger and frustration. They have been killed, one by one, in heartless, premeditated acts of violence. Smitty, Ivan, Alpha, Roosevelt, Van, John, Jerome: our friends. Human beings created in the image of God. Through them we have been gifted to know the life-giving power of God's forgiveness. The dignity and heart-breaking strength of each one has made me wonder how the rest of us could ever dare to consider giving up the struggle.

To think back over these five years is to take in an overwhelming series of events: sometimes exhilarating, sometimes numbing. There has been an endless procession of people—from the streets, in prison and jail cells, from churches, from Brazil, Australia, Germany, Central America, Ireland, South Africa, Sri Lanka . . . people from everywhere. People coming with great needs, and people bringing great gifts.

The years have seen a series of failures: failure to love enough; failure to really address the needs of the homeless; failure to stop the execution of our friends in particular and the death penalty in general; failure to meet the expectations and needs of those who have come seeking community and a shared life and work; failure to admit our mistakes: failure to pray enough; failure to be kind, joyful . . .

The years have been an experiment in love. An experiment in learning how to love God, our suffering neighbors, each other. An experiment in weaning ourselves from the cultural addictions so that we might seek a life of freedom and resistance to death and oppression.

But when all is said and done, here we are after five years at 910: weak, vulnerable, and precarious. We still wonder how we'll get the work done next week and where the money will come from to pay the bills. It often seems that we spend more time burying the dead, saying goodbye, and dealing with tragedy than celebrating victories. How strange it seems to affirm that this is precisely how God has gifted us. If we had somehow become a successful ministry, we surely would not have moved into such close familial ties with the poor.

We have had to be reminded again and again that any love shown through our ministry is simply because of God's grace. When put to the test, we fail as often as not. Again and again we must lay aside our selfishness and brokenness, and seek healing. The world says this is foolish. To accept vulnerability is stupid; to confess and seek forgiveness is wimpish. Certainly, left to our own devices, we would not accept this path. But it is precisely our vulnerability, our precariousness, our inability to see ahead, our instability and insecurity that keep us close to the poor. And it is among the poor that God comes to us in a distressing disguise.

The only ones who stay here are those of us who have to stay. As Jeff Dietrich once said of the Catholic Worker, this is a place that no one would stay unless they were very poor, or very insane, or very committed to the values of poverty and service. (I often think that some combination of poverty, insanity, and commitment is helpful.)

It's been five years at 910. If we could have seen ahead we never would have had the courage to begin. But how good it is. Life here is full of grace: laughter, singing, children playing, lots of food, people talking, crying, working together. The demons that hurt and divide by race, sex, and class are challenged by our shared life and love for each other. And we learn, day by day, to forgive and accept forgiveness. It is wonderful to get a taste of God's reign.

It's not at all like I thought it would be. But it is very good. And we are grateful.

The Open Door Community:
A Common Life, Vision, Hope, *by Ed Loring*

A U G U S T   1 9 8 5

On a Friday night in July, visitors Allen and Yvonne King stood in the hot kitchen taking orders from Sye. A homeless, middle-aged black man, unemployed since half of his body was severely burned by french-fry grease in a short-order restaurant, Sye kept the Kings busy until midnight cooking a birthday cake for one of the partners at the Open Door. Allen and Yvonne did more than bake cake during their visit to the Open Door Community. They helped to feed one hundred people at the soup kitchen in addition to aiding forty homeless and haggard men and women who came for a shower and a change of clothes.

The Open Door is a residential Christian community which ministers to the homeless and hungry on the streets of Atlanta and to prisoners across the state of Georgia. The roots of the Open Door Community stretch back to a small inner-city neighborhood congregation, the Clifton Presbyterian Church. I was pastor, and Murphy Davis, my wife, who is also a Presbyterian minister, directed the Georgia office of Southern Prison Ministry from the church. The Clifton congregation numbered thirty members, mostly young adults who came together seeking a disciplined and active Christian life. Living in the midst of the poor, and in a city with thousands of hungry and homeless people, the church decided to open its doors to thirty homeless men for shelter from the mean streets and bitter nights. Every night since November 1, 1979, Clifton Presbyterian Church has fed and sheltered homeless men in the sanctuary.

The need for shelter discerned by the Clifton congregation was, and continues to be, much greater than any one church could resolve. In 1979 there were approximately 1,500 homeless people in Atlanta; today there are 5,000. By the winter of 1980–81 several churches had followed the Clifton example and began offering hospitality, food, a blanket, and a foam mat to the poorest of the poor. A movement was now underway to shelter the homeless. During the winter there are now thirty churches, representing most denominations, feeding and sheltering 1,500 men, women, boys, and girls.

During the second year of Night Hospitality Ministry at Clifton Church, Rob and Carolyn Johnson joined Murphy Davis and me to form the Open Door Community. We felt a new vocation emerge from our experience of serving God in the midst of the poor. We wanted to live with those whom we sheltered and we wanted to form an alternative style of Christian commitment—a residential community.

After a long and prayerful search for a building, the Open Door and Atlanta Presbytery purchased an old fifty-six-room apartment building from the Atlanta

Union Mission. Located at 910 Ponce de Leon Avenue, the new community began feeding the hungry on Christmas Day 1981, when one hundred homeless folks came for dinner. Since that day more than four hundred thousand meals have been prepared in the kitchen.

Community and service are the two foci of common life at the Open Door. Wanting to live a life of discipleship based upon the Bible, the members are molded by the experience of the early church as found in Acts of the Apostles 2 and 4. Partners are those members who covenant to give their lives and resources to the community. Resident volunteers are persons who join the community for six months to two years for experience and education as they follow different paths on their life pilgrimages.

Faithfulness to the scriptures and resistance to the greed and materialism of contemporary society demand a lifestyle of simplicity and compassion. To that end, each member of the community receives basic needs plus a small weekly stipend. The Open Door is supported by contributions from churches and individuals. Although no government money is received, gifts are tax-deductible. No member has an income-producing job.

Common life, the shared life in community, is more than work and rest. Each week we worship, study the Bible, plan advocacy for the powerless poor, and play together. Each month a speaker joins us for an analysis of a current social issue and every sixth week we go to the nearby monastery for a retreat. Life together is often difficult, but the joy and purposefulness are resources deeper than our complaints. In addition to the partners, novices, and resident volunteers, twenty-six street people live at the Open Door. Most residents are unemployable due to their physical and/or mental disabilities. Many have spent years on the streets, have served in the armed forces, are black, have been displaced by either agricultural technology on the farms or urban renewal in the cities. The majority of the homeless are neglected by churches, government, and business. They have nowhere to go. Although families, teenage boys and girls, and single men and women constitute the homeless population, the vast majority are single men.

Let me introduce you to a couple of our friends. Tim is thirty years old; he looks fifty. He is blind in one eye, crippled in his right leg. Tim is white. After his father ran off some years ago, economic necessity put Tim on his own. He worked day labor and developed a terrible alcohol problem. After ten years on the streets he was reduced to a beggar who often fell victim to beatings and abuse. A year and a half ago Tim came to live at the Open Door. Slowly his life is being pieced back together. He has not taken a drink since entering the community, and he works each day in the soup kitchen. Tim is a stronger person, often joyful and happy, but the streets still hold the specter of joblessness, alcoholism, and violence. It is a simple truism that haunts the lives of many homeless: on the streets a drink of liquor is easier to find than a slice of bread.

James's story is quite different. A sixty-two-year-old black man, James came to the Open Door two years ago, exhausted from a fruitless search for a regular job. Shortly after his arrival, Murphy realized that she and I had been visiting his son on death row. Through Murphy's ministry, father and son reestablished a loving and supportive relationship. On James's sixty-second birthday, about a year ago, he became eligible for Social Security benefits. A lawyer friend of the Open Door worked hard to get James an efficiency apartment in public housing. James now has his own home, but he returns to the community five mornings a week as a volunteer. He often answers the phone and front door.

Each person who enters the community has a story of failure and triumph. Some folks, like James, experience victories in the battles for survival and for a life of dignity. Others with whom we have lived return to the streets and freeze to death or die a slow and desolate death from privation.

Volunteers from the Atlanta area also constitute a part of the community. Some people come monthly, others come weekly to serve soup, prepare supper, sort clothes, or bandage hurts. One hundred fifty volunteers work at the Open Door each month.

Servanthood among, with, and on behalf of the poor is the purpose of the Open Door Community. The biblical understanding of justice informs the mission and shapes the service performed in the name of Jesus Christ:

> The kind of fasting I want is this:
> Remove the chains of oppression and the
> yoke of injustice, and let the oppressed
> go free. Share your food with the
> hungry and open your homes to the
> homeless poor. Give clothes to those
> who have nothing to wear, and do not
> refuse to help your own relatives.
>
> (Isa. 58:6–7 TEV)

The day begins early at 910 Ponce de Leon Avenue. At 6:00 A.M., one of the partners or resident volunteers begins to cook the Butler Street Breakfast. By 7:30 A.M., the meal is ready to be put into the van and taken to an exceedingly impoverished area of the inner city. In the basement of the Butler Street CME Church, between 135 and 200 people, mostly black men, line up for the coffee, eggs, grits, a piece of fruit, and a vitamin C tablet.

At 9:00 A.M., as the van loaded with empty pots, pans, and dirty dishes returns to the Open Door, other community members are starting to open the clothes closet and shower room. Five days each week up to forty men and women who have slept in abandoned buildings or vacant lots come in for a change of clothes and a hot shower. Simple bodily hygiene is most difficult for those with little access to toilets, running water, clean clothes, and showers. Often we must turn people away, for there is not enough time and room for all.

As sheltering the homeless is the focus of our ministry at night, feeding the hungry is the heart of our day. Seven days a week the soup kitchen is filled with folk. Preparation begins at 9:30 A.M. (as the Butler Street pots are washed!) and the tables are full between 11:00 A.M. and 12 noon. Ten thousand meals per month are served from the kitchen.

Various ministries supporting the homeless are carried out as well. Ann Connor, a nurse who teaches at Emory University, comes each Wednesday to bathe and to care for injured feet. Dr. Jerry Hobson fits used glasses on those with dimming eyesight. And on the first Saturday of every month, Eric Kocher organizes several lawyers in a legal clinic for the poor.

The poor are not only locked out of the mainstream: they are also locked into prisons. Jesus proclaimed that God "has sent me to proclaim liberty to the captives and recovery of sight to the blind, to set free the oppressed" (Luke 4:18b). Wanting to be partners with God in this majestic view of human liberation, community members join with Murphy Davis, who provides the leadership for the Open Door's prison ministry. Death-row prisoners are the focus. However, transportation for families and loved ones, support groups, and visitation with prisoners throughout the state are important aspects of the ministry.

Opposition to the death penalty is the primary political focus of the prison ministry. Through speaking engagements, legislative lobbying, Bible study, and public protests, the Open Door attempts to change human hearts and human law toward life-sustaining structures of justice. "Why do we kill people who kill people to show that killing people is wrong?" is a question often asked.

Advocacy cannot be separated from direct personal involvement, which is the highest form of love. Murphy spends a day each week on death row near Jackson, Georgia. Her ministry of visitation includes personal counseling and support, and responding to prisoners' needs. For instance, because everyone on death row is poor, and the state provides no legal counsel for court appeals, Murphy must locate lawyers who will, without financial remuneration, represent the convicts.

Burying the dead is one of the works of mercy. Three of the men executed in Georgia during the past year and a half have left their tortured bodies to the Open Door. As a community of faith we have gathered in love and hope to bury our dead brothers.

Death tries to come more secretly into Georgia in another way that the Open Door resists. For years, trains carrying nuclear materials have passed through our state on their way from a munitions factory in Amarillo, Texas, toward the Charleston, South Carolina, naval base. Thanks to a national network of people along the "Nuclear Train" route, we in Atlanta have been able to witness for life several times a year as Death comes near. Like Germans who saw trains carrying innocent people toward death in concentration camps, we are witnessing concentrated death carried toward innocent people of the future. Our belief in life will not let us keep silent.

Living within the struggle of life and death, we, like all of God's children, are constantly in need of healing. Donna Pickens, a deeply gifted artist, leads us to discover ourselves and to explore the inner relationships between art and spirituality. There is now emerging a new aspect of our vision, as homeless guests and community members mold clay and paint pictures that depict the love of life in the context of the quest for justice.

John Pickens is also bringing a broader shape to the life and work of the Open Door. Beginning as a lawyer on the twenty-first floor of a very tall building, he now guides us in our Legal Defense Ministry. John walks the streets, visits the jails, serves soup in the dining hall, and, out of personal relationships with the homeless, he represents them in court. Liberty to the captives and rights for the widow and orphans are directions of John's discipleship.

The Open Door is home. It is a small portion of the Body of Jesus Christ. We have nothing and we are nothing, except for Jesus. You, our readers, are a constant source of hope and strength. Please visit us and pray for us and join in the works of mercy, that love may reign.

The Open Door Community: Purposes and Aims, *by Ed Loring*

N O V E M B E R   1 9 9 1

PURPOSES

The Open Door Community is a tiny part of the wounded body of Jesus Christ. We grew out of the womb of Clifton Presbyterian Church and, from our move ten years ago to 910 Ponce de Leon Avenue, we have been a partnership ministry with Atlanta Presbytery. We are, like the Body itself, ecumenical, diverse, a bit wild, and deeply loved by most of you. We thank you.

The Open Door Community is a residential Christian community of thirty folk living in a sixty-room home. We are formerly homeless, ex-convicts, and middle-class Christian resisters to mainline America: that culture which crushes the prophets for profits and calls the most powerful hunger for possessions ever unleashed upon God's good creation "The American Way Of Life."

But Jesus Christ is alive, well, and Lord! He resides in the flesh and feet of the homeless poor, not far from where you are sitting right now. Our crucified Lord lives caged in the state prisons with girls and boys, women and men. He lives, the one who out of the manger in a barn (and out of the parking garage behind the Hilton Hotel) suffers the little children to come unto him. But the too-busy disciples clamor against him and keep their eyes on the clock and their hearts on the weekend. (They would rather be sailing than walking on the water.)

Our childlike, donkey-riding leader gathers early each morning before us at 910 and Butler Street and everywhere with the poor, ill-clad, hungry folk that yuppies hate and fear: citizens of this great land and subjects of the Kingdom of God.

Yes, in the cries of the oppressed we discern the groan of God whose fierce and fiery womblike love calls us at the Open Door into a life of community in solidarity with the poor; into joy and dance with each other; into the political dominions to root out the powers and principalities that encourage some to eat too much while famine stalks the ghettos and streets of every town and city in this nation which is, according to Mr. George Gallup, God-fearing. Political and economic hunger encourage some to enlarge their homes and to panel their attics in cedar while others shake and shiver on the streets, or turn, twist, and tumble from the blasting fury of a sun whose air is unconditioned.

So, in the name of the Lord Jesus Christ, by the power of the Holy Ghost, to the glory of Yahweh whom we know as mother-love, father-love—we at the Open Door Community live, serve, worship, play, and die together. And because of you, our faithful friends, we are thankful folk. We thank you for helping to make our lives possible, and we hope that you will come and visit us.

AIMS

Now that I have shared the purposes of our little community, let me tell you of our doings, our aims.

First, we live together. If ever there were a mark of the church which needs to be joined to the classical notion of preaching and sacraments, it is diversity. Ironically, we are given the gift of unity in the midst of diversity. We meet our God in otherness. We at the Open Door Community are old and young; Black, Brown, and White; men, women, and children; strong and weak; highly educated and illiterate; gay and straight; mentally ill and supposedly sane; married and single; short and tall, fat and skinny; joyful and sad—all the joys and agonies that this fool flesh is heir to! In the midst of our sin and brokenness, our blessing and curses, our light and shadows, each of us and all of us are claimed by the grace of God, who calls us into a family of faith to live in this household of hope. Wow! What a miracle we are at Ponce de Leon!

Second, we work together. We serve up to ten thousand meals each month to famine-stricken folk who are starving on our streets. We provide, by God's love and your support, more than three hundred showers and changes of clothes every thirty days. Most of the fifteen thousand homeless men and women, boys and girls who are dying on the streets of Atlanta, Decatur, Sandy Springs, East Point, College Park, Stone Mountain, Tucker, and Roswell have no access to showers, shoes, toilets, razors, hot water, towels, or toilet paper. Because of your love and compassion we have now completed tiling and renovating our public bathroom, where many come every day to pee for free with dignity.

We visit in the prisons and build caring friendships with folks under the sentence of death. Each month we provide transportation for one hundred people to visit loved ones in the most racist of American institutions: prisons (houses for the homeless; jobs for the African American male). Let us all remain faithful to this fundamental fact of faith: "I was in prison and you visited me."

Third, we struggle not against flesh and blood but with the powers and principalities in high places. Dan Berrigan is correct. He says that the church is the church when the people of God are at worship and in conflict with the state. Often we follow our Prince of Peace into the streets to demonstrate against policies and practices that reward the greedy and maim the marginalized. There are powers willing to pay for a professional basketball franchise, but that scream, "No taxes!" when it comes to building homes for families living in station wagons. They would build more prisons rather than bring restitution and reconciliation among the perpetrators of crime and their victims. Loudly cries our Lord against such vile and hideous thievery. So with the gift of boldness straight out of the Book of Acts we present our bodies as a living sacrifice and cry, "No! No! No!" to death-dealing economic structures and political folly.

Most often we fail. The shadow of Christ's cross falls into the streets, and every twenty-four hours there are more homeless people (why?), more unemployed people (why?), more people in prison (why?), and more men and women under the sentence of death (why?). We must, oh people of faith and justice, stand together in the Lord's love to structure the mission of the church into the lives of the poor and onto the side of the oppressed.

Finally, and most important, we worship together. Every day of every year we gather together. Every day of every year we gather to worship our God. We are grateful folk, so we are people of doxology. We are trustful folk, so we depend entirely on donations from friends and churches for our support. We are broken folk, so we ask our God for healing and salvation. We are selfish, blind, and judgmental folk, so we live by the new covenant, which is the forgiveness of sins wrought by the cross of Christ. We are servant folk, so we wash one another's feet. We are Christian folk, so hungry and hurt we come again and again to the Lord's table for God's broken body and shed blood. From this feeding, this Eucharist, which is our daily bread, we are given the love and the power to live together, to serve together, and to worship together.

Thank you for making our lives and ministry possible. Please pray for us. Please support us.

Loving the Poor and Embracing the Radical Gospel: Matthew 25 as a Liberation Spirituality,
by Murphy Davis

OCTOBER 1994

There are many different ways to serve and work with homeless people, prisoners, victims of violence, and other marginalized people; and there are a great variety of motivations that bring various of us to the work. Issues in the city have pushed us once again to think through the basics: what Dorothy Day and Peter Maurin of the Catholic Worker movement called "Aims and Purposes." What is at the root of our call and vocation that simply cannot, must not, be compromised?

Matthew 25:31–46 is at the foundation of all we hope to do and be in the Open Door Community. In 1977, when we started Southern Prison Ministry in Georgia, we looked to the Committee of Southern Churchfolk who, in the persons of Will Campbell and Tony Dunbar, had started the ministry a few years earlier as a simple, unpretentious effort to respond to the gospel mandate to visit the prisoner. It was promised, after all, that in doing that we would meet Jesus Christ. Everything else would flow from that.

A few years later, when it was time for the Open Door to be born, we looked to the Catholic Worker tradition. There again, the founders insisted that it was in the sharing of bread with the poor that our own eyes would be opened to see God in our midst. Christ comes in the stranger's guise. This is the tradition we were called to follow.

The passage from Matthew's Gospel is Jesus' story to his followers shortly before his execution. He tells of final judgment: a time when all the people and nations of the world will stand before him and be divided into two groups. To one group he will speak words of welcome and blessing: "For I was hungry and you fed me, thirsty and you gave me a drink. I was a stranger and you received me in your homes, naked and you clothed me; I was sick and you took care of me, in prison and you visited me." When the blessed ones were surprised, he said, "Inasmuch as you have done it for one of the least important of these sisters or brothers of mine, you have done it for me." The other group, who had neither fed, welcomed, clothed, nor visited the marginalized, had already chosen the sentence of isolation and apartness that the judge now pronounced on them.

In other words, Jesus said to his followers, "The time is coming when I won't be physically with you anymore. You need to know how to follow me, know my suffering, comfort me, and be with me. I live with you and among you in the presence of the poor and the outsider. Serve them and you are serving me. Befriend them and you will be friends of God. Shut them out, harass them, deny them what they need to sustain their lives, and you deny God." Simply put, Jesus was teaching the disciples that God is present among us in the poor and suffering ones: the sickest, hungriest, smelliest, most neglected, most condemned. How we treat them is a direct indication of our love of God.

It is a simple teaching, really. When I was in seminary, I heard the story told of Shirley Guthrie, our Reformed-theology professor, who was speaking in a church somewhere. A church member asked him what this passage really meant. Shirley said (no doubt tapping his pipe and shrugging his shoulders), "Seems to me it says 'if you don't feed the hungry you'll go to hell.'" Simple enough, indeed.

Generally we read Matthew 25 as a mandate for action. But it is about more than action. It is a description of a spirituality: a liberation spirituality that teaches us about the complete transformation, conversion, change of orientation that scripture calls for. As the Latin American liberation theologians teach us, a spirituality that is not concrete is not real. Our spirituality is a manner of life that gives unity to our thought, prayer, and action. It has to do with a way of seeing, being, understanding, and interpreting. It has everything in the world to do with the language we use to describe life and reality, the choices we make, and what and whom we value.

Our spirituality is how we hammer out the meaning of our encounter with God in the particularity of our present context: here, now, in this place, with these people, in the midst of this struggle. Whatever our circumstances, God comes to us in the poor and oppressed and invites us to open up our lives. When we do share, welcome, and invite, we find ourselves in the glad company of a loving God. We are no longer alone. We are not abandoned. When we reject the invitation, we choose the path of isolation. We cut ourselves off. We might still have the food or whatever we didn't share clutched in our hand, but when we look up, there is no one to share the meal with us. We are alone. This is essential to the nature of a liberation spirituality: always we are invited *in,* invited into community. How we respond to the presence of God among us in the most unsightly, the uncomely, the least, defines for us a quality of life. This spirituality involves an invitation to a complete change of orientation.

Sometime around 1980, Ed and I went to Emory University to hear Professor Jürgen Moltmann lecture. It was before we got to know him as a friend, but the event deeply shaped us. He was articulating, I think, a Matthew 25 spirituality. The poor, said Moltmann, are subjects of the Kingdom of God. Subjects! It took some time to appropriate it. Almost always, the poor in the ministry of the church are objects. We the church members and leaders define the need, we plan, we get the resources, we serve, we decide when we're burned out, when to quit, when to move on to another project or to set up another program. They are, after all, *our* programs, so naturally we are the subjects.

Not so, said Moltmann. The poor are the subjects of the Kingdom of God. In the poor, the oppressed, the stranger, we encounter the crucified Christ. Jesus Christ is the subject of our worship and our discipleship. And if we understand that we meet Jesus Christ in the poor, then the poor are transformed in our eyes, and we see that they are the subjects of our love, not the objects of our mercy or action.

Objects can be moved around, manipulated, acted upon, withdrawn from, seen as an optional activity, and related to at will—at our will, on our time. Subjects, on the other hand, have priority. The needs and agenda of a subject in our lives set the agenda for us. In a subject-subject relationship (or an I-Thou relationship, as Martin Buber wrote), the pain that the other suffers, or the rejection they experience today, probably will give definition to how I spend my day tomorrow. In a subject-object relationship, I have the option of responding, but no one is likely to think it strange if I choose not to. Our friend Don Wester calls this "drawbridge ministry": you let the bridge down, go out, and "do" ministry; then you come back in and pull the bridge up tight so nobody can get to you except on your turf and your terms.

There are three implications of a liberation spirituality that we must explore further: first, the need to listen; second, the need to be very careful with our language; and finally, liberation spirituality as resistance.

People of faith who come from privileged backgrounds need to be very quiet and listen to scripture and to the poor. If God really is present to us in the presence of the poor, then we need to be quiet and hear what she has to say. This is not to say that everything that poor people say is the word of God. The task is, rather, as Gustavo Gutiérrez says, to listen to the poor with an ear well-trained by the scriptures. What we can hear is God's lively Spirit, which transforms us, changes us, and leads us into deeper solidarity with the wretched of the earth.

Second, a liberation spirituality demands that we speak differently: we need to speak the language of love; we need to speak with a tongue well-trained by the scriptures. Modern technocratic culture has its own language, which demands precision and conformity. It is the language of management, and its function is, at least in part, to distance people. It makes people objects. Those who come to us for help are called "clients," and we are "service providers" or "case managers." We should interview them for a "needs assessment" so that we can better plan and manage their "rehabilitation." (Once Randy Loney heard me describing these language patterns, and he said, "You know, it sounds like a sort of urban renewal of the soul.") If we decide to cut back on the services provided we call it "downsizing." If somebody gets fired, they are "terminated," and on and on (ad nauseam). One of the worst examples of this I ever saw was in a *Creative Loafing* article several years ago on Grady Hospital. It quoted from a report from Emory Medical School: "The patients at Grady Memorial Hospital constitute a wealth of clinical material not available elsewhere to Emory. . . ." Human beings: sick, needy, hurting human beings, described as "clinical material"! It's one reason that we often sing the spiritual: "If anybody asks you who I am, just tell 'em I'm a child of God." ("Ain't no clinical material!") It is a far different reality to welcome guests as sisters and brothers in community. While the language of modern technological culture distances, the language of love binds us together and helps us open our eyes to see each other as kinfolks.

Finally, a liberation spirituality is necessarily a spirituality of resistance: a life well-trained by the scriptures. If the poor are subjects in our life, if we really do believe that God is present to us in the poor, then it is a given that we are against the system that hates, punishes, and crushes the poor. To serve the poor and not to confront the injustice of the system that causes poverty and oppression is ultimately to insult the poor and to denigrate the presence of God among us. It is to say that your poverty and victimization is an individual problem (i.e., your fault), so obviously the agenda must be to rehabilitate you, not to reform or transform a sick society. If Jesus comes to us in the poor, and we are working to rehabilitate the poor, what are we doing: trying to rehabilitate Jesus Christ?

Loving the poor, the Christ in the stranger's guise, means having to confront injustice because we cannot stand to see Jesus being hounded, put out, humiliated, hurt, starved, caged, cuffed, laughed at, poked with a billy stick, or neglected. We cannot live quietly or comfortably in a world that tolerates, much less condones, injustice.

But let's face it. To love the poor and to embrace the radical gospel is very clearly to choose sides. It is to side with the poor and oppressed, yes, against the systems of the rich and powerful. It is neither a comfortable nor an easy place to be. It means struggling mightily not to give in to hatred, cynicism, bitterness, and despair; and it means living in hope always for grief and love to express themselves in joyful, hopeful action.

It is in such a place that the gospel can become food and drink to us. In such a place we know day by day our need for the gifts of grace, mercy, and forgiveness in our own lives and the gifts of justice and righteousness to cover the broken earth. When God comes in the distressing guise of the stranger, it is never the same for us again.

The Open Door Community
and the Sins of the World, *by Ed Loring*

O C T O B E R   1 9 9 3

We have often confessed that the Open Door Community is not a place for those seeking a way out from the sins and demonic powers of modern America. For inside our lovely home reside the same racism, sexism, classism, greed, desire for comfort, and hunger for shortcuts that feed the fiery engines of evil and oppression outside our house and yard.

The difference at 910 is not in the presence or absence of sin and iniquity, but in our response to its presence and power in our lives. First comes confession. All European Americans (and European visitors) are racists. We are sorry; our hearts are broken. We repent. We commit our lives to the long, slow, error-prone process of undoing our racism and its concomitant prejudice, as well as the racism which infests the social structures of our society. We also understand that our progress when it does occur is partial, paltry, and ambiguous. We believe with sorrow in our hearts that we shall die racists, and only our children will finally see this land washed of its guilt and blood.

The confession of racism and its hold on the lives of European Americans is only one part of our life together. African Americans and people of color confess that their bodies and souls have been oppressed, distorted, and confused by racism. People of color cannot be racist in this society because racism is prejudice plus power, and people of color have been outside the structures of power. People of color, then, must concern themselves with the painful task of undoing the consequences of racism. As the lies of superiority and privilege are benefits of racism for whites, so feelings of inferiority and judgments about societal disabilities shape the lives of people of color. Repentance and a lifelong agenda of personal conversion and radical social restructuring fill the lives and vocations of those oppressed by racism and who live lives of undoing its consequences.

Within this tiny toe of the Body of Christ, this piece of the Beloved Community, we make the same movements of confession and repentance and commit our lives to undoing demonic realities as we grapple with sexism, classism, and the idols of our affluent but dying culture.

The biblical tradition and the leadership of Jesus by the power of the Holy Spirit give us two very particular resources for the struggle. Although the demons and powers have not been removed by casting our lot as rich and poor together in residential Christian community, our courage has been strengthened.[1] We find here in this community the gift of love and openness, and the power and persistence to look the devil directly in the eye. What a gift from God! What a joy in the midst of the death and pain of this tragic and broken world! Eye contact with the devil promotes "I" contact with love and justice. The biblical injunction "be not afraid" is practiced in our little household of hope. Granted that we often fall and fail, and some days our eyes avoid our sin, we can nonetheless claim a taste of God's good gift and promise to the church. Courage. God is with us!

Second, we have a practice that encourages courage and frightens the Evil One. We often admonish each other: "There is no such thing as a stupid question. Ask, ask, keep on asking." There may be, and often there are, lots of stupid answers. But we encourage our children, visitors, new community members off the streets and out of the prisons, and us partners, too, to keep on asking questions. This biblical truth is often put into practice in our house and in our yard.

"Suppose one of you," said Jesus, "should go to a friend's house at midnight and say, 'Friend, let me borrow three loaves of bread. A friend of mine who is on a trip has just come to my house, and I don't have any food!' And suppose your friend should answer from inside, 'Don't bother me! The door is already locked, and my children and I are in bed. I can't get up and give you anything.' Well, what then? I tell you that even if your neighbor will not get up and give you the bread because you are a friend, yet she will get up and give you everything you need because you are not ashamed to keep on asking. And so I say to you: Ask, and you will receive; seek, and you will find; knock, and the door will be opened to you. For everyone who asks will receive, and the one who seeks will find, and the door will be opened to anyone who knocks" (Luke 11:5b–10).

At the Open Door Community we have been given the gift of courage by the grace of God. We are thankful and joyful and often we put this gift, this courage, into practice by looking racism, classism, sexism, greed, and comfort directly in the eye and saying "No!" to the Evil One. This courage also enables us to keep asking questions—unashamed—until our neighbors get out of bed and feed the hungry, house the homeless, give liberty to captives and sight to the blind. Our Holy Parent gives the Holy Spirit to those who ask.

---

1. Leonardo Boff, *The Lord's Prayer: The Prayer of Integral Liberation*, trans. Theodore Morrow (Maryknoll, N.Y.: Orbis Books, 1983), 24.

The Cry of Dereliction, *by Ed Loring*

M A Y   1 9 8 8

My God, my God, why have you forsaken me? are words which have a long history and profound meaning in the Old Testament and throughout the entire experience of Israel. We, too, live in the days of dereliction. We live in the days of abandonment.

Often "derelict" refers to old, forgotten, alcoholic men on our streets, but the epithet also points toward a profound existential place in our own lives when we see and hear how our society is relentlessly pursuing the abandonment of the poor, the abandonment of civil rights, the abandonment of affirmative action. As we abandon our sense of history—the common purse in Christian communities, the Bible as God's radical word on behalf of the poor, the stigmata of the poor in our servanthood and protests—we participate in the power of death named *dereliction.*

We members of the family of faith need to remember that a fundamental responsibility of the spiritual life is to listen to the cry of dereliction and then to pronounce it to the powers of this world. We must position our lives so that as we serve, read the newspaper, study scripture and poetry, as we dance and have babies, we are shaped in our bowels by the experiences of homeless and hungry derelicts. The cry of dereliction then becomes our own cry. We graft that cry into our lives, into our hearts, into our wallets, into all our choices.

My God, my God, why have you forsaken me? Why is there dereliction and abandonment in our days? Dereliction is a very important perspective from which we are called to live our lives.

In addition to hearing the cry of dereliction among the hungry and homeless on our streets, our little family named the Open Door Community also listens to and visits among prisoners. We have a particular focus on those under the sentence of death. Tonight 120 men and women sit in the shadow of death by electrocution in the name of all the citizens of Georgia: a sentence upheld by the American Constitution although the pagan rite of bloodfest and revenge is outlawed in almost every society that finds its cultural and spiritual roots in the Judeo-Christian heritage. Most of our friends are guilty of terrible crimes, several are innocent (as were Jerry Banks and Earl Charles), all are poor, neglected by friends and Christians, and they are human beings created in God's likeness.

As we have learned to sit in prison and listen to those daily dying in iron cages encased in concrete slabs, we have discovered that homelessness, too, is a death sentence.

Homelessness, like the sentence of death, is abandonment, dereliction. Our society, through laws and lawyers, courts and judges, has evolved and maintained structures for legally keeping and killing the poor. This is the explicit, and, among many, the righteous way to control, frighten, and obliterate those we wish did not exist. Homelessness, on the other hand, is society's implicit decision to abandon hundreds of thousands of people to die on the streets.

Homelessness is a sentence of death. The fundamental bond between death row and the streets is abandonment: poverty is death.

As the streets are the places of residence for increasing numbers of American citizens, jails and prisons are houses for hundreds of thousands of other poor and minority folk. Prisons are the high-income housing for the poor, and in an almost direct proportion over the last six or seven years, as low-income housing funds have become less available, allocations for new jails and prisons have skyrocketed. We have a new city jail in Atlanta, and Fulton County plans to open its new home for the homeless and poor, the Fulton County Jail, in a few months. Of course, with the largest city shelter closed on April 1 due to warmer weather, and with the Democrats on the way to town this summer for their national convention, every jail cell, iron cage, holding center, and detention facility will be filled to overflowing. Is the Democratic Convention simply a practice period for the city before the grand opening of Underground Atlanta? Let us listen to the cries of dereliction for the answer. The cries of the poor are the cries of Christ.

My God, my God, why have you forsaken me? "I have not forsaken you, my child. I am in the flesh of Henry, walking your abandoned streets. I am in the body of Annie Ruth, sitting on death row. Why won't you listen? Come, follow me."

Dorothy Day: The Only Solution Is Love,
by Murphy Davis

JANUARY 1998

Editor's note: In May 1933, Dorothy Day, along with the French peasant philosopher Peter Maurin, started the Catholic Worker movement with a newspaper, the Catholic Worker, *and the first house of hospitality. Today there are some 120 houses of hospitality in the United States and several other countries. The Open Door Community is listed among them as the "Protestant Catholic Worker house" in Atlanta.*

From the time of her conversion until her death in 1980, Dorothy Day practiced a life of voluntary poverty, pacifism, daily practice of the works of mercy, and re-

peated acts of nonviolent resistance to war and systems of oppression. She was last ar-rested at the age of seventy-three in the struggle for fair working conditions and just wages for California farm workers. Always a teacher, her disciples have included Daniel Berrigan, Robert Coles, Cesar Chavez, Michael Harrington, Thomas Mer-ton, and others. She has been generally acknowledged as the founder of the Catholic left in the United States.

In honor of Dorothy Day's one-hundredth birthday on November 8, 1997, eight members of the Open Door gathered with some four hundred Catholic Workers in Las Vegas. The three-day celebration culminated with a Mass and civil disobedience at the Nevada nuclear-test site.

The following is an adaptation of Murphy Davis's talk at the Las Vegas gathering.

I come to celebrate the life of Dorothy Day with a sweet sense of irony. It amazes me when I remember that I spent several years studying church history. Ed's Ph.D. is in American church history, and I was working in the same area; but in all our studies in seminary and graduate school, we never once heard of Dorothy Day. It was only after we left the academic life that we began to hear of her life and work. Now I look back over the last twenty years and realize that no one person, living or dead, has had a more profound effect on my life, my work, my belief. This formidable woman, this Yankee Catholic anarchist, has been a primary source of conversion for this born-and-bred Southern Presbyterian!

In 1977, Ed and I read William Miller's *A Harsh and Dreadful Love: Dorothy Day and the Catholic Worker Movement*, and knew that we wanted to learn more. In 1979, we went to New York to try to raise funding for our work in Georgia with people on death row. We knew that we wanted to visit the Catholic Worker while we were in town. When our free afternoon came around, we were tired and grumpy but got ourselves together enough to get to Maryhouse. Mike Ha-rank was "on the house," and he generously took time away to sit down and talk with us. When he heard that we had interest in starting a work of hospitality, his advice was simple: (1) the work should have its foundation in love, and (2) we should always keep it small in order to preserve hospitality and personalism. As Mike spoke at length about love as the beginning and ending point, my grumpi-ness began to melt away, and the tears began to roll down my cheeks. My heart of stone softened, and the more Mike talked, the harder I cried. I've often thought of that conversation and wondered what Mike must have thought of this Southern woman dissolving in a puddle of tears in the newspaper office in the front of Maryhouse. But after a while, he gave us a big stack of Dorothy's books, and we were on our way.

The following fall we opened the Clifton Presbyterian Church night shel-ter. A year later we visited the Catholic Worker again, this time with our infant daughter, to spend a week deepening our understanding of this movement that was beginning to shape our lives. At the Friday night meeting that September in 1980, Dan Berrigan came to celebrate Mass and to tell of the King of Prussia Plowshares action, in which he and others had taken hammers to disarm a missile. And though we never really met her, Dorothy Day came downstairs to receive the Eucharist. She died two months later. I have always felt so very grateful for sharing that time of table companionship with her. I'm especially glad because I think that table companionship and the eucharistic vision were the center for Dorothy. Everything else flowed from this experience.

Dorothy often spoke of coming into the church as an experience of coming home. This coming home was being welcomed to a meal—to the companionship of the table. The Mass was central. For much of her life she went to Mass every day. When she became too ill and weak to go, it was brought to her. The work of hospitality was also a daily practice: inviting the poor, the hungry, the forgotten to come in and share food, drink, and table companionship. It all started and ended with a meal for Dorothy. And so it starts and ends for us. We are fed with abundance. We share what we have, and others are fed. Sometimes there seems to be so little that we cannot see the way. But when we give thanks and break the crust, again and again we find that there is enough.

When we read the Gospels, we see that Jesus was always interested in getting people together to eat. We have stories of Jesus feeding the multitudes; the great banquet when people were brought from the highways and byways; eating with friends like Mary, Martha, and Lazarus; the Passover supper; fish for breakfast on the seashore; and, of course, the meal at Emmaus.

Table companionship brings us to some of the central conflicts of our own culture as we think about growing numbers of us struggling with obesity, anorexia, bulimia, and filling ourselves—our mouths, stomachs, and spirits—with junk. Several years ago I spoke to a class at Mercer University. I was speaking of the despair that grips the lives of poor and rich alike—making a connection between the suffering of children in the inner city of Atlanta and a recent rash of teenage suicides that had occurred in eastern Cobb County, an affluent white suburb. There was a great deal of press attention to the suicides because the adolescents, who had shot themselves, were children who had been given every material advantage: clothes, cars, entertainment, everything they could have wanted. After the class a young student waited patiently to say to me, "I know why those kids in East Cobb are killing themselves." I was very interested and urged him to tell me. He said quietly, "Because they have no idea that they can be anything but an appetite."

At times it indeed seems that we have become little more than an appetite for the boundless consumer mania of our culture. And as the prophet Isaiah says, we spend our money for what does not satisfy; we spend our wages, and still we are hungry.

Dorothy Day, as we understand from her own reflections on her early life, was given a sort of sacramental sense about life. This sense of the holy is what made her a restless wanderer until she found her home in the church. She came home to the Blessed Sacrament, as she always called it, and everything else flowed from that.

This has been true to our experience and journey as well. Everything about our work with the homeless poor, and much of our work with prisoners, began with sharing meals together.

I do not come from a sacramental tradition. In the Presbyterian Church of my youth, we celebrated communion four times each year. But when we began to work with and among poor and suffering people, we began to experience the need for the sacrament. And Dorothy's theology was basic to understanding that our solidarity, our hospitality, and our journey into community must be rooted in the experience of being fed at the table. We came to learn from her that table companionship, the eucharistic vision, would provide the basis for every-thing else.

In the eucharistic vision, the bread and the cup are at the center, and diverse companions are gathered around. At the table we are bound together and find our identity as sisters and brothers. The first thing that happens is that we circle up and we are fed—a gracious plenty! At the table we are invited and empow-ered to bind our lives to the lives of the others—most of whom are poor and op-pressed. At the table we are invited to make covenantal vows to struggle against the powers that kill and maim and oppress our companions, our friends.

This is how the table companionship becomes a basis for solidarity. Soli-darity is our affirmation—our assent—our Yes—to life in the Mystical Body of Christ. One of the most important gifts of the Eucharist is receiving the eyes of faith to see God in our midst. Matthew 25 teaches us that what we do for the least of our sisters and brothers, we do for God. When we are fed by God, we are given the eyes to see God—especially in the suffering of those who are poor and forgotten and condemned. This is the basis for solidarity, the basis for a preferential option for the poor, the basis from which the poor and oppressed can begin to set agenda in our lives.

Jerome Bowden was one of the memorable characters of our twenty years of visiting on death row. Jerome was a clinically retarded African American man who had grown up in Muscogee County, Georgia, where his mother worked as a maid for the county sheriff. Jerome and his sister grew up eating surplus com-modity food because his mother was not paid a living wage. His whole life was something of a death row even before he got to prison. There he remained for a number of years before he was executed in June 1986.

Jerome had a simple, childlike approach to life. And the way he saw what was going on inside the prison was always so basic, that I often learned from him. I loved the time he told us about the Bible study they were having in his cell block, on the Book of Revelation. Jerome wanted to understand Revelation so badly that he kept going to the others, saying, "Look, can't you just break this down for me just a little bit? Can't you explain this thing to me?" Finally, one of his friends drew a chart of Revelation. I really wish I could have seen that chart because I would like to have seen exactly how the Book of Revelation was reduced to a chart and explained to Jerome.

We went to see Jerome one day, and he was dying laughing. He started to tell us the story of how the guards had come into the cell block for a shakedown. They threw his stuff all over the floor and looked for contraband and weapons. One guard came across Jerome's chart of Revelation. He was convinced that it was an escape plan! So Jerome's chart was confiscated and taken straightaway to the warden's office, where numerous prison bureaucrats put their heads together over this chart of the Book of Revelation. They tried to figure out how Jerome Bowden was going to escape from death row with this chart. And Jerome couldn't stop laughing. But he never got his chart back.

When Jerome's execution date was set, the Georgia Association for Retarded Citizens took his case and began to advocate for him. A stay of execution lasted for several days. During that time the Board of Pardons and Paroles sent an Emory University psychologist to study Jerome and to determine just how retarded he was. The conclusion drawn by this eminent psychologist was that Jerome Bowden was retarded, but not quite retarded enough to be spared. What an ironic twist that the test the psychologist used asked Jerome to define the word *sanctuary*. And Jerome said, "A place to go and be safe." And it killed him. . . . *Sanctuary*—because he knew the word, Jerome died.

We sat with Jerome on the day before he was scheduled to die, and he was telling us another story. He was a great storyteller. He described a series of mean things that one of the guards had done to taunt one of the prisoners on the cell block. Jerome was confused; he couldn't understand people being cruel to each other. And as he thought about it, he stopped and said, "You know, peoples was not made to dog around. Peoples was made to be respected."

Jerome Bowden was retarded—clinically retarded. But I think his statement is one of the wisest things I have heard in my life. I think it's one of the best summations of the dignity of the human creation that you will find. "Peoples was made to be respected." We can learn this respect as we come to table companionship and let our eyes be opened to see the presence of God in each other. This respect is the basis of our love and solidarity.

Our task in these days is that of loving the poor in a time when the poor, in attitude, in words, and in policy, are hated. We hear so much talk about wanting to make poor people work; getting people off welfare and making them work. But just being poor is the hardest work in the world. So many people in mainline culture don't have any idea what that means. And it cannot be understood apart from solidarity—sharing life with the poor.

Being poor is the hardest work in the world, but all we can think of is,

"What's going to be our next mean policy to pass, our next law to dog people around, harass them, and chase them out of our central city, and get them out of one neighborhood or another?" To love the poor in our day is going against the odds, probably more than in any other age we know.

The Eucharist is a foundation for solidarity: an ongoing assurance that God has never abandoned us, giving us the faith and the hope that we might find strength to be faithful in our love for the poor.

These are confusing days. Things have changed so much in the last several years that it is difficult to keep up. In the past twenty years the prison population in the United States has tripled! Three times as many people are in prison today as when we began to do prison ministry in 1977. And prison has become the model for our attitudes and our frame of reference for the poor. We have come to blame the poor for their own plight and to assume them to be criminal. Our policy approach has moved to one of punishment, despair, fear, hate, revenge, and retribution.

We seem to have lost our minds and have let our spirits be worn down again and again by the constant hype and the fear. What would have been unthinkable to us five to twenty years ago is now routine. It is justified and undergirded by the sort of vague fear and disease that grips our spirits and paralyzes our minds.

But still Matthew 25 says, "What you do for the least (not only for the innocent poor, but for the guilty poor) is what you do for me." By our solidarity that grows from our table companionship and our eucharistic vision, we're called to reduce the distance between ourselves and the poor, to reduce the distance between the privileged and those without the basics to sustain human life. We are called to renounce privilege, to step back and step away from the privilege that is given to those of us with white skin, to those with a formal education.

Two and a half years ago I became very ill and had emergency surgery at Grady Hospital. I was diagnosed with what was thought to be a terminal case of a virulent cancer called Burkitt's lymphoma. Since all of us are without medical insurance in the Open Door Community, we had known for many years that anyone with a major medical need would go to Grady Hospital, our public hospital, whether we came from privilege, or from the streets, or from prison, or from poverty.

Now, of course, the public hospitals have closed their doors in some cities. Grady Hospital has not closed, though it is under serious attack. Grady is on Butler Street in downtown Atlanta, the place to which we were called fifteen years ago to begin serving a breakfast to 250 hungry and homeless people every weekday morning. Butler Street is a sacred space in our life.

I had very extensive surgery and hospitalization, and then five months of a rigorous, mega-chemotherapy. And I am so thankful that my life was spared. I was prayed for by so many friends and family, including the Catholic Worker communities, and I know that was a great source of my healing.

Though I had spent a lot of time around Grady for twenty-five years, I had always been on my feet. For the first time I was a patient. I began to realize what was meant when I heard an Emory doctor who practiced at Grady Hospital describe the patients as "clinical material." There were a few times that I felt like "clinical material." But I must say that, for the most part, my care was wonderful, and I was absolutely amazed by the compassion and the excellent care of so many medical staff in that place.

Now we pray for the power and the capacity to renounce privilege. Dorothy Day often pointed out that sometimes we don't know what we're praying for, but we can count on the fact that our prayers are answered. And there was one time in particular that was a real comeuppance for me. I was sitting in the hall with Ed one day, waiting for my chemotherapy treatment, when a woman bustled up to me with a clipboard and said, "How do you do? I am your social worker." And I thought, "My social worker?" The first thing I could think was it was one thing to be told that I had cancer. But it was something else to be told that I had a social worker! I had worked with social workers for years, so I had this immediate surge of "wait-a-minute-I've-got-to-tell-her-who-I-am." We talk with Grady social workers when they are trying to place somebody, or trying to find somebody's family, or to meet some need. Now I was struggling to hear this word: "I have a social worker." Finally I realized that my prayer for solidarity was being granted: I was really a poor person in that moment. I had a social worker just like everybody else I knew at Grady Hospital. All the patients at Grady have social workers, and now I had my own. In fact, she has become a good friend, and has sent us other patients from the oncology clinic to live at the Open Door. At one point, there were three of us in the community from the oncology clinic, and with the same social worker.

God does answer our prayers, and we can move toward solidarity with our sisters and brothers who are poor. If there is anything that the scriptures and the Eucharist teach us, it is that the poor are not a problem to be solved, as we hear so often in the parlance of our day. The poor are not a problem to be solved, but a mystery to be loved. They are a sacramental presence among us.

In the eucharistic vision we are given the eyes to recognize and to love God's presence among us—Jesus Christ in the stranger's guise. It all, of course, becomes a joke without the Eucharist. It is incomprehensible to the rest of the world, to those who lack a vision of the holy in the ordinary. The table companionship and the eucharistic vision are the bases for our hospitality. If, as Dorothy always said, solidarity brings us to the table with the poor, then the grace is that at the table we can learn to love the poor. Love is the only solution. Here we come face to face with the depth of the vision of hospitality. Solidarity is the political expression of the eucharistic vision. Hospitality expresses the love of table companionship. By hospitality we are drawn into the Mystical Body of Christ.

Ed Loring, my partner, the love of my life, is known from time to time to adopt a certain refrain that he repeats again and again. Last year's refrain, which we heard several times, was "Justice is important, but supper is essential." Without supper, without relationship, without love, without table companionship, justice can become a program that we do to other people. So justice is important, even crucial. We hope to give our lives to the justice struggle; but supper is essential. What we must do, what we are graced and gifted to be able to do, is to sit down and to eat together, to open our doors, our homes, our hearts, and our very selves to the needs of others.

Dorothy Day found her home in the church, her home at the table. She knew that the works of mercy and hospitality are the best antidotes to the empty, despairing acquisitiveness of our lives in twentieth-century America. A friend and volunteer in our community, Horace Tribble, prays every day for an "attitude of gratitude." That is what we are given with the table companionship which brings us to open ourselves in hospitality.

The works of mercy and hospitality are important, not just in and of themselves, but in a particular way in our times as a social and political expression. There needs to be a public character to our work of hospitality. It must be done in the open so that it is seen, so that everyone can remember that it is possible to love and welcome each other.

All we hear is how to buy the next mechanism to protect your home and your family and your property and your car, whether it's a lock on the steering wheel, or an alarm system, or whatever. All we hear is that we should protect ourselves from our neighbors because they are scary, and they are out to hurt us and take from us. Hospitality, practiced publicly, says that even in 1997 we can welcome one another in love and in care. In our hearts, we need to open our own doors. We need to confront our own racism, our own misogyny, our own class hatred. As we welcome our sisters and brothers, we learn how to take on these battles within ourselves.

And finally, table companionship and the eucharistic vision bring us to community. When we find the holy in what is ordinary, when we share what is ordinary in love, we become companions. Companions are those who share bread, from the Latin roots *com* (with) and *panis* (bread). Companions on the journey are those who eat together and share the bread.

Bread, of course, is the most ordinary of foods; the staff of life. When we share bread, it becomes, in the midst of the community of faith, manna, the bread of heaven. And the sharing of bread creates community—where we can practice confession and forgiveness, where we can be formed to "practice the presence of God," to renounce privilege, and to depend on the Mystical Body of Christ. Community, sharing bread, is an antidote to the despair and isolation of our time.

As Dorothy said, "It all sounds very wonderful, but life itself is a haphazard, untidy, messy affair." We have to disarm our own hearts. In the life of companionship and community we learn how much in our own hearts has to be disarmed day after day. That disarmament is as important as the disarming of a nuclear-test site.

Dorothy Day also spoke often of holy folly. She said, "We are fools for Christ and wish we were more so." I think sometimes in community that prayer is granted more often than any of our petitions.

In 1985, we at the Open Door hit a most difficult and painful period in the life of our community. We were founded by two families, and one family decided that it was time to leave. It was painful and wrenching. We came to the point when Ed suggested that we change the name of the community from the Open Door to the Open Sore Community. We often remembered the story of Teresa of Ávila. She was traveling to another convent on a donkey. It was wintertime, the beast balked in the middle of a river, and Teresa fell into the cold water. She sat in the water, and is said to have cast her eyes heavenward and said, "Lord, the way Thou treatest Thine friends, 'tis no wonder Thou hast so few."

We had gone into community, thinking of it as an endeavor of people who were like-minded—coming together and making something together. Frankly, we had in mind people who looked like us, smelled like us, acted like us, came from the same kind of backgrounds. So when in 1985 all of that fell apart, we thought very seriously of closing down quietly, sneaking out the back door, and finding something else to do.

But during that time, God gave us a new vision that was pure grace. We realized that we did live in community with Willie Dee Wimberly, Ralph Dukes, Joe Owens, Barbara Schenk, and Harold Wind, who had come out of institutions and off the streets. We had been community together for some years by that time. We were living in community, but our limited, narrow vision said, "The others that came with us have left; it's over." We were given such a gift because God helped us get our narrow, squinty eyes open to see the rich gift that was there. From community we were able to rebuild, to heal, and to pray for a strengthening of that new vision.

Dietrich Bonhoeffer in *Life Together* offers his own articulation of love as a harsh and dreadful thing. He says that to be shaped into community with each other, we have to come to the point that all of our dreams of community are dashed. They have to die. We bring our dreams into this endeavor and try to make this thing happen, but it can't start to happen until those dreams fail and God can begin to bring life out of the ashes. I think that's part of what Jesus meant when he said, "Unless the seed fall to the earth and die . . ." We have to get past all of our dreams and plans before the real life can begin.

The good gift that God gave us in 1985 is borne out in fruits here today, in the leadership of Phillip Williams, Ed Potts, and Ira Terrell, who have come to this gathering and are leaders at the Open Door Community. They give shape, structure, and vision to our life together because God helped us see each other. Our lives are full of ironies. I love the story that is told about the wedding of Dorothy's daughter, Tamar. They say that Peter Maurin got up to make a speech that was a discourse against raising pigs for profit! That's kind of like life in community. You never quite know where the other person will be coming from. But we learn to endure, to find a sense of humor, and to go on with each other.

❖   ❖   ❖

I want to tell you about another friend on death row, a man named Alpha Otis Stephens, who died in the electric chair in Georgia in 1984. It took them twenty minutes to kill Alpha, and they said that he didn't have the right body chemistry. I thought, "Lord, have mercy. He couldn't even die right to fit these folks."

Alpha didn't get anything but the short end of the stick. He grew up in a very poor area of Macon, Georgia. He had an abusive and violent, alcoholic father. He and his mother were beaten regularly. But when Alpha was about six, he began to try to get between his mother and his father to defend her. His mother saw the handwriting on the wall, so one day she packed him a little lunch, dressed him warmly, and put him outside. That was it. He was on his own from age six, basically a street kid in Macon. Sometimes he would stay with another relative or hide in an abandoned house. But he was never again "at home."

It wouldn't come as a tremendous surprise to learn that Alpha grew up to be a violent person, and he took the life of Mr. Henry Asbill. Alpha was guilty; there was no question about that. Death row seems like a dead end, where everything is over. But we have been privileged witnesses over the years to the fact that growth and change can still come, even among people on death row.

On one visit, Alpha told us about Charlie and his persistence, and how God used Charlie to move Alpha toward hope and redemption. This is kind of the way Alpha said it: "Yeah, I changed. The thing that made me change was what Charlie did. When I came to Jackson Prison I was violent—good Godamighty I was violent. Most everybody here just left me alone, except Charlie. I stayed in my cell all the time. He started coming sitting in front of my cell, just sitting, looking at me. Finally, I say, 'What you starin' at?' 'You,' he said. 'Just trying to figure out how can anybody be so mean. You crazy? Or just ain't got no sense?' So I didn't say nothing. He didn't go away. He didn't never go away. Seem like he just worked so hard to make me be his friend. Finally, I just give up. Me and him always been friends after that. That changed me. Man, I just couldn't be mean around old Charlie. Everybody in prison call me Stephens. But Charlie, he call me Brother Alpha."

That story didn't have a happy ending because Alpha Stephens was electrocuted with 2,300 volts, three different jolts. But I've got to tell you that it wasn't all bad news in Alpha's life. He lived a life where hope was reborn. The prison called him #D9164, but some of us got to know him as "Brother Alpha" because of what one man did with his persistent hospitality.

Resurrection hope is a gift anytime and anywhere that the power of love is shown to be stronger than death. Anytime love overcomes death, despair, and hopelessness, we see truth and hope reborn. That's a hope that all of us have in community. Dr. King used to quote the folk saying: "We ain't what we oughta be; we ain't what we wanna be; we ain't what we gonna be; but thank God we ain't what we was." There is that hope: We ain't what we was, none of us. Even though we haven't gotten to where we're going, we know that we're on the way. In the meantime, we are encouraged by the stories, the memories, and the hope of love prevailing in whatever small ways, and sometimes even in the big ways. Just like old Charlie encouraged Brother Alpha through the work of loving patiently, unobtrusively, and persistently.

One of the great gifts that Dorothy Day gave us for the journey of community is companionship with those living and working out her vision. The community that we get to share and celebrate is one of the best and truest gifts. In the end for Dorothy, as for all of us, the work comes back to the table, to the companionship with our God and with each other. Here we receive food and drink for the journey, which gives us the eyes to see God's presence among us and on the road. When the burden seemed unbearable, and for Dorothy at times it most certainly did, her response was that she had to deepen her spiritual life. Her daily celebration of Mass was a part of that. The joy to be celebrated, for Dorothy and for us, brings us again to the table, just as Jesus shared the Passover meal with his disciples before his hard and tortuous journey to state execution. That vision of the banquet is ours to share, because when Jesus sits at the table, he says, "This is my body." What we are fed is the substance, the material, of God's presence. God is love, the scriptures say, and the Feast is a Feast of Love.

One way to understand the Eucharist and table companionship is to know that we are fed by love. We are eating bread and drinking wine that we pass to one another, but we are being fed with love—a love that sustains us and becomes the basis for all that we have, and are, and do. It helps us to remember always that God's loving-kindness is present even in this violent, warmongering, broken world. God comes and tells us that the cosmos, at war with itself, is still shot through with the glory of God. We need the table companionship, the sacrament, because we live with a mystery so deep that we do not have the words to define it. We have to act it out. We need a drama to try to approach the depth of this truth, to appropriate this truth in bread and the mystery of holiness.

In the depth of the mystery, we remember the story, and we are "re-membered"—put back together again, in solidarity, in hospitality, in community—healed, restored. Dorothy Day said, "We know our God in the breaking of bread, and we know each other in the breaking of bread, and we are not alone anymore. Heaven is a banquet and life is a banquet, too, even with a crust, where there is companionship." Thank God. Amen.

When Did We See You? *by Elizabeth Dede*

JUNE 1989

The question of seeing comes up often in the New Testament, because it seems that a big part of Jesus' ministry was to help people see. Some of that work was restoring actual physical sight. We know many accounts of Jesus healing blind people. The New Testament is also full of spiritual eye-opening experiences, in which people who were blind to the truth suddenly recognize it. Perhaps the most famous of these is the Easter story of the walk to Emmaus, when two of Jesus' followers walked with the risen Lord, speaking of the events of the past week, yet not recognizing Jesus until he broke bread with them. Then, the story goes, "their eyes were opened, and they recognized him." So the question, "Lord, when did we see you?" is a question of recognition, which, with understanding, is an act of faith in the post-ascension world. Jesus has left this earth, and we can see him now only with the eyes of faith.

Often at the Open Door we read Matthew 25 and ask the question, "Lord, when did we see you?" In the answer to that question—"Whenever you did this for one of the least important of these sisters and brothers of mine, you did it for me!"—we find a clear explanation of our calling and work: to feed the hungry, to give a drink to the thirsty, to receive strangers in our home, to give clothes to the naked, to take care of the sick, and to visit the prisoner.

On Sunday, April 30, 1989, I had the privilege of reading Matthew 25 during our worship. It was a special Sunday because we were celebrating the partnership of Jay Frazier, Carl Calford Barker, Willie London, Willie Dee Wimberly, Ralph Dukes, and Robert Barrett. All of these members of the Open Door Community have been committed to our life together and to the work of the Kingdom for many years. So it was clearly a faithful act of seeing, recognizing, and acknowledging their partnership when the leadership team decided to invite them into a fuller relationship as they signed the covenant of the Open Door Community. Yet as I read that scripture my eyes were not completely open.

The words of Matthew 25 spoke to me of our vocation—of the work that we do together—and I was blind to the words about seeing. A few nights after this celebration of partnership, I had a strange dream. I dreamed that a new person moved into our community. He was blind, and everybody tried to introduce him to me. But I couldn't see him. Pat Fons would lead him to me and say, "Elizabeth, I want you to meet this new member of our community." And I would try hard to see him, but he was invisible to me. I was blind to his presence. When I woke from that dream, the words "Lord, when did we see you?" were running through my head, and I began to think about Sunday's worship when I had read those words from Matthew 25.

Suddenly, the significance of that scripture for our celebration of partnership struck me. I had lived and worked with Jay, Carl, Willie, Willie Dee, Ralph, and Robert for three years, yet I hadn't recognized fully their partnership with me; I hadn't seen completely how they were my family. Acknowledging their partnership publicly was my first step toward sight. Now I know that I had been blinded by the things that make me different from these new partners: my education, the color of my skin, my comfortable existence, and the privilege to choose to come to the Open Door. But with the eyes of faith, given by our brother Jesus, we can see Jesus in everyone, and so recognize our partnership.

I wonder where our other blind spots are. When do we not see our brothers and sisters? When do we not see the Lord? I'm sure my brother Jesus takes a shower at 910. Jesus eats at the Butler Street Breakfast, and maybe is imprisoned in an office building downtown. I think my sister Jesus is in prison. I just haven't seen her yet. Perhaps it will be revealed to me in a dream.

Prison Ministry: Sorrows and Celebrations,
by Murphy Davis

JANUARY 1988

Last spring marked ten years in prison ministry. Like many who fast approach forty I have become sentimental, and marking anniversaries has become more important to me. So we decided to throw a celebration on May 15. I talked with our old friend Will Campbell, who helped to start Southern Prison Ministry, and we decided that a lot of us should mark the time with an evening of stories, singing, and recollections. So much of the prison work is overwhelmingly sad, depressing, fatiguing; this time we would schedule an evening to bring together some of the wonderful people who make the wheels turn—prisoners' families, lawyers, ministers, former prisoners, visitors—and celebrate the good gifts of the struggle: remembering how our unity and commitment is strengthened in the heat of the movement. Sounded like a great idea.

And then May 15 arrived. At 10:00 that morning we buried Viva Lamb—our dear friend and a leader in the movement against the death penalty—who had been killed three days earlier in an automobile wreck. At 7:00 that evening our good friend Joe Mulligan was executed in the Georgia electric chair. At 7:30 in the evening, 250 friends gathered in the church hall at Central Presbyterian Church for the "celebration."

Bill Tucker's family was there; his execution was two weeks away. Richard Tucker's execution was one week away.

Good people. Good food. And Will Campbell's stories were good. But it was a hard evening to pull off, to say the least. A number of friends who would have been there were in jail as a witness against Joe Mulligan's execution. For some who had wanted to tell stories, the grief overwhelmed any remembrance of the hopeful signs or happier times. I was simply numb—and exhausted with the realization that within the two weeks to follow, the funerals would probably total four. And they did: Viva, Joe, Richard, Bill. It was a rather brutal reminder: in the work with and on behalf of the oppressed, the celebrations are spontaneous and often unexpected. You can't be sure about scheduling them.

But this still has been a time of looking back and looking forward in the work of our prison ministry. It began for Ed and me at Clifton Presbyterian Church. We had gone to this tiny congregation soon after we were married in 1975, thinking of it as a stopover while I finished doctoral work at Emory. Ed would serve as interim pastor to what was classified a "dying inner-city church." And then we would move on as teachers.

We were unprepared for much of what we learned. A newly formed Bible-study group that met on Sunday evenings took on Isaiah. What was this relentless theme of liberty to the captives? Go to those who sit in dark dungeons! Hear God's word of freedom to all the people! And Matthew 25 began to pound in our ears: Feed! Clothe! Welcome! Visit! A seed began to settle in our hearts.

A Supreme Court decision in July 1976 upheld the Georgia death penalty laws, and Ed got involved in a little group called Georgia Christians against the Death Penalty. He also began to visit a man in prison. In November 1976, we rode with Austin Ford to Macon, Georgia, for a meeting on the death penalty. There we met and heard from the mothers of several death-row prisoners—Viva Lamb, Betty George, and Marian Butler.

Henri Nouwen describes the task of liberation spirituality as a constant listening to the people of God—especially the poor and oppressed—with ears that are well-trained by the scriptures. That was the context for my call to prison ministry. Bible study was training my ear. The mothers of death row gave voice to the cry. Mercy!

Within six weeks of that meeting with Viva Lamb and others, Emory Graduate School was behind me, and I had been employed to organize "Witness against Executions"—a national demonstration against the death penalty, held in Atlanta during Easter weekend in 1977. Clifton provided the office space. "Witness against Executions" brought together more than three thousand people from around the country to say *no* to executions, *no* to vengeance and blood retribution, *no* to a law of death, *no* to the lack of forgiveness that kills.

From there the work of Southern Prison Ministry in Georgia began. Most of death row back then was in Reidsville, a five-hour drive into South Georgia. So every month our old blue van would pull out, filled with mamas going to visit their sons, with huge baskets filled with fried chicken and potato salad. It seems like it was always 102 degrees when we would roll through Vidalia and turn right onto the prison reservation.

By the spring of 1978 we were ready to celebrate when Earl Charles, a young black Savannah man, walked out of the Chatham County Jail after three and a half years of death row. It finally had become clear—even to the judge—that Earl had been wrongly convicted. So Earl and his mother, Flossie Mae Charles, came to Atlanta, and we had a liberation celebration at Clifton. That little church rocked and sang. Then, of course, we ate dinner. We learned a lot from Earl. The infamous Chatham County Jail was a rat-infested dungeon that had once been the Savannah slave market. Slave shackles still hung from the wall of each cell. He spent three and a half years there waiting to die for a crime he did not commit.

How did you make it, Earl? What brought you through? "You know," Earl said, "I had to get up every morning, and I'd wash my face and I'd shave and I'd comb my hair and get dressed. Then I'd look in the mirror and say, 'Today might be the day of my freedom. Today I might go home. And I'm ready.'" Thank you. We need every lesson we can learn about how to live like people ready for freedom.

We learned how to mourn. John Spenkelink's execution was the first of many in the late 1970s and into the 1980s. Forming friendships with the condemned, their families, and the victims of violence gave us a new hunger and thirst for righteousness. It gave us new gratitude in hearing, "Blessed are those who mourn, for they shall be comforted."

And then there was Jerry Banks, a gentle, quiet man who sat—again wrongly convicted, innocent of the crime, young, and black—on death row for six and a half years. I knew Jerry well. He became a friend to Ed and one who welcomed little Hannah's birth and held her, rocking her gently from side to side. Through our concern and that of Jerry's lawyers—Wade Crumbley and Steve Harrison—and, finally, through Tom Wicker of the *New York Times,* many people followed Jerry's story.

We went to court with him, prayed for him, and visited his wife, Virginia, and three children. And what a day it was—Christmas week of 1980—when Jerry walked out of prison—free! Once again a large crowd gathered at Clifton for a knock-down, drag-out freedom celebration. A busload of family and friends came from Stockbridge, Georgia. We packed the church and raised the roof. And then, of course, we ate dinner.

But it was just over three months later when the procession moved the other way—from Atlanta to Stockbridge. We traveled to Bentley Hill Methodist Church to bury our friend Jerry in the red clay of Henry County. Six and a half years had taken their toll. Virginia really didn't want Jerry back. She had, after all, been forced to build a life of her own. She had survived by learning not to think about Jerry, just as he had survived by thinking of nothing but her and the children. After so many years, the damage was too deep. The court's sentence of death had settled into the fabric of the family structure. And so on March 29, the day before their divorce would be final, Jerry shot Virginia and used a .38-caliber bullet to destroy what was left of his own broken heart.

The biblical sense of the powers and principalities became more real. Death is very powerful and very present in the lives of the poor. And we learned that to live in solidarity with the poor and oppressed of the earth is to live with broken hearts—hungry and thirsty for the day of Justice.

"Blessed are those who mourn, for they shall be comforted." To visit the prisoner is to learn to weep for sisters and brothers, to learn to mourn our lost humanity. Twelve times our friends have gone down, murdered by 2,300 volts in the Georgia electric chair. For all the strategy, planning, public witness, and legal maneuvering in the struggle against the death penalty, the time comes when all we can do is stand in a little group on the steps of the Capitol or the prison yard or with the family, and mourn one more deliberate act of violence.

We struggle for justice for women—especially women who, as prisoners, are at the bottom of the social and economic heap and suffer the raw violence of sexism. In one three-year period, five men were fired from the staff of the Georgia women's prison for raping prisoners. The five included the chaplain, the head counselor, and the assistant warden for *security.* We could not protect our sisters from the violence.

Linda Rogers, doing hard prison time in 1979 for making harassing phone calls, died in a fetal position. The only viable explanation seems to be that she was drugged to death by prison authorities. Nancy Sims died this fall of breast cancer. Nothing was done about it because the prison doctor kept saying the lump was "nothing serious."

Executions continue with great public support. There are more than twice as many women in prison this year than when the work of Southern Prison Ministry in Georgia began. And this month the Department of Corrections will ask the state (which already locks up a higher percentage of its women, men, and children than the Soviet Union and South Africa!) for another $201 million to build additional prisons.

Perhaps this is not what you would call—in any traditional sense—a successful ministry. I often remember St. Teresa, who said once, "O God, the way you treat your friends, 'tis no wonder you have so few."

Not a whole lot of people these days are attracted to work on behalf of prisoners. There is a lot more appeal to issues that unite us with innocent victims. Solidarity with the guilty pushes us to the limits of our theology and self-understanding. For we come to know the guilty one within ourselves, and this pushes us to our knees, crying out, "Lord, have *mercy* on me, a sinner."

We prefer, of course, to pray like the Pharisee, "I thank you, God, that I am not like others . . . like *them!*" Good guys and bad guys. Just like the movies. Us and them. The hard part of the gospel is to accept that we have been God's enemies, and only by grace have we been "brought near" and changed into friends. So—who is in a position to condemn? The church? The state? Who is in a position to condemn?

Jerome Bowden was executed in June 1986 in spite of the outcry against killing a retarded person. A professor of psychology from Emory University determined that while Jerome indeed was retarded, he was not retarded enough to have his life spared.

Retarded he was, but also very wise. On the last day we saw Jerome before he died, he said, "You know, peoples was not made to dog around. Peoples was made to be respected." Too bad the Emory psychologist was too busy, or too blind, to understand such a profound appreciation of human dignity.

Peoples was made to be respected. And in the struggle for justice and human dignity the scriptures promise us joy. That sounds crazy, but it's true. "Remove the chains of oppression and the yoke of injustice and let the oppressed go free . . . and God's favor will shine on you like the morning sun, and your wounds will be quickly healed. . . . The darkness around you will turn to the brightness of noon."

Looking into the wounds of the Crucified Christ—who made himself indistinguishable from the guilty and condemned—we see the brightness of resurrection power. And we know—in some strange and mysterious way—that our own healing and joy is tangled with the question of whether and how we reach out to those who carry the wounds of Christ: those who are broken by the chains of oppression, the yoke of injustice, and by every gesture of contempt. The promise is true. And the promise is good. Visit the prisoner with merciful healing and a passion for justice. Proclaim liberty to the captives. And discover God—who is mercy within mercy within mercy—among you.

I doubt that we'll ever plan another Southern Prison Ministry anniversary celebration. We have learned again to await the unexpected celebrations, the presence of joy, the taste of fulfillment, the moments of comfort that come as we mourn. Yet as I, a woman-child of God, bound in chains yet free by grace, reflect upon the years, I know how our cup overflows with goodness. Each day fills us with thanksgiving and celebration as we are graced to share life and love and merciful healing amid the prisoners of this society.

You Gotta Serve Somebody, *by Murphy Davis*

August 1990

Editor's note: The following address was delivered at Converse College, Spartanburg, South Carolina, on May 4, 1990, at a symposium, "The Challenges for Women in the Twenty-first Century."

As a way of introducing my remarks to you this morning, I want to say just a word about my life in the Open Door Community since this so deeply affects anything I would say to you.

We are a residential Christian community of thirty-two folk. We are African American, white, Hispanic, young and old, women and men, formerly homeless, formerly prisoners, and those of us who have always been housed; Ph.D.s and illiterates, from backgrounds of the middle class, obscene wealth, and utter poverty. As a family we live together, eat together, worship, work, and sing together, share our money and other resources, and try to understand, learn from, and love each other.

Out of our family life and shared faith we live a life of servanthood and advocacy among and on behalf of the homeless poor of Atlanta—more than ten thousand men, women, children, and families who have nowhere to go—and of servanthood and advocacy among and on behalf of prisoners in our state: the increasing thousands of women, men, and children who live in cages. We work particularly among the 111 people who are on death row in Georgia.

As a way of beginning to talk about the challenge of service I'd like first of all to introduce you to three friends that I more or less brought along with me this morning.

First, there's Charlie. When I left home yesterday morning, Charlie was lying in the sunshine in our front yard waiting for the soup kitchen to open. He is, like hundreds of thousands of men and women and children across this land, homeless. Charlie has been a working man since he was seventeen years old. The last job he held was one that he had had for five years, and he had worked up to four dollars an hour. But at forty-five, Charlie was slowing down a little, and the employer realized that there were any number of twenty-two-year-olds to be had at the drop of a hat—and for $3.35 at that!

So Charlie was fired. He was forty-five. It would be seventeen years before he would be eligible for Social Security, and none of his jobs had offered any benefits. The weeks and months of job-hunting were fruitless: "Sorry," they all said, "but you know we're really looking for somebody a little younger." The strain on Charlie's marriage grew to the breaking point. By the time he found himself with no job and no family and no home, he began to wonder—in this macho culture—what kind of a sorry excuse for a man he was anyway.

He gets an occasional job out of a labor pool. He crawls out of his cat hole at 4:30 A.M. and goes to sit in a dingy room full of hopeless humanity and prays for eight hours of work. Usually there's nothing for Charlie. But if he does go to work, he goes out hungry, and the soup kitchens will be closed long before the time he gets back. The best he can expect, though the company might pay the labor pool seven dollars an hour for his work, is $3.35 an hour minus a few bucks for transportation, hard-hat rental, and all—maybe he'll have nineteen or twenty-one dollars at the end of a day. The only place that will cash the check is a liquor store across from the labor pool—with a purchase, that is. So, by nightfall, the best he's looking at is a bottle, a pack of cigarettes, and sixteen bucks. Try to live on that.

Charlie gets locked up a lot. From time to time he does twenty to forty days in the city prison farm for the terrible crime of public urination. We jail those who relieve themselves in public even though Atlanta has not one single public toilet. In other words, there is not a legal alternative, even though with the money we spend in one year on punishing this heinous crime we could build and maintain public toilets all over the city. But for doing what every human body must do, Charlie goes to jail.

Charlie also did ten months of a one-year sentence for criminal trespass. That was from the time he was caught sleeping in an abandoned warehouse. He has another court charge pending because he went into Underground Atlanta and walked down the street. The police told him he didn't belong because he stank. So he was arrested.

When the pain gets to be too much for him, Charlie drinks. As he lay in the sunshine in our front yard yesterday, a car drove by. A young man stuck his head out the window and screamed with venom, "Get a job, you bums!" Charlie raised his aching head for a minute and then dropped it on his arm again.

Next, I'd like you to meet Jerome. Jerome was young, African American, poor, and retarded. He was executed by the state of Georgia in June 1986. He was convicted of being involved with another man who killed a woman in Columbus, Georgia.

When Jerome got his death warrant, the Georgia Association for Retarded Citizens got involved in his case. They examined him extensively, confirmed that he was clinically retarded, and made a passionate appeal on his behalf.

But our society had long ago given up on Jerome. I read one school record from the time he was about eleven. A counselor wrote this advice to Jerome's teachers and guides: "Jerome is slow and probably unfit for anything other than simple factory work. He's not worth your time."

The admonition was apparently heeded. Nobody wasted any time on Jerome. His mama loved him, but her life was hard. She was a maid for the county sheriff and, though she worked more than full-time, she was paid so little that they had to depend on government-surplus powdered eggs and milk to keep from going hungry.

His life was one of degradation and neglect, but Jerome, in his own simple way, tried to do right. When the state set his execution date they sent their own psychiatrist to examine him. Jerome tried to do the best he could on the intelligence test, and he was very proud. The shrink said that he wasn't quite retarded enough to be spared from the electric chair. The doctor was paid and Jerome died with 2,300 volts of electricity through his body once, twice, three times.

But before he died, Jerome said one of the wisest things I think I've ever heard from anybody. We had been talking about prison life, and Jerome looked at me and said: "You know—peoples was not made to dog around. Peoples was made to be respected."

And third, I'd like you to meet Nancy. If you had met Nancy a few years back, you would not have expected her to end up with a ruined life. She was a schoolteacher, and her second marriage was to a prominent lawyer in a small Georgia town. He had once worked for the state attorney general's office and had friends in high places. But for all his prominence, Nancy's husband was a violent man. Soon after they were married, he began to have outbursts that would leave Nancy bruised or with an occasional broken tooth or bone. Didn't Nancy's coworkers and friends and family wonder that she was "falling down the stairs" so often?

But we learn from Nancy that the problem of male violence against women and children cuts across every class line and every racial line. Our leaders like to talk about Willie Horton and violence by strangers against women on the streets, and it's a problem. But we most often avoid the most obvious truth. And that truth is that the most dangerous place for a woman to be in the United States of America is in a relationship with a man. The most dangerous place for a child to be in the United States of America is in a family. Hear it! Most women and children who are victims of violence are victimized at home. That's how deep our sickness is.

And for Nancy, the sickness was eventually fatal. One night her husband came across the room with a two-by-four in his hand. She turned, picked up his gun, and shot him dead. She was convicted of first-degree murder and sentenced to life in prison.

She really and truly tried to make the best of her life in prison. She taught other prisoners to read. She wrote letters for the illiterate. She helped set up a special program for mothers and solicited transportation for their children to visit.

The prison doctor told her that the lump that developed in her breast was benign. When it grew he insisted that it was "nothing to worry about" and accused her of malingering. When she finally got another biopsy, it was too late. This "dangerous criminal" was sent home in a wheelchair to spend the two remaining months of her life with her teenage son and her elderly parents.

Now that you have met my three friends, I can go on to talk about the challenge of service. My title this morning should actually have been, "Gotta Serve Somebody." Bob Dylan sings that song:

> You might like to wear cotton
> Might like to wear silk
> Might like to drink whiskey
> Might like to drink milk
>> You might like to eat caviar
>>> You might like to eat bread
>> You may be sleeping on the floor,
>> sleeping on a king-sized bed
>> But you're gonna have to serve somebody . . .
>> It may be the devil or it may be the Lord
>> But you're gonna have to serve somebody.[2]

The point is this: everybody is serving somebody or something. Not having made a decision does not mean we are not serving. Because, you see, I really believe that anyone, especially of the middle or upper class, who is not serving her oppressed neighbor is serving the status quo. In other words, as long as our neighbors are being oppressed among us—and they are—and we are not serving them, then we are serving those who benefit because of our neighbor's oppression.

We would not have homeless people if it did not benefit someone. We would not be spending millions, billions of dollars a year at every federal, state,

---

2. Lyrics from "Gotta Serve Somebody," *Slow Train Coming*, Columbia Records (© 1979, Special Rider Music). Used by permission.

county, and municipal level to build prisons and jails if it didn't benefit some-body. Do you mean to tell me that we've got all these billions and we can't build housing for people? Where do you think crime comes from? Despair! But prison construction is big business. Beware when you raise a question.

The oppression of some benefits others. Our government speaks, for exam-ple, of "acceptable levels of unemployment," meaning, of course, that a certain level of unemployment is actually good for the economy. Tell that to the unem-ployed person!

You gonna have to serve somebody. The question is whom do we serve? Now, in traditional terms, when we talk about serving our neighbors we really have charity in mind. That's a great word, *caritas,* and it means love, passionate caring, compassion, advocating love, stand-up love. But charity is often taken to be serving someone a bowl of soup and thinking that's it. Don't get me wrong: the bowl of soup is critical. (I live in a soup kitchen, for heaven's sake!) A hun-gry person has to eat and the sooner the better.

But let a love for justice walk hand in hand with charity, so that at the very same time we serve the food we ask, "Why is my neighbor hungry?" What cre-ates so much hunger in a land where we throw away more food than any peo-ple in human history ever dreamed of? Charity and justice together provide a night's shelter while asking Why? Why? Why all these thousands of people homeless? Why these women and men and boys and girls and families? We have huge quantities of construction materials—buildings everywhere, church build-ings, government buildings, college buildings, so many of them standing empty most of the time.

At many points in history, women have taken important roles in the strug-gle for justice for the oppressed. I'd like to take a moment to mention one group of foremothers who are a resource for us in these days: the ASWPL—the Asso-ciation of Southern Women for the Prevention of Lynching. After the Civil War, African American people were freed from the institution of chattel slavery. But southern white people were bound and determined to maintain a tight control. In three decades after the war, it is estimated that more than ten thousand African American people were lynched.

Gradually there emerged the myth of the Black rapist, threatening at every turn to deflower southern white womanhood. It became the excuse for lynch-ings that continued well into the twentieth century. And it was done in the name of southern white women. Ida B. Wells, Mary Church Terrell, Mary Tol-bert—bold, courageous, outspoken African American women—stood up, protested, pleaded with their white sisters to take up the cause. "Because it is done in your name," they argued, "you are the very ones who can stop it."

It took about thirty-five years to get some real action. But in 1930, Jessie Daniel Ames joined with white churchwomen from around the South to form the ASWPL. Their motto as they picked up the crusade against lynching was

"Not in Our Names." They were tireless in their petition drives, meetings, letter-writing, and demonstrations and in taking on their own men. Their effectiveness in bringing an end to the public acceptance of lynching is a reminder to us of the power of women working together to end oppression. The crusade against lynching had its problems, but it was genuinely an interracial women's movement: the sort we need so desperately today.

Do you know? Do you have any idea how much the poor and your oppressed neighbor need you? Do you have any idea how much your life, your service, your compassion and love are needed by the many who suffer because of injustice?

Oppression in the form of racism, sexism, war, and poverty is causing death and destruction around the world and right under our noses. The flagrant destruction of the earth and its precious resources and the destruction of human hope and human dignity are a part of the same death-dealing spirit that says: "Serve yourself. Take what's yours and then get yourself a gun and an insurance policy to protect it. Use up whatever you want right now and let somebody else worry about tomorrow."

Our earth and the earth's people (most of whom are at this very moment poor and hungry) need us to give our lives to serve our neighbors, toward the goals of justice and social transformation. It is easy to be blinded by our class, our privilege, and, yes, even to be blinded by our education and our educational institutions.

But in these days our ignorance of our neighbor's plight—whether willful or unwitting ignorance—our silence, and our inaction mean, literally and powerfully, service to a public policy that is killing our neighbors at home and around the world.

You gonna have to serve somebody.

Please. Let us abandon exclusive travel on the predictable path. Go into the shelters, the streets, the jails and prisons, and the substandard housing. Don't let fear and oppressive myth control your life.

Meet your neighbor. Listen. Hear her story. Learn of her life.

Serve her!

Part II

HOSPITALITY
TO THE HOMELESS

There's not enough of us in this city, or in this society, who are black enough. We've got to get blacker.

—Ed Loring

Entering the World of the Homeless, Hungry and Angry, *by Ed Loring*

MARCH 1996

Editor's note: The following transcribes a lecture at Denison University on October 10, 1995, delivered as part of the school's Goodspeed Lecture Series.

I come before you on this evening as one of sixty people who live at the Open Door Community in downtown Atlanta. There are thirty-five of us who live in the house, and there are another twenty to twenty-five who live outside, some in our backyard and some in our front yard. I come before you on this evening to bear witness to you. I am a white man. I am a well-educated, middle-class person. But I come to you tonight bearing gifts, great gifts that have been given to me by homeless men, women, and children, by prisoners, some of whom have been executed by the state of Georgia. I come to share with you those gifts that these people have given me.

One of the gifts I have received is hunger, given to me by hungry people. It is a powerful gift in this culture to hunger for justice, to be thirsty for community, to be moved in your life and in your dreams and in your visions by a hope for a coming future, where as sisters and brothers, in the midst of an ever-deepening diversity, we may be one as we chew upon the bread of life.

Another way that I can speak of the gift of homeless people and prisoners in my life is that I am pissed off. I am angry. I am furious. It is absolutely stupid that in the United States of America there are men and women, boys and girls who sleep outside. It is unconscionable that there is hunger—even a famine—that stalks this land in the midst of good, nutritious, happy food. What gifts!

Hunger and manna. I hope if you came into this room tonight, and you were not hungry for justice, and you were not angry at injustice, that you will be so when you leave.

I want to speak tonight on entering the world of the homeless and the hungry, the oppressed and the marginalized. As I do that, as we walk through a door

53

into a reality, I want to say something about our world—the world that we bring as we enter the world of the homeless and the hungry. We, as middle-class people, are infested with ignorance. We have been removed by powers and forces, desires and hungers in our own lives, from the front line of suffering and oppression and deprivation in this society. We are ignorant. I was at a college last week, and I was having lunch with some of the faculty, and we were talking about homelessness. One professor said to me, "You know I think that homeless people ought to go out and get jobs. What's wrong with them?" I said, "Well, what kind of jobs do they get? People are struggling for jobs." The faculty member replied, "They could go out and get a lawn mower and they could cut grass." I said, "My Lord, man! We've got twenty thousand homeless people in Atlanta, Georgia. Could you see twenty thousand people walking down Peachtree Street, pushing lawn mowers, asking, 'Can I cut your grass?'" This was a well-intentioned, highly educated faculty member.

Our worlds are so far apart that we are ignorant of the world of the hungry and the homeless. The kinds of ideological explanations of suffering and poverty in our society, rooted in the belief that some people are unwilling to work, simply divide and separate us further and further. Not only are we ignorant in our world; often we are contemptuous. Often we find those who are other to be our enemy. We are afraid most particularly of African American men. They frighten us. The poor frighten us. They are our enemies. Even if they ask for a crust of bread. Even if they ask, and many do all over Atlanta, "May I cut your grass? Could I clean your gutters?"

Newt Gingrich has touched a deep and spiritual chord in the United States. He knows that in responding to middle-class pain, you're going to move one way or another. Either you take the pain, suffering, and insecurity of the economic stress that is growing in middle America and blame it on the big, multinational, bomb-building corporations sucking off more and more tax-free profits. Or you will say it is pregnant Black girls in housing projects. And Newt Gingrich has done a brilliant piece of work to say it is not the powerful and the rich and the international interests that are sucking the life of this nation. It's not the multinational corporations that are taking manufacturing jobs and moving them to Mexico and Taiwan. It's the people who get food stamps that are threatening your life. And more and more Americans believe these lies even as they feel their fears and watch their wallets shrink.

The world in which we live also shackles the poor. Not only are we ignorant and contemptuous, but we're slaveholders. We must continue to find ways to be abolitionists.

There are two basic ways that we are slaveholders. First, a minimum wage of $4.25 an hour is slavery. The laborer cannot afford both food and shelter. We make people work against their will and do not give them enough. Think of this: I come from the Deep South; my foreparents were slaveholders. Before 1860, when we owned slaves, and evening would set, and darkness would come, people would leave the cotton fields, or the corn patch, or come out of the barn or the kitchen in the big house after the children had been put to bed; we had some care about what happened to those people because we wanted them to work the next day. They had food, cabins, clothes, and rest. We wanted their market value of $500 to $2,300 in the flesh. But in this country we have no such interest anymore. We don't give a damn if, after eight hours of work at $4.25 an hour, workers spend all that money on crack cocaine, because we don't care whether it's the same person doing the work tomorrow that did it yesterday. It doesn't matter to us because there are so many people hungry and homeless, begging for work. There is a demonic force in the slavery of the twentieth century that, through economic self-interest, did not exist in the nineteenth century. Prisons, public and private, are a part of this slave system as well.

Second, in the world in which we live, there is a moral mystery. How in the world, with our gospel, with our founding documents, with the movements in democratic institutions and the resources for human compassion, how is it that some time in the 1970s there emerged a new phenomenon in the urban areas of the United States of America, called homelessness? And how is it that by 1990, homelessness has been institutionalized and accepted by the middle class? We simply expect it. Why do we not scream when we see boys and girls, men and women, mothers and daughters, fathers and sons outside at night? It's a mystery. With our poets and novelists, our singers and preachers, our lovely parks, how has homelessness been institutionalized in the United States?

Now let us enter, from that world of the well, into the world of the poor, the homeless. Let us go out onto the streets, where people struggle. Let us learn the most important spiritual disciplines and political tools of listening to the cry of the poor.

It is midnight in an urban setting like Atlanta. There are people lying on the streets, trying to sleep. Between them and the concrete is a piece of cardboard. How wonderful it is, sometime after eight o'clock at night, when the dumpsters have been emptied and you are still able to find a piece of cardboard that is six feet long and a couple of feet wide! Cardboard is precious at midnight on the streets because it is insulation. Have you ever slept on concrete? Even in the summertime it sucks the heat right out of your body. Praise God for cardboard!

What a wonderful experience at two o'clock in the morning to find a neglected piece of cardboard. The business community instructs those who collect the garbage, "Don't leave any cardboard around. You know it brings those damn derelicts down here. When you empty that garbage you make sure there is no cardboard!" You find a piece of cardboard, and it's two o'clock, and you take your cardboard to some place where you will not be seen, and you lie down. Maybe in a parking lot. You sneak into a covered parking lot, and by two o'clock the security guard is nodding her head, and you can move past, as though you are a fast car, in the fast lane, to find a corner where you can sleep until the sun breaks forth in the sky.

Or perhaps today is a lucky day. We have twenty thousand homeless people in Atlanta. In the wintertime with our winter shelters, we have five or six thousand places in churches, in basements, in other buildings for night shelter. Sometimes at the city shelter, we'll put three hundred people in the old city jail. Or at the women and children's shelter at First Iconium Baptist Church on Moreland Avenue, we'll put 175 people in a gymnasium. And you've worked all day, a lucky day. You go down to the church shelter, and you're given some food, and you lie down on the floor on a mat, not on cardboard!

You've got a chance for a job, for a repeat ticket out of the labor pool. You want to get some sleep. It's early, it's only ten o'clock. You lie down in the muffled moans of the night shelter, moans of parents separated from their children, of nightmares that grasp and hold you, in a room with thirty people coughing and sniffling and crying. You cannot sleep.

It's five o'clock in the morning now. Most shelters close, and people begin to look for work. Forty percent of the homeless people in Atlanta, Georgia, work regularly. People who are poor work. People who are homeless work.

At the Open Door Community we have a breakfast program. This afternoon I learned that we served three hundred people there this morning. We generally serve about 250. We almost ran out of grits. We serve a good breakfast: grits, boiled eggs, coffee, oranges, multivitamins.

When I was speaking of the college professor and the lawn mower, I wanted to tell that story because it is so reminiscent of me when I began fifteen years ago working on the streets of Atlanta. I did not know that one thousand to three thousand people every morning must make a difficult decision when they seek work, when they leave a shelter or a cat hole or an abandoned automobile or an abandoned building. If you get day labor, you lose your access to the soup kitchens, so you make a choice, "Shall I eat today, or shall I work?" I didn't know that. When I found out that homeless people were forced to make that choice between food and work, we started the Butler Street CME Church breakfast. For thirteen years now we have been serving breakfast in the basement of that church in downtown Atlanta.

A labor pool is a modern slave market. It is where people who are desperate for work go in the dark, dark hours of the morning. If a contract comes to a labor pool for a job that's worth ten dollars an hour, the labor pool becomes a labor broker, and says, "I will accept you for this job. You come up here, and I will pay you $4.25 an hour." The labor pool, a private enterprise, gets the market value of the job minus the $4.25 an hour.

In Atlanta, for instance, we send many, many hundreds of people out from the labor pools into neighboring counties to collect garbage. We have a county just north of Atlanta, Gwinnett County, that will not allow public transportation, and that works hard to keep African Americans and poor people out, but that still has the regular work we need poor people for. Who in the hell is gonna empty the garbage can? So they bus and truck people out of labor pools in the morning to collect the garbage, and then get them out of the county in the evening by the time residents get home from work.

Now after sleeping on a sidewalk it's difficult work to empty garbage. It's difficult work any time of the day or night. It is difficult work after sleeping in a night shelter. It is difficult work! But think what it would be like when, so often, as you are on your way to work, someone passes you in a car, rolls down their window, shoots you a bird, and yells, "Why don't you get a job, you lazy bum! You worthless freeloader!" The work becomes even harder. For students it would be as though you were on your way to class, having spent the night, not in student housing, but outside. And it had been raining. You were cold and wet and your books and papers soaked and ruined, and your professor looked at you and said, "Why are you coming to class, you dumb student? You've got an IQ so low, I don't know how you got into Denison University." It is that level of op-pression, pain, and marginalization that greets the homeless as they walk to work.

This morning, when I was flying in to Columbus, Ohio, from Atlanta, I looked out a window and saw a golf course. This was before lunch, and on that golf course I saw a whole bunch of these little golf carts running around and great big grown men with a little stick, chasing a little ball. Now how come they aren't lazy bums? What are these qualified, strong, gifted people doing out here before lunch playing golf?

A friend of mine, who works out of a labor pool named Temporary People, was very upset one morning at five o'clock because he couldn't get a job. I said, "Why not? What happened?" He said, "Well, I got sent on a construction job a couple of days ago, and when I got there they told me to go down into this hole to do some digging. The hole had not been reinforced in an adequate way." Cave-ins cause a lot of injury and death on construction jobs, I learned through this conversation with my friend. He told the supervisor that he would not go down in the hole, so they told him to sit and that he would not get paid one penny. At 6 A.M., when he was leaving Temporary People to go to this con-struction site, he had accepted a brown-bag lunch with two baloney sandwiches on white bread, a soda, and chips for three dollars. They also charge $1.25 for transportation to the site and back. When he returned he owed the company more than five dollars, and he had lost a day of his life. He had no redress.

One morning a number of years ago I was sitting in a labor pool. It was late; usually the labor pools are most active between 4:30 and 7:30 in the morning. If you're not out by eight o'clock, your day is pretty close to finished. I was sitting in the labor pool, and I was just amazed. One man turned to another at about 8:30 or nine o'clock, and said, "Well, I guess my day is over." He knew in that situation that there would not be anything for him to do. He trudged to a soup kitchen, to the public library, to a corner where people were gathered around a dumpster, passing a vodka bottle. Maybe he went out into the weed patch, where lots of vines are growing, to smoke some grass. He went somewhere and did something to numb himself from the assault of poverty and homelessness. And as he wandered he would have to know, to hear, and to experience being unwanted.

In fact, by the year 1990 in the United States, homelessness was accepted as an issue that did not relate to housing. Homelessness is considered a public safety issue. When you have a lot of homeless people you need a lot of police. And when you need a lot of police, you need a bigger budget to build more jails. We have just quadrupled the size of the city detention center in downtown Atlanta, which almost exclusively holds poor people.

We have a place in Atlanta called the vagrant-free zone. You get rid of the vagrants there because they're bad for business, and white people won't come to downtown Atlanta when there are aggressive panhandlers, especially beggars of color. Housing and hunger are understood in this country to be public safety issues. Rather than house the homeless, we build more jails and prisons and hire more police. Rather than feed the hungry, we take food stamps away. That means death for poor people. It means prisons. It means the loss of hope and the development of despair that lead to drugs and alcohol and mental illness and crippling disease. And we have accepted this hell, this injustice.

Please be hungry for justice and angry at injustice!

When we leave the world of the homeless and the hungry and come back to our world, to our place, to the university, to the Open Door Community, to the church, to the civic organization, to the sorority or the fraternity, we need to find resources for hope and vision in our lives and relationships. We can in community, in life together, develop an ethic and a walk in life that makes us thankful and joyful people. We can live out the image of God in dance and celebration as we reach out to one another.

Let me give you a wonderful example. You probably know Harriet Tubman, a woman, a slave, who struggled, fought, demanded, and got freedom. She got out of it; she beat the system; she got free. And at the moment when she was free, and she had to choose the course her freedom would take, she turned her back on Ohio (the place of freedom) and returned to the South to free other slaves. Nineteen times she came South, and nineteen times she came out of the South.

We are forced and pushed in this society to get a college education, to get a job, and to make a lot of money. We are pushed when we achieve freedom to use it for our own betterment. Harriet Tubman says, "Wait! I didn't pull myself up by my own bootstraps. I was lifted up by voices of the ancestors. They created in me a hunger for justice and an anger toward injustice! I must go south

to work for the freedom of my brothers and my sisters." At the moment of freedom, not slavery, she turned back to achieve solidarity with the oppressed and
the slave. She refused the distance that pushes us away from the poor, the sick,
the prisoner. Harriet Tubman came back to free others from the oppression she
had known.

That is what we can do. It is what we must do. We must involve ourselves
with homeless people as the way to respond to homelessness. We must be involved with hungry people as the way to respond to hunger. When you come to
know hungry people, fasting is a powerful discipline. When you come to know
homeless people, sleeping outside on a piece of cardboard is a wonderful practice. In the quest for solidarity, we can bring hunger and suffering into our flesh.
Fasting in these ways is a necessary spiritual discipline.

As we look for an ethic that makes us joyful in solidarity and thankful as we
reduce the distance, we give thanks for the role of women and sisters in our lives.
If there are going to be resources in North American culture for an ethic that
will not tolerate children living under Interstate bridges, that says, "No! Hell,
no!" to old people withered on sidewalks, fallen over, as they're already doing in
Los Angeles, where the public hospitals are closing, the hope is help from sisters.

Work with our hands is another resource for hope and vision. Habitat for
Humanity gives us a place to join with our bodies and with one another to build
houses. But homeless people, just like you and me, need a lot more than a house.
We need home. Housing precedes home. We will not find ways to live together,
to overcome the deepening rifts between Black and white, rich and poor, male
and female, and straight and lesbian and gay, until we build houses so that we
can be about the work of making home. What a great human vocation! Are we
not all homemakers? Certainly we are.

We are blessed at the Open Door Community by the numerous people who
have come to live and to die with us, who have been HIV-infected, and who
then died from AIDS. All of us in this room can find ways, as we struggle, to
build hope and vision. We need to stand, to sit, to eat, to live, and to die with
those who have AIDS. When we commit our lives to the dying, there is a quality of life—life, not death—of energy, not fatigue, of a capacity to rest rather
than to be busy all the time.

I thank you for listening to me. I have come before you to bear witness to
my listening. Where will my next meal come from? I heard that yesterday afternoon on Peachtree Street. Where will I sleep tonight? How can I stay dry when
it rains? Where can I get a drink of water? Where is the bathroom? We all gotta
pee for free with dignity! Where can I take a shower? Where can I wash these
filthy hands of mine after I have worked out of a labor pool at a construction
warehouse? Where can I find work? I want work! I'm not a lazy bum! Where?
How? When? Who? Where's my daughter? I'm not a deadbeat dad. I just can't
make it, man, on $4.25 an hour. I love my son. I'm not a deadbeat dad. I just

can't give 'em my name at the night shelter, but I want to see my child. Where's my child?

Here we are. We are hungry for justice. Let us, please, be angry at injustice. Let us build a better world. We can do it. Harriet Tubman will lead us there. We have sisters and brothers. We can stand in solidarity, reduce the distance, and be filled with the life of joy and thanksgiving, of song and prayer, of hope and affirmation. I thank you.

Homelessness Is Hell, *by Ed Loring*

SEPTEMBER 1987

Homelessness is absurd. Homelessness is unnecessary. Homelessness is hell. Homelessness is Ralph, Jay, Brenda, five-year-old Jimmy, sixty-five-year-old "Pop," black Willie, brown Juan, white Jane. Ah, homelessness is you and homelessness is me, even as we bite the bullet to pay for home repairs on the beach cottage. Homelessness is dereliction, frostbitten toes, crooked and lost fingers, burning, bleary eyes with 20/200 vision and a pair of Eckerd reading glasses to mask the shame and blindness. Homelessness is an effort to squeak out an identity where one has no place and where one has nothing to do.

What do you do when you have nothing to do? Something? Then you know little of the spiritual and political plight of the 8,753 boys and girls, women and men who roam downtown Atlanta to the chagrin of Central Atlanta Progress and the horror of the Chamber of Commerce and the dread of the banker who just sold one more risk-free bond for the development of Underground Atlanta, where doctors and lawyers and businesspeople will soon be able "to do anything they want," and never have to see, touch, hear, smell, or taste the slowly dying, hidden lives and bodies of the homeless.

We have learned in modern America that to have the poor available and ready is a good for the well-to-do. That is why we want them as a source of blood plasma for medical research or for the manufacture of medicines, and as bodies for teaching hospitals, and as an ever-ready pool of cheap labor. However, to have them present as anything other than objects for our benefit is bad for business and a blight on our pleasure. Therefore, we will not feed the hungry in a land that produces so much food that it pays farmers not to farm; nor will we build houses for the homeless in a nation that has more than enough construction supplies to house everyone.

Homelessness is Henry. He grew up in North Carolina and, twenty years ago, came to Atlanta in search of work and his shot at the American Dream. Black, strong, easygoing, Henry now finds himself a resident of nowhere while a member of a human community that names itself Atlanta. Henry lost job after job, as all unskilled workers in our economy do. Henry drinks alcohol to ease his pain and to grasp once more at his dream in the same way that others do at the Falcons football game or at the Hilton Sunday brunch.

Henry sleeps under a bridge near the municipal market just off 1-75/85. Sleep comes only in bits and pieces in such a spot, so he is exhausted when he arises at 5:00 A.M. and stumbles toward the local private-enterprise labor pool.

"Shall I get work today? Do I want work today?" These questions haunt not only Henry, but the two thousand other men (and some fifty women) who sit in the various downtown labor pools each morning. If a job is offered, most folk must make a choice: to eat or not to eat. To go out on a job means the worker will miss the opportunity for two meals at the soup kitchens. Stomachs, already groaning from digestive juices sloshing against empty stomach walls, say, "Go for the soup kitchen." A labor-pool job, that last glimmer of hope, has its attraction—"maybe today the break will come." Torn between another day of hunger and a twenty-five-dollar paycheck, Henry, today, chooses food. So he will not work. At 6:00 A.M., sitting in a metal chair not far from the greasy hand-written sign, "No Sleeping Allowed," Henry falls asleep.

At 7:30 A.M., Henry pulls his aching body out of the chair and heads to Butler Street CME Church for the "grits line." There he meets two hundred others who stand in line until the door is opened. By 8:15 he has had a cup of coffee, a bowl of grits, a boiled egg, and a vitamin C tablet. Just as he is ready to hit the streets his bowels yell out. Where can he go? The church has locked its doors, not wanting the poor and the dirty to use its facilities. He clunks upstairs, walks outside, and quickly hides himself behind the dumpster. Atlanta refuses to provide public toilets. One theory offered by an intelligent leader is that if we provide public toilets, homeless from all over North America will come to Atlanta. Yet we spend fifty thousand dollars each year processing the average of four arrests per day for public urination. Henry hopes, with his pants below his knees and feces dropping from his bottom, that no one will see him. When finished, a flicker of desire passes through the broken black man's heart—"Oh, if only I had a sheet of toilet paper, and maybe . . . just a piece of soap and a little water." But he does not. Now he stinks. Now, as daylight has filled the city streets, Henry is an enemy of the professional—a discarded person, a punk, wino, and bum in newspaper columnist Lewis Grizzard's terms. He can't even keep himself clean!

Henry wanders toward Grady Hospital. If the guard is nice or sleepy, Henry can wash off. If the guard is absent he can sit in the waiting room until discovered. There he can get some of that wet and cold out of his torn socks. He sits and looks at his filthy feet. Damn, how I wish my left shoe had a sole, he thinks

silently to himself, for there is no one with whom to share this most human wish.

When one is poor and carries the terrible burden of poverty—which is having nothing to do but to wait—time moves so slowly. The single most important distinction between the well-to-do and the poor is this: the rich have too
little time and too much to do while the homeless poor have too much time and
nothing to do. In contemporary culture this distinction leads in many instances
to the same spiritual states: despair, alcoholism, stress, violence, sexual abuse,
and an ironic dimension of hatred whereby the rich hate and fear the poor because they have too little to do and the poor hate and envy the rich because they
have something to do.

Henry, now with nothing to do except shuffle his way uptown, heads for St.
Luke's soup kitchen. Walking hurts; hunger hurts. He now longs to travel the
mile so he can stand and wait for the soup and sandwich. Henry joins seven
hundred men and women, boys and girls who climb the fifty stairs to the dining hall. Music plays in the background, crazy people mumble to themselves
about love and lost children, young men search in a macho, violent-prone society for a way to test and prove their manhood with no tender fathers there to
help. Henry eats his soup.

It's 11:00 A.M. Henry's day that really never began is almost over. He now de-
cides to go for the big eight-dollar job, which the medical board allows twice a
week. With eight dollars he can get cigarettes, a half-pint, and a chicken supper.
So Henry, reduced to a man who can only muster the energy and hope for survival, heads to the blood bank.

After a two-hour wait, his name is called. Slowly he rises from the floor,
where he has watched a *Perry Mason* rerun, interspersed with advertisements
that promise a good life if you will only buy their useless product. Henry walks
to the hospital bed and lies down. Finally, for the first time in five days, he is
comfortable. A nurse stands beside him and applies the needle. His blood begins to drip out of his body. Tired, and without recognition that he is bleeding
to feed forces beyond his control, and perhaps beyond the control of anyone in
this society, Henry sleeps. Sleep at the blood bank is unlike sleep anywhere else
for the homeless. Here, bleeding, he is safe. The temperature is warm, and the
noise of the TV and the din of voices from those waiting to sell their blood after
Henry are muted by the closed door. Yes, the most comfortable and the safest
place for a homeless person in all of Atlanta is on the blood-bank bed. It's a pity
that one can only be there four hours per week.

Henry's day is over. His life, according to many who understand human ex-
istence to be rooted in meaning and purposefulness, has been over for years.
Homelessness is death. Homelessness is absurd. Homelessness is unnecessary.
Homelessness is Hell. Homelessness is Henry. Ah, homelessness is you and me.

Homelessness and Slavery, *by Elizabeth Dede*

J U N E   1 9 9 0

During April at the Open Door we learned a lot about homelessness. Our time on the streets taught us much about the daily and nightly struggles of our friends who have no homes. At the same time, I began reading a book by Lerone Bennett Jr. called *Before the Mayflower: A History of Black America.* From this book, I learned and relearned much about the constant struggles of our African American sisters and brothers to be free and full citizens of the United States. When I connect my experience on the streets of Atlanta, in solidarity with homeless folk, with my reading of *Before the Mayflower,* I can only conclude that, despite the abolition of slavery, notwithstanding the repeal of Jim Crow laws, and while recognizing the victories of the civil rights movement, white Americans continue to find ways to enslave our African American brothers and sisters.

The comparisons between slavery and homelessness are frighteningly close. Some are obvious, dealing with the similarities in physical conditions. Examples come readily. The vast majority of American slaves had their roots in Africa. The vast majority of homeless people in Atlanta today are African Americans. Slaves owned nothing, and everything they had, down to the clothes on their backs, belonged to their white masters. They were sometimes given used clothing, handed down to the slave from the owners. Our homeless friends fit the same description. Their possessions are few, and the clothes they wear are most often used, handed down from a white person who has outgrown them or grown tired of the style or color.

We can also consider the kinds of work slaves did in comparison to the work our homeless friends find, and again there is a frightening similarity. Slaves did the hard and dangerous "physical labor" so that their owners could enjoy an easy, comfortable, prosperous existence. Homeless people who find jobs through labor pools are sent out to load trucks, clean hotel rooms, load garbage, wash windows on skyscrapers, and remove asbestos (to name only a few of the hard and dangerous jobs they do) in order to make life more pleasant and safe for the mostly white population that looks out the windows of the skyscrapers or attends the convention at the hotel.

Apart from the physical descriptions of homelessness, we can also look to the spiritual, emotional, or mental conditions of slaves and the homeless to find similarities. Imagine what happened to the spirit of slaves each time they realized that they had nothing, or that all they had belonged to the master who enslaved them. Even their children and spouses were sold, so that the most intimate relationships were torn apart. Slaves must often have struggled against the feeling that they were nothing or nobody. Now imagine a strong young man who sleeps in the backyard at 910 Ponce de Leon three nights each week so that he can be here early enough to get his name on the list for a shower and a change of clothes. Imagine what it must feel like to wait three hours between the time he signs his name and the time he gets called in for a shower. Imagine the humiliation as the rush-hour traffic crawls by on Ponce, carrying the well-dressed, freshly showered, and breakfasted businessfolk to work downtown while he waits for the coffee to be put out, for a place in the shower room to open up, and for the used clothes to be handed to him from the clothes closet. Imagine what happens to the spirit of that person each time he realizes that he has nothing. Homeless folk struggle daily against the same feelings of nothingness and "nobodyness" that their slave ancestors struggled against in the nineteenth century.

While on the streets during Holy Week, we were shocked by the overpowering police presence we encountered in downtown Atlanta. We heard from an African American friend that he spent nearly a month in jail because he had dropped a cigarette butt on the ground in the park. We were told that we could not stand on a public sidewalk or sit on a public bench. We watched the police kick sleeping homeless folk until they woke up, while across the park businessfolk on lunch break enjoyed a peaceful nap. We have heard that the police often require homeless folk to show identification or leave the park. And we know of several proposals to license homeless folk, including a "Ponce Pass," which a homeless person would be required to have in order to walk down Ponce de Leon Avenue.

Lerone Bennett writes in *Before the Mayflower* about a similar police state:

> Arrayed against rebellious slaves was a police apparatus of unparalleled severity. Each slave state had a slave code which was designed to keep slaves ignorant and in awe of white power. Under the provisions of these codes, slaves were forbidden to assemble in groups of more than five or seven away from their home plantation. They were forbidden to leave plantations without passes and they could not blow horns, beat drums or read books. A free black, when challenged by a white person, was obliged to produce papers proving that he was free.

Bennett explains that the slave codes were developed and enforced to make slaves believe that they were slaves:

> Each slave was taught . . . that they were totally helpless and that their master was absolutely powerful. Each slave was taught that they were inferior to the meanest white and that they had to obey every white person without thinking, without questioning. Finally, if these lessons were learned, slaves

looked at themselves through the eyes of their masters and accepted the values of the masters.

It seems to me that ordinances and proposals to create and sustain the vagrant-free zone in downtown Atlanta accomplish the same purpose as slave codes. Homeless folk are arrested or harassed or pushed around with the desired outcome that they will no longer appear on the streets downtown. They will see themselves as vagrants and will stay away from the vagrant-free zone. Those in power today are using the same tactics against the homeless poor as those used against slaves in the nineteenth century.

Just as there was an abolitionist movement in the nineteenth century, we must begin to abolish homelessness now. Bennett shows that the crusade to abolish slavery happened in two phases. The first was characterized by "muted rhetoric and reformist demands for limited improvements in the slave system." We seem to be entrenched in this phase in the abolition-of-homelessness movement. Much of the work and talk about homelessness is about improving homelessness. So to advocate for year-round, twenty-four-hour city shelters is an improvement, but it does not end the slavery of homelessness. For Mayor Maynard Jackson to talk about his concern for the homeless and his plan to provide single-room occupancy housing is a sign of hope, but the talk does not build homes. To provide a soup kitchen makes life better for homeless folk, but it means that there are poor and homeless folk who must depend on others to provide them with food. The labor-pool reform movement seeks to make working conditions better, but, in reality, reform results mostly in improvements to a system that continues to oppress people. Central Atlanta Progress plans to develop a computer network for alternative labor sources so that laborers can keep more of their pay. However, I am cynical enough to believe that even with reform and networks, homelessness, or some other form of slavery, will continue to exist, because the labor-pool system—free-enterprise slavery—depends on the exploitation of the poor. Therefore, a second phase, which involves a change in the system and not just improvements, and which requires action and struggle and not just muted rhetoric, is needed.

According to Bennett, the second phase of abolishing slavery was a more militant phase that called for universal emancipation and action. It required not only belief in the words that all people are created equal and have the right of liberty, but it also necessitated a movement into the streets to force action and change.

The rhetoric of the second phase was clear and uncompromising. Bennett quotes from William Lloyd Garrison's first editorial in the *Liberator:*

> I will be as harsh as truth, and as uncompromising as justice.
> On this subject [slavery], I do not wish to think, to speak, or
> write, with moderation. No! No! Tell a man whose house is on

fire to give a moderate minim; tell him to moderately rescue his wife from the hands of the ravisher; tell the mother to gradually extricate her babe from the fire into which it has fallen; but urge me not to use moderation in a cause like the present! I am in earnest—I will not equivocate—I will not excuse—I will not retreat a single inch—AND I WILL BE HEARD!

It is time for us to use such rhetoric. We must enter the second phase in order to abolish homelessness. We must now act decisively to stop police harassment, to end the oppression of laborers, to produce affordable housing, and to make sure that all people share in the good things of life—food, clothes, safe dwelling, family, friends, health, and meaningful work.

However, this major change in our system will not come without struggle. Frederick Douglass, one of the great abolitionists and a former slave, would sum up the protest movement toward freedom, again quoted in Bennett, in one word—*struggle:*

The whole history of the progress of human liberty shows that all concessions yet made to her august claims have been born of earnest struggle. . . . If there is no struggle there is no progress. . . . This struggle may be a moral one, or it may be a physical one, and it may be both moral and physical, but it must be a struggle. Power concedes nothing without a demand. It never did and it never will. Find out just what any people will quietly submit to and you have found out the exact measure of injustice and wrong which will be imposed upon them, and these will continue until they are resisted with either words or blows, or with both. The limits of tyrants are prescribed by the endurance of those whom they oppress.

We can no longer quietly submit. It is time to enter the struggle, to speak loudly against the injustice of the slavery of homelessness, and to act firmly. Our homeless friends have endured enough.

So with protests and actions we will struggle for change. We will have words and come to nonviolent blows with the system until there is freedom. The powers will know by our noise and our action that the limit has been reached.

We invite you to join us in the struggle. When homelessness has been abolished, when we stop oppressing the poor—particularly the African American worker—then slavery will finally be abolished, and we will find ourselves living in a beautiful society of free people, where all are equal.

Sobering Up: How to Clean Up the Streets in America, *by Ed Loring*

F E B R U A R Y   1 9 9 2

This article began in April 1979. Carolyn Johnson and I had completed our first research project on the numbers of people without houses in Atlanta and on resources for folk in such a crisis. I shall continue writing this article long after I lay my pen on my desk. For as a response to our findings in the spring of 1979—1,200 men and women, boys and girls living on the streets or at the Salvation Army and the Union Mission, eating at St. Luke's Community Kitchen and finding no free shelter space in the city—I committed my life to the houseless folk of Atlanta.

Housing is a critical social problem in American society. Everyone accepts that fact today. We continue to debate the numbers and causes of people residing on streets in Atlanta. Some suggest a very few thousand. They tend to believe that having no place to live is a breakdown of personal morals, such as addiction to alcohol and drugs. Others, like the Atlanta Task Force for the Homeless, paint the picture on rougher canvas: 15,000 on any given night; 45,000 to 60,000 different people during a twelve-month period. The causes, never unrelated to personal choice and behavior, lie within a political system which executes public policy that results in increases in the number of people on the streets every twenty-four hours. This public policy is buttressed, according to the task force, by cultural values rooted in individualistic habits of the heart; the resulting social analysis rarely goes beyond blaming the victim for her situation. Notwithstanding the ongoing debate over numbers and causes, we have reached an American consensus: (1) housing is a critical social problem, and (2) folk without housing are in personal crisis.

Martha is a twenty-five-year-old African American woman. She is unmarried, the mother of two little boys, Timmy and Odeka. She lives in a shelter two miles from the central business district. Martha, like more than 40 percent of the homeless, has a job. She works five nights a week, from 5:00 to 9:00 P.M., for a janitorial company which contracts to clean office buildings. Her pay is minimum wage. She gets no benefits and no vacation. The company's employment policies mandate reliance on part-time temporary labor. Full-time employment at a living wage for Martha, Timmy, and Odeka is not an option. The bottom rung of the ladder is the top rung. Martha has a bed; she wants a home. Martha is a mother; she wants private space, a yard, and a nearby school for Timmy and Odeka.

Occasionally, Martha goes to the blood bank to pick up an extra twelve dollars selling her plasma. From entrance to departure requires four hours; she earns three dollars per hour. She has been known to have a drink in Woodruff Park (bars and restaurants charge too much for her), get feisty, and to get locked up for a couple of days; then she is fired from her janitorial job and put out of the shelter for a week. Then Martha, Timmy, and Odeka start over again.

As despair grows among the street population, so grows aggressiveness, hostility, and contempt. Yet there remains a majestic quality to the endurance, suffering, and survival among the urban exiles and nomads. Their pain and grief is beyond the imaginings of those of us who sleep well, eat what we want, and know, from calendars too filled with marginalia, what we will be doing the day after tomorrow. Though no Anne Frank, Martha represents the secret resources and mystical qualities of human nature available to cope with and endure this homeless hell. Unfortunately, she, like Anne Frank, is doomed. Martha lives under the death sentence of homelessness. The streets may be neither concentration camp nor oven, but Martha's fate is sealed. She shall die from houselessness, hunger, and underemployment. Timmy and Odeka, African American males, though no Willie Horton, will, if they survive eighteen more years, end up in prison.

The resources available in American life to resolve social problems have not been able to end homelessness, nor to slow its development. We have not designed a therapy to halt the insidious progress of a cancer gone too far. Our elected leadership has discovered no public policy which can house the one million to three million American citizens living on the streets. The business community has been unable to develop an equitable distribution of work, a living wage, or market incentives to address the death and waste of human life in every urban area. Communities of faith have failed to mobilize their membership into a cadre of compassion which could inform our politicians and inspire our business leadership. People of faith have done better at confessing sins than opening their homes to the homeless poor (Isaiah 58; Romans 12). Why?

The vast majority of people in the United States are housed and have access to many benefits of living in the most privileged society in history. Not only do we possess material abundance, but political liberty and economic mobility keep our nation the envy of more than a billion people. Deep are our problems; lofty are our accomplishments. Yet the political powerlessness among the 2 percent of our population who are houseless and the 23 percent in poverty is devastating.

In our democratic society, public policy reflects the will of the majority represented by Congress, which in turn is checked and balanced by the Supreme Court's interpretation of our rights guaranteed by the Constitution. Dr. Martin Luther King Jr., between 1964 and 1966, was able to build a coalition among Blacks and whites, rich and poor, which established desegregation as the will of Congress and thence as public policy. Unusual indeed! No person, party, or movement has ever been able to enlist majority support to house the homeless, to feed the hungry, or to employ the jobless as public policy. The New Deal moved in this direction during the Depression, when formerly middle-class citizens were in shelters and soup-kitchen lines, without work. John Steinbeck's novel *Grapes of Wrath* pictures graphically the limitations of the trickle-down theory.

The majority of Americans are well-to-do. We are housed, fed, and working. There is little inclination on the part of the majority to shape public policy so that decent housing, nutritious food, and full-time employment are accessible to the poverty-stricken. Therefore, democratic political structures are not effective means for addressing the interests of homeless people. Housing the homeless as public policy will not be achieved democratically unless the majority of voters are personally threatened by the loss of their housing. Apparently, we will not alter the way things are until the self-interest of the majority is employed in response to their own material loss. People without housing, adequate employment, or food will continue to be born, to grow, to serve their time, and to die on the streets of America. Even now, our streets, prisons, hospitals, public libraries, parks, and charitable institutions are filling up with poverty-stricken folk. Yet houseless men and women know pain and resentment, suffering and rage, hope and resistance. God is on their side; so, too, the implacable forces of fairness. But for now . . . we stand and wait.

The political problem, then, for the houseless and poor citizens of the United States is their minority status. The poor lack the means to change the systems through the democratic electoral process. That they can is the terrible and poverty-producing myth of the American System. The Voting Rights Act, the idea of one person, one vote, and the Nineteenth Amendment, which invited our sisters into the democratic process, are all achievements in the pursuit of justice. But to admonish the poor to organize and to vote their way off the streets into houses is illusion. The antislavery movement tried daily between 1830 and 1860 to end slavery through the democratic process. It failed. It was not the will of the majority to set African Americans free. John Brown rode into Harper's Ferry only after every legal means to abolish human bondage had been attempted. What will it require of us to house the homeless?

❖ ❖ ❖

Now for the good news! The absolutely astounding news! There is no housing shortage in Atlanta. On any given night there are, according to the Task Force for the Homeless, fifteen thousand men and women, boys and girls without living space. On the very same night considerably more than fifteen thousand boarding-house rooms, apartments, and houses are on the market in the metropolitan area. In fact, during the fall of 1990 a leading economist from the

University of Georgia announced a housing glut across the state. His research revealed that the Georgia economy is threatened by the tremendous number of vacant apartments and houses. The Georgia economy and our quality of life are also threatened by men and women and children living and dying on our streets.

Fifteen thousand people in Atlanta are homeless, and more than fifteen thousand vacant properties are on the market. So we have a simple solution to homelessness in Atlanta. Make the vacant housing available to those with no housing! Simple arithmetically, complex economically. If we lived in a feudalistic society (God forbid) the houseless could go to an overlord, make a fealty oath as a serf, and move into the vacant housing. In a capitalistic economy it is not the pledge of life and labor, but money, which provides access to housing. Ah, dear Hamlet, here is the rub. We have a money shortage, not a housing shortage, in Atlanta. The fifteen thousand people who live on our streets do not have money to rent or purchase the available housing.

The capitalistic solution is to make more money available among the poor. We need an equitable sharing of money so that all U.S. citizens will have access to decent housing, nutritious food, adequate medical care, and joyful life. We do not need a new system of government or new economic structures. Democracy and capitalism already have the mechanisms to provide housing, food, and jobs for all citizens.

First is the system that is the barometer of our nation's commitment to fairness, economic sharing, and the democratic way of life: the graduated income tax. As a nation we have no money shortage. We do have an imbalance between the well-to-do and the poverty-stricken. In this society, where there is enough for everyone to have enough, a revision of percentages within the tax system could redistribute income so that homelessness would be a memory. Put the money in the market.

Our second resource is the minimum wage. The bottom line for setting the amount needs to be determined by the market costs for a decent life. How much money does it take to have access to the necessities of life—housing, food, medical care, and so on—plus surplus for crisis, old age, and leisure?

The good news for the poor is that we have no housing shortage and that the political and economic mechanisms to end homelessness are already in place. A problem we well-to-do folk face, however, is our addiction to poverty. The benefits of poverty we reap—a cheap pool of laborers, bodies for medical teaching and research, middle-income jobs for rendering assistance—are not worth the costs of prisons, police, violence, crime, fear, and the decay of human values inherent in innocent suffering and needless death. Poverty is no more beneficial to our society than the numbing effect of alcohol is to the person.

Like an alcoholic family, we are afraid of sobriety and health. The impulse and inclination of drinkers and nondrinkers alike is to quickly point out the reasons why they need to continue drinking, or to deny that they drink at all. (U.S.

Attorney General Edwin Meese just a few years ago denied that hunger existed in the United States.) Addiction to poverty, with the concomitant inability to halt its growth or to eradicate its presence, is destroying the American way of life. Blaming the poor will not heal our addiction. Intervention—the graduated income tax equitably applied, and a living minimum wage—will.

The homeless and those, like myself, who stand with them are failing. We are losing the battle against poverty and death. How can we as a nation sober up? How can we clean up our streets? We need help; we need leadership.

Shelter from the Storm: Why Do People Live in Houses? *by Ed Loring*

M A R C H   1 9 9 2

I've heard newborn babies wailin' like a mournin' dove
And old men with broken teeth stranded without love.
Do I understand your question, man, is it hopeless and forlorn?
"Come in," she said,
"I'll give you shelter from the storm."

—Bob Dylan[1]

"Ebbie, come on in now. It's suppertime."
"Aw, Mom, can't I play a little longer?"
"No, your supper is ready and it's getting dark."
"Aw, Mom . . ."
"Come on in now."

What wonderful grace! I grew up, and now I am growing old, well-housed. I have tasted homelessness a few bleak and desolate times, but never houselessness. A place of one's own is a means of grace. It's where sacramental things happen, like learning to trust your mom's voice at eveningtide, beckoning you inward toward a shared meal and family warmth.

Because Yahweh is who she is and because Jesus does what he does and because the Holy Ghost blows through my window, I, like my mother, call people

---

1. Lyrics from "Shelter from the Storm," *Blood on the Tracks,* Columbia Records (© 1974, Ram's Horn Music). Used by permission.

inside. "It's eleven o'clock, come on in now. It's lunchtime," I shout to the 125 folk in our front yard on the mornings Gladys lets me do the door. Through Dorothy Day's amazing book *The Long Loneliness* I fell in love with the homeless poor—Yahweh's chosen ones—thirteen years ago. Since then a basic aim and a fundamental purpose of my life has been to get folks inside, that is, off the streets.

Everyday now there are fewer Americans who deny that we are in the midst of a storm. Certainly the very rich continue to live in the eye of the storm, but the raging waters, the fierce winds, and the ferocious fire are demanding the attention of many middle-class Americans.[2] Every one of us, even the most well-to-do, needs shelter from the storm. The homeless and houseless on our streets are among the most vulnerable. The winds are blowing them and our communities apart; the waters are drowning them and our families; the fires burn our very souls and char our compassion, which should constitute any mature and decent life.

We all need shelter. The need for housing is not a class, ethnic, or gender issue. We all need shelter from the storm. The word *shelter* has an interesting etymology. It comes from Old English (400–1100 C.E.) and is a military term. *Shield troop* is the original word, meaning a large body of people who gather together and interlock their arms; thus their many shields form one large shield for protection. Images of cooperation, mutual support, and shared resources for security are rooted in this word, *shelter*. Also implied is a communal response to threat, challenge, and war. To face the storm, the community made shelter available for all. As is often the case, word history is a source of hope. Today, when prophets for housing as a human right gather our bodies and voices, we have a particular image in our hearts.

Human domicile must be warm when the weather is cold and cool when the weather is hot (that leaves Georgia prisons out), always dry, safe, healthy, and accessible. To be human shelter, a significant amount of private space must be included. Migrant workers who pick peaches in Spartanburg County, South Carolina, each summer—you can see them and their little white slave quarters from Interstate 85—do not have human shelter. Over the years at the Open Door Community we have lowered the number of people who live together. When we began there were fifty. Tonight there are thirty. As we have loved and

---

2. In a democratic society in which public policy reflects the will of the majority, the problems of minorities like the homeless are ignored until the consequences begin to affect the status quo. The first response of the American people was to help the homeless charitably; the second was to condemn them and blame them for their poverty, unemployment, addictions, and houselessness. Now even Jimmy Carter and his handpicked alter ego, Dan Sweat, of Central Atlanta Progress—a downtown businesses' organization—say we need to respond to the poor, not only for the sake of this minority but for our own, that is, the majority's, welfare.

fought, served and been served, grown old and died together, we have come to grasp more profoundly the interplay between shared space and private space. So we now have no bedroom in the house with more than two people. All of us have access to private space. I note this fact because of the growing greed in government to control the lives of the poor through zoning laws and behavior ordinances. To be poor is a crime in the United States, and shelter is often a quiet little jail or a spot in a nighttime concentration camp. But we all need shelter, freedom, community, and private space. But why? Why do we live in houses? What twists of fate and freedom would the response to such a question mean? Let's see where the answer will lead us. "Ebbie, come on in now. It's suppertime."

❖ ❖ ❖

We live in houses primarily because shelter is a necessity of physical life, of survival. Our shelter links us historically and mythically to our earliest ancestors: the cave dwellers. Human beings, to exist, require shelter. Unlike the turtle, we do not carry our homes on our backs; unlike dogs we are not covered with hair; unlike fish we cannot stay under water. Shelter is a necessity for survival.

About two million years ago, when we took the agonistic and glorious leap to become humankind, climbing out of trees, cleaning off the mud, and losing lots of fur, we realized that those who looked like us (i.e., other human beings) needed what we need: shelter. For the most part we shared caves, igloos, tents, wigwams, and houses. Only since the Industrial Revolution, and its concomitant movement of people from land to city concrete, has civilization accepted the existence of people without shelter.

Our minds and hearts, however, have through dreams and myths—one ancient and one modern—retained an impulse toward houselessness. One idea is that we were originally cast to live naked in the woods without shelter. The biblical story of Adam and Eve at home with themselves, God, and nature, before the fall into sin, is often experienced as a story of innocence and how we would like to live if we did not have to deal with modern life. Adam and Eve before the fall have been basic symbols for interpretation of American life. A modern imagining of the Adam and Eve story comes from the British invasion of Africa by Tarzan and Jane. This story also reaches us in the places of our fatigue and disgust with urban life and bureaucratic strictures. Don't we all wish we could live in the absolute freedom of the jungle, with chimpanzees to protect us, pure water to drink, and clean air to breathe, swinging from tree to tree with the love of our lives?

One consequence of this primordial dream is that as you sip cool coffee and listen to the latest Washington scandal on the morning news, sitting in your car during rush hour while we know you would rather be sailing, you experience a slight twinge of envy when you glance out the window at a group of homeless men warming their hands over a primitive fire in a modern garbage can. The envy is quickly concealed by anger and, with certainty, you know that these homeless men choose to be homeless. They like it like that. In fact, they are all that is left of Adam and Eve, Tarzan and Jane. Then the car behind you blows its horn, waking you from your reverie; you move down the road with your mind still on the savings-and-loan scandal. Perhaps this fantasy is a creative way to deal with the boredom of our transportation system, but it is a dangerous source for social analysis and political policy.

Notwithstanding our dreams and myths of childlikeness and innocence, without housing a human being cannot live. Shelter is a matter of life and death, a physical necessity. Without shelter from the storm, disease, freezing weather, or the blasting sun will kill you. Houselessness inevitably leads to death.

> Houselessness is murderous.
> The causes of houselessness are murder.
> The causers of houselessness are
> murderers.

Why do people live in houses? Housing is a basic necessity of physical survival; we want to live. What about the homeless?

Labor Pools: Holy Places in the Belly of the Beast, *by Ed Loring*

APRIL 1995

A Labor Pool is a holy place. If you are, like me, well-fed, housed, and employed, you may never have visited a Labor Pool, much less turned to one for a day's work. Labor Pools are foreign territory to most of us, and Labor Pool workers are foreigners and fugitives in this land.

A most important step on our journey in faith is to reduce the distance between ourselves and the poor. Herein lies the hope for our personal and societal transformation toward love and justice, toward what Martin Luther King Jr. called "The Beloved Community." To reduce the distance requires us to journey into the Land of Nod, the turf of the poor and dispossessed, rather than to invite them to our table. Videos, the Internet, books, computer software, photos, or speakers won't reduce the distance, although they can certainly build tools and provide bread for the trip. We must go in the flesh, just as Yahweh decided to do in 4 B.C.E. Information can travel as fast as the laser beam; prophetic truth cannot move much more than three miles an hour. You have to go to the Land of Nod yourself, walk and talk, touch and be touched, listen, and unveil your nasty wound. For there is a balm in Gilead to make the wounded whole, to cure the sin-sick soul.

There is power and healing when we reduce the distance and enter holy places where the poor are dying because of our sins. Labor Pools are holy places.

Over the last several years I have asked college students and seminarians, "What are you willing to die for?" I follow that discussion with, "And what are you willing to kill for?" Most replies to the latter tend to resemble (1) "I will not kill for any reason," followed by a discussion of the nonretaliation ethic of the Sermon on the Mount, or (2) "I will kill for my family," followed by a reasoned argument justifying self-defense. Only once have I met a seminarian, a woman, who would be willing to kill for the protection of the congregation or Christian community. Dr. King preached that we must discover what we are willing to die for in order to know what we shall live for.

In these nights of murderous assault on the poor, we need to know how far we will reduce the distance to them. The minimum wage kills the poor. The minimum wage is a wolf that devours the sheep. Shall the shepherd only stand and watch? Shall she only pick up the bones and entrails after the wolf is satiated and then perform a funeral service rooted in the theology of the resurrection of Jesus Christ? Is every funeral an Easter event? When U.S. Representative Dick Armey (R-Texas) introduces a bill calling for removal of the minimum wage or Newt Gingrich (R-Georgia) removes the crumbs from the table already intended for dogs, my guts growl and I feel the fear of death rumbling down the road into the hellholes of poverty and prison.

Two reasons that Labor Pools are holy places are the three-mile-per-hour prophetic truths of God and the biblical leadership that we have as guides and models. One of the great gifts Yahweh gives to modern America is the thirty-fourth chapter of Ezekiel. This chapter has had a special relevance since World War II, but has been a burning light since April 4, 1968. Listen to a little and then read all thirty-one verses.

> Says the Sovereign LORD: "You are doomed, you shepherds of Israel! You take care of yourselves, but never tend the sheep. You drink the milk, wear clothes made from wool, and kill and eat the finest sheep. But you never tend the sheep. You have not taken care of the weak ones, healed the ones that are sick, bandaged the ones that are hurt, brought back the ones that wandered off, or looked for the ones that were lost. Instead, you treated them cruelly. . . . So listen to me, you shepherds, I, the sovereign LORD, declare that I am your enemy."

Ezekiel not only saw wheels over his head; he saw the future food banks of developed nations.

> Some of you are not satisfied with eating the best grass; you even trample down what you don't eat. You drink the clear water and muddy what you don't drink! My other sheep have to eat the grass you trample down and drink the water you muddy. . . .
> I will rescue my sheep and not let them be mistreated anymore.

God is present in Labor Pools. God is angry, on fire with passion on behalf of Yahweh's beloved poor and wounded. God hears the cry of the poor, sees the death of the minimum wage, eats trampled grass and drinks muddy water. God has made a choice; God has joined the Labor Pool worker and calls us to follow suit: "I, the Sovereign LORD, declare that I am your enemy." The Labor Pool is a Holy Place.

Prophetic truth can't move much faster than a prophet can walk or a jackass can carry him. One hot afternoon after having been raised in what Malcolm X calls "the big house," Moses went for a walk to see how his people, the slaves (i.e., Labor Pool workers), were doing. Dangerous is the act of reducing the distance. We are forced to see what we have not seen, to hear what we have not heard. We, like Moses, must, if we "visit our people" (Exod. 2:11), make a choice. Either we will affirm slavery or we shall be transformed into brothers and sisters of the prophetic Beloved Community. When Moses reduced the distance, when he visited the turf of the poor, he became a murderer. He discovered what he was willing to kill for.

When Moses opened his eyes while standing on new ground, he saw that his community consisted of slaves and that they were forced to do hard labor. No longer could he eat the best grass or drink sweet water at Pharaoh's table. In discovering the slaves at hard labor, Moses met Moses. But that's not all. "He even saw an Egyptian kill a Hebrew, one of Moses' own people. Moses looked all around, and when he saw that no one was watching, he killed the Egyptian and hid his body in the sand" (Exod. 2:11b–12).

Word got out. Moses fled, became a fugitive, made a new life, got a wife, and they had a child. Moses became a shepherd. One day Moses came to a place not unlike a Labor Pool. A Holy Place. A bush was burning, but not consumed. Moses' murder of the Egyptian slave driver must have impressed Yahweh, for out of the bush came two hot gifts. The first gift was vocation and commission. Said the God of Sarah and Abraham:

> I have seen how cruelly my people are being treated in Egypt;
> I have heard them cry out to be rescued from their slave driv-

ers. I know all about their suffering and so I have come down to rescue them [to reduce the distance] from the Egyptians and to bring them out of Egypt to a spacious land. . . . Now I am sending you to the Pharaoh of Egypt so that you can lead my people out of his country. (Exod. 3:7–10)

Moses met this God who hears the cries of those at hard labor at a wage that does not satisfy. But this God does not channel surf; rather, she reduces the distance, plans a shift in the labor market, and calls a leader. The place of the burning bush was holy ground, for there God spoke and dreamed of freedom and economic justice. Labor Pools are holy places run by Egyptian slave drivers but visited by the God who rescues the workers from Pharaoh's grip.

The second gift God gave to Moses was God's very own name—Yahweh: I Am Who I Am. Just tell the slave owners and labor bosses that I Am sent you. Ah, what power to behold, even though many plagues and much death were necessary. The one who visits, upon hearing the cries of the poor, is I Am—Yahweh—reducing the distance so that freedom and justice, love and salvation, houses and food may abound for all God's people. We, like Moses, must listen. We must go into the places where God's name is burning hot, like the passion of a mother's love when her child is being abused. A Labor Pool is a holy place, for there we learn the name(s) of God.

Labor Pools are holy places, for that is where Jesus is crucified. I have known people to pay more than three thousand dollars for a trip to Jerusalem. They have wanted to go to the Holy Land and to walk the walk that Jesus walked. They have stood on Golgotha, and unlike the women in the Gospels, have not fled when seeing the spot where Jesus was crucified. Perhaps with imaginative insight and intuitive power they have even experienced the shriek of dereliction: "My God, my God, why have you forsaken me?" But one doesn't need to fly to a far country, for in the center of the city, in the belly of the beast, Jesus is crucified today.

Yahweh reduced the distance when she came to Moses in the bush, giving him truth (liberty to captives) and her name. But that was not enough. Words are important, but visitation in the flesh is a necessity. God still had, as we all have, some distance to go. So God was born in a barn, taking on not simply human flesh, but the flesh and life of the poor. For God to be the one named Yahweh—the I Am—who comes to those held at hard labor, God had to come in a stranger's guise. Had Jesus been born to parents of power, wealth, or prestige, Yahweh would not be Yahweh and the gospel would be nothing more than a song of saving souls and maximizing profits, which it is not. The character of God is such that for God to be human, Yahweh had to be a poor and marginalized person. The crucifixion follows the necessity of Yahweh's birth as naturally as death follows a minimum wage of $4.25 or $5.15 per hour. As Moses was transformed when he visited those at hard labor, so God was transformed in Jesus Christ. When we reduce the distance to the poor, we are transformed, converted, and made new; we are made into brothers and sisters in solidarity with the poor and marginalized. The minimum wage is a cross, a slow hanging death. People yell to "come down from that cross" or, said in today's business language, "Get a job, you lazy bum, you welfare cheat." The minimum wage is the economic infrastructure of the Labor Pool. Here Jesus, in the flesh of those forced to labor, is crucified. Here Jesus dies. The Labor Pool is a holy place. Come and see for yourself.

❖ ❖ ❖

The most powerful place in scripture for an articulation of God's work in Jesus to reduce the distance to the poor is Matthew 25:31–46. Here Jesus speaks of his solidarity and identifies with those assaulted by the U.S. Congress, the Olympic Committee, the multinational corporations, and by those who work to gain while others do not have enough.

Matthew 25 is closely related to Ezekiel 34. There is judgment. God separates the sheep, or sheep from goats. God declares solidarity and life with the oppressed and declares Godself an enemy of those who have not met the needs of the poor. In Ezekiel 34:16b, Yahweh says that "those who are fat and strong I will destroy, because I am a shepherd who does what is right." In Matthew 25, Jesus teaches: "I tell you, whenever you refuse to help one of the least important ones, you refuse to help me. These, then, will be sent off to eternal punishment, but the righteous will go to eternal life."

Of whom is Jesus speaking? He speaks of those who are not helped: the hungry, thirsty, naked; the prisoner; the sick, lonely, homeless; African Americans; many women; all the poor; and, of course, Labor Pool workers. Jesus is in the flesh of the poor. He stands with the hungry in our soup-kitchen line. He died at Grady last month with Piedmont Joe. Jesus works at hard labor for $4.25 an hour at the most dangerous and boring jobs our system produces.

Jesus preached the powerful liberation sermon—the Nazarene Manifesto (Luke 4:16–30)—in his hometown, where he said, "God has sent me to proclaim liberty to the captives and recovery of sight to the blind, to set free the oppressed. . . ." Long before he preached these words, he had reduced the distance. Matthew 25 precedes Luke 4. Before we preach or make public policy, before we seek salvation for others or sell goods in the marketplace, we must enter the terrain of the poor and abandoned in our cities and across the land. From visiting holy places such as jails, we may proclaim liberty to captives. From sitting in the Labor Pool, we may learn how to join the long, hard battle to free the oppressed. One step begins to reduce the distance. Let it be so among us.

Butler Street Breakfast, Part 2, *by Ed Loring*

Editor's note: The following is a transcription of a sermon preached on September 17, 1995.

Since 1982, the Open Door Community has been serving breakfast to hungry people on Butler Street, in the basement of the Butler Street CME Church. Today's meditation is on Butler Street. We serve the breakfast five days a week, and we serve between two hundred and three hundred people each morning.

The first lesson today is from the twelfth chapter of the Book of Genesis and the first five verses:

> Then the Lord said to Abram, "Leave your country, your relatives, and your father's and mother's home, and go to a land that I am going to show you. I will give you many descendants, and they will become a great nation. I will bless you and make your name famous, so that you will be a blessing. I will bless those who bless you; I will curse those who curse you, and through you all bless the nations."
>
> When Abram was seventy-five years old, he and Sarai started out from Haran as the Lord had told them to do, and Lot went with them. Sarai took Abram with her, and their nephew Lot, and all the wealth, and all the slaves they had acquired, and they started out for the Land of Canaan.

Now *Canaan,* like the words *Butler Street,* is an image. We hear "Butler Street," and we think of more grits than anybody can eat. We think of abundance and gifts and hot, steaming coffee on cold and needy mornings. Canaan in the Old Testament is a symbol of abundance, a land that flows with milk and honey. It is a place where, later in the story, the Hebrew slaves, moving out of Egyptland and across that torturous wilderness, would struggle, as they struggle even now, to make home in Canaan land.

There are two New Testament lessons. The first comes from the Gospel of Luke in the second chapter, beginning at the first verse:

> At that time, Emperor Augustus ordered a census to be taken throughout the Roman Empire. When the first census took place, Quirinius was the governor of Syria. And everyone then went to register themselves, each to their own hometown.

Joseph went from the town of Nazareth in Galilee, to the town of Bethlehem in Judea, the birthplace of King David. Joseph went there because he was a descendant of David. He went to register with Mary, who was promised in marriage to him. She was pregnant. And while they were in Bethlehem, the time came for her to have her baby. She gave birth to her first son, wrapped him in cloths, and laid him in a manger. There was no room for them to stay in the inn.

And from the ninth chapter of Luke:

As they went on their way, a man said to Jesus, "Jesus, I will follow you wherever you go." And Jesus said to him, "Foxes have holes, birds have nests, but the Son of Humanity has no place to lay his head and rest."

Then he said to another, "Follow me." But that one said, "Sir, first let me go back and bury my daddy." Jesus answered, "Let the dead bury their own dead. You go and proclaim the Beloved Community."

Another one said, "I will follow you, sir. But first let me go and say good-bye to my family." Jesus said, "Anyone who starts to plow and then keeps looking back is of no use to the Beloved Community."

As we relate the New Testament to the Old Testament, as we try to tell a story of continuity from one covenant to the other, we must face this fact: in the New Testament there is a big disappointment in the place and social location of Jesus. How they had hoped and struggled, and how we yet dream in our own lives of a land flowing with milk and honey—a place as was promised to Sarah and Abraham—where we shall be great.

When we jump into the New Testament there is an embarrassing and disastrous change: for this one there is no room in the inn. So seek him in a manger. There is disappointment when we come to the New Testament as we drive our way through Egyptland, across that wilderness and into Canaan, and then on to Palestine. We think of the leadership in the Old Testament, and we know those dreams deep in the collective unconscious of the Hebrew people: for King David, dreams of a kingdom mighty, powerful, and strong. But in the New Testament, the one who has the mantle of David is a vagrant, a Messiah, a Christ; he is Jesus the peasant. And that's not really what, or who, we want.

There's even disappointment in our building programs. How much sense it makes for great architecture to be our goal, when we're rooted in the Old Testament. We dream dreams, and we build great temples in Jerusalem. But when we come to the New Testament, we find one who is more destitute than foxes, who have holes, and than birds, who have nests. He has no place. Even in his adulthood has he forgotten the manger in the barn? "No place," he says, "to lay down my weary head to rest these tired bones."

Cat holes, basements, and old buildings represent the dreams for church architecture in the New Testament: a disappointment. We want nice buildings. You can't have church growth without pews with cushions! It is after all a burden to interest people in the gospel of Jesus Christ, especially in such an affluent society as we have in North America. We face disappointment about the location of this God; the leadership this God offers; and the place, architecture, and building of worship, community, and common life.

We have been blessed at the Open Door Community because we have been called and sent to Butler Street. When we started the Open Door Community, we didn't even know where Butler Street was. And yet we've been sent, and we are sent, and we believe that we shall be sent day after day to Butler Street. God sometimes whispers and sometimes shouts, "Go down, little people of the Open Door, to Butler Street, and there in my name feed the hungry." God didn't ask us to go anywhere and everywhere. "Go to Butler Street! And there in my name welcome the stranger. And in the midst of the breakfast on Butler Street, visit the one who is sick, listen to the wounded describe her wounds, stand beside the drunk. Go down to Butler Street! And there in my name be nonviolent in the midst of strife. For I have already been whipped, nailed, struck, denied, beaten, spat upon, rejected, and am dejected for all of you. So stick there in the strife. Don't run! Don't build a fence or wall around your house. Go on," says this God, "and when you get there, hurry out of that van, and run inside, and unlock those bathrooms because we've got to have another place where we can pee for free with dignity!" Christ is always in this city looking for a place to urinate, and the Atlanta newspaper keeps spewing lies and trash, belittling those who have no place to pee. They are talking about Jesus. "Quick, quick!" says God. "Get down those steps and unlock the bathroom doors, and turn on the water fountain. I'm thirsty!"

"Listen," says our God on Butler Street, "to the cries of the homeless poor. Listen to the Labor Pool workers, who can't be workers if they're waiting in line to eat breakfast, even though they've waited in line for labor at the Labor Pool, but there is no labor, so they're called lazy bums. Go!" says our God, "not like Abraham and Sarah, with all your wealth and nephews, and slaves, and good memories. Go!" says our God, "almost empty-handed, but for some grits, and listen! Listen to the Labor Pool worker, who can't find work."

So it is that we leave morning after morning. Someone has gotten up early to cook the breakfast, and Ralph Dukes has brewed the coffee. We go down to Butler Street, a place of disappointment for many, a place for some of encounter with the Lord Jesus Christ. We leave the dining room at the Open Door Community, where we worship, where we share Eucharist, where we feed, where we have community meetings. This room is the center of the common life of the Open Door Community. We've had baptisms in this room; we've had funerals.

We drive down to Butler Street, and we pass Dr. King's crypt, where his bones lie restless in the grave, waiting for people with guts to stand up and say again, as he said, "Let my people go!" We arrive on Butler Street, and there is God, waiting for us. There is Jesus, standing by the gate, just above the "No Loitering" sign. Butler Street.

I am very interested in names and love to find out their histories. So this summer I found that Butler Street is named for William Orlando Butler. We also have a town in South Georgia named Butler, which is the seat of Taylor County. This won't come as any surprise to you because you know of the struggle in Atlanta about the names of streets and whom we honor: Butler was a slaveholder. He was also a soldier and a lawyer. In 1861 he ran for the vice presidency of the United States, hoping a Southern slaveholder would keep the Civil War at bay. So we stand on the street, Butler Street. And we know by that name that we honor a past for which we have not fully repented; nor have we restored this nation to health and reconciliation.

Butler Street intersects some other streets of noteworthy name, for instance, Coca-Cola Place. At the corner of Coca-Cola Place and Edgewood was the first office of the Coca-Cola company, and in the basement (which later became a day shelter for homeless people) was the first laboratory for the company as it labored to find a formula, so that you could drink many Cokes and not quench your thirst. It worked! Coca-Cola is the most successful multinational corporation in the world, and its product is worthless. It has no food value.

In front of Grady Hospital is Gilmer Street. George Gilmer was governor of Georgia in 1830, shortly after gold was discovered in Dahlonega. The rules of jurisdiction changed, the state brought in the land lottery, and we took the land from the Cherokee. So we honor his name.

It is important for us to know and remember the history of that asphalt and the naming of that street. Whether the place is named Calvary or Golgotha, whether it is Galilee or Butler Street, God calls us to go where there is no room in the inn. If God is leading you and your camels somewhere spacious, you've got the wrong map.

The color of Butler Street is black. Black asphalt. The color of God is black. Most people who live on Butler Street are black. God sends us to Butler Street so that those of us who are not black may become black, and those of us who are already black can get blacker. There's not enough of us in this city, or in this society, who are black enough. We've got to get blacker. Not being black enough makes it possible for the Christian Coalition to proclaim in the newspaper that racism isn't a problem in our society, or in this city. And it's a lie! We've got to get blacker. Not being black enough makes it possible for Atlanta newspaper columnist Colin Campbell to blame the problems of downtown Atlanta on those of us who are homeless. We've got to get blacker. We need to be as black as Butler Street. We need to be as black as the bowls into which we pour those white grits.

On the other side of the church, down Coca-Cola Place, is the morgue. Across the parking lot and beside the morgue is the municipal market, and in the other direction is Grady Hospital. And just past Grady Hospital is the police department. And just across from Grady Hospital is the Fulton County Health Department, where many spend the night and sleep. If you go to Grady Hospital after dark, you'll see people stretched out in open spaces. Beside the Butler Street CME Church is the Hughes Spalding Hospital. And there is the Butler Street CME Church.

This church is composed of members who perhaps at one point belonged to Mr. Butler. It was in South Georgia that a group of African American former slaves, in the midst of Reconstruction, were still told in church to go up to the gallery: "You can't worship down here with white flesh. Our social location is good. We love Abraham and Sarah with all those camels and goats and sheep. We're going to bring our nephew Lot over here and have a bigger steeple next year than we've got this year! I don't know about those people up in the gallery, but we're going to have comfortable pews down here. We don't want you down here with us! The next leader in our church is going to be stronger than Robert Edward Lee!"

And those former slaves said, "We don't want that. We don't want that kind of God. We don't want this kind of place. We don't want this kind of gospel. We don't want this kind of social location. The one we want to follow is the one for whom there is no room in the inn."

There was born a new denomination. It is now a national denomination, and in the early 1870s was called the Colored Methodist Episcopal Church. The name was changed from Colored to Christian in the early 1950s. And there that black church stands on Butler Street to witness for another way. And we praise God for that place. We praise God most especially because it has a basement. And because it has a basement, they let us go down those stairs to serve this meal. We need to be aware of and thankful for how good it is to meet our Jesus. Two thousand years ago he was born in a barn and laid in a manger because there was no room for him in the inn.

It's a lie to say that Jesus has changed. It's a wish. There's no question about it: we'd really like to have the gospel's social location somewhere else. Wouldn't it be nice to go north of the city? And take our grits to an air-conditioned place? To have all those businesspeople come in and eat our grits?

But I'm convinced that God is on Butler Street, and that's where God calls this community. God sends all of us on journeys. For those in seminaries, maybe you haven't yet discovered the Butler Street in your lives: Seek it! Knock! Ask! Shout! You'll find it where people are turned away; where prisoners languish;

where there's not enough to go around, though most people have too much. Where is your Butler Street? Among the poor and the dying, the hungry and the rejected. God sends us, all of us, where those for whom there is no room wait. There we encounter the vagrant Christ—the one who comes in a stranger's guise.

When we find our Butler Street, we are reshaped and made new. Out of basements and cat holes and gutters and prisons, and from under bridges, we are grasped by a mighty power that makes us struggle for justice. It incorporates in our very beings a loud cry for righteousness: "Let my people go! Repent, for the Beloved Community is at hand!"

Hunger on Butler Street:
The Butler Street Breakfast, Part 3, *by Ed Loring*

APRIL 1996

Butler Street is a road, and we are on a journey. Butler Street is Black, and we are a community which has been empowered to see Jesus in Blackness. It is important to be on a road that is Black as we encounter Blackness in our lives. Encountering Jesus in Blackness is a very important part of our journey together.

Our God is a God who despises hunger. Several weeks ago we were on a street tour. Early in the morning we left the Open Door and went to a labor pool near Jefferson Street. Then we went to Joe Miller's and Ralph Dennis's home in the hut community and visited them. After that we rushed as fast as we could to make it to the Butler Street Breakfast.

We had a wonderful time. We were cold, and we were already tired, although we had only been out on the streets for three hours. How wonderful it was to go down those steps into the basement to share that meal.

When the group that I was with had finished eating, we went outside and sat on the steps of the Butler Street CME Church with hungry and homeless people. We had a great blessing that descended and appeared to us, like the dove of the Holy Spirit coming down on Jesus at baptism. We looked up, and, lo and behold, right in front of us, already on the second or third point of a sermon that had begun years and years before, Sye Pressley was preaching to us. It was a wonderful experience.

At the conclusion of his meditation there on Butler Street, Sye made each of us, looking each in the eye, to say what it is we hate. We were caught off guard at such a call so early in the morning. Naming what we hate does not exactly fit into mainline American manners. Yet everyone in the group spoke, and we spoke from our hearts.

An American diet is a diet of death. The food that God gives us is enough for everyone, everywhere on the earth. God did not create a world in which there is hunger. Jesus comes to us again in faith, giving us nothing more than everything we want. In Mark 6, Jesus tells his disciples, even as he tells us, "You, yourselves, give them something to eat." With five loaves and a couple of fish, Jesus thanks God, the Creator of enough for everyone, and sends his disciples to feed the people. Everyone ate, and there was enough. Twelve baskets of fish and bread were left. There is enough for everyone: it's the miracle of the presence of Christ; it's the goodness of the Creator; it is the movement into liberation that leads us to a life in the wilderness rooted in faith and struggle against oppression. There is enough! There is no reason for hunger in this land. We will never accept hunger, because those who do are blind and have not seen by the glorious light that lets us see in darkness. Let us be filled in our hunger! Let us be nourished and strengthened on our journey.

Oppression and greed are the causes of hunger in our land. Power and affluence lead to oppression and greed. Hunger is not a class issue. One thing about rich people is they get hungry. Poor people get hungry. The issue is who gets to eat. This world that God loves so much is filled with people who have too much and others who do not have enough. Some people are consumed by overeating, while others starve.

In Ezekiel 34, God tells the shepherds, the leaders, the policy makers that God is their enemy because they have not cared for the sheep. They have eaten the best grass and trampled what remained. A couple of weeks ago we went out on a Saturday night to check the dumpsters for cardboard because we were spending the night in the backyard. Cardboard is a good insulation against the cold ground. We checked the stores in this neighborhood. Dumpster after dumpster was padlocked. "You even trample down what you don't eat. You drink the clear water and muddy what you don't drink. My other sheep have to eat the grass you trample down and drink the water that you muddy."

Our liberating God says, "When I break my people's chains and set them free from those who have made them slaves, then they will know that I am the Lord their God. I will give them fertile fields and put an end to hunger in the land."

A primary source of hunger that we face in this land, in this city, in this community is the disproportion of power that allows some people to have too much money and influence. Their excess comes from the backs and the bellies of the poor and the hungry.

A second source of hunger is found in the Book of Isaiah, chapter 55: "Why do you spend money on what does not satisfy?" What is at the heart of America that drives us to exploit the natural resources of the world? We eat and eat and eat, and we are not satisfied. God says, "Listen to me and do what I say. You will enjoy the best food of all." Come to me and you will have life. Each of us in our journey must continue to choose life—abundant life—that satisfies as we pour out our lives in servanthood, in solidarity with the oppressed.

Throughout the Bible, God feeds the hungry. Jesus calls us in Matthew 25 to concern ourselves with that work, which is a mark of the gathering of Christian people. Christians eat and invite all sorts of folk to join them. Fundamentally, the biblical response to the hunger on Butler Street, and in our own lives, is to feed the hungry, to share the food that we have, and to be happy, even when it's only five loaves and two fishes.

Tomorrow morning this community will go to Butler Street, and we will feed the hungry. We do that in the name of Jesus. We are sent to feed. We have been graced. Though we are still deaf, we have heard little bits: "Go to Butler Street, feed the hungry. For when you have fed the least of these my sisters and brothers," says Jesus, "you've fed me."

We are taught by Jesus, commanded by God in joyful obedience, day after day, to pray for food: "Give us this day our daily bread." The prayer that we must pray for the world is that the plenty will be shared with everyone. We cannot stop praying for our daily bread, believing that there is enough for everyone. It must be shared, distributed, harvested—good, healthy joy for everyone.

God teaches us through the scriptures that we are God's chosen people, who must demand that the hungry be fed. It won't do us any good just to go to Butler Street and serve 250 people every morning, then to come and pray, "Give us this day our daily bread," and then to go about our usual lives. We must demand that the hungry be fed in the name of God.

You remember the story in Luke when Jesus teaches the disciples how to pray. After he teaches them the words of the Lord's Prayer, Jesus suggests prayer is like having a guest late at night. You find that you're out of bread, so you go to your neighbor's house to ask for bread. The neighbor won't come to the door because it's too late. You persist in knocking. Jesus teaches us, in the midst of our going to Butler Street, to join the prophetic community. We become those who won't quit knocking on the doors of City Hall, along the streets of Atlanta, in the state legislature, on the doors of those running this Congress—who won't feed the hungry but who will take their food stamps and their medical care, who suck the life out of the poor.

If we don't feed the sheep at Butler Street, God will be our enemy. But God is not our enemy; God is our Beloved Friend. God empowers us, invites us, and loves us into being those who understand that there's enough for everyone. We understand that hunger is rooted in oppression and in choices about what we do with our lives. We know that this God calls us and sends us to feed the hungry, to pray for food, and to demand that the despicable and hated hunger of so many women and men, boys and girls come to an end.

The Politics of Cleanliness, *by Mark Harper*

J u l y / A u g u s t   1 9 8 7

The poor must wait. Because our culture has embraced a political and economic system that overfills the pockets of the rich while denying poor people access to the goods and services that would meet their most basic needs; because our society's moral behavior is dictated by corporate Goliaths who proclaim that the earth is theirs and not the Lord's; and because we define our humanity using the standards of those who have accumulated the most and not by how we are treating the least, the poor must wait.

In our city, the poor are forced to wait for scant low-cost housing to become available. The poorest are forced to wait for police vans to take them to crowded night shelters, only to be forced out at 5:30 A.M. to wait some more for low-pay, low-dignity jobs in day-labor pools. Despite the clear biblical teaching that the fruits of creation be made available to the entire human family, God's poorest children are forced to wait in long soup lines, hoping to receive the leftover fruit that Goliath could not digest. And, three mornings a week, as commuter traffic rushes by the front yard of the Open Door, the poor must wait for a chance to take a hot shower, to put on clean clothes, and to wash away the dirt that dehumanizes them and causes doors to be closed in their faces.

As is the case for most people who live in the Third World, water for bathing, drinking, clothes-washing, and flushing human waste is scarcely available for the homeless poor of Atlanta. Like parched fields in a season of drought, the streets of our city do not offer life for the people who must call them home. Rather, they crack open and swallow our sisters and brothers whose spirits become dry and broken as they search for work and affirmation day after day after day.

If a homeless woman or man is able to find space at a night shelter that has showers; or if the one city day-labor center happens to have clean towels; or if that person is among the thirty-five people that the Open Door is able to welcome for a shower and change of clothes on Monday, Wednesday, or Friday morning, then becoming clean—even for a few short hours—is cause for hope: hope for a renewed sense of dignity, hope for better health, hope for a job. While the maxim that "cleanliness is next to godliness" is debatable, the hard reality in our culture is that only when people are clean and neatly dressed will Goliath permit them to sit at table and enjoy some of our country's economic pie. Thus, when we open our door for folk to come in and wash themselves, it is more than a simple act of mercy or charity; it is, in fact, a political act.

It seems significant, then, that one of the most powerful proclamations about justice in the Bible should use water imagery: "Let justice flow like a stream, and righteousness like a river that never goes dry" (Amos 5:24). Indeed, water is a symbol and vital resource for life. And while offering hot water, soap, and towels to our tired and dirty sisters and brothers cannot wash away the injustice of a world that forces them to line up at our door in the cold morning hours, it is an offering that we must continue to give. For in this simple work of mercy, we are not only seeking to make more economic fruit accessible to those who have been denied it; we are also seeking to know the vagrant Christ who is standing, tired and dirty, in that same shower line.

You Are the One! *by Elizabeth Dede*

SEPTEMBER 1991

Recently the Open Door had a Bible study based on 2 Samuel 12:1–14. It is a powerful story about King David's recognition of his sin. The prophet Nathan is sent to tell David a story about a rich man and a poor man. The rich man has everything, including much cattle. The poor man has nothing, except a lamb that he loves dearly and cares for as part of his family. One day, the rich man receives a visitor and does not want to kill one of his own animals to serve his guest. Instead he steals the poor man's lamb and slaughters it.

When David hears the story, he is outraged and says that the rich man deserves to die. Nathan simply and starkly replies, "You are that man."

Indeed, it was true; David had done a terrible thing. He had lusted after Bathsheba, slept with her, and gotten her pregnant while her husband, Uriah, was fighting in the king's army. When David couldn't get Uriah to abandon his post as a loyal soldier and to sleep with Bathsheba to cover up David's sin, King David had faithful Uriah killed.

The parallel to Nathan's story is all too obvious, and David cries out, "I have sinned against the Lord!" In a powerful moment of self-awareness, David says to himself, "I am that man." He is brought to repentance and learns of God's forgiveness.

Since that Bible study, I've been listening for the prophets in my life who say to me, like Nathan said to David, "You're the one!" and bring me to repentance. I observed at the Bible study that we had a difficult time naming the prophets in our lives and telling about the prophecies that we receive.

It was easy to identify ourselves as prophets, because then we are the good guys, speaking the truth to power, and telling off the oppressors. So the occupation of the Imperial Hotel came readily to mind as one of our prophetic actions. It was a simple truth that we had to tell: Tens of thousands are homeless in Atlanta while the business community spends billions of dollars on entertainment, with leadership from city government. Buildings that once provided housing now stand empty and abandoned. We said, "House the homeless here!" and showed clearly and simply how God's justice should reign in the city.

More recently, this summer we've had to speak a prophetic word to the city, the police, and the neighborhood as we've gone to sit on our wall. "The poor and homeless will not have their rights stolen from them in front of our home," we've said. As long as some classes can stand on the sidewalk, or sit on a wall, then all people will be able to do it at our house. We dramatized that by having a group of comfortable, housed students sit on our wall with us and our homeless friends for a morning. At least on that day, the police did not harass us.

At the Bible study, we talked about feeding people and decided that, even though it is charity work, feeding the hungry is prophetic because powerful people in this city cannot forget that too many are hungry. "God's justice comes when the hungry are fed," we proclaim to the city.

So it is easy to see ourselves as prophets, as I suppose it was easy for David to see himself as a prophet—he had, after all, stood up to Goliath and brought Goliath's destruction. David could even identify the injustice in the story the prophet Nathan told, but he didn't recognize injustice in himself until Nathan said, "You are the man!"

Those times of self-discovery are rare, and even more rarely do we tell about them. If we tell about ourselves, we make ourselves vulnerable. Our confessions can be saved and used against us in our weakness. That is often our experience.

So in the Bible study, when we talked about the prophets who say to us, "You are the one!" suddenly we were able to share about the times that we've said that; but nobody wanted to talk about things they had been forced to learn about themselves: it's too hard and painful—look what happened to David. He learned, "I am that man," and his child died.

But the purpose of the prophet is to cause recognition, repentance, and change. We don't sit on our wall because we want to annoy our neighbors. We sit on our wall because we want the neighborhood to recognize how unjustly it treats the homeless, and we want our neighbors to stop and, instead, to walk on a new path, when we will see them organize to build affordable housing, even in our neighborhood.

In the same way, prophets come into our lives and say, "You are the one! You need change. You need to repent."

For a couple of years now I have dreaded the Butler Street Breakfast. I go out of a sense of duty and responsibility, but I don't like going because it depresses me. Standing in the doorway, I look into that room full of people, and I see only emptiness and nothing. It is a room full of people who are, for the most part, young, strong, bright, capable, and willing, but who will waste their day waiting in lines. We have arrived at a point in this country of feeling that we have been too nice to the poor. The poor, this way of thinking says, need to feel the pain of being down-and-out in order to get their lives in order.

None of this, I must say, is new. In fact, we can look at this view as a modern version of the idea that poor folks are lazy. This way of thinking represents a mean-spirited and morally bankrupt value system that flows from values this culture promotes. Chief among these values is the idea that the individual controls their personal well-being. That is, society and the "haves" are not to share any blame, or responsibility, for the presence of homeless people. Therefore, as "haves" we should not be placed in a situation in which the "have-nots" can spoil our enjoyment of privilege by begging or smelling bad.

I want to close by quoting one of my favorite addresses by Dr. King:

> Jesus told a parable one day, and he reminded us that a man went to hell because he didn't see the poor. His name was Dives. He was a rich man. And there was a man by the name of Lazarus who was a poor man, but not only was he poor, he was sick. Sores were all over his body, and he was so weak that he could hardly move. But he managed to get to the gate of Dives every day, wanting just to have the crumbs that would fall from his table. And Dives did nothing about it. And the parable ends saying, "Dives went to hell, and there was a fixed gulf now between Lazarus and Dives."
>
> There is nothing in that parable that said Dives went to hell because he was rich. Jesus never made a universal indictment against all wealth. It is true that one day a rich young ruler came to him, and he advised him to sell all, but in that instance Jesus was prescribing individual surgery and not setting forth a universal diagnosis. And if you will look at that parable with all of its symbolism, you will remember that a conversation took place between heaven and hell and on the other end of that long-distance call between heaven and hell was Abraham in heaven talking to Dives in hell.
>
> Now Abraham was a very rich man. If you go back to the Old Testament, you see that he was the richest man of his day, so it was not a rich man in hell talking with a poor man in heaven; it was a little millionaire in hell talking with a multi-millionaire in heaven. Dives didn't got to hell because he was rich; Dives didn't realize that his wealth was his opportunity. It was his opportunity to bridge the gulf that separated him from his brother, Lazarus. Dives went to hell because he

passed by Lazarus every day and he never saw him. He went to hell because he allowed his brother to become invisible.

Kinship, *by Elizabeth Dede*

SEPTEMBER 1993

When Dick Rustay leads worship at the Open Door Community, he often prays that we will all be able to recognize our connectedness. This is a good prayer because it implies thankfulness for God's gracious diversity in creation, and it seeks forgiveness for our foolish belief in our own superiority. Often in prayer at the Open Door we say, "Open our eyes so that we can see Jesus in each person," but I think this is not an easy prayer for God to grant because our vision is clouded by our strange notions of Jesus and by our unwillingness to see in a new way.

Flannery O'Connor wrote a story about kinship and the recognition of Jesus called "The Partridge Festival," which, in O'Connor's humorous way, teaches us about seeing and about the pitfalls as we look for Jesus. I read it again this summer with the new eyes that come with seven and a half years at the Open Door. I didn't see it the same way I had when I first read the story as a college student.

"The Partridge Festival" is about how two young people come to recognize their kinship with each other, with the ugly and vulgar, and with polite society; and when they see their family ties, they are no longer able to condemn or romanticize; they can only accept the kinship. Calhoun and Mary Elizabeth are intellectual snobs whose chief interest in the Partridge Azalea Festival is a crazy man named Singleton, who killed six of Partridge's townsfolk because they had cruelly made fun of him and had abused him for his unwillingness to participate in the festival. Without a trial, Singleton was imprisoned in the mental hospital, and Calhoun and Mary Elizabeth intend to write an exposé about Singleton, whom they see as a Christ figure, innocently suffering for the guilt of others. Each is disdainful of the other's intellect, and both condemn the townsfolk for their shallow interest in business and appearance, rather than human suffering and need.

Neither Calhoun nor Mary Elizabeth has ever met Singleton, but they are convinced that "he's the scapegoat. He's laden with the sins of the community . . . sacrificed for the guilt of the others. . . . He was an individualist. A man who would not allow himself to be pressed into the mold of his inferiors. A non-conformist. He was a man of depth living among caricatures and they finally drove him mad, unleashed all his violence on themselves."

Often we are tempted to the same romanticizing of the poor. We want desperately for them to be completely innocent and blameless, because the picture would be easier to look at if there were a clear villain and an obvious victim. But life is seldom that simple, and we, along with Calhoun and Mary Elizabeth, must recognize the ambiguities. Then we can forgive ourselves and others, without trying to blame or assign guilt. In forgiveness we are able to recognize our kinship with each other.

Before Calhoun and Mary Elizabeth come to that recognition, however, each accuses the other of cowardice and stupidity, and they dare each other to visit Singleton. Faced with the reality of a crazy man who has murdered six people, Calhoun and Mary Elizabeth find that they can no longer be romantics. Mary Elizabeth is afraid and Calhoun is appalled. But they cannot back out from the visit without appearing cowardly or stupid, so they go through with it.

The Singleton they meet is not the innocent they have imagined. He curses, swears, and yells at Calhoun, "Whadaya want with me? Speak up!! My time is valuable." And when Mary Elizabeth explains that they came to say "we understand," Singleton begins to say lewd things, grabs at her, and lifts his hospital gown over his head to expose himself. Both Calhoun and Mary Elizabeth are shocked and frightened, and they jump up and run out of the hospital to get away from this man, who moments before had been their Christ figure, a sacrificial lamb.

When Calhoun and Mary Elizabeth finally stop running, they stop to look at each other, and they are shocked to see Singleton in each other's face. This is the kind of recognition we have when we look at reality without romanticizing the poor. It is a recognition that leads to redemption; both Calhoun and Mary Elizabeth recognized their common humanity: they are bound to each other, to Singleton, and to the greedy townsfolk. None is innocent, and neither is more guilty than the other.

Sometimes at the Open Door we have such eye-opening experiences, when it is no longer so simple to see Jesus in each person who comes through the soup-kitchen line, when we can no longer find an easy villain, and when we no longer have all the answers.

Not too long ago, Dick Rustay had one of these experiences of recognition at the Butler Street Breakfast. More than likely, before Dick left that morning, he had prayed that God would open his eyes to Jesus in that line and to see his connectedness with everyone there. The answer Dick received to his prayer was a punch in the mouth. One of the homeless people who eats with us didn't want to get in line for a breakfast ticket, so he hauled off and slugged Dick.

To be punched at seven o'clock in the morning will open your eyes, but it's not usually what we have in mind in our prayers. Most of the time anger and violence don't help us recognize Jesus. Such an experience causes one to pause and reflect. Sometimes you have to ask yourself, "What am I doing here anyway?"

While reflecting on his morning at Butler Street, Dick asked himself, "What hit me? Was it a demon, or was it God?" It would be very easy to call this angry, violent man a demon, or at least someone temporarily possessed by a demon, and thus to dismiss the episode as one of those things that happens from time to time in this line of work. Perhaps it was that simple, but Dick received a revelation like Calhoun's and Mary Elizabeth's. First, Dick learned about himself. He saw that while he shared a common humanity with this angry person, there were also some key differences. Dick is a white man, from the oppressor race and class; he eats well, sleeps in a bed, has a place to call home, and doesn't have to line up to get a ticket for breakfast. Obviously, Dick knew all of this about himself, but it took the punch to open his eyes so that he could see himself in a different way: rather than seeing all of those features in the mirror as he trims his beard, Dick saw all through the eyes of a young African American man who can't claim any of the things for himself that Dick claims.

But Dick's revelation didn't end with new self-knowledge. He also found new meaning in the prayer about our connectedness. For a peaceful, nonviolent person like Dick, it's hard to see a connection with someone who punches you, and life at the Open Door sometimes makes it difficult for us white folk to identify ourselves with the oppressors. But when he came to understand the rage of this young man, who was sick and tired of being told what to do, and who had been left out of the privileges and rights of being a human in this wealthy city, Dick saw how a racist system connected him to this angry man and to the oppressors. A common humanity links them all, and a common humanity empowers Dick to struggle, not only to continue to serve the Butler Street Breakfast, but also to change the oppressive system so that everyone at that breakfast will eat well, sleep in a bed, have a place to call home, and not have to line up to get a ticket for breakfast.

Finally, God's love was revealed to Dick. When Dick recognized that he was not struggling with a demon, he learned that God's love reaches us where we are, no matter how vulgar and ugly, no matter how angry, no matter how greedy, no matter how peaceful and generous. God's love is expansive enough to encompass all.

Like Calhoun in O'Connor's story, Dick saw in his own face and in the face of the angry man a "face whose gift of life had pushed straight forward to the future to raise festival after festival." These festivals won't just celebrate flowers, but they will mark the day when all God's children live in justice and peace, and there is no more hunger, no more homelessness, and no more death penalty. We will all celebrate our kinship on that day.

Jeannette Lewis: A Debt Which I Can Never Repay,
by Elizabeth Dede

MARCH 1996

On Monday, January 8, 1996, our friend Jeannette Lewis died at Grady Memorial Hospital, less than twenty-four hours after she had been taken there in an ambulance. Her last day, like almost all the days of a homeless woman, was spent in grief and shame, given to her by a white, racist society that can spare no love for the least of Jesus' sisters.

On January 7, the weather was cruelly cold, and snow was falling. Jeannette came to eat breakfast with us, as she often did on a Sunday morning. But she was very ill and could not eat much of her food. Her companions were concerned for her, saying to us that Jeannette was sicker than she was saying. She told us that she had the flu and asked us to call an ambulance to take her to Grady Hospital, the only place where a poor person can receive medical treatment.

When the ambulance arrived, the emergency medical technician (what a cold and technological name for a person) was enraged that anyone would call an ambulance for a person with the flu. He berated her, yelling, "You want me to take you to the hospital for the flu?!" Jeanette could only reply weakly that she needed to go to the hospital. Her friends spoke up on her behalf, telling the EMT that this illness was more serious than the flu. He stood in the center of this group of friends and said derisively, "Take her to Grady then," like the people who passed by Jesus and hurled insults at him as he hung on the cross: "You were going to tear down the Temple and build it back up in three days! Save yourself if you are God's Son! Come on down from the cross!" Jesus could no more come down from the cross than Jeannette's friends could take her to the hospital.

The next day we learned that Jeannette had died. After her death, I began to recollect Jeannette's life, and I sadly realized that I knew very little about her. She was called "Pony" by all her friends, but I had no idea where the name originated. Did Pony have children? Did she have a family other than her homeless friends on the street? Where was Pony born? How old was she? These are questions that a friend should have answers for, but they knocked around unanswered, echoing in the emptiness of my head and heart.

Pony is a word with many meanings. It can be a small horse; anything small of its kind (even a small liqueur glass); a literal translation of a work in a foreign language, often used dishonestly by students; or a racehorse. Or it serves as a verb: to pay (money), as to settle an account—as in "pony up." Fascinating stuff! An account must be settled. Why didn't I know anything about Jeannette Lewis, even though she lived in our yard for years and years?

Ed Loring taught a course at Columbia Theological Seminary during the January term, and I have learned a lot by listening to tapes of his lectures. On the fourth day of the class, just a week and a half after Pony's death, Ed helped solve the mystery for me and his students, and I am ashamed for my innocence and ignorance, which make me guilty of Pony's invisibility.

If women and children form the fastest-growing group among the homeless, why are there so few women and children at the Butler Street Breakfast, at St. Luke's soup kitchen, here at the Open Door? If Pony had children, why did I never see them with her? Why didn't I ask these questions before Pony died? The answer is clear and simple to those who have eyes to see and ears to hear. It is as blinding as the tears poor mothers shed; it is as deafening as their cries for their poor children.

When the Egyptian slave masters wanted to control their Hebrew slaves, they sent out an order that all the baby Hebrew boys were to be drowned in the Nile River—a slaughter of the innocents much like the one Herod ordered when Jesus was born. Hebrew mothers went to great lengths to hide their children; Moses' mother hid him in a floating basket on the river. Homeless mothers in the United States face a similar death for their children: if children are seen at a soup kitchen with their mother, or in the public library, or dragging wearily down the street when they should be in school, the children will be shuffled from agency to agency, passed from foster home to foster home. Surely this is a death no mother can bear for her children. So Pony and her sisters are in hiding; we do not see this invisible mass of hungry and homeless humanity; we do not hear their cries and stories.

In a recent faith history from an Open Door resident-volunteer applicant named Sarah Moses, I read the following astute observation: "In the current welfare debate we see the double standard of a society that wants women in the upper class to 'stay at home' and nurture the children, but that wants to put the single mother on welfare 'back to work.'"

On the first Sunday in February, the Open Door Community began its celebration of African American History Month. We listened to the proud voices of our ancestors who have struggled in the movement toward liberation. I thought of Pony as I heard these words spoken by Sojourner Truth:

> America owes to my people some of the dividends. . . . America can afford to pay, and America must pay. I shall make them understand that there is a debt to the Negro people which they never can repay. At least, then, they must make amends.

We must pony up. There is a huge debt white Americans owe to our African American sisters and brothers. We must pay for the hundreds of years of time and labor stolen. We must pay for the lives that were destroyed. We must pay for the children who have died in poverty. We must pay for the men who were lynched. We must pay for our ignorance and apathy. We must pay for Pony's lack of medical care. But it is a debt we can never repay because the time is gone, the children are dead, the men hang from the trees, and Pony is in her grave. We can only make amends.

I am sorry, Pony. You died on Christmas Day as it is celebrated by Orthodox Churches. You died because there was no room for you. Even the hospital didn't want your poor, sick, tired body. I sing this Christmas hymn for you:

> Ah, dearest Jesus, holy Child,
> Make Thee a bed soft, undefiled,
> Within my heart, that it may be
> A quiet chamber kept for Thee.

Ah, Jesus, enlarge my heart, and melt it, and make it soft and warm, a welcome place for you to rest, so that Jeannette, and Judy, and Jennifer, and Glenda, and Lena can find a home of warmth and welcome and safety were they can live joyfully with their children.

Ah, Jeannette, I can never repay the debt I owe to you. But I will pony up with my life and dedicate it to the struggle for liberation. I long for the day when you and your children will be safe from Pharaoh.

Pony up, good people! Jeannette and Moses are on the other side in the Promised Land, watching over their children.

Bringing Love and Justice Together, *by Ed Loring*

J U N E   1 9 8 7

Editor's note: The following speech was delivered on April 4, 1987, at the Southern Christian Leadership Conference Poor People's Crusade.

It's very good to be here today with all of us. We come, I know, with a sense of grief in our lives because we come on the anniversary of the assassination of Dr. King. We come here today to remember. We come today to find ways to channel our grief and our anger so that we can move forward. The Dr. King that was killed on April 4, 1968, is not the Dr. King whose birthday we celebrate as a national holiday. He was a man who became increasingly radicalized after the passage of the Voting Rights Act of 1965. His dream was being translated into something new across the face of this land; and it was bringing a new voice for the whole world. That was the Poor People's Campaign, rooted in a stance against war, saying "No" to Vietnam, and "No" to that violence, and "Yes" to whites and blacks and poor coming together and holding hands and marching a new march. And that's why we come here today. We come for a new Poor People's Crusade which will change the USA!

We're happy even in the midst of our grief. We are hopeful even in the face of despair because in this room we come together because we're ready to move forward. Now we're saying "No" to the death at the Lorraine Motel in Memphis, Tennessee, and "Yes" to the Poor People's Crusade, because it is going to emerge now, in a new way, with an agenda for justice and for peace and for equality. So it is. Amen.

I come today to stand before you, for by my life and work I represent the 8,753 homeless people who walk and wander our streets for no right reason here in Atlanta, Georgia. I stand as one who lives among, and with, and on behalf of those who early this morning climbed out of filthy cat holes, abandoned buildings, and church shelters which are now ready to close for the summer months. Leaving stinky places without breakfast, they had to make the choice: do I go to a labor pool and accept the crummiest, crappiest kind of work available at less than $3.35 per hour, or do I go down to Butler Street CME Church for a bowl of breakfast? Here in Atlanta, to choose to work is a choice not to eat. And so I come before you with the voice of the hungry and the homeless.

There are three causes of homelessness. The first reason we have homelessness in the United States of America and in the city of Atlanta, Georgia, is that homeless people are a social benefit for us. There's money in homelessness. People benefit from homelessness, and that is why we have homelessness. In this hour, as we talk, many bodies across this city lie in plasma banks with their arms stretched out like our Savior on the cross, and there's a needle stuck in their veins. Blood is being sucked out of them. Because that blood is dripping out right now, we benefit in the production of medicine and medical research. There is homelessness in this land because it is a social benefit. We must come together to find ways to empower the poor so that we can say "No" to the selling of the poor and of their bodies for our access to medicine and medical research.

Another social benefit of homelessness is labor. There is much work in this society that is so dangerous that labor-union forepersons won't allow their union members to do it. Instead, they telephone a labor pool—a modern slave market that works mainly in the dark, dim hours of the morning. The foreperson says, "Send me somebody to climb way up on this bridge and paint it. I don't want somebody I'm going to see again." Or they call, breaking the Civil Rights Act and fair-employment practices, and they say, "I tell you what I want. I want three workers, and don't send me a Black woman. I want three workers, and don't send me a Black. And I tell you what I'm going to do. I'm going to put 'em right to work with acid. And on the third day, even wearing big rubber gloves, the skin's going to break out in sores, and don't you send 'em back to me." We benefit from homelessness! That's why we have homelessness in this land.

And there's a third social benefit from the horror of homelessness: middle-class people have a large investment in poverty. What would happen to all the jobs that middle-class people have if all of a sudden we got rid of homelessness? Why, to get rid of poverty in the United States would be as bad for the middle class as a Second Coming of Jesus would be for preachers just before the offering. We sense that our comfortable middle-class existence and our secure jobs are safe only because the thousands of unemployed homeless do not compete with us for our work. Thus, we do not struggle to end poverty, unemployment, and homelessness. We need to know that we, you and I, benefit from poverty and homelessness.

With social benefits as the first cause of homelessness, let us now look at a second factor which causes homelessness. In this nation, we lack the political will to feed the hungry and house the homeless. Hunger has nothing to do with agricultural production. There's no shortage of food. Hunger has to do with the fact that our political system will not distribute the food so that everyone has enough to be healthy. The reason there are not enough homes doesn't have anything to do with the material resources to build houses. We have plenty of hammers; we have plenty of nails; we have plenty of shingles; we have plenty of men and women crying, "Give me some good work to do!" We lack the political will, and the political agenda must be, "Let's do what we can do. Let's house the homeless. Let's feed the hungry. There's no reason not to."

The third and final reason that we have homeless people is that we are scared. We are people who are really inhibited. We do not hate the homeless; we fear them. Hate is just weak love; when you hate somebody, you love in a negative way. But the opposite of love is fear. Further, we live in a system and in a city that teaches us not to be satisfied with our daily bread. We pray for daily bread, but we are gripped by hunger-full accumulation, and the need to have more and more turns strangers into our enemies. We fear the poor because they come to us and ask for our daily bread—those crumbs that we no longer desire. But we do not have the love for strangers that provides the courage to give, so we push them away. We build vagrant-free zones. We build prisons. We build death holes. We are scared, and we're so scared we take money from the bowels of our children to build bombs that will burn and kill anyone who would want that which we cannot use. Fear drives us to abandon the poor and to let our sisters and brothers die homeless on the streets.

Now let us look at some responses to the problems of homelessness. First of all let me remind you that we are coming now to the bicentennial of the American Constitution. We don't want to follow Warren Burger down to Disneyland and whoop and holler and sell plastic and cheap copies of the Constitution. Instead we want to listen to Sojourner Truth. You remember that Sojourner Truth rose up one morning and got rid of her slavery name, Isabella. Then the Holy Spirit came to her and said, "Travel." She went. She said, "Lord, what's my name?" And God came and said, "You're a Sojourner," and she said, "Lord, what's your name?" And God came and said, "Truth." She said, "Well, I'm Sojourner Truth." And she went and told people, "The American Constitution ain't a bad document, given what it's looked like, but it's got a worm in it. We gotta stomp that worm out, and that worm is right there in this document. It says that people of color, black folk, slaves, ain't but three-fifths of one human being, and we got to stomp it out." And it got stomped out.

But we must come in these days to know that there's another worm in the American Constitution. In our documents we define equality as equal opportunity, and we limit our rights to speech, assembly, freedom of the press, and others like them. These are excellent rights, especially for powerful people. The middle class understands the Bill of Rights according to these limits. These rights assume that our basic needs have been met. We have freedom of speech, so we can stand here on Ponce de Leon in the Big Star grocery store, and we can talk in freedom about hunger and starve to death. We can gather together and have freedom of assembly. We can get fifteen or twenty or two thousand people, stand outside of Grady Hospital, and say, "What we need is adequate, decent medical care, and I can die of disease while I'm talking." Yes, there's a worm in the American Constitution. We don't simply need opportunity. We need equality. We need human rights which guarantee the basics of life. That's what we need as people.

We need equal rights to *shelter,* to *food,* to *medical care,* to *education,* to *transportation,* and to *good work* for *just pay.* We want people to have houses, so they can build homes and families. We want food—it's a natural right. You know, hunger doesn't have anything to do with class analysis. Everybody gets hungry three times a day. The class analysis has to do with who eats. Not everybody eats three good meals a day. The American Constitution must provide that every human being who is made in the image of God should have three nutritional meals a day that they can cook in their own home. People don't need to be standing out in front of my house and some damned soup kitchen. Food should be a human right. Medical care should be a right. Not only should we receive care when we are bleeding and dying, but also we should receive preventive medical care so that we may be a healthy and whole community. Medical care should not be an equal opportunity if we are able to buy it, but medical care should be a human right.

Education all the way through college must be a constitutional right. I'm not talking about child care alone, but I mean education that makes mature men and women. Through the power of knowledge and education we can hold our bodies straight and high and say "Yes" and "Amen" to the liberating power of education and knowledge, which brings sisters and brothers together as we work for justice. Transportation must be a human right in this mobile society. Did you know that there are fifteen thousand people in this city who must take a cab to get to Grady Hospital? Do you know why health care costs so much? Why do we charge somebody to get on a MARTA bus? It ought to be free for us all. Human mobility is a need that ought to be a right in the American Constitution. How are we poor people going to get to Washington? We don't need to follow a mule. We can all ride up there together. It ought to be a right. It ought to be a right.

Finally, let us reflect as we think about the bicentennial of the American Constitution: not only do we need the separation of church and state, but we need the right to good work. People do not need to produce bombs or work with acids or with waste that will not rot. We need the right to work in ways that build the Beloved Community, that nurture children, that care for the elderly, that visit the sick and make the weak strong. Good work needs to be a human right in this society. During this two-hundredth-anniversary year of the American Constitution, more and more people are underemployed, and those of us who find jobs are working more and more in death production. Let's stop! We can stop it!

Poverty—we can get rid of 37.5 percent of the homeless in this city tomorrow, and even more than that within a few months if we had a minimum wage that was a living wage instead of a death wage. We need to pay people an amount that is not only fair but that re-creates the economic order and brings an equitable redistribution of goods. Yes, we want to work in ways that build families, that build homes, that build justice, that make for peace. A minimum wage of ten dollars an hour is the bottom line when we seek life and fairness.

Our response to homelessness must be the eternal struggle for love and justice. We must put together love and justice, because love without justice is a sentimentality that we want nothing of. And justice without love becomes political infighting, ego-tripping, a dead society. We want love and justice together. We will walk together the road toward freedom as we love one another and struggle for justice. So, let me say, I want to invite all of you to come on March 15, 1988, to the opening of the Al Smith Memorial Park. And we'd better come together and celebrate love and justice in Al Smith Park. We'll dance and we'll holler and we'll be together and then we'll hear the Republicans and the Democrats both saying, "The main part of our platform is human rights and equality with a roof over every head, a job for every hand, food for every stomach, education for every mind, medicine for every illness, and a bus token for every trip."

In Defense of Band-Aids, *by Ed Loring*

NOVEMBER 1988

Sometimes I feel caught in a whirlwind of unfortunate dichotomies. Recently I listened to some juxtapose the concern for the whales trapped off the shores of Alaska with the concern for the homeless trapped on the streets in Atlanta. That juxtaposition is unfortunate, because the God of Creation cares for each and every creature, like a shepherdess who seeks for one lost sheep. The God of Redemption, whose justice demands shelter for whales from Arctic winds, is also the God of the Bible, who demands the benefits of our society (i.e., houses, jobs, medical care, etc.) for the sojourner and the outcast.

I vividly remember standing before a committee of the Atlanta City Council during the winter of 1983 and being horrified that a city that would not respond to the homeless (although twenty-one persons froze to death in one week) had purchased extra heaters for the animals at the city zoo. I did not, however, begrudge the elephant her heater; I simply felt grief and anger toward the city officials whose lives are so isolated from the poor that it took frozen corpses to get their attention.

Most of those who care for our earth and all its inhabitants also struggle for justice; just like those who pollute the air and defend TV commercials or cigarette sales are the same folk who blame the poor for their poverty and believe the ACLU is an enemy of the Bill of Rights.

There are a myriad of dichotomies that seek to split us in two and to make our already unfocused and confused lives more schizophrenic. (The biblical word for the devil is the "Confuser.") Some folk pit spirituality and prayer against a life of activism and political effort. In our churches remain those who seek lost souls and others who understand the mission of the church in terms of social concerns. Within the camp of socially concerned are those who seek to aid hurting persons and others who fight to change the systems of abuse and injustice. This latter split is often referred to as the charity-justice polarity, or the Band-Aids versus root-causes approach. I wish to address this latter issue with the understanding that all these divisions need healing. All these divisions need to be woven into the single fabric of wholeness from which they were rent. Activism without spiritual discipline and prayer? Absurd.

Band-Aids are wonderful. Cuts, scrapes, blisters, and sores hurt. Band-Aids help stop the pain and suffering. Band-Aids also retard, if not halt, infection and thereby often save toes, fingers, hands, and lives. We use Band-Aids everyday. A friend comes out of a weed patch with a shallow rodent bite, and we are able to bathe the wound and put on a Band-Aid. You cannot do that, however, if you do not locate your body in close proximity to the homeless ones of God. Of course, Band-Aids include much more: the use of the telephone, a bowl of soup, a meat sandwich prepared by a downtown law firm, a slice of bread delivered by a monk or a neighborhood baker, a shower and clean underpants, a pair of eyeglasses, a MARTA token, a bed with clean sheets, a short visit with a friendly smile and hopeful ear, a coat. . . . Band-Aids are sacramental leftovers which sustain and nourish those who have been left out. Said simply: Band-Aids are charity.

The reason I titled this apologetic "In Defense of Band-Aids" is that some among us, in their very fine pursuit of justice, and in their dedication to root out the causes of suffering and oppression, disdain charity. I have known workers against hunger who have never shared a meal with a hungry person, never even met one, never even seen one in the flesh! But hunger is hungry people.

Charity is love. Charity is Band-Aids. Charity is the basis of justice and its fulfillment. When our days are over and Jesus has returned (from what I hear, he will return as a Black woman), charity will characterize our lives and the demand of justice will be finished. Oh, what a day . . . !

Charity means reducing the distance between ourselves and those who are poor. Charity cannot take place apart from those who freeze on the street and sit in the jails. When a church responds to homelessness by opening a shelter, the congregation invites Henry and Martha into their building and into their lives. We must work for affordable housing for the poor. That is a good response to the root causes of homelessness. But tonight what the homeless need are a warm welcome and a friendly space in which to eat, shower, and sleep. Those who separate the Band-Aids of shelters from the systemic, root-cause advocacy for affordable houses tend to be those who have not yet reduced the distance between themselves and the poor.

Charity—that way of life which reduces the distance between those of us who have money and those who do not—is friendship. The Beloved Community, for which we all work and toward which the path of peace and justice leads, is one in which we are all friends. Sleeping with the homeless, eating with the hungry, waiting with the convicted, and putting a Band-Aid on an open sore create wonderful friendships. What more could we want in life? That is exactly what God is doing in Jesus Christ: making God's enemies into God's friends. Have you ever thought of the atonement as a Band-Aid?

Charity—those little Band-Aids that are the filaments of the web of justice—brings an unexpected gift that can be received nowhere else. A life of charity receives more than it can give; the gift received is the immediacy of the presence of God. God lives in the flesh of the poor. Jesus speaks in the voices of the least. The Holy Spirit heals our wounds and weaves us into community through the gifts of the oppressed to the oppressor, from the poor to the rich. The energy for the long-haul battle with the powers and principalities of death comes from life among, with, and on behalf of the poor. The forgiveness of sins and new life on this earth (today!) are the unexpected fruits of charity.

The person with cancer eating his lungs out because of the asbestos work he did for the city ten years ago needs medical care. We must struggle to see that he gets it now, even as we struggle for guaranteed medical insurance for every woman, man, and child.

In the Bible, laws exist to restrain the rich and to control the greedy. Charity is the beginning of the New Jerusalem, of the Kingdom of God on earth. Tonight in Atlanta, 12,354 people will have no place to sleep. Why? What are you doing about it? What about a Band-Aid? Invite just one to spend the night in your home. It just might deepen your hunger and thirst for justice. Thank you.

Band-Aids and Beyond, *by Ed Loring*

MARCH 1989

There is a famine in the land.
There is a famine in the land.

When Mrs. Durant came to live with us at the Open Door Community, she most often came in the back door, because that is where we have our handicapped-access ramp. Mrs. Durant lacked a leg, so she rolled along in a wheelchair. Why? Because she was dying, like thousands here in Atlanta, of invisible starvation. Long and harsh years of lousy food had ruined her body. Mrs. Durant had developed diabetes, and the sugar in her system left her sour, not sweet. She stank. It is hard to move from a wheelchair onto a toilet, especially in a city which welcomes few poor and homeless to share its white porcelain commodes. Often she just peed in her pants and let it dry on her shabby clothes.

One day she rolled her wheelchair into the cement canyons and asphalt rivers which are Atlanta. I never saw Mrs. Durant again. Street stories say she rolled that chair straight up I-75 to Detroit, Michigan. I don't know.

But I do know this: Some years before Mrs. Durant came to the Open Door, she walked—strong of limb—and with a loud voice she entered my office at Clifton Presbyterian Church. She wanted a bag of food from our food shelf. "Yes," I said, and I went to the pantry and gathered cans and bags of food: beans, tuna, dried milk, five pounds of grits. When I returned to the front of the

church to hand her the "bag of life," she hesitated, and then in a wailing cry—
like Rachel weeping for her children in Ramah—she said:

> "Oh Pastor Loring
> There is a famine in
> the land.
>
> There is a famine in
> the land."
>
> "Yes," said she,
> "I see children
> stalking the streets
> Women wandering in the woods
> Men motionless in the morning
>
> Attacked and beaten
> bruised and broken
> by violent death."
>
> She wept and clamored
> She stomped her feet
> And like a wild woman
> Set aflame with fear
> and indignation
> She reached down into the
> Abyss of her soul
> and touched the primordial
> depths of lamentation
> like a woman whose breasts
> have gone dry
> while her little one starves
> in her arms
>
> She yelled,
> "Alah beganda Abtu re Now
> woc Tim la Kata
> Alah beganda Abtu re Now
> woc Tim la Kata . . ."
> And walked away.

Because Mrs. Durant taught several of us that in the land of plenty "there
is a famine in the land," and because Dorothy Day and Mitch Snyder led us to

hundreds and hundreds of starving people in our streets, we formed the Open Door Community.

A home. A refuge from the storm. A sanctuary and shelter. And we feed folk. Yes, yes, we feed folk! We serve more than ten thousand meals per month! (Thank you, Lord.) This morning, before the sun streaked saffron in the eastern sky, 250 cold and wet human beings tumbled and stumbled down the steps into the Butler Street CME Church basement. Elizabeth stood smiling at the door with a welcome on her face. Larry poured steaming-hot coffee. John handed out bright white boiled eggs. Ruby Evans poured gallons of cheese grits. Carol served oranges while Chet spooned out the vitamin C tablets.

By 8:15 A.M. the sky was blue and the sun had peeped over I-85/I-75. The van headed home toward 910. Amid those waiting for showers and soup, the empty pots were brought to Carl, who waited at the pot sink. Sarah Floyd had already begun the soup and sandwiches for the 11:00 A.M. serving. In the hallway a woman cried as her feet bled. Thank you, Mrs. Durant.

Band-Aids are receiving unfair press these days. During the 1960s the word for personal response and responsibility was *charity*. Like Band-Aids, charity was considered bad, weak, and the easy way out. The call was for justice. But during the 1960s those who called for racial justice could not meet the challenge of their own arguments. So rather than justice they chose to bus children across town and to let them graduate and face the meaning of justice as it affects housing patterns, jobs, and medical care.

During the classical period, Band-Aids were called love. The good Samaritan is the fullest image of the Christian love ethic, which is charity, or Band-Aids. However, as the rich and powerful became Christians, the opposition between love and justice arose. Some argued for love without justice (the opiate-of-the-people theme) as a way to keep the status quo safe from systemic change. In the last fifty years, liberals and activists have called for justice, not love (systemic change, not Band-Aids), as a way to force the powerless to change while at the same time keeping their own lives separated from God's poor, prisoners, and hungry friends.

The Band-Aid response to hunger and oppression is helpful in three overlapping ways. First, love brings healing and reconciliation. Interpersonal love, which is friendship, brings to the other what no law or revolution can: understanding and acceptance. Band-Aids heal us from our hurts and stop our wounds from bleeding. Oh, how I hope that those who threw parties and filled with rage as Ted Bundy was executed will find some good Samaritan who has time to help them from the ditch of their murderous way of living. Neither the abolition of the death penalty nor the quick killing of killers brings wholeness to the victims, or to those who thirst for revenge and feed off the carrion of the executed. Only love and friendship can redeem us from ourselves.

Second, Band-Aids bring us home to the poor, the stranger, the despised one. All of a sudden, the hungry and homeless become Beth and Henry. We eat with them and they with us. Again, we make friends. We are transformed little by little into companions.

Finally, Band-Aids, charity, or love bring us toward conversion. It is in the voice of the poor that we hear the cry of Christ. The flesh of the hungry ones is the very body of our Lord, who feeds us his broken body and serves us his spilled blood. We do not so much take the gospel to the poor as we receive the call to conversion through the poor. One reason many leaders in this society are so arrogant and immature is that, by belittling Band-Aids and the direct relationships fostered by charity, they have grown deaf and blind, and see only in the "white male system" the answer to the social problems of injustice.

But to stop with Band-Aids and not, at the same time, to move toward the demands for systemic change is hideous. Band-Aids alone hide the structural roots of injustice. As Reinhold Niebuhr has written, "Love without justice is a sentimentality." To say it another way, love without equality is oppression. Without the fight for justice, those of us who love the poor are likely to use them for our own purposes and agenda: ego status, jobs, research, scapegoats, stoop labor, guinea pigs for medical schools . . .

Another pitfall of love without justice, or Band-Aids without systemic change, is that we become confused and unable to identify the enemy. Most often in our society, and even among many good Samaritans, the hungry person or the victim—rather than the structural reality of hunger—is deemed our enemy. When the hungry, rather than hunger, are the locus of the problem, and Band-Aids become an end rather than a means, then we find money in the treasury for new prisons: we want to punish the poor for their poverty! Or we hear 1960s liberals calling for the reinstitutionalization of the mentally ill. And we want to build homes for the aged and infirm, and a multitude of other segregations of the hungry and poor, rather than encounter the economic and social structures that cause us to fear and flee the homeless and even our own parents who, try as they may, continue to grow old and withered and infirm. To stop at Band-Aids only leads us to see the hungry person as our enemy, when our enemy is actually the political system which produces hunger. While we give charity and live our lives of personal responsibility we must also demand justice.

The great danger of Band-Aids is that they hide our hate of the hungry. Charity does not disguise the recipients, but it may cover up the investments we treasure in the status quo. Love without justice can turn our aims and purposes upside down, so that we despise the hungry and live with the reality of hunger. It is damnable that in the United States we tolerate hunger today.

What I am suggesting is that we must love the hungry and hate hunger. We must make friends with those who do not have enough to eat, and we must declare war on the causes of hunger. I beg you to make a vow to go to war! Make a vow that you will not rest until the systemic causes of hunger are rooted out of our capitalistic system. Until the values of the American way of life will not tolerate the lack of three good, nutritious meals for every man, woman, and child everyday, make a vow that you will not rest.

> Be lamb-like
> gentle, kind, loving to
> the hungry.
>
> Be a snarling lion, or a growling
> bear to hunger.
>
> How? How shall we—
> makers of Peace—
> make Peace with the hungry?
>
> How shall we—
> demanders of justice—
> make war on hunger?

First, let us never separate charity and justice, Band-Aids and systemic change. Let us live out our lives with the poor while they set the agenda for our personal and social decisions. Those of us who serve the hungry with bags of food from the pantry or bowls of soup from the kitchen must experience and feel hunger. We must know what it means to be hungry. Hunger is a great, though harsh, teacher. Before the filming of the movie *Ironweed,* Meryl Streep put ice all over her body for thirty minutes so she could know the agony and pain of the street woman Helen. Ms. Streep wanted to be Helen, to feel Helen— yes—to love Helen. We who feed the hungry must fast often. We must know hunger, be hungry, hate hunger. Personal hunger—my hunger, your hunger— must be our position: a committed stance in life by which we make decisions and live out our lives.

Charity and love are expressed and given to others as our hunger meets the hunger of the hungry. This shared suffering in our bellies and bowels becomes a fundamental source of passion and commitment to wage war on hunger.

But charity is not enough. We must travel beyond Band-Aids into the land of justice. Hunger is a political problem, not an agricultural problem. We have plenty of food and resources to feed everyone. Because hunger is a political problem, we must change the economic structures by political means to feed everyone. We must wage a political war on our hated adversary: hunger.

Public education is not only a right in the United States, but it is a requirement to attend school between the ages of six and sixteen. This law is based on a Jeffersonian idea that the democratic process cannot maintain itself unless the voters are educated enough to make wise decisions for themselves and the nation. What about starving voters? Hungry citizens? And what about the soul of the nation that is so anesthetized to the suffering of 20 percent of our sisters and brothers that we find funds for construction of a domed stadium while people perish on the streets?

The political response to hunger must be the same as our political response to ignorance: hunger must be against the law. We need to pass legislation which will guarantee three nutritious meals per day for everyone in our society for as long as they live. We need not only Head Start, but stomach start and stomach finish, too.

This then is war against hunger in our democratic society. We must overturn the forces and the politicians who vote against such legislation. With good food available we may then listen to the empowered poor as we discern the next steps toward a more just society: housing, full employment, child care, medical care . . . And each step will be fought for with love, with Band-Aids by friends who care for and heal each other as we walk together on the road toward justice.

Therefore, let us go forward and meet the enemy. Let us say *no* to this suffering.

Hunger is our enemy.
Hunger is violence.
Hunger is death.

This is a call to arms,
A call to war.
We are already on the way.

Let us come closer to the front lines.
Let us present our bodies
and get into the battle!

What Is the Problem with Underground Atlanta?
by Murphy Davis

J U L Y   1 9 8 9

Underground Atlanta has opened amid fireworks, fanfare, and public response that exceeded the fondest hopes of the project's developers. In the first four days, more than a million people visited Underground, and who knows how many millions of dollars were spent in the restaurants, bars, balloon and T-shirt shops? "The fun's back in town," screamed the billboards and politicians.

In the midst of all the hoopla, some of us went to jail. Others of us, along with homeless advocates from around the city, leafleted and picketed in a driving rain. Why? When everybody was having such a great time, why would we want to be the spoilsports who insisted on raising the unpleasant issues? Why interrupt the speech of Mayor Andrew Young, civil rights hero and successful politician? And what does Underground have to do with homelessness anyway?

Underground Atlanta is an unequivocal statement of what is important to our city. It has been the primary agenda of the Young administration and the centerpiece of the business community's plan. But development of Underground has not just ignored the poor; Underground has been developed at the expense of the poor. It is an entertainment center (only, of course, for those who can afford it). But at the same time, 32 percent of the people who live in Atlanta live below the poverty line (only Newark, New Jersey, has a higher percentage of poor people). In this year, 35,000 to 40,000 men, women, and children have slept in Atlanta's private and public shelters for the homeless.

One hundred forty-two million dollars has been spent, and the city anticipates spending another twenty million to thirty million dollars to subsidize the project over the next ten years. Eight and a half million dollars spent on Underground Atlanta came from community-development block-grant funds: federal money specifically allocated for housing and jobs for the poor. Serious efforts were made to persuade Mayor Young to put that money into housing, which this city so desperately needs. The excuse has been that Underground is creating jobs. But what kind of jobs? Jobs that provide a living wage? Surely not. Forty percent of the men and women living in Atlanta's shelters for the homeless are employed. But still they cannot afford a place for themselves or their families to live. Twelve million dollars came from city sales-tax revenues. Tax money belongs to all of the people of the city. Surely some of that could have been used to address the increasing suffering of the poor. Without even a vote on the matter, Atlanta taxpayers were committed to backing eighty-five million dollars in revenue bonds. If Underground fails, the home and property owners of the city will pay off a debt of $7.5 million per year for twenty-five years.

In the seven years that the new Underground was planned and developed, the city has sunk deeper into crisis. The schools are a mess. Drugs control the lives of thousands of people and entire areas of the city. Many recreation centers and playgrounds around the city are closed down and boarded up, as are thousands of units of public housing. The soup kitchens' lines are longer and the shelters more crowded as the number of homeless men, women, and children grows.

In the face of it all, we have chosen to spend our major resources on an entertainment center for the well-to-do. There is, of course, nothing inherently wrong with entertainment. Good food and music are among life's good gifts! But how can we justify such expense for entertainment in the face of ever-increasing human suffering?

Plaza Park was for years a home—a sanctuary of sorts—to hundreds of homeless people, most of them older black men. In March 1987, Plaza Park was closed so that it could be transformed into an elegant entrance to Underground. Replacing the older men on park benches are cascading fountains and a bronze statue of a homeless man. He sits, frozen in time, feeding a pigeon with his bedroll beside him.

The stated policy of Underground is this: If a "derelict" comes into Underground s/he will be asked to prove their legitimate business there. Anyone unable to prove legitimate business will be warned; if the "derelict" fails to leave immediately or returns to Underground s/he will be arrested on a criminal-trespass charge (the sentence for which is up to a year in prison and/or a one-thousand-dollar fine).

Such policies concerning Underground are part of a larger plan, introduced two years ago, for what was called a "vagrant-free zone" in the downtown area. (In the face of public criticism, the planners changed the name to the "sanitized zone.") The plan, if not the terminology, was endorsed by the mayor and the city's business leaders.

Homeless people and other poor people are not welcome in downtown Atlanta. To keep them out, police arrests for sleeping on a park bench, panhandling (begging), public urination (despite the continuing lack of any public toilets), and criminal trespass (for sleeping in an abandoned building or daring to enter Underground) have been stepped up. To visit Atlanta's municipal court is to see the "vagrant-free zone" at work. The city jail and prison farm are literally stuffed with poor people—a large percentage of whom have "offended" with their mere presence downtown.

Underground Atlanta has become a statement that the rich of our city are willing to be cruel and greedy to find a good time. If the poor are in the way, or are seen frightening suburban shoppers, then city policy will be mustered to move them out of the way.

We cannot allow this to go unchallenged. We often sing a spiritual in our community, "If anybody asks you who I am, just tell 'em I'm a child of God." And so we are. When God's children are humiliated, degraded, insulted, and when what is rightfully theirs is taken away, we should never stand for it.

And we will not.

Underground Atlanta and Daily Bread, *by Ed Loring*

JULY 1989

Give us this day our daily bread.

—Jesus, March 18, 32 C.E.

I ask you, God, to let me have two things before I die; keep me from lying, and let me be neither rich nor poor. So give me only as much food as I need. If I have more, I might say that I do not need you. But if I am poor, I might steal and bring disgrace on my God.

—Proverbs 30:7–9

The United States has 6 percent of the world's population and controls and consumes 50 percent of the world's resources. This imbalance creates a problem: because we have more than we need, we no longer need God. The biblical God did not die; our God just faded away behind the loaves of bread. Isn't it ironic that we have more bread than we need, yet we steal from the wretched of the earth? We disgrace our God.

Therefore, the fastest-growing faith in the United States is the Muslim faith, which offers another way to live, and the largest religion today is the worship of television and obedience to its lies that you deserve more bread; that the good life is a materialistic life of consumption and comfort; that those who are not well-to-do, beautiful people are bad and deserve the plight in which they find themselves, so it would be wrong to help or care for them.

Thirty-two percent of the people in Atlanta live below the poverty level. Atlanta is a city in crisis because of the sheer quantity of homelessness, hunger, and unemployment among African American teenagers and men. Atlanta is the home of Andrew Young, SCLC, the Martin Luther King Jr. Center for Nonviolent Social Change, the regional office of the NAACP, Ralph David Abernathy, and the greatest consortium of African American educational institutions in the United States. Yet we have no leadership in the local political community (mostly Black) or the business community (mostly white) that gives voice or vision (much less policy) for the poor. In fact, with the opening of Underground Atlanta, our leadership not only celebrated all that food but the silent victory of the vagrant-free zone.

Isaiah, wonderful old prophet who seemingly was neither poor nor rich, tells us that if we forget our God and turn away from the Lord, we will meet the following devastating punishment: "The LORD will let the people be governed by immature boys" (Isa. 3:4). This is certainly true in Atlanta today. In the government and business community we are led by "immature boys." Our leaders appear in the grown bodies of men and women, but they are selfish, spoiled, greedy, and deaf to the poor and the demands of love and justice. That is the fundamental reason why 32 percent of the boys and girls and the men and women in this city live a life of squalor and die a death of degradation. We have no mature and courageous leadership. Andy Young has sold his birthright of civil rights leadership and visionary Black leadership of all people for a bowl of porridge served in a chic cafe in Underground. Why? Watch television; it will tell you.

Hunger in Atlanta is a paradox. We have entirely too much food, but we have more than twenty thousand hungry people. Why? Watch television; it will tell you. The Atlanta Community Food Bank has to relocate every few years because of ever-increasing needs for warehouse space. We cannot even store the stuff. We have too much food in Atlanta, and that is a primary reason that we are faced with starvation and malnutrition on the streets and in the ghettos. (On Memorial Day we were the only soup line open in the city. We, with a dining hall that seats forty-two folk, served 619 people. We served from 10:00 A.M. until 4:00 P.M. Why? Watch television; it will tell you.)

Hunger in Atlanta is a political issue, not an agricultural issue. The opening of Underground Atlanta will increase poverty and hunger because it was built and now is maintained at the expense of the poor. If we are given more food than we need, according to the scriptures, we reject God and that, of course, brings despair and death through the leadership of "immature boys."

So what can we do apart from turning off our televisions? First, we can love our God and obey the words of life which we have been given. An immediate social norm should be "enough for everyone." That is one aspect of biblical justice. Second, we can love the poor—an amazing 32 percent of our city. Love of the poor means to stand in solidarity politically with the poor. Let our lives be "good news for the poor." Where we eat, where we play and work, how we vote, with whom we live—let it be "good news to the poor."

But politics is not enough. We must also serve the poor with our hands and hearts. Love builds community, and the one who loves God is one in community with the poor.

Finally, we must love and live in a way that will help the "immature boys" (many of whom are female) grow up. Good leadership, faithful to all people, taking care of the weak and limiting the power of the strong, is a part of both the biblical and the American traditions. There is no reason on earth for a city to lack moral vision and a commitment to justice for the poor and Black. I believe that the tons and tons and tons of bread (and money) that have come into Atlanta since World War II have blinded and crippled our leadership. But God is faithful and can restore sight to the blind and give to us—the flock—a good shepherd.

Let us be neither rich nor poor. Let us have only as much as we need. Then we can eat and dance and play at Underground with no one homeless, and hunger will be only that rumbling we hear before we sit at table.

Woodruff Park and the Search for Common Ground,
by Murphy Davis

MARCH 1996

Woodruff Park is a 1.7-acre tract of land in the center of downtown Atlanta. Like many other valuable pieces of real estate in American history, it has become the subject of hot debate, quiet deals, great expenditure of funds—both public and private—and has seemed to require, along the way, a military presence to secure its function for those who hold the power and intend to define the park's use.

The park, formerly known as Central City Park, most recently emerged from behind a curtain of chain link with a five-million-dollar facelift. This new park is, more than anything else, a spot to look at. It is not a public gathering place: indeed, there is no area of the park that encourages gathering, conversation, play, human exchange, or interrelatedness of any kind.

While the old park never seemed like a spectacular place to me, its walkways were wide and spacious, lined with benches and grass. People walked to and through, stopped and talked together, waved to, and even hassled, one another. But it was at least somewhat inviting, friendly, and spacious.

The new park is mostly an expanse of concrete, stone, and some grass. The walkway is narrow and has a greatly reduced number of benches (all of these face in the same direction). The benches, of course, are a crucial symbol and reality.

In 1993 we won one of the only (narrowly defined) major political victories in the history of our political action and advocacy. We tested the city ordinance that prohibited lying on a city park bench (or against a tree!). In two actions in September and October of 1993, twelve of our number were arrested and went to jail for "slouching" or lying on the benches of Woodruff Park. The city council rescinded the law. Amazing.

Exactly one year later, the park was closed for a five-million-dollar renovation. Nimrod Long, whose firm was paid three hundred thousand dollars for a new design, was frank. He said that they were charged with the mission of creating a park that would be inhospitable to homeless people. This, of course, must include park benches with armrests spaced so that it is impossible to lie down.

Well, we can be proud of the fact that they darn well did their job. This park clearly does not invite homeless people to gather. Trouble is, if we mandate a public space inhospitable to any one group of people, we end with a public space that is inhospitable to everybody.

Woodruff Park is unfriendly space. This is not, for instance, a place you would think to bring children to play. There is no play equipment, no bathroom, no drinking fountain, no convivial space for parents to gather while the children play, and it simply is not clear whether or not the grass is an inviting space to run and tumble.

Gone are the wraparound-bench tree planters that invited long chess games and spontaneous lunch gatherings. What is left is a narrow walkway, a relocated *Phoenix* statue (the post–Civil War image of Atlanta rising out of the ashes), a huge, very expensive thirty-foot cascading waterfall, and a stretch of grass. The grass will be nice if people are allowed to sit for picnics, naps, and conversation. But it will not do to replace the benches, especially for the elderly, the disabled, people in business attire, or for anybody when the weather is wet or cold. Neither will it do if the powers that be decide, as they did with the old park, that people cannot sit or play or walk or lie down on the grass. In fact, in the old park they installed what our street friends call "pneumonia grass"—sprinklers buried invisibly that come on without warning, drenching anyone who might be unwittingly sitting or sleeping.

The park is intended to be, as Mayor Campbell proudly proclaimed at the opening ceremony, "a beautiful place to look at," which seems a gross concession to the suburban mentality that controls our city. Downtown Atlanta is designed more to entertain tourists and suburbanites who want to drive through, with doors locked and windows rolled up, than to foster an urban life and culture. In addition, you might be led to question Mayor Campbell's sense of beauty.

Perhaps the opening ceremony was somewhat premature, and more trees, shrubs, and plantings are yet to come. But for now there is much less greenery. From the northeast corner the park looks like a fortress. And when the water is turned off, the "cascading waterfall" actually resembles the exposed, barnacle-encrusted, pocked, and rusted hull of an aging battleship. Beautiful this place is not.

It could be that this "battleship," this lifeless wall, is indeed a fitting monument for the center of Atlanta. The city government and controlling business interests have pursued a course of destruction in the central city for several generations now, displacing people seen as undesirable. When these policies of removal began in the 1950s, it was clear that race was the motivating factor. The powers in Atlanta did not want African American people in the downtown business district. So neighborhoods were broken up and gave way to interstate highways; housing was destroyed, little shops and businesses were forced out, and a stadium, a civic center, and countless parking lots rolled over the poor. These practices, which began thirty years ago, resulted in much of the poverty and homelessness in the African American population we see in our city today.

This pattern of destruction has been repeated, and there is little beauty, culture, or humanity left. What we have instead is precisely what the powers say they want: a "sanitized zone," "vagrant-free," and deserted enough to appear safe, devoid of the color of a rich, urban culture whose life has never been antiseptic, colorless, cold, and heartless.

Eight years ago, the rebirth of Underground Atlanta brought a similar enthusiasm for displacement and destruction to this current renovation of Woodruff Park.

Plaza Park, once a lively place filled with street vendors, preachers, homeless folks, and pedestrians on their way to the Five Points MARTA station, was razed to make way for the cement, light tower, glitz, and security guards at Underground. A large number of people made homeless by the destruction of their neighborhoods were once again displaced from Plaza Park.

Within a stone's throw of Woodruff Park, thousands of units of single-room occupancy housing have been demolished since the late 1970s. These SROs were places where many who would now like to rest in the park could have lived, and where some of them probably did at one time. Where was the outcry when the Avon and Capital Hotels were destroyed and replaced with parking decks? Where were the protests when the Francis Hotel was closed, mysteriously burned, and replaced with John Portman's latest gleaming tower? Where now is the outcry from any Atlanta government or business leader for housing for Atlanta's homeless? Their silence is deafening. Instead, editorials and columns whine, "City Doesn't Belong Just to Bums and Winos";[3] countless city laws have been thrown in place to empower police to hound the homeless and to move them from one corner to the next, and the next.

Now we see this same forced removal in Atlanta's Olympic zeal. Hundreds of public housing units were lost as Techwood Homes was torn down to make room for dormitories for Olympic athletes. Where did all those people go? Why is housing for transient Olympic visitors more important than homes for the people of Atlanta?

Additional examples abound. Seventy-two acres of a low-income, mixed-use area (with shelters, labor pools, day-care centers, small businesses, and warehouses) are now being plowed under to make way for Centennial Olympic Park and to clear this space of undesirable elements. The area, so that no one would question its removal, was labeled a "cancer" by the former head of the Atlanta Chamber of Commerce. But the lost housing has not been replaced, businesses have folded, and shops and restaurants have nowhere to relocate. Of the seventy-two acres, twenty-five will remain after the Olympics as space for a park, at an estimated cost of fifty million dollars. The space will be given, not to the city, but to the state of Georgia for management and control. Why? Could the reason be to up the ante and to make any infraction there a state offense rather than a violation of municipal laws? The rest of the acreage will be developed as commercial property, and if past patterns remain the same, African American people and businesses that were displaced will not find a welcome. The park and surroundings are being redeveloped, not because Atlanta wants to cultivate public space, but because the world is coming to town, and Atlanta wants a clean façade; the "garbage" will be swept under a rug temporarily.

How do these decisions about public space and policy get made? As a citizen of Atlanta, I have no recollection of being asked for my opinion. Whose park is Woodruff Park? Like most of the important decisions about Atlanta's life and future, this was one more deal cut by the powers in a back room. There was never any public discussion, debate, conversation, or exchange about the park. Why does this autocratic method of decision making exist in a democratic society? The answer seems clear: including everyone in a discussion about the use and regulation of public space might not bring the desired results for those who already have so much and who stand to gain much more. Atlanta is in fact one of the poorest cities in the United States, but the super glitz we put forward is a thin, often convincing, veneer for the rest of the world. If the real poverty were known, would the world come to Atlanta to fill Billy Payne's pockets? Could the world of Coke continue to deceive the world, or would we all realize that the veneer covers an ugly, rat-infested, festering bleakness?

How can we have a truly beautiful, friendly city that welcomes all people,

---

3. Richard Matthews, *Atlanta Journal*, 20 October 1994.

without regard for race or economic status? We can all agree that nobody likes to be assailed by an "aggressive panhandler." But why do we like to be, or allow ourselves to be, assailed by the pages of a respectable newspaper, which refers to the poor in epithets laced with strong racist implications? While the columnists complain bitterly about their loathing for the poor and homeless, where is the public outrage and protest that people in Atlanta do not have the food, medical care, housing, and good work they need to sustain life? Instead, we dismiss these poor folk as mere trash to be moved around and pushed out of sight and mind.

The task for those of us who love the city is to transform Woodruff Park into a beautiful, friendly space. Welcoming hospitality cannot be found through another design firm, or with an army of bulldozers. We need to move in with play equipment, music, chairs and benches, picnic tables and blankets, and then all the people of the world can come to celebrate the true urban culture of At-lanta. We need to put up bathrooms and drinking fountains right away. Woodruff Park could yet become a welcoming space for the women and men and boys and girls of the city. Can't you see the rich and poor, the Black and white, the homeless and well-housed, dancing and laughing and clapping their hands to the music of Blind Willie McTell, while the smell of smoked ribs wafts on the breeze, and children swing high enough to touch the sky, as the old folks play a hand of dominoes? Who knows? Such a party could inspire us to build a city with housing, justice, and care for all of its people.

Toilets, Justice, and Hospitality:
The Case for Public Toilets, *by Murphy Davis*

NOVEMBER 2000

I'd have to say that it has come as a surprise to realize how much time and attention I have given to toilets in the past twenty years. I guess I never thought it was something I would do when I grew up. But if you work with people who are poor or oppressed, sooner or later you get to the subject of where bathrooms are located and who has access to them.

Those of us who grew up in the Jim Crow South learned early that every bathroom was not available to every body. The signage was complex: White/Colored, White Ladies, White Gentlemen, Colored Only. There were bath-rooms where the signs cut to the chase: Whites Only. For bathrooms lacking signs, the message went without saying: Black people did not have to ask. Water fountains were similarly marked, although without the gender specificity. Any

African American who traveled in the South before the Public Accommodations Act of 1965 can tell stories of how they got along without bathroom access on the road. I recently heard a man about my age refer to "traveling with the Maxwell House coffee can." When the Public Accommodations Act passed Congress, the distinguished Mrs. Sadie Mays heard the news and reportedly said, "Oh, thank goodness, I won't have to travel with my chamber pot anymore."

In the spring of 1968, the small southern women's college from which I graduated accepted its first Black student. She was my roommate. At a dorm meeting (my roommate was not present), one sweet belle contorted her face and snarled, "Well, maybe I can't stop her from living here, but I'll never share the same bathroom with her." That harsh memory caused me particular pain when, some fifteen years later, the African American congregation in whose church we were going to serve a meal locked its newly renovated bathrooms so they could not be used by the poor people (mostly Black) who were coming to eat. *Poverty. Race. Germs. Unclean. Protect the Bathrooms.* These words and ideas seem to keep coming together.

In 1983, our fifth year of working with homeless people, we began to advocate for public toilets in Atlanta. We had heard the story again and again of men and women who, caught in the humiliating act of public urination or defecation, had been arrested, jailed, and sentenced to serve time in the city prison farm (now the city jail). Public urination is a violation of a city ordinance, punishable by up to 180 days in jail or a fine of up to $1,000 or up to six months of work on public streets. Most people arrested for this "crime" are the homeless poor. They do the jail time.

Joanna Adams, then associate pastor at Central Presbyterian Church, was president of the Christian Council. She responded to our advocacy by having the council sponsor a debate on public toilets, held at City Hall. Ed Loring of the Open Door spoke in favor of public toilets, and Dan Sweat, director of Central Atlanta Progress, spoke against them. Ken Burnett, police zone commander of the downtown area, was also present to speak. Ed made a case for installing toilets at five "pressure points" in the downtown area. This, he said, would cover the most crucial areas, providing everyone access to bathrooms, cleaning up the streets, reducing the odor and health hazard of urine and feces underfoot, and reducing arrests and costly imprisonments. The toilets would also go a long way toward easing the life of the poorest of the poor.

Dan Sweat declared, "We will have public toilets in Atlanta over my dead body." He went on to explain why the concept was distasteful and would cause poor people to come here from all over the United States. (This is known as "the Mecca theory": Do something nice for the poor, they come in droves, and we are overrun.) He would not hear of it.

Major Ken Burnett spoke and, much to our surprise, he said, "I agree with everything Ed Loring has said here today." He described how foolish he felt as a police officer having to arrest someone for what for every human being is a necessity. He supported public toilets for the dignity of the poor and of police officers, too.

A proposal, sponsored by council members John Lewis and Elaine Valentine, was brought before the Atlanta City Council. There were several committee meetings. Representatives of the downtown business district took notes on the debate, and at each meeting we seemed to lose one more supporter on the council. Lewis and Valentine persisted but lost the battle.

Finally, a compromise was struck. There would be one "experimental" toilet (a PortaPotty) set in the old Plaza Park (now part of Underground Atlanta). It was no victory, since the compromise was clearly designed to fail. One toilet where thousands of people passed everyday! Sure enough, the toilet had been removed within a few months. It had been used so heavily that the company that owned it could not clean it fast enough.

Over the years there have been many conversations, many letters and articles, many meetings, and many direct actions. In the time that has passed, hundreds of thousands of dollars have been squandered jailing people for this "offense," when a fraction of those resources could have put toilets all over the city.

In December 1983, we held a twenty-four-hour fast and vigil in front of City Hall, calling on then-Mayor Andrew Young and the city council to take leadership in providing public toilets. In 1984, we specifically took on the city's day-labor center on Edgewood Avenue. The center had been one of the few places where, at least during business hours, homeless people had access to a bathroom. In 1983, federal funds had been allocated to renovate the center and to repair and improve the bathrooms. By June 1985, the toilets in the center had been dysfunctional for many months, and there still was no movement toward renovations. No one in City Hall could explain why the federal funds sat in a bank account while the toilets backed up. Our political organization, the Atlanta Advocates for the Homeless, had written countless letters, gone to endless meetings, and made zillions of phone calls, but nothing happened. Those among the Advocates who had insisted on "working through the system" reached their limits along with the rest of us. We found a toilet and carried it into the mayor's office, where Ed Loring sat on it and read scripture (rather loudly). The rest of us sang and chanted. Before the end of the day, Ed, Will Coleman (now a writer and professor of theology), and Dick Stewart, a retired Wycliffe Bible translator, had been arrested and carted to jail, and a contract for the renovations had been signed (pure coincidence, according to the mayor's staff!). At the hearing in municipal court the next day, Judge Barbara Harris interrupted the police account of our actions to lean over the bench and ask, "Reverend Loring, do you *usually* take a *toilet* along when you make business calls?" Ed answered quickly, "Oh, yes ma'am!"

During those years, we felt that, while we advocated for the city to take action, we needed to do something ourselves. We had always made bathrooms in our home available during hours our door was open. But we needed to provide more. We rented a portable toilet and put it in our backyard, behind the parking lot. We paid to have it cleaned twice each week, and we cleaned it ourselves several times each day. It worked well. But that was during the years that several business folk in our neighborhood had organized to try to get rid of the Open Door, thereby (they hoped) cleaning homeless people out of the neighborhood. The city inspectors visited and declared our outdoor toilet a "health hazard." It was mind-boggling! You mean that people urinating and defecating on the streets and behind dumpsters is better for public health than having a portable toilet? But the inspectors were not there to talk sense. The toilet was removed. So we built a public bathroom with direct access to the driveway. It is open for homeless people (and cleaned frequently) during the day. But we are not able to open it at night. It is less than a great solution.

Since the mid-1980s, we have engaged in numerous street actions, countless meetings, conversations, articles, and commiserations. We have consulted with activists in other cities and visited public toilets in numerous places. Friends who have supported our campaign have sent photographs of public toilets from Europe, Canada, Indonesia, and other places I cannot remember. Several years ago, Ed and I went to Quebec with friends Erskine and Nan Clarke. After a few days, Erskine said, "You know, I don't think I've ever traveled with anybody who photographed all the toilets." But public bathrooms were everywhere: in the cities, parklands, and small towns, clean and readily available.

In 1995, it appeared that the 1996 Olympics would finally bring the occasion for the city to build public toilets. The world was coming to town, and even those who did not want to provide toilets for the homefolks acknowledged that they would be a necessary part of our hospitality. City Council President Marvin Arrington sponsored a plan, and he was so thrilled when a contract to build a number of freestanding, self-cleaning toilets was signed that he brought refreshments to the Open Door for a celebration. But the plan was abandoned when the contract fell through, and a millionaire businessman put up big bucks for portable toilets that disappeared as soon as the crowds were gone. It was a missed opportunity of grand proportions!

But it appears that a possibility exists again. Are there perhaps leaders in our city who recognize the ludicrousness of our situation? We promote ourselves as a tourist destination; the real estate interests are furiously marketing downtown as the hottest residential choice; we call ourselves an "international city." But the lack of access to toilets means that our city is *not* hospitable space.

The issue is largely one of race and class. An ugly fact about our society is that many white people still don't want to share bathrooms with people of color. Middle-class and wealthy people don't want to share toilets with the poor. There is still a feeling around the city that, if we do anything to help the homeless poor, there will automatically be more of them. So rather than risk that happening, we make our public spaces inhospitable to everyone. It is a big problem for the elderly, for people with small children, for those with kidney and bladder problems, and, at one time or another, for everybody.

But the city's approach is also a way to make certain groups continually experience indignity. Our friend Tirso Moreno, who organizes farmworkers in central Florida, has told us of the ongoing struggle to have the growers provide portable toilets near the fields. A law finally passed requiring growers to provide toilets; but without constant enforcement, the growers often let it slide. The workers must take care of their personal needs in the fields. Is this humiliation really unintended?

Mr. W. W. Law, one of the heroic figures in the civil rights struggle in Savannah, Georgia, has often told of his work as a mail carrier. He walked all day, but he never had easy access to a bathroom. Did white people know the real effect of reserving bathrooms for Whites Only? Was the indignity forced on Mr. Law's daily life an unintended consequence of the white supremacist structure of Savannah in the 1940s? I doubt it. These days, privileged people often talk about how homeless people are dirty and smell bad, and how disgusting that is. But what would any of us do if we got up in the morning and had no access to a toilet, toilet paper, running water, soap, and a towel? What if we didn't have a shower and a sink and a mirror? *To condemn people for a condition about which they can do little or nothing is mean and pointless.*

The real problem for homeless people, of course, is that they don't have homes. Affordable housing is what homeless people need more than anything. In all but the very worst housing, people have access to their own bathrooms— at least when they are at home. In the meantime, it is punitive, mean-spirited public policy to punish the poor for what every human body must do. Public toilets would provide a modicum of relief from the indignity of homelessness. As our friends Alice Callahan and the Los Angeles Catholic Workers said in their (successful) campaign for toilets on Skid Row, "We need outhouses for people without houses."

It is way past time to have public toilets in Atlanta, Georgia. We could do the right thing to alleviate some of the misery of homelessness, or we could do it because we want to be a decent city that provides hospitable space for all its citizens. Either way will do. Let's just do it.

Trouble at Grady: Local Symptoms, National Crisis, *by Murphy Davis*

J U N E   1 9 9 9

The county commissioner looked perplexed. "You understand, don't you, that we're the bottom of the food chain here. You're coming to us because you know who and where we are. But we're not the *real* cause of this crisis at Grady Hospital. It's much bigger than DeKalb and Fulton counties."

She is absolutely right, and she is absolutely wrong. Grady Memorial Hospital, our local public hospital, faces a $26.4 million deficit for this calendar year. To cut costs, the administration recommended that the hospital board begin to charge even the poorest of the poor five dollars for each clinic visit and a ten-dollar copayment for each prescription and medical supply. This disastrous policy attempted to solve the budget problems on the backs of the poor and amounted to a death sentence for many Grady patients, especially the poorest, who are elderly and/or who have chronic illnesses that require several medications to sustain life and health.

These problems at Grady are a local problem with local causes; they are also the local symptoms of a national crisis with national causes. Local governments are both responsible for and victims of the problem. The national health care crisis is being played out on a local level, and I have begun to wonder if health care will be the issue on which we come together nationally to seek significant change.

Over the past twenty years, the United States has undergone sweeping change that increasingly has consolidated resources in fewer hands. The wealthiest 1 percent of our people have amassed fortunes in the millions and billions. A significant number of people near the top have accumulated more money and possessions than anybody could need in one lifetime; the middle class is more vulnerable; the working class is close to falling over the edge; and the poor have sunk deeper into the misery of substandard housing, homelessness, prison, and limited access to good schools, proper nutrition, and health care.

Since the early 1980s, a persistent legislative and judicial program has given every advantage to wealthy individuals, corporations, and institutions, putting the working class and poor at a greater disadvantage. Public institutions and services have been opened to the forces of privatization, increasing profits for the already wealthy and destabilizing the work environment. All services and institutions are becoming fair game for the market, and all space is becoming commercial space. The values and language of the market have come to dominate our common life to the extent that ethical discussion, or religious or moral discourse, has begun to seem quaint, if not irrelevant. The bottom line is everything. Consumers are the only ones who matter. Since they are not consumers, poor people (by definition, those without capital) literally do not count. They do not exist except as commodities in the prison-industrial complex.

At the same time, at national, state, and local levels, we have cut every program that in any way helps the poor and vulnerable. The results have become increasingly disastrous for individuals, families, public institutions, and, yes, for the common good.

The Grady crisis is part of this unfolding drama. As a single example of the national trend, two pieces of federal legislation, the Welfare Reform Act of 1996 and the Balanced Budget Act of 1997, cost Grady Hospital $28 million in 1998—more than this year's projected deficit. As people have been moved from "welfare to work," they have, more often than not, moved into low-wage, dead-end jobs that almost never provide health insurance. Without access to Medicaid, these families continue to depend on Grady for medical services; the patients, however, cannot pay for services and medication, and the hospital can no longer be reimbursed by Medicaid. Grady's plight is one that, to some degree, affects teaching hospitals across the country. Even Harvard University's several teaching hospitals are in trouble.

The state of Georgia has absorbed the federal cuts and made deeper cuts in Medicaid and Medicare. The DeKalb and Fulton County Commissions, who are legally responsible for Grady, have voted less support for Grady every year since 1992. Simply put, the emergency that Grady faces has been created by specific policy decisions, at every level of government, over a period of years. Some folks knew doggone well what they were doing. A few people protested in vain, and the rest seemed to be watching TV and shopping at the mall. But as the cuts continue to trickle down to the local level, they are deadly for the poor, the sick, and the vulnerable.

The crisis is local, so the organizing has to begin locally. Elected officials closest to home must take the heat first for this multilevel assault on public institutions and poor people. They are responsible for their own malicious policy decisions. And they are responsible for not raising Cain with state and federal decision makers who helped them craft this disaster.

For the Open Door there is a rich privilege in being part of a diverse and growing coalition that is confronting the local health care emergency and crying out for those who cannot cry out for themselves. When we forced a discussion with the Grady board, it voted temporarily to rescind the copayments. We made a commitment to work with them and to help advocate for additional funding to meet the deficit. We knocked first on the door of the Fulton County Commission, and we were received by those commissioners, who are friends of the poor and advocates for Grady. They allocated an additional $3.5 million. When we went to the DeKalb County Commission and CEO with the same appeal, we met a stone wall. More than a month since we first asked for a response, the

DeKalb Commission has directed arrests of thirty-seven advocates, but it still has refused to put the hospital's $1.1 million request on the agenda.

We are continuing this struggle on several fronts. We will knock on De-Kalb's door until it opens and until this additional funding (small change in a county budget) is allocated. In the meantime, we are appealing to Governor Roy Barnes to get involved, and to make state resources available that would move toward long-term resolution of support for this regional and state resource. We understand that this proposal must include discussion and action on behalf of public hospitals across Georgia.

We are also looking toward public dialogue about the responsibility of private institutions for Grady's long-term health. Emory University *made* its international reputation as a medical school and as a research center at Grady Hospital. The medical school has been a major source of Emory's growing wealth and power. At $6 billion, Emory's endowment is the fastest-growing among the nation's private universities. It is time to share the wealth and to endow Grady's future as a resource for health care for the poor *and* as the excellent teaching context it continues to be.

Other private sources that must be called to accountability are the many for-profit hospitals in the Atlanta area that sometimes send their patients to Grady when insurance monies have run out. We understand that some cities and regions levy a tax on for-profit hospitals to help support public hospitals. Drug companies and insurance companies must be called to account for their massive profits and for pricing based on market feasibility rather than their own costs. Finally, Morehouse Medical School and other smaller teaching institutions and programs must be called into the discussions to explore shared responsibility for this precious community resource.

As all the local partners are called to account, we must be seeking new ways to advocate together in Washington. The Balanced Budget Act will bring deeper cuts in coming years. We must stop the damage and move toward a national health insurance plan.

On May 11, thirty members of our activist coalition were arrested for praying and singing when the DeKalb Commission again refused to discuss Grady. It was, without a doubt, the largest and most diverse group arrested for an act of civil disobedience in Atlanta since the 1960s. We were clergy and layfolks; Christians, Jews, and Buddhists; women and men; gay and straight; Black, white, and Asian; students and retirees (the oldest were seventy-nine and eighty-one!); medical professionals in white uniform; and members of organized labor taking the day off. While we were loaded onto the police bus and taken to jail, two hundred or more supporters sang and prayed. Then they moved the vigil to DeKalb County Jail. When Rev. Stalmacher, a local pastor, heard about the action, he brought a candle along with signs saying, "Letting the Light Shine for Grady Hospital." He walked and kept vigil all night in front of the jail and greeted us when we were released the next morning.

The diverse and lively coalition that has formed around the Grady crisis is a long-haul group of committed activists. We are working and planning together with clear knowledge that we have a long road ahead. We look forward to learning more about how this struggle has taken shape in other cities and regions. And we hope to be part of a growing movement that will struggle not only to guarantee decent health care for all God's children, but for justice, housing, freedom, and peace for every woman, man, and child.

Please help us cry out for Grady patients. No more clinic charges and co-payments! Nurture the public health. Support Grady Hospital.

Power, Privilege, and Privatization, *by Murphy Davis*

JULY 1999

Looking back over the years and at the political issues that have claimed my attention, it occurs to me that some social, political, and economic forces will simply not go away. They might go underground for a while, but not to die, to be buried and forgotten. They rest and mutate before emerging again in another guise.

Twenty-three years ago, I went to a small town in South Georgia for a trial. I had traveled with several other folks, including a bright and enthusiastic Yale law student. When we got out of the car and walked toward the courthouse, we came to a chain-link fence surrounding a little, kudzu-covered building and an open space. The law student, who had spent part of the previous week in town helping with trial preparations, said, "You'll never believe this! This used to be the town swimming pool, and . . ." I interrupted to finish the sentence for him, ". . . and somewhere between 1954 and 1960, the town council, fearing that the pool would have to be integrated, closed the pool, filled it in, boarded up the bathhouse, and abandoned it."

The young man looked at me in astonishment. He knew that I had never set foot in this little town. "How did you know that?" "Because," I said, "I grew up in a Southern town."

When I was in the seventh grade, our junior high school band practiced in a little brick building that previously had been the bathhouse for the municipal swimming pool. The pool itself had been closed in, paved, and turned into a parking lot. That was 1960, and the pool had been closed four or five years earlier.

Brown v. Board of Education, which the U.S. Supreme Court decided in 1954, struck down the "separate but equal" basis for school segregation and mandated the racial integration of public schools. Town and city leaders all over the country, but especially in the South, saw the writing on the wall. They knew that all segregated public institutions had been called into question. Wasting no time, local authorities decided to close public facilities like swimming pools rather than wait for a court order mandating their integration. If we have to swim with Black folks, white folks figured, we won't have a swimming pool at all.

Except that the decision makers *did* have a pool. The upper-class white folks had the Greenville Golf and Country Club. The middle-class folks had the Moose Club. Poor whites, as usual, were left out of the deliberations; as programmed, many of them resented Black folks for the loss of all-white public amenities. And Black folks continued to be excluded from the decision making *and* the facilities.

In other words, when threatened with sharing something they never intended to share, the powerful privatized their resources and abandoned the public institutions in question. Through the late 1950s and 1960s, the same sort of thing happened to public schools in the South. In one town, city, and county after another, private schools and academies sprang up. Often they were called "Christian" schools. They were all-white. (Jesus, the dark-skinned Palestinian Jew, would certainly not have been welcome.) In some towns and counties, the public schools became all-Black; they were essentially abandoned and received only nominal support. It was a swell deal for wealthy whites, because they maintained control of their own institutions and paid less to support public institutions—especially the ones that no longer existed.

I cannot remember anybody using the word *privatization* in the 1950s and '60s. But that is what is going on now. Government services, parks, utilities, schools, and other institutions are being contracted out to private, for-profit agencies and corporations. Prisons and jails are being constructed and managed by corporations whose stocks are soaring. (The Corrections Corporation of America is currently building two prisons in South Georgia that nobody asked for. The corporation appears confident that, as was said in the movie, "If we build it they will come.") Vendors who provide services for the public or formerly public institutions are operated by private interests for private profit. And while corporate America bites off larger chunks of public funds, the strident resistance to government "interference" through planning or regulation is a steady theme.

The mainline media, which ought to help us think about and discuss these issues in public, are owned and controlled by corporate interests as well. So the real changes that occur, as public money moves into private pockets and as public institutions are eviscerated, are not covered, and dissent from the prevailing trends and ideologies is treated as non-newsworthy.

There has been in recent years a programmatic assault on *all* public institutions. This assault intends to assert the intent of the privileged elite to protect and multiply its own resources. It is also an assault on the poor themselves. Private hospitals and schools, like all private institutions, serve those who can pay for their services. Public hospitals and schools are provided for every citizen— those who can pay and those who cannot. To attack public institutions with the intent of dismantling them is nothing less than a direct assault on the poor.

Grady Memorial Hospital is, by charter and definition, a hospital for anybody and everybody in Fulton and DeKalb counties. Any resident of these two counties is entitled to medical care at Grady, regardless of ability to pay. Those who can get medical care nowhere else turn to Grady. Those who could not otherwise see a doctor or receive medications or have surgery or undergo chemotherapy can generally find a welcome at Grady. That is the way it was intended to be. But things are changing.

❖ ❖ ❖

Health care has not all of a sudden become an issue of privatization. Much to the detriment of the common good, health care in the United States has long been understood as a commodity. More often than not, it has been a problem for poor people to find adequate care. But we have had at least some sense that the government had an obligation to care for the public health. For several generations, for instance, it has seemed imperative that we sustain agencies that monitor, test for, and treat infectious diseases. It has been an acceptable notion that all children, regardless of economic circumstances, should be immunized to protect them from preventable illness. We have even supported programs like Medicaid and Medicare to insure at least minimal care for the very poor, the disabled, and the elderly.

But even this minimal level of care provided from public resources is now under fire in the United States. Medicaid and Medicare continue to be cut. All public programs are under assault while market-driven, for-profit managed-care systems move to control an increasing portion of the health care "market." The poor, disabled, elderly, and prisoners have no place in the market. These people, because they are not "consumers," do not exist. What horrible language and concepts to use for human beings! What are we doing to ourselves and to each other?

Aside from dehumanizing the poor, we are creating a system that increasingly funnels public resources into private pockets and that depends on silencing public debate, decreasing democratic process, and eliminating accountability. Privatization is intended to build and protect privilege for the benefit of those who already control the power and wealth in society. The word *privilege* means, literally, "private law"; the motivation of the privileged is to become "a law unto themselves." Along the way, democratic process suffers, and the institutions of democracy are damaged.

We in the United States spend some four thousand dollars per person per year for health care, more than any other people in the world. The cost is nearly twice that of our nearest competitor and much higher than that in industrialized countries like Canada and Great Britain. Expenditures in those countries pay for a health care system that provides access for everyone. Despite this enormous expenditure, there are forty-four million uninsured women, men, and children in the United States—a number said to be increasing by 125,000 per month. (If this occurs during an economic boom, what will happen when the downturn comes?) In countries that provide a national health system, the infant-mortality rate is lower and life expectancy longer than in the United States. One finds healthier people in such national systems.

But how can this be? If we spend more government *and* private money on health care in the United States than Canada, and Canada has healthier (and considerably less anxious) people, why wouldn't we move immediately toward a national health plan? The answer seems to relate to the fact that the lion's share of our health care dollars are pouring into enormous corporate profits. These dollars include enormous government subsidies for the health care system that move public money into private coffers rather than toward the common good. We are paying through the nose to maintain the obscene wealth of the elite rather than the general health of the people.

How many people do you know who are anxious about their health care? The problem does not only affect the poor. Many middle-class and working people know that they are paying more and getting less every day. They also know that they live in danger of not getting necessary care or of losing insurance coverage altogether. The anxiety is growing along with corporate profit margins. A sense of paralysis and futility seems to grip the body politic. The electoral process is controlled by the same corporate interests that reap benefit from the health care system, so movement seems almost impossible.

The market-driven, for-profit system intends to build the privilege of the few and to increase a sense of powerlessness among the rest. But we do not have to accept the powerlessness that we are supposed to feel. We can move toward a healthier life together when we remember and practice this truth: a healthy life is possible only when we live with a sense of community and mutual care. Without such a commitment we are pitted against each other, and we get sicker. When Dr. Martin Luther King spoke to the Selma-to-Montgomery marchers in 1965, he said, "What we seek is a society at peace with itself." What medicine for our anxiety-ridden society! What a balm is this medicine that we take with every step toward the Beloved Community.

The drive toward privatization will not go away, because human greed will always be part of the human story. But it is never the whole story. The struggle for justice and human dignity is also part of the story, and the struggle is healing. When we refuse to cooperate with the system that "takes necessities from the masses to give luxury to the classes," we begin to restore the health of our body politic. We can have health care—*good* health care—for every girl and boy, every woman and man in the United States. We can live together and share the wealth and the good gifts of the land. Until that day comes, we can struggle together to live into the vision. We experience the joy of this truth as we continue in the struggle for our beloved Grady Hospital. Please join us! We'll all get better together.

Part III

HOSPITALITY
TO THE IMPRISONED

The spirit of the Lord GOD is upon me,
because the LORD has anointed me;
he has sent me to bring good news to the oppressed,
to bind up the brokenhearted,
to proclaim liberty to the captives,
and release to the prisoners.

—Isaiah 61:1 NRSV

You will soon learn that there are more drugs available in prison
than in the free world.

—Georgia state prisoner

The Soul Stealers, *Anonymous*

F E B R U A R Y   2 0 0 0

Editor's note: This article was written by a man who has been a friend of the Open Door since his sentencing to a long prison term in the 1970s. Since being incarcerated, he has graduated from college, pursued various vocational programs, and maintained relationships with numerous friends outside prison. We publish this article anonymously for his protection. This clearly is one man's account, gleaned from experience in various men's prisons and jails. At some points, the essay represents experiences shared by men and women. At other points, the writing comes from a distinctly male experience. We are grateful for his willingness to share this experience in such painful detail.

In Matthew 10:28 it is written, "and do not fear those who kill the body, but cannot kill the soul. But, rather, fear the one who is able to destroy both soul and body in hell."

For years, I have read this verse of scripture and wondered about it. I can easily understand how a person can kill the body of another person. And I can understand that God can destroy both the soul and body of a person in hell. But it has taken me years to learn how human beings can destroy the souls of other human beings.

I'd like to spend a few moments sharing my thoughts as to how a person can destroy or "steal" another's soul. In fact, I'd like to shed light on an institution that, as a by-product of its day-to-day operations, steals tens of thousands of souls.

You may scoff at this idea and question, "How can this be?" Bear with me a few moments, and I will shed light on who is responsible for stealing these souls and how it is accomplished.

In the United States, we look to a number of governmental agencies and organizations to preserve the integrity of our society. Laws are created and enforced to define the parameters of acceptable behavior. Agencies are created and developed to enforce and uphold these laws. Those who violate these rules are brought to task and punished for their transgressions.

Police officers are sworn to "protect and serve" society. They fulfill their duties by arresting violators of our laws. Judges and prosecutors are elected to bring to trial a person accused of a crime. Ideally, prosecutors present the evidence against the accused, while judges insure that this is accomplished in a fair and just manner. When a person is found guilty of a transgression of the law, they are punished. One of the ways this is accomplished is by sending the lawbreaker or criminal to prison.

What transpires when a person is sent to one of our nation's ever burgeoning prisons? One would think that our prison system would educate and train the prisoner to be a law-abiding, productive member of our society. But this is far from what happens. What happens is that the person who enters prison is emotionally, psychologically, spiritually, and sometimes physically attacked. You are humiliated and dehumanized. Everything is taken from you—your dignity, your thought processes, even your sense of right and wrong.

Many wise thinkers have postulated that in order to understand another person, we first should walk a mile in their shoes. Following this line of thinking, I portray the path the average prisoner walks and the experiences they encounter. Search your heart and mind as you ask what you would feel and think if this happened to you.

❖ ❖ ❖

During your trip to prison you are placed in chains. Your hands are cuffed and fastened to your waist by a waist chain. Leg irons are fastened around your ankles. Your movements are vastly curtailed. You are uncomfortable. The handcuffs bite into your wrists; the inability to move your hands from your waist aggravates the condition. The ankle chains impede your steps. To walk you must take short, half-hobbling, half-shuffling steps. Each step brings pain as the chain between your ankles tightens and causes the ankle bracelet to bite into the flesh.

You feel the contempt of the transfer officer as he or she yells and rails at you to climb into an already overcrowded van or bus. If you have worldly possessions, you must carry them with you. Among your meager possessions may be a Bible (or Koran), a writing tablet, pen, envelopes, stamps, and perhaps a few old letters, pictures, and an address book. Also, you carry a few articles to help maintain your hygiene. You carry a toothbrush, toothpaste, shampoo, and, perhaps, some shower shoes.

Being chained this way makes carrying your possessions difficult. If you drop anything, more often than not it is trampled and left behind as you are herded along. If you stop and try to retrieve a dropped article, the transfer officer yells and curses at you to hurry up. The chains restrict your movements. This leaves you feeling put out and frustrated.

On the bus or van trip to prison, the atmosphere is filled with quiet trepidation. No one really knows what to expect. Horror stories have been passed around, and fear creeps into your heart. You hope and pray that none of these situations will befall you, and you wonder how you will react if they do.

Arriving at the prison, you see a fortresslike structure. You notice the high fences and the abundance of barbed wire and razor wire. You also notice the evenly spaced guard towers and the guns. Your mind and heart probe the prison for some hint as to what is about to happen to you. Your eyes linger on the men already confined, whom you see either on the yard or performing some unknown tasks. Your heart sinks as the gates close behind the bus, and you wonder how you will fare.

As you get off the bus, the chains and cuffs are removed. You are told to take what possessions you have managed to hang onto and to stand in a line. Moments later, a prison guard with a clipboard comes by, calling out names. Most names are mispronounced. If your name is garbled or mispronounced and you do not answer, the guard yells and curses until you finally overcome your bafflement and reply. People whose names have been called are instructed to line up next to a door. What lies behind the door seems forbidding. After the line forms, an ominous jingling of keys announces the opening of the door.

Several guards step out and start screaming at the people in line. These guards start haranguing the men to enter the building, to keep against the wall, to keep their mouths shut and their eyes straight ahead. As you walk down the hallway, your spirits plummet. In noticing the prisoners already confined, one observation stands out. Most people avoid eye contact and keep their heads lowered abjectly. Whether through humiliation or a broken spirit, their dull gazes stay focused elsewhere. With quiet resolve, you shore up your spirits and wonder what has reduced these men to this state.

Walking down the hallway, the line of men turns and enters the ID room. The new arrivals are instructed to sit on a row of benches and to keep quiet. You do so, observing all that is transpiring, hoping to glean some information that will ease the situation. The guard who escorted you into the prison hands his clipboard to another prison guard. A few of the new arrivals sit beside you and begin a quiet conversation. Suddenly, an explosion of profanity erupts as the two conversationalists are berated for opening their lousy mouths. With a profusion of expletives, the guard admonishes and browbeats, telling all to remain silent unless spoken to by a guard.

After an interminable period, more hapless men file into the ID room. They take their seats on one of the rows of wooden benches. In time, all the available bench space is filled, and men start finding places on the floor. When fifty or sixty men are crowded into the seating area, a guard with a clipboard comes over and starts calling names. As the names are called, men are instructed to stand in an adjoining area, on one of the lines painted on the floor.

As all the new prisoners shift from the benches to one of the painted lines, individual comfort zones are violated. Some say that to feel comfortable around people we do not know, most of us need two or three feet of space. Prison officials have no comprehension of this fact—or perhaps they do. The new prisoners stand crowded, shoulder to shoulder, with a two-foot space between rows.

The guard with the clipboard comes over while other guards circle the closely packed group of standing men. Again, names are called and checked off the clipboard. After all the names have been called, and everyone has been accounted for, the men are told to place their property on the floor at their feet. One guard starts yelling a list of rules, while another starts sending the new prisoners to one of several barber chairs. In prison everyone gets the same haircut—your head is shaved. After that, you are instructed to stand at your spot on one of the painted lines.

In less time than you would imagine possible, fifty or sixty men have their heads shaved and are standing on the line. When the last head is shaved, everyone is ordered to strip naked. You can forget common decency. As long as you are in prison, you will be asked to strip naked almost daily. Humiliation seeps in as, layer by layer, your dignity is stripped away.

Standing in a crowd of naked men is indescribably uncomfortable. The first row is handed razors and soap out of a communal box and sent to an exposed wall of showerheads. The men are ordered to shave their faces and to wash their bodies thoroughly. When finished, they return the razors and soap for the next group.

As one person showers, the next group has more layers of humanity removed. They will be introduced to what is called a "strip search." You will be expected to submit to strip searches frequently and on demand as long as you are in prison.

Several guards move in front of the row and conduct their humiliating search. Standing naked, you are asked to open your mouth and raise your tongue. You are then instructed to raise your scrotum, then to turn around and spread the cheeks of your buttocks. Finally, to add insult, you are asked to squat and cough. The purpose of all this, you are informed, is to look for weapons.

After everyone has showered and been humiliated, the men are placed back on line in their crowded, emotionally injured group. A guard walks by and "inspects" the property at your feet. He picks up an item and looks at you slyly. If, while the guard fingers your property, you show concern or indicate that any item has value, he curses and yells at you as the item is thrown to the floor and trampled.

The result is that most, if not all, of the valuables that you brought to prison are damaged, destroyed, or confiscated. You are told repeatedly that you do not merit owning anything of value, that you are a useless piece of crap. Get used to it. You will be treated this way the entire time you are incarcerated.

In a flurry of activity you are given an ill-fitting set of underwear from a communal clothes bin and an equally ill-fitting uniform. When everyone is dressed, you are divided into small groups and escorted to your respective cell blocks.

When you arrive at your cell block you receive bed linen and are assigned to a cell. Most people are placed in a two-man cell. As you are locked into your cell, you nervously introduce yourself to your new cell mate. You are highly apprehensive about how you will be received and about what attitude this new person thrust into your life will have.

In your cell, if it is a small one, there will be one bunk and a mattress on the floor. If you are in the cell first, you grab the bunk. But if you are a late arrival, you are placed on the floor. By the head of the bunk is a sink and a toilet. The front of the cell is open, with only a wall of bars. There is no privacy. You had better get used to using the toilet and to showering with numerous sets of eyes on you.

❖ ❖ ❖

As the weeks turn into months, then years, you learn more about life in prison and adapt yourself accordingly. Many people will speak about their legal cases, and you come to one blinding realization: Justice is a mockery and an illusion in this country.

You will meet people who are in prison for all sorts of crimes. A number of these people are in prison for drugs. Many will have life sentences. Yet, while you speak to them about their downfall brought on by selling drugs, word will pass around of a guard who will bring in any type or amount of drug, for the right price. You will soon learn that there are more drugs available in prison than in the free world.

At any given moment, you are subject to a shakedown. This is a cell search and/or the humiliating strip search. But it is appropriately named. Often a guard will come to your cell and inform you that he is conducting a cell search. Looking into your locker box and seeing that you have purchased a few food items from the inmate store, he will say, "Give me a Coke and honey bun, and I won't search your cell again for a week." If you consent and give up the Coke and honey bun, you will be left alone. But he'll be back. If you refuse to give in to these rapacious demands, you will have to submit to the strip search. The guard will go through your property with a fine-tooth comb, often damaging stuff as he conducts his search. It's your call as to which indignity you'd prefer to suffer.

While in prison you may seek to turn your life around and to better yourself. Before you get your act together, you will have to face several cold, hard truths. Nothing beneficial to you comes easily in prison.

Let's start with the education department. If you want to study for and take the GED, you must cross several hurdles. First, the prison system doesn't encourage you to better yourself. To get into a GED class, you must get on a waiting list. Then you must keep an impeccably clean record while you await placement. In prison, guards hand out disciplinary reports like popcorn in a movie theater. If you receive a disciplinary report (DR), you can't get into a GED class. You must have a clean record for ninety days to be admitted.

Before I continue, let me explain how easy it is to get a DR. In your day-to-day routine, you will come into contact with numerous prison guards. "Sanitation" (as in highly polished floors and shiny surfaces) is a big deal in prisons. That being the case, you may be assigned to clean something. A sergeant or lieutenant on one of their rounds may tell you to clean something in a specific manner. After they leave you with instructions, a lower-level prison guard may come and question your actions. If they give instructions contrary to what the sergeant or lieutenant said, you must comply with them. This leaves you in a situation in which two or more people are telling you to do something different. So, regardless of what you do, you will fail to follow someone's instructions. When one of the officers walks by and sees you doing something different from what they instructed, you will receive a DR for failure to follow instructions. If you try to explain the conflicting orders, you will be given an additional DR for insubordination.

The DRs, when they are investigated, may be thrown out. Still, you are charged four dollars for each DR. Additionally, receipt of a DR makes you ineligible for a GED or vocational-trade-class waiting list for ninety days. You must have a clean record for ninety days to be admitted.

Once you are placed on the list and then admitted to a GED class, this in no way means you will get your GED. To take a GED, a prisoner several years ago had to score 225 on the pre-GED test. Quite a few men studied and struggled to bring their scores up to that point. When a lot of men were ready to take the pre-GED—confident that they could pass with 225—something happened. The state overnight changed the score needed to take the test, raising the hurdle from 225 points to 250. A lot of men were frustrated and disappointed at having the rules changed when a GED was within their grasp.

At one time, college-level courses were taught in prison. A study had determined that less than 2 percent of prisoners with some college under their belts returned to prison. At the time it cost $7,500 per year to provide the books and instruction required for a prisoner to receive a four-year degree. It costs the state roughly $30,000 per year to house one prisoner. When college-level classes were offered, prisoners had to work during the day and go to class at night. In addition to keeping up their grades, they daily had to run the gauntlet of guards that resented the prisoners bettering themselves. For political reasons, college-level courses were removed from prison.[1] Once again, national and state leaders and prison officials had denied prisoners a means to better themselves and to improve their chances of staying out of prison once released into society.

Most prisons have a vocational-education department. In theory, prisoners with few or no job skills can obtain vocational training and licensing to help make them employable in areas such as auto-body repair, auto mechanics, cabinetmaking, masonry, heating and air-conditioning repair, small-engine repair, computer repair, welding, food services, food preparation, and so on. The problem is that most, if not all, of the vocational-trade instructors were fired, laid off, or forced into retirement. Again, this is frustrating if you wish to better yourself.

You are told that the state doesn't have the money to pay these salaries. Yet you see many prisons with a salaried coaching staff. Soon you face the grim realization that prison officials would rather see a prisoner playing basketball or softball than earning a GED, college degree, or job skill that would keep him out of prison.

Do you wonder why men and women in prison are bitter and angry? Do you wonder why so many prisoners, when released, commit new crimes and return to prison? Do you wonder why so many in prison are caught in a cycle of self-destruction?

Let's say you want to join one of the group sessions offered in prison. These groups address topics like substance abuse, anger management, and cycles of violence. The first thing in which prison counselors try to force you to believe is that you are mentally defective and in need of their help. Men are taught in these groups that it is an error in thinking to strive to be independent from government assistance. Instead, you are taught that, since you are defective in your thought processes, you should give up guilt about leaning on government-assistance programs. What gets you labeled as having a defective thought process? Frankly, if you express your desire to stand on your own two feet and to work for yourself, you are told that you are not dealing with reality.

If, in being in prison, you have the misfortune of experiencing the death of a loved one, whatever you do, *do not* tell one of the prison counselors. If you do, the following is likely to transpire:

Your counselor will ask if you feel sad or are grieving over your loved one. If you say yes, he or she will make an appointment with one of the prison psychologists. If you say no, they will say you are having problems expressing your grief, and they will make an appointment with one of the prison psychologists.

---

1. For many years, Senator Jesse Helms (R-N.C.) pushed to make federal Pell Grants unavailable to prisoners. Although less than 1 percent of Pell Grant funds ever went to prisoners, Helms finally prevailed, and most college programs in prisons were crippled or gutted (ed.).

If and when you do see a prison psychologist or psychiatrist, he or she will say that they are going to prescribe a little pill to help you cope during this difficult time. If you refuse the medication, they will say that you are refusing treatment and will have it forced on you. If you take the medication, they will say that the medication is to help just one of the numerous psychological problems you are having. In time, you will be "zombie-fied."

Staff shortages occur frequently in prison. When this happens, all the so-called mental health patients will probably have their dosages increased. The result is that they often are destroyed psychologically. The treatment is forced on them; if they refuse, they are physically restrained and given an injection.

If you follow the "logic" of the prison system, a man or woman who has spent ten or twenty years in prison should be the safest, most stable person around. But the American Psychiatric Association has said that anyone who spends more than five years in prison qualifies for psychiatric disability. Why?

For those ten or twenty years the prisoner is under constant supervision. The prison system controls what they read, where they work, and what types of education and job training they receive—not to mention what types and degrees of counseling. Literally every aspect of a prisoner's life is controlled and monitored. Those who have been in prison a long time should be the most stable people alive.

Yet instead of stability, most of us who have spent many years in prison are filled with fear and anxiety. Deep down, we known that officials in charge of our prisons are not there to help us become stable, competent citizens. In fact, these people have carried out their duties in such a haphazard, horrendous manner that we recoil in fear at *their* product: the bitter, aged convict.

❖ ❖ ❖

In the late 1960s or early 1970s, the psychology department at Princeton University conducted a behavioral study on mice. They put mice in a pre-constructed maze to see if they could "learn" their way through. After the mice learned this task, the psychologists sought to determine how well the mice could adapt to a change in the rules; thus, they changed the construction of the maze. In time, the mice adapted to a new set of rules and learned a new path.

The psychologists then sought to learn the adaptivity of the mice's learned behavior. To do this, they changed the rules of the maze repeatedly. This is when they made a startling discovery. Eventually, the mice would reach a limit to their ability to adapt. They would, in time, approach a wall that previously was open and try to push through it. When they failed, they would sit and begin to tremble. In effect, the psychologists found that they could drive the mice insane. All they had to do was to keep changing the rules.

This is the environment in prison. The rules change from day to day, from prison guard to prison guard. For examples, let's consider how you would respond to various events.

Every prison has a commissary. In this prison store you may purchase a limited number of items. You may do this *if and only if* you have the funds in your inmate account. How do you receive these funds? Most prisons have what they call an "inmate's approved receipt-of-funds list." If you want to receive funds from anyone, you must submit their names for approval before it is allowed. Assuming that you have parents or a sibling placed on your receipt-of-funds list—forget receiving money from friends, as only immediate family members are approved—what do you do when they send you a money order and the mail-room officer tells you that their name is not on your receipt-of-funds list? The officer sends the money order back, and you are left fuming. If you ask your counselor about it, they say they will check into it, but they never do. If you file a grievance, the warden will deny your grievance and say there is no proof that this event took place.

Let's say you want to order an electric razor. The mail-room officer has you fill out the appropriate forms, the officer signs them, and the business office deducts the funds from your inmate account. Yet when the razor arrives, don't be surprised when the mail-room officer tells you that you can't have the electric razor because it isn't approved. Do you think you would be angry?

What if you've run the gauntlet and managed to acquire a few certificates of accomplishment? To demonstrate to the parole board that you are trying to get your life together, you send these certificates with a letter requesting that they be placed in your file. Don't be disappointed or angry when the parole board returns these certificates with a letter stating that they don't have room for them. If you get a disciplinary report, don't be surprised when they have plenty of room.

The point is that neither the prison system nor the parole board will keep on file any paper that demonstrates positive accomplishments. But they will keep anything and everything negative about you. Do you think you would feel frustrated, disappointed, or angry?

If you have loved ones who care about you and who wish to help you develop the right attitude toward life, they can have a publishing company send you books on this topic. But books aimed at opening your eyes and mind to changing your self-destructive attitudes are frowned on. On occasion, you might be able to slip one of these books through the mail room. But if the book is found, be prepared to suffer for it. The prison administration may tell you that the words are offensive and inflammatory. If you point out similar words in other books in the prison library, you may be told that the cover of your book has tape on it; therefore, it has been modified and, as such, must be confiscated.

If you point out that placing tape on the covers of books is the method of re-pairing and preserving books in the library, be prepared to hear another reason why you cannot have the book.

How would you feel about having books that promote taking responsibil-ity for your actions either censored or confiscated outright as contraband?

In doing time in prison, you will learn that many people swallow their pride, bite their tongues, and bow down to the humiliating demands of over-bearing prison guards. On occasion, you might meet a prisoner who challenges the dehumanizing brutality of the guards. This person will speak out and say the things that you feel, but that secretly you are afraid to say. In time, you will see that this prisoner is always harassed and that he winds up in and out of the iso-lation unit ("the hole").

If this person refuses to give up the struggle, you'll soon hear that he went back into isolation. Then one day you will see the prison CERT (Corrections Emergency Response Team), dressed in black, with body armor and electric shields, making one of their frequent trips to the isolation unit. How would you feel if, one day after seeing the CERT go to the isolation unit, you learn that your rebellious friend, who always spoke up and challenged the system, had a "seizure" in his isolation cell, fell, hit his head, and subsequently died? Will you be disgusted, sad, frustrated, or angry at such an unfair system?

❖ ❖ ❖

Prior to coming to prison, you are led to believe that you will encounter all sorts of prisoners. You are told that you will meet drug dealers, rapists, robbers, and murderers. You are made to feel afraid of these predators. But, on arriving, you learn an astounding truth. Yes, there are a few prisoners who prey upon weaker prisoners. But it isn't as widespread as you have been told. The real threat is not from fellow prisoners but from the prison staff. They will steal your prop-erty, force you to pay protection money, and try to ensnare and destroy you with their drugs.

If you have the misfortune to come to prison, you will be tested. If you are weak, you will fall prey. If you are strong and willing to stand up for what you believe in, you might find yourself being asked to sit in on an underground meeting of prisoners. You will be asked your thoughts and beliefs, and you will be challenged on them.

Don't be surprised to learn that, in prison, members of the Aryan Nation sit down with members of the Nation of Islam. Christians, Muslims, Buddhists, and atheists alike come together, eat from a common bowl, and identify a com-mon enemy. The enemy is a state-sanctioned organization oriented toward the destruction of humans. This organization is the Georgia Department of Cor-rections and its evil sister, the Georgia State Board of Pardons and Parole.

Both organizations seek to oppress and dehumanize the prisoner. Countless thousands of men and women come to prison guilty of having made a few bad choices. After years, if not decades, of mentally and morally crushing treatment from prison officials, they leave filled with bitter hatred toward society.

In prison you soon learn that prison officials have failed miserably in helping the men and women there get their lives together. If you are fortunate enough to sit in or to associate with one of the underground groups, several things will be required.

First, you will be required to open your eyes to the truth of the world. Evil comes in many colors and many forms. You will need to recognize the evil of this world.

Second, you will need to educate yourself. In prison you learn first and foremost that, to succeed in life, you must educate yourself for success.

Third, you will learn to fight like you've never fought before. You are fighting a system aimed at your destruction, so you are fighting for your very life and soul.

Fourth, you must learn to keep secrets. Educating yourself to the truths that will help you stay out of prison and build something for yourself will be frowned on, discouraged, and even punished by prison officials. Books are passed around and discussions held that will benefit you. The prison administration, however, does not approve of this activity.

Many people in prison are dead spiritually and mentally. The system encourages this spiritual death, so much so that prison officials are called "soul stealers."

The Holy Bible says, "The greatest commandment is to love your brothers and sisters as yourself. Failing to do this, you will live in darkness instead of light." The Bhagavad Gita says that whether one's path is paved with harmony or destruction depends on one's thoughts.

Because the prison administration fosters hatred, the system causes countless thousands to lose their souls. With a heart filled with hatred, the Christian lives in sin.

Officials of the Georgia Department of Corrections and the Board of Pardons and Parole are employees of state agencies; therefore, their administrators represent the will of the citizenry. This makes the citizens in part responsible for the actions of these agencies.

For those who call themselves religious, these agencies are stealing souls in your name. What excuse will you give when, on that day of judgment, you confront your Creator, who asks why you did nothing or so little while so many souls were stolen?

A Bag of Snakes, *by Murphy Davis*

FEBRUARY 1994

Go to the Lord, and you will live. If you do not go, God will sweep down like fire on the people of Israel. The fire will burn up the people of Bethel, and no one will be able to put it out. You are doomed, you that twist justice and cheat people out of their rights!

The Lord made the stars,
the Pleiades and Orion.
God turns darkness into daylight
and day into night.
God calls for the waters of the sea
and pours them out on the earth.

God's name is the Lord.
God brings destruction on the
mighty and their strongholds.

You people hate anyone who challenges injustice and speaks the whole truth in court. You have oppressed the poor and robbed them of their grain. And so you will not live in the fine stone houses you build or drink wine from the beautiful vineyards you plant. I know how terrible your sins are and how many crimes you have committed. You persecute good people, take bribes, and prevent the poor from getting justice in the courts. And so, keeping quiet in such evil times is the smart thing to do!

Make it your aim to do what is right, not what is evil, so that you may live. Then the Lord God Almighty really will be with you, as you claim God is. Hate what is evil, love what is right, and see that justice prevails in the courts. Perhaps the Lord will be merciful to the people of this nation who are still left alive.

How terrible it will be for you who long for the day of the Lord! What good will that day do you? For you it will be a day of darkness and not of light. It will be like a woman who runs from a lion and meets a bear! Or like a man who comes home and puts his hand on the wall—only to be bitten by a snake!

The day of the Lord will bring darkness and not light; it will be
a day of gloom, without any brightness. . . .
    "I hate, I despise your feasts, and I take no delight in your
solemn assemblies. Even though you offer me your burnt offer-
ings and cereal offerings, I will not accept them, and the peace
offerings of your fatted beasts I will not look upon. Take away
from me the noise of your songs; to the melody of your harps I
will not listen. But let justice roll down like waters, and right-
eousness like an ever-flowing stream."

—Amos 5:6–15, 18–24

As the Georgia state legislature convenes, Atlanta begins to hear from a new mayor, the U.S. Congress goes about its business, and we are being treated to increasingly strident truckloads of political rhetoric that suggest police and punishment are the simple answers to the deepening darkness of our social disintegration.

What does Atlanta, Georgia, one of the poorest cities in the United States, need? "More police," says Mayor Bill Campbell. What does Georgia—the state whose children are the hungriest, most illiterate, sickest of any in the country—what does Georgia need according to our leaders? More prisons, more mandatory sentencing, more occasions to use the death penalty, and automatic life in prison for those convicted of a second violent offense.

What does our country need? Our country where the guns proliferate, the violence is overwhelming, the schools are broken, the libraries are closing, the community centers cutting their hours, and we are all scared to death of each other—what do we need according to our "leaders"? Police. Prisons. Harsh sentences. Death as punishment. Provisions that allow us to try thirteen-year-old children as adult criminals.

The Sentencing Project has figured that the crime bill already passed by the U.S. Senate would cost $6.5 billion for construction of new prisons and an additional $1.3 billion per year to operate them. That's on top of the sixteen billion dollars per year we're already spending. If an ever expanding criminal-control system were the answer, the United States would be the safest place on earth. No other country even approaches our out-of-control use of prisons to respond to every problem. But we doggedly ignore the facts while the political boondoggle further rips at the very fabric of our society. Few of the politicians who spout the get-tough rhetoric believe what they're saying. But the thinly veiled racism and call to class hatred fuels the hell-bent machinery, and we're selling our children's future to keep it going.

Dan Berrigan said some years ago that trying to tell people the truth about prison is like trying to hand them a bag of snakes. Nobody wants it, and it seems like a tacky thing to do to nice people—especially people you like. It's simply no fun—we don't want to touch it or look into the bag. We'd rather settle for the accepted political line.

That's probably true of the fifth chapter of Amos, too. The prophet's tirade against the people of Israel was as unwelcome as the raggedy shepherd himself in polite eighth-century society. So why? Why bother with these unpleasantries? Why push beyond what anybody is interested in hearing? Why not leave the prophet on the shelf as a historic curiosity—a quaint word from the past, in the past, about the past?

Well, first of all because it's a living word for us now. And second, it's the finest methodology for political analysis that you'll find. Amos has this basic assumption for prophetic social, economic, and political analysis: if you want to understand what is going on in any society, then go to court and see how the poor are treated. You will see in the court system, implies the prophet, more than you want to know. Amos rants and raves about what he sees. It is corrupt. It is stacked against the poor. Then he delivers this zinger: "And so, keeping quiet in such evil times is the smart thing to do!"

He follows with this image, which is apt for our culture—an image of a day of darkness:

> It will be like a woman who runs from
> a lion and meets a bear.
> Or like a man who goes home and puts
> his hand on the wall, only to be
> bitten by a snake.

We have a choice, and it's clear. If we don't turn to God, says Amos, God will turn to us—like a fire, a fire that will burn everybody up.

Look, if you dare, at the court system—and see what happens to the poor. Look, if you can stand it, at the intent of our criminal-control system—look at the message for the poor. Look, if you can, at the power of the laity from your church and mine: mainline church folks are generally the lawyers and judges and prosecutors and decision makers. Look at how the decisions that come from high benches and big offices crush the life and hope and human dignity of the poor, women, African Americans, Hispanics, Native Americans. Ah, perhaps keeping quiet in such evil times is the smart thing to do!

What will you see if you look into the courts, into the jails (we euphemistically call them "detention centers"), into the prisons (do we really believe they are "correctional institutions" or "diagnostic and classification centers?")? What will you see if you look into the children's prisons ("youth-development centers")? What will you see? Please consider the question long enough to look, ask, and listen, and to get at least some of your information from sources other than judges and lawyers and the mainline news media.

One thing you will see if you look into the criminal-control system is absolute continuity in our history since the Civil War. Our prisons are racist from top to bottom. The criminal-control system is one of the major factors in the fracturing of the African American family in this society. More than one-half of all prison and jail admissions in this country are nonwhite. One in four African American men aged twenty to twenty-nine are under the influence of the criminal-control system—either in prison, jail, or on probation or parole. Half of all African American men will be arrested at some point in their lifetimes.

The facts are there. Please look. The criminal-control system, including the death penalty, is the main unfinished agenda of the civil rights movement. If you look, you will see that prisons are now the major government program for the poor in the United States. Prisons are our housing program for the poor. In the Reagan-Bush era, thirty billion dollars was cut from housing budgets, while, of course, the need has grown. Much of what remained was squandered and stolen by high-level bureaucrats. In the same era, from 1980 to 1990, the prison population in the United States doubled, while the overall crime rate increased only 7 percent.

We now spend sixteen billion dollars each year to lock up more than one million Americans in prisons and jails; that's like locking up the entire population of San Francisco or Cleveland. The United States has the highest incarceration rate in the world: 426 per 100,000. That is far more than South Africa's 333 per 100,000, not to mention the Netherlands' 40 per 100,000! In the 1980s our rate surpassed the Soviet Union's.

Prisons are our only remaining social program for the poor. Prisons are our dumping ground. A reality that reflects what's going on in the rest of the United States is the Los Angeles County Jail, which houses 3,600 people who are seriously mentally ill. In that jail are more mental patients than the total number in California's four state hospitals. As we have cut health and social services, jails and prisons and, yes, death row have become our dumping ground for the mentally ill and the retarded.

Lois, a woman I know who is the mother of a man on death row, says: "My son, who is a chronic schizophrenic, was turned out of a mental hospital because our health insurance ran out. They knew he wasn't well but the money was gone so his treatment was over. His condition got worse and he killed someone. Now the state is spending four million dollars trying to kill him. There's all this money to kill him but there was none to help him. What kind of sense does that make?"

Prisons are taking everything. During a recent three-year period, the people of Georgia spent $350 million for new prison construction while we cut programs and fired state workers and couldn't adequately fund our schools. George Bush's last budget slashed $100 million from public libraries and another $800 million from low-income housing and rent subsidies, while asking for $250 million more to build new prisons. We are literally trading family housing and school textbooks for more prisons.

Given all this growth, prisons have become, after war, the number-two industry in the United States. An entire industrial structure has grown around them, including professional advantage and opportunity for architects, academics, food-service vendors, social workers, weapons companies, security-equipment companies, health care firms, corrections bureaucrats, psychologists, psychiatrists, construction companies, fence corporations, engineers, and on and on and on. This is to say that, to keep the wheels turning, our economy is undergoing radical shifts to build a long-term dependence on human bondage.

The prophets are right: To understand who we are and what is going on, we have to look at what happens to poor people in the courts. We have to look at prisons. And then we need to ask, "Why?" The social, cultural, political, and economic landscape of the United States is undergoing massive change—and it's being done without our acknowledging it. Why?

On the local level, people are increasingly tired of, and frustrated by, the ongoing and growing presence of the poor. And so we use police and jails to sweep the poor out of sight, never bothering to ask, of course, what happens to the least of these after they're swept from our neighborhoods. Sanctuary is shrinking with a private and public policy that is increasingly hateful toward the poor.

Underneath the numbers is a well of human suffering and social disintegration that is beyond description: hundreds of thousands of shattered lives and hopes, broken families, and broken dreams. Built shakily on top is the privilege of a shrinking number. Ah, yes, perhaps keeping quiet in such evil times is the smart thing to do.

But there is no need to be afraid, because we have the rich resources of a biblical faith and a great cloud of witnesses that would look familiar to any Georgia prison warden: Jesus the prisoner—sentenced to death as a common criminal—Rahab the hooker; Mary Magdalene the psychotic; Jacob the thief; Moses the murderer; David the murderer; Saul the murderer.

Don't you think that God must sometimes chuckle? All these stories from scripture and still we don't get the point! God loves to come to the most broken, the most wasted, those least likely to be fixed or rehabilitated or "mainstreamed" and say, "You! You! Tell Pharaoh to let my people go! You! Find the Risen Christ at the empty tomb and run, tell the others, proclaim the resurrection! You! Plant my church. Go to the ends of the earth!" We have the story! We know it! We just forget that it has anything to do with the culture and politics of today. And so the story sits on a shelf and shrivels for lack of vitality.

The prophet is clear about the stakes. If we don't turn to God—if we don't plumb the resources of our biblical faith to sort through the political baloney that misleads and that continually sacrifices the poor for our corporate lack of imagination—then Yahweh will come like a fire. . . . And friend, it will burn! The fire is already burning. We've denied it; we've been quiet; we politely pretend it's not there, or that it won't touch us. But it's burning.

We're running from a lion—straight into the jaws of a bear. We've been zealous, even frantic, to keep our neighborhoods safe, and now in the sanctuary of our home we put our hands on the wall and are bitten by a snake. Such are the consequences of a corporate life based on greed and fear, on a willingness to keep quiet and to give our silent consent as the poor and people of color go down the tubes; and then to pretend it has nothing to do with the rest of us.

It doesn't take much imagination to realize some of the things we must do to create a safe society. We need to house the homeless, to provide care and a healthy, safe environment for every child; we need to feed the hungry and to see that everyone has access to health and medical care. We need to stop the proliferation of violence and weaponry in the U.S. military, on the streets of every city, and in the American home. We need to persevere in seeking the language, the behavior, and the public policy that will move us past the racism, the violence against women, the homophobia, and the class hatred that divide us more deeply every day.

But the language of reconciliation and justice doesn't seem to sell in the political marketplaces. Keeping quiet in such evil times is the smart thing to do! Why is it smart for you and me? Why does it make so much professional sense to turn our heads from the reality of prisons in our midst? Why do the people you and I know not talk about it? Why is it impolite to begin to ask questions about Episcopalians and Catholics and Presbyterians in the court system of your county—or whatever county? What is in this bag of snakes anyway?

It's your question. It's my question. It's our question.

Why?

Dollars and Sense, *by Murphy Davis*

JUNE 1989

In the past two months the state of Georgia has released, with a flurry of publicity, some three thousand prisoners. Each was given a clean set of clothes, twenty-five dollars, and a bus ticket to somewhere, or to nowhere. Nobody wanted to release them, but the governor, because of serious overcrowding in the prisons, agreed to do it to avoid a suit. In a recent two-week period the Fulton County Jail released more than one thousand prisoners. Each was given two dollars and a bus token. The releases were ordered by a federal judge because of the jail's dangerous overcrowding.

The Georgia legislature met again this year. They didn't have much money to go around, bless their hearts, so they couldn't give significant raises in Aid to Families with Dependent Children, or fund the indigent-defense system, or help the homeless. But miraculously, at the end of the session, the governor found one hundred million dollars to set aside to build new prisons. This was, of course, over and above the millions already appropriated for the Department of Corrections budget for the coming year.

Nine economically depressed rural Georgia counties have recently landed commitments from the state to build new prisons in their communities. In Hancock County, where 40 percent of the residents live below the poverty line, the twenty-one-million-dollar, 750-bed prison will bring an estimated 350 jobs! (To imprison two people creates one job. What if we could marshal such resources for education or health care or home building?) There has been no opposition in Hancock County to building the prison. As the governor's executive assistant said, "People are beginning to realize it's a good, clean industry."

Everybody has something to say about prisons these days. And most of what's said is that we need more of them. "Surely if we could just build a few more . . . if we could just keep more people in for a little longer . . ." So every time lawmakers convene, stiffer criminal sentences are the order of the day. And the most popular way to campaign for public office is to promise to throw more of "them" in jail and to throw away the key, if not to throw the switch on them. Where are leaders who can admit that we will never build our way out of the problems we've created?

The rich are getting richer and the poor are getting poorer. With increasing numbers of desperately poor people, the issue of social control becomes more critical to those in power. So we use prisons. If we wanted to address the deepening problems of the poor, we would. Instead, we, as a society, are making the choice to try to control the poor so that the middle and upper classes will be disturbed as little as possible.

We will spend our money on what is most important to us. If it were really important to house the homeless we would begin to do it. But we do not have the political will. I heard Parke Renshaw say recently: "We cannot build affordable housing, but we can afford buildable jails." We—as a people—like jails. We want more jails. And we want to put more and more people in them. So we build them. When we want housing, we will build housing. When we want decent health care, we will provide it. When we want education in the schools, we will get it.

In Atlanta, we would rather spend our money to arrest, jail, process, and then imprison a person for twenty to forty days for urinating in public than to provide one public toilet. For the amount we have spent punishing people for this "crime" in the past five years we could have built a hundred public toilets to make the crime unnecessary. But we buy what we want. And what we want is to put poor people in cages. So we do.

Yes, we do have a problem with crime. And it will get worse. We have in our society a deadly combination of extreme wealth and extreme poverty, drug and alcohol abuse in every social strata, and a proliferation of weapons. As long as we maintain a narrowly focused law-enforcement approach, crime will get worse and worse—everything from petty crime to serious violence. Former Atlanta Public Safety Commissioner Lee Brown once said, "Too many people just want the police to be janitors—to come along and clean up the mess we've made as a society that nobody else wants to touch."

We must demand a more serious look at the big picture. We need to demand leaders who will stop playing games with their tough talk. Surely we can come up with a "good, clean industry" not totally dependent on human bondage. We will not find peace in our land until we narrow the gap between the rich and the poor. We will not have a "safe" society until people have houses to live in, food to eat, health care when they're sick, and decent work.

"Why?" cries the prophet. "Why spend money on what does not satisfy? Why spend your wages and still be hungry?" How long will we pretend that problems are caused by bad people who need to be put away? At points of desperation any of us could be capable of crime—stealing, selling drugs, or even murder. Our task, as Dorothy Day often reminded us, is to build a world in which it's easier to be good.

Of the ever increasing numbers of people sent to prison, most will eventually be released. To what? And with what hope? Some will return to homes, families, and caring communities who will help them toward a restoration of life. But many, if not most, will come out with nowhere to go, nobody to meet them when they get there, and nothing to do—which is probably a large part of the reason they ended up in prison or jail in the first place. Some will turn to violence. Prisons only exacerbate the problem of violence.

When Jesus began his ministry, he read from the prophet Isaiah: "God has sent me to proclaim liberty to the captives and recovery of sight to the blind." Prisons and jails stand as monuments to our refusal to live the good news. Until we open ourselves to the healing word of God's justice, we will choose harsh judgment and a deepening violence, rather than a compassionate response to victims and healing for those who hurt or offend. We are captives to our blindness, but the good news is that the blind can recover their sight. And when we claim the healing that God has promised, then the captives can be liberated.

Prison Labor, *by Murphy Davis*

Our friend Thony is locked up for a sentence of 481 years in an infamous southern plantation–style prison. He spends his days with a swing blade, cutting grass on the edge of ditches over the 23,000 acres. For his labor he is paid two cents per hour. One penny per hour is banked until his parole consideration (the year 2070); the other penny per hour is his to spend at the prison store.

Mary Louise sews blue stripes down the pants legs of prison uniforms at the garment factory near the Hardwick women's prison. For her eight hours a day she is paid nothing. She begs stamps from friends to write to her children.

Charles stands day after day in front of a machine, watching it stamp out license plates. The work is monotonous, and he is paid nothing for it. The prison tells him he is building "work skills." But since license plates are only made in prison industries, he is not being prepared for any work on the outside market.

Frank sits on death row. Day in, day out, he is, for all practical purposes, idle. Television, exercise, writing letters, playing checkers pass the time. Frank, though young, strong, and energetic, is not allowed to work. He has spent the past ten years of his life unable to do anything of use.

Thony, Mary Louise, Charles, and Frank, like hundreds of thousands of men, women and children in the United States, cannot control their own labor. They are slaves. *Slavery* is, of course, not a fashionable word in the latter part of the twentieth century. We assume ourselves to be rid of it. But the Thirteenth Amendment to the Constitution did not abolish slavery in the United States. It simply narrowed the practice. The amendment reads: "Neither slavery nor involuntary servitude, *except as a punishment for crime* whereof the party shall have been duly convicted, shall exist within the United States, or any place subject to their jurisdiction." Prisoners are, by mandate of the U.S. Constitution, slaves.

Prisons are rarely called "prisons" anymore. We have "correctional institutions," "diagnostic and classification centers," "youth-development centers," and so on. Wardens have become "superintendents"; guards have become "correctional officers"; prisoners have become "inmates." Solitary confinement, or the "hole," has become the "adjustment center." The language of scientific penology attempts to mask harsh reality. Prisoners are people from whom most rights of citizenship have been taken. They have no rights to control where they are, with whom, or how they spend their time—in forced labor or forced idleness. They are given over to the prison system presumably to be "corrected" or "rehabilitated." In fact, they are in the system to accomplish only one goal: punishment.

Why? And for whom? Can we be satisfied to live with the commonly held assumption that people are in prison solely because they have done bad things? If this assumption were true, then why would there be such wide variation in incarceration rates around the world and even within the United States?

The United States stands third in the world in its rates of imprisonment. We follow only South Africa and the Soviet Union. But within the United States, a few jurisdictions—including Georgia and the District of Columbia—exceed the incarceration rates of South Africa and the Soviet Union (state prisons, municipal and county jails, and children's prisons are counted in this measure). That is to say that some of us in the United States depend—more than any other government in the world—on caging people as a response to our problems.

Prisons have not always been such major institutions in the United States. A bit of history: The first state prison opened in Milledgeville, Georgia, in 1817. The prison was based on the "Auburn plan"—named after the system at the Auburn State Penitentiary in New York—which assumed that hard work would simultaneously punish and reform. The average number of prisoners stayed around two hundred—all white. Black people, of course, were slaves and were dealt with inside the system of private ownership. This development in Georgia roughly coincided with the opening of state prisons in other states. Thomas Jefferson took from Italian philosopher Cesare Beccaria the notion of confined-convict slavery and designed a prison for Virginia that opened to receive prisoners in 1800.

Centuries earlier, governments had learned that the punishment of slavery could be used to benefit the state. Galley slavery of ancient Greece and Rome was used again in France and Spain during the fourteenth and fifteenth centuries. In the nineteenth century, slavery as punishment was tailored to the needs of the American system. The benefits of this form of punishment to general social control were frankly admitted. A prison report in 1820 stressed that convict submission was "demanded not so much for the smooth functioning of the prison but for the sake of the convict himself, who shall learn to submit willingly to the fate of the lower classes."

As the system of American prison slavery was honed, the controversy raged over the practice of chattel slavery. At the close of the Civil War, the controversy focused on the wording of the constitutional amendment to legally abolish slavery. Those who argued for the complete abolition of slavery in the United States lost their struggle. The Thirteenth Amendment as it was passed, and as it stands, forbids slavery "except as a punishment for crime." Rather than legally abolishing slavery, the amendment changed the system to permit the state, not private citizens, to be slave owners.

After the Civil War, southern planters thought themselves lost without their slaves. The one legal form of slavery still available to them was imprisonment.

Some states passed "black codes." But others, including Georgia, passed vagrancy laws and similar laws as a way to lock up black people who were seen to be out of their "proper" place. In 1868, Georgia established by law the convict-lease system, modeled after the Massachusetts system begun in 1798. Convicts could be leased to counties or county contractors for use on public works. In 1874, the Georgia law was altered to permit leasing convicts to private individuals and companies. By 1877, Georgia had 1,100 prisoners. Nine hundred ninety-four (90 percent) of them were black.

In 1878, former Confederate Colonel Robert Alston, serving as state representative from DeKalb County, visited convict work camps all over the state. As head of the Committee on the Penitentiary he wrote a scathing report:

> The lease system at best is a bad one, and seems to have been forced upon the State by an inability to provide for the great increase in the number of criminals growing out of the changed relations of labor. . . . To turn the prisoners over to private parties, who have no interest in them except that which is prompted by avarice, is to subject them to treatment which is as various as the characters of those in charge and in many cases amounts to nothing less than capital punishment with slow torture added.

Alston encouraged leading citizens to withdraw from the companies leasing convicts. He was promptly murdered by a man who leased convicts.

As difficult as it must have been in the harsh days of the post-Reconstruction era, the black community found various ways to protest the lease system. One of their methods was an annual memorial service and "decoration of the grave" for Alston as the first white person to "condemn and denounce the workings of the abominable, blasphemous and vile penitentiary lease system, under which so many of our race are doomed to horror, agony and pollution."

In 1908 the Georgia Prison Commission reported that in the penitentiary and chain gangs combined there were 4,290 Negro males, 209 Negro women, 461 white males, and 6 white women. In that same year a committee report to the legislature on corruption and cruelty in the lease system led the legislature to abolish the lease.

From then on, chain gangs worked on public works rather than for private individuals and companies. But abuses and cruelty continued. One infamous warden used to send black trustees out with a pitchfork to make the hogs squeal, so that the townsfolk would not hear the human screams as the warden beat a prisoner with hose pipe. Submission to the "fate of the lower classes" seems to have continued as an agenda in the prison system.

In 1957, forty-one prisoners at the Buford Rock Quarry broke their own legs with their sledgehammers to protest harsh working and living conditions. When the investigations promised by prison officials never took place, a second and then a third group of prisoners broke their own legs.

As recently as 1979, a number of prisoners at the Wayne County "Correctional Institution" cut their own Achilles tendons in protest of working conditions.

I will never forget my first visit to the Georgia State Prison at Reidsville in the spring of 1978. We drove onto the prison reservation and there, as far as I could see, were groups of men (mostly black) bent over, working in the fields. Over them sat a uniformed white man on horseback with a rifle across his lap. I was utterly amazed to see this picture of slavery. I did not realize then that slavery still existed as a legal institution in the United States. Most people probably still do not. But as the Committee to Abolish Prison Slavery has said, "In any form, slavery dehumanizes, cripples, and destroys anyone who willingly, or unwillingly, partakes in its practice."

Prisons and prison slavery are crucial institutions in this country for controlling labor in the interest of the powerful few and to the benefit of us all. It is beyond dispute that imprisonment rates go straight up and down with unemployment in the lower class.

But we should be clear about the damage done to the human family by the increasing dependence on prisons. When a breadwinner is taken to prison, her/his children often become wards of the state—by foster care or welfare. Family ties are damaged and sometimes completely broken. Because prisoners earn nothing, or nearly nothing, for their labor, there is no possibility of helping to support their own families or of making reparations to their victims.

Because prisons on state and federal levels have become multimillion-dollar industries, an increasing number of individuals and institutions are dependent on their continued existence.

Most important is that prison slavery infects all of us, whether we make ourselves aware of its use or not. Prisons are off the beaten path for most people. Middle- and upper-class people have little reason to know anything of prisons or prisoners except when it's time to keep a new prison from being built in "our neighborhood." But pretending to be untouched by systems of degradation and dehumanization can only be a self-defeating game.

Prison slavery must and will someday be abolished. Until then we will not even begin to take an honest look at questions of labor, employment, fair wages, and good work.

Let us be about the task of seeking human dignity and liberation for all of God's children.

Thony Green: Prison Worker, *by Ed Loring*

FEBRUARY 1989

Thony Green is a beautiful Black man. He is big and strong. Thony's human frame is full of African features: meaty lips, a flattened nose, coal-black eyes that twinkle with mystery and love. He is dirt poor—Mississippi River, South Louisiana–side poor: where the dirt is rich but the poor people are depleted. Thony completed the eighth grade in poor schools as he grew up along the levee from LaPlace to Norco. This area is part of the infamous Cancer Alley, where petroleum companies belch their waste into the grey sky, and the earth, water, vegetation, animals, and human beings mutate, suffocate, and die. Last year, Thony's younger sister perished from cancer.

During the winter of 1982, Thony Green became a member of the Open Door Community. Immediately he became a friend and coworker. He took care of our daughter Hannah and her friend Christina on a regular basis. He also worked in the kitchen and, as the strongest member of our family, Thony was often asked to help with the heavy work of hauling and moving. As is the case so often when God's love is the basis of family life, we began to love one another deeply and profoundly.

One morning, a few months after his entry into our lives, and just before the soup kitchen was to open, two men from the Georgia Bureau of Investigation jumped the front hedge, broke into our home, grabbed Thony, threw him to the floor, stuck a pistol into his neck, cuffed his hands together, dragged him to their automobile, and drove off almost as fast as the daily commuters from Decatur and Tucker who chase the death-dealing, sickle-wielding second hand of the clock down Ponce de Leon Avenue. (It is not the fountain of youth that secular, faithless moderns chase along this ancient, now-asphalted pathway, but the job, so that they may pay part of a bill for a product long-ago consumed, broken, and forgotten. Ponce de Leon also, I think, traveled along Cancer Alley beside the Mississippi River. But I digress. That is really about tomorrow.)

News moves slowly out of jails and prisons. We learned over the next few weeks that Thony had escaped from jail in St. John the Baptist Parish. The local authorities were mad. At the conclusion of his trial, the judge, robed in black garments but covered from head to toe with white skin, had leaned forward and, beetle-browed, hissed to the defendant, "Four hundred eighty-one years. Parole is possible in the year of our Lord 2070."

Thony Lee Green, man-child and hungry for the simple amenities which make life good, had robbed the Bucket of Blood Tavern. In the course of the robbery a fellow human being was shot in the shoulder. To understand an event is not to justify the event. Thony's desperate act is understandable. Armed robbery is wrong.

On a warm Thursday morning not long ago, Murphy, Hannah, and I took our annual trip to Angola Prison to spend a few hours with our loved one Thony. The road from Baton Rouge is long and winding. The last twenty miles are especially difficult. But a nun-friend in New Orleans had loaned us her car and we were filled with joy and expectation as we reached the prison; our year-long longing was about to be released.

Angola Prison is an enormous plantation. Twenty-three thousand acres of land, with eighteen thousand under cultivation, comprise the layout. Seventy percent of the prison population is Black. Almost everyone there is dirt poor. However, there is one great difference between Angola and our state plantation in Reidsville, Georgia: financial payment for work. The U.S. Constitution upholds human bondage for punishment, but historically there has been no agreement among slaveholders that slaves should not receive any payment for services. Throughout Western history there exist systems of slavery including pecuniary reward for the slaves' forced labor.

Thony works for eight hours a day, five days each week. His job is to cut grass around the drainage ditches by hand. He uses a scythe. The state of Louisiana pays Thony two cents per hour for his work. One penny is put into a savings account, and one penny is put on the books for him to spend any way he wants at the prison store. The prison store, for instance, sells stamps. The prison does not allow convicts to receive stamps from any other source.

A very pleasant guard escorted us toward Thony's camp. We had been driven by prison bus for a couple of miles and now we were walking into the compound. Everywhere we looked we saw Black men. I don't think I saw five white convicts during the entire visit. As we walked down the concrete and steel-barred corridor, I felt again that pang of pain and sipped from my cup of anger at George Bush and his filthy lies. Here were some of the Willie Hortons of our nation. Black men broken and battered by people who are simply too far removed to grasp the significance of poverty and racism and sexism in the human personality. Willie Horton's name and image became for the Republicans what the image of a Jew was for the Nazis. Willie Horton—the Black male of the United States of America—became an incarnation of fear, rape, death, and violence to white middle-class America.

Thony Green is Willie Horton. So am I, and so is Jesus Christ. Hannah reached her little hand up to the thick screen, and through the wire mesh bulged tiny pockets of flesh that touched Thony's hard hands. As tears streamed down our cheeks, we laughed with joy. Together we were, and after so long a time. The bars, the wire, the very different lives we led could not separate us from the love we shared. Then, suddenly, that death-dealing, sickle-wielding second hand cut us off. We had to leave. Thony back to the ditches at two cents per hour. Ourselves back to 910—home, where we receive all that we need.

I am eternally thankful for the love and friendship of Thony Green. My wounds are healed and desert places inside my rib cage are made oases of delight because many in prison love me. I invite you who read this article to join me in setting your life against prisons and slavery. Let's join to bring love and justice to this land.

Angola Bound, *by Ed Loring*

J A N U A R Y   1 9 9 3

Too many mornings gonna wake up soon
Oh, Lordy eat my breakfast by the light of the moon
Oh Lord by the light of the moon

If you see my momma
Tell her this for me
Oh, I got a mighty long time
Lord knows I'll never go free
Oh Lord I'll never be free
Angola Bound now
Angola Bound
Angola Bound now
Angola Bound.

102340. Thony Lee Green is black. So is the sky. A nimbus of orange dances to the bumblebee buzz of the insecurity lights as I load my black boom box singing black man's blues into the backseat. Nibs hits the starter. We roll into the blue-black soft morning even before the radio's Mara Lyason begins to describe the damage done during the darkness.

102340. What would Thomas Merton think? A man has become a number by no will of his own, and his manhood is eroding in the floodwaters of hell, where survival is resistance. Death is the program. Death is white. I wonder in the parking lot if computers and numbers are used among the Trappists. I'll ask Father Tom Francis in October gold. Penitentiary.

102340. Rev. Stroupe lowers the steering wheel so that he may peer above his meaty hands as we turn onto Airlines Highway. Baton Rouge is asleep except for the very poor and devout who, bent, pray for bread. We swing silently onto the white concrete of I-10 as signs sing of Natchez and we dream of Huck Finn, Sal Paradise, and Jack Burden. Flames jump and dance from garbage gases along the Mississippi River. One must tour Cancer Alley when Angola Bound.

102340. June 1982. 5:30 A.M.: Thony got his beautiful black body out of bed. Ambled to the kitchen to fix coffee. (This was in the morning before Ralph Dukes was the high priest of Java at 910.) 6:00 A.M.: Thony mopped the hall, dining-room, and living-room floors. 9:00 A.M.: A sprightly man, he climbed the stairs to the Loring-Davis apartment, where Mama Murphy handed Thony our two-and-a-half-year-old bundle of love. We were off to a meeting in down-town Atlanta. An hour later (and three diaper changes!) Carolyn brought Christina to Thony while she finished the soup and sandwiches. At 10:45, Thony put our girls down for a nap and sped to the soup kitchen to ladle life to the starving ghosts and spooks of the kudzu patches and cat-hole cages along Ponce de Leon Avenue, N.E. Suddenly, horrible, deformed-looking white men broke down the porch door. Yelling like injured weasels, guns aloft like Salvadoran death squads, they race through the dining room to the kitchen. Throw Thony to the floor. One actor in this nightmare puts his pistol to Thony's neck, holler-ing that he will blow his head to pieces if he moves. Another man bends and beats Thony's arms behind his back while a third cuffs his gentle wrists with steel. Carolyn shouts, "Who the hell are you?" "None of your business, lady," snarls a snake who, boa-like, is hugging Thony to his feet. Another member of the posse flashes a Georgia Bureau of Investigation picture ID (I wonder if his number was 102340). They drag Thony out the front door, through the line of hungry humans whose hope is hopeless and throw him in the back of their car. His sentence: 102340, 482, Louisiana State Penitentiary, Angola, Louisiana.

> I got lucky last summer when I got my time
> Angola Bound
> Oh my fally got a hundred
> I got ninety-nine
> Angola Bound
> You've been a long time comin' but
> you're welcome home
> Angola Bound
> Angola Louisiana get your burden on
> Angola Bound

102340. Nibs swings onto Highway 61. We speak of Bob Dylan's "Revisita-tion" and the mass migration of Blacks and blues up this highway—North, North, North, North—yearning, seeking, fleeing, dreaming, traveling for justice in a white man's land. Muddy Waters. Malcolm X's dad, perhaps. Fannie Lou Hamer remained, we recall, as conversation rolls toward Ruleville, Mississippi, and the weeds of Sunflower County. Catholic ghosts peer at us. We hit all three traffic lights in St. Francisville. I dream: When was it that Christians agreed that one baptized Christian could own another baptized Christian? Do white men make black decisions? Is my visit to Thony a continuation of the Christian theology that built and maintains St. Francisville? Do I really hear hope banging at my back door when I step over African American men curled together on my back porch?

102340. The sky is black and begins to bleed as the shortest Presbyterian minister in America steers us onto the brown gravel parking lot in front of the steel gate and concrete guardhouse of the Louisiana State Prison. Twenty thousand acres of rich farmland stretch and groan before us. An Old South plantation, really. Five thousand two hundred men are slaves here. Four thousand three hundred are people of color, 4,160 are African Americans. Nine hundred are European Americans. Everyone is poor. Unlike our Georgia prison plantation system, the slaves at Angola are paid for their labor. Thony receives four cents per hour. Two cents goes into his savings account and is his upon release; two cents goes into his draw at the prison commissary. After 3,723 days and nights at Angola, Thony has accumulated less than two hundred dollars. His primary job during these past ten years has been cutting brush along the many ditches that lace this land in the Mississippi Delta.

> Oh captain, Oh captain, don't you be so cruel
> Angola Bound
> Oh, you work me harder than you work that mule
> Angola Bound

I step toward the metal detector, which shrieks at me. Strip off my boots. Unstrap my belt buckle. Leave my glasses on the counter. Ah, finally the machine is silent. I can now redress. Nibs takes my notebook, three-by-five cards, and pen, which were not approved for the visit, and turns toward the pouring rain. He is not allowed to visit. Angola allows no "special visits" whatsoever. What would Tertullian think? Moving westward Nibs spends the next five hours listening to the Mississippi River moan and grieve. He drank from this river every day of his life for eighteen years. I sit beside some man's mother. We wait for the bus which will take us deep into the belly of this beast. Suddenly, roaring like a mad lion, the bus crawls up to us. After we are seated the driver closes the metal-cage door and loops but does not fasten the padlock. We are ready to roll.

102340. Maybe John Brown was right as he sat polishing his rifle before riding into Harper's Ferry. Blood must be shed for redemption—an idea expressed by Yahweh in the days before Mr. Brown saw red. The sky continues to bleed and weep as we visitors are carried toward the ones we love. The land is rainwater wet and wonderful for weary workers. The big boss man, as Jimmy Reed would sing, has called the slaves in from the fields; it's Sabbath Rest in cells and dorms. I peer out the filigreed and filthy window and see my South. Surely the year is 1845; two men, one white, one black, on horseback with rifles. Forty convicts in two parallel rows marching with hoes on their right shoulders.

In front of the men is another overseer riding with rifle ready. The horses skitter as the bus roars past. Again and again we come upon this configuration of brothers walking away from their ruined fields. I recall that in the American mythology of meaning we have not yet decided just why we fought the Civil War. John Brown was certainly clear.

> Oh, they always talkin' 'bout dangerous blue
> Angola Bound
> If I had my shank
> I'd be dangerous, too
>
> Angola Bound
> Oh, the captain says, "Walk"
> and the boss say, "Run,"
> Angola Bound
> If I had my pistol I'd do 'nary one
> Angola Bound

102340. Camp D. I enter the visiting area alone. All the other visitors tumbled out of the bus at the main prison. The guard at the front desk is a large African American woman. She is reading her Bible as I approach; she welcomes me. I sit alone at a small table for fifty minutes waiting, waiting, waiting for Thony. In front of me a man and a woman make love with their eyes. I try to stare out the window but the chain-link fence and concertina wire frighten me. I dream of Murphy Davis and wish I was home: "Christ if my love was in my arms and I in my bed again."

Finally Thony bounds into the room from a secret passageway beside the Coca-Cola machine. He is six-foot-one, two hundred pounds, Black as an African King, shaved head. He is beautiful! We embrace. We are the only mixed couple in the room. Glances glance off my arms and the side of my head. I am the child of that man who rides the horse, with rifle ready to kill. I am white.

"No, no, no! It's not cancer. I have arthritis in my back."

"How great! God, I've been worried. Thank God for arthritis!"

"Little Bobby came to see me in March. He is six feet tall. Gone man. The streets are hell. When I was out there we only did beer and whiskey. Not these damn drugs. Oh, God. My boy, my boy. This country's coming apart, man. Dead. White. . . ."

"Yeah, two bleeds equals one case of Bugler. Four bleeds equals one carton cigarettes."

"What!"

"Yeah. We have a plasma bank right here at the prison. Course you gotta be tested first, but if you can bleed, you can make eight dollars to ten dollars per week."

"Damn. I can't believe this!"

"Yep. Two bleeds or four bleeds, but you gotta keep coming or they'll drop your butt fast."

We feast. Our cups runneth over. Cokes, french fries, hamburgers, fish sandwiches, coffee, and candy bars . . . We are free and joyful. We are not even at Angola State Penitentiary at all. We are almost home.

> Thou preparest a table before me in the presence of mine
>   enemies;
> Thou anointest my head with oil;
> my cup runneth over
> surely goodness and mercy shall
> follow me all the days of my life
> and I will dwell in the house of the
> LORD forever.

"Here, Thony," my mind plays games with me. "This french fry is my body of Christ broken for you." He munches away. "Thony," my heart murmurs to my bowels and my guts grieve, "this Cherry Coke is the blood of the New Covenant, shed for the remission of sins." "Sure wish I had a woman," he slurps. I'm not yet quite ready for reality, so bound by truth am I.

> "Christ has died
> Christ is risen
> Christ will come again" (Damn)

102340. The gift of the clock is complete. The bus is waiting in the lot. The guard informs us. I go. Thony stays. But . . . we embrace. We kiss. "I love you, Ed." "I love you, too, Thony." "Good-bye." "See you in February." "Yeah, I hope so." The iron door closes behind me and in front of Thony. On the bus is a man angry at George Bush but who proclaims that he will never vote for a Democrat. He tells us of the problems in Israel. "We need to kill either all the Jews or all the Arabs," he pontificates. "Those people have never been able to get along. I think if we kill all the Jews then the Arabs would fight among themselves, so it would only work if we kill all the Arabs." John Brown's body must be tossed a turn or two.

I sit in the back of the bus and try not to listen. Thony's face comes and goes as I bump along. The sky is healed now. The sun shines and there is an odd beauty shimmering on the fields. Nibs sits waiting in the car for me. He waves as I walk toward him to fly away from this piece of hell, from Thony Lee Green.

> If it wasn't for the captain
> Oh, Lord, and shaggy hounds
> I'd be with my woman, yeah
> before the sun goes down
> They come up here skippin' and a jumpin'
> Oh, Lard, they won't last long
> gonna wish they was a baby boy
> In their mother's arms.
>
> Angola Bound now
> Angola Bound
> Angola Bound now
> Angola Bound[2]

Tantamount to Torture, *by Murphy Davis*

JANUARY 1993

The long days and endless nights of prison life piled up on her shoulders like a dead weight. The noise seemed never to stop, and a minute of privacy was an almost impossible pleasure. Memories of the endless terror of her life and now the separation from her three small children pulled at her in the meaningless, idle hours that stacked themselves like a brick wall around her. Suicide— once only a fleeting thought that she could chase like a cat out the kitchen door—settled in and took the shape of a reasonable option.

"Oh?" said the psychiatrist. And nothing more. She was led from his office and down the hall. The guards pulled mechanically at her clothes until they lay in a crumpled heap around her and she shrank in her nakedness. The cold metal of handcuffs snapped her arms behind her back. Shackles gathered her ankles and, metal to metal, the chain connected and snapped behind her. Then came the football helmet. "This way, you see, you can't bang you head. . . . We don't want you to hurt yourself. . . ."

---

2. The song "Angola Bound" is from *Warm Your Heart,* A&M Records (© 1991, Aaron Neville and Charles Neville, Irving Music, Inc. [BMI]). Used by permission.

The heavy metal door slammed behind them, and her mental health treatment began. Only mealtime broke the cold concrete and steel isolation. The tray arrived. One time the guard unlocked her handcuffs long enough for her to eat. The next time the tray was simply left on the floor. If she wanted to eat she did it by shoving her face into the food, gobbling like a dog and salting it with her tears.

Then it stopped. How many days and nights? Who knows? God knows, there was no sun, moon, or stars—only a fluorescent sky. But she was better, they declared. Back down the hall she shuffled. Back to the dormitory with forty-nine other women. And this time if she had any thoughts plodding through her numbed brain she kept them to herself.

Since last spring the news has trickled out of the Georgia women's prison: sometimes one allegation at a time; sometimes a flood. It has been a seemingly endless horror story of sexual assault of prisoners by prison staff, coerced abortion, forced prostitution, and mental health "treatment" tantamount to torture. The light is shining on these allegations, thanks to a suit filed against the women's prison by Georgia Legal Services in 1984. The allegations over the past year have kicked the suit into high gear.

I often quote Dan Berrigan, who said years ago that trying to tell people about prisons is like trying to hand them a bag of snakes. Nobody wants the bag, and we'll do anything to avoid it. But this time the snakes are in our face. The well-concealed world of the prison system is being exposed and we have to look, like it or not. The silent screams and muffled suffering of captive women have come uninvited into our living rooms, and it's time to hear what they are saying.

As of late 1992, well over one hundred women in the Georgia prison system have come forward to tell of the treatment they have received. Most of these incidents have been at the Georgia Women's Correctional Institution at Hardwick, but other reports are already coming from the just-opened women's prison in Washington, Georgia.

Acknowledged, even by prison staff, is that a large majority of the women who go to prison in Georgia arrive in need of serious counseling for the physical, emotional, and sexual abuse they have already received. It would be bad enough to realize that the prison system does not give, and never has provided, this needed help. It is nearly incomprehensible that large numbers of women instead have received added abuse of every kind and description. We are hearing from hundreds of women prisoners that large numbers of women have been raped by prison staff; that prison employees have offered special favors and even favorable parole recommendations in exchange for sexual contact; that mental health "treatment" has regularly included stripping, hog-tying, chaining, and isolation of mentally ill and suicidal prisoners; that drug and prostitution rings have been operated to the benefit of prison staff. On one occasion we hear that, when the warden learned that a prisoner had been impregnated by a staff member, he forced her to have an abortion. We must remember that these reports come only from women currently in prison; they don't include the women who have been released from prison, those who have not been able to summon the courage to tell, and the women who, because of abuse and torture, are unable to speak out.

It would be reasonable to assume that our state's elected officials would take these overwhelming allegations with utmost seriousness. We would like to think that every elected official and state worker in a position to do anything would be at work to ensure that anyone and everyone who participated in, had knowledge of, or tolerated such despicable behavior would be fired immediately. And we would want to think that we would all work to make sure that such a thing never happens again.

Instead, for months on end, the governor and Department of Corrections staff have shuffled, covered for each other and, overall, have denied the seriousness of the situation. One warden has been replaced; some guards and maintenance workers have been fired. One worker, who has spoken with the Georgia Bureau of Investigation about his own misdeeds, and who is said to have promised to give testimony about involvement of other prison staff, was found dead in his truck—poisoned. The Department of Corrections has hired Allen Ault, former commissioner of the department, to come back at seventy-five thousand dollars a year to "handle" the scandal.

When it became clear that a deputy commissioner knew about, but did not stop, the stripping and hog-tying of mental health patients who were prisoners, the department spokesperson shrugged: "We didn't feel it was inappropriate because it was in line with standard operating procedures of the [prison] system." Then, to add insult to injury, Terry Coleman, chair of the Appropriations Committee of the Georgia House of Representatives, said that the women who had taken the risk of reporting their victimization should themselves be investigated and punished. It is clear that our elected and appointed officials are unable to respond to this situation in an appropriate manner.

We seem to have a group of men in charge who are incapable of understanding what is going on. They scramble and hope the publicity will cease, without acknowledging that the conditions in our women's prisons are major violations of basic human rights and human dignity and will require a housecleaning, top to bottom. A similar but quieter scandal occurred in the women's prison some ten years ago when five men were fired, or "allowed to retire," for sexually violating the women. They included the head counselor, the chaplain, the assistant warden for security, and two other staff. The Department of Corrections rearranged things a bit and went on. Obviously, the problem was not addressed.

We need to understand that in an institution in which men hold keys and power, and women are completely without power, there will be abuse. A women's prison is simply an exaggerated expression of our society and its values. Sexism is violent and deadly and cannot be addressed by firing some "bad" guards and hiring a fresh batch. The system must be overhauled and must include stringent safeguards that guarantee the safety and dignity of women prisoners. The problem will never be adequately addressed by a group of white male political appointees who, to begin with, do not view the sexual abuse and violent domination of women as a problem.

The suffering inflicted on women in the Georgia prison system has gone on far too long. May we join our voices to demand a change of heart, mind, and practice that will guarantee health, safety, and dignity for each of our sisters in prison. If we keep at it, the walls will tumble.

The Hardwick Trip, *by Joanne Solomon*

M A Y   1 9 8 6

The pre-printed postcard was returned to the Open Door as expected, only the message this time was different. The top line on the card showed no check mark, telling us that "Jessie" (as well as a daughter and six grandchildren) would not be visiting her other daughter, Mary, at the Hardwick prison in March. But when I noticed the bottom line, there was a moment of unexpected joy. Jessie had put a check mark in the space next to the words, "Sorry, I can't make it this month," and had crossed out the word "Sorry." Above it, she had written the word "Glad." To the side was the explanation. She wrote: "Mary is home! Thanks for everything."

Home. Family. Special words to many, but most meaningful and poignant to those who know the loneliness and difficulty of a forced separation. Jessie's family knew what this meant, and she had for many months made the daylong trip with us to Milledgeville for a two-hour visit with her daughter in the women's unit of the prison in nearby Hardwick. This meant rising very early on a Saturday morning, gathering her large family, meeting us by 9:30 A.M. for the trip, and returning home after 6:30 P.M. that same day. It meant riding the bus from her home to meet us, and, at times, even walking the long distance when her resources did not include adequate bus fare. The resources Jessie did have were care and concern for the daughter she would visit in prison, a place for her when she returned, and, most certainly, a *welcome home!*

The trip to the Hardwick prison in Milledgeville, Georgia, is one aspect of the Southern Prison Ministry at our Open Door Community. We provide family members of inmates the opportunity to visit their sons, daughters, mothers, fathers, husbands, wives, grandsons, or granddaughters. One Saturday each month, volunteer drivers in an assortment of cars and vans depart from the Open Door and wind through the streets of Atlanta in a caravan, arriving at the MARTA Five Points station at Alabama and Peachtree Streets, where we greet and are greeted by our fifty to seventy friends who will be making the trip. It is here, on this windy, bustling corner in the middle of Atlanta, where our friends have arrived by bus, by train, by foot. Often they share with us moments of thankfulness for times when *"it's not raining (Hallelujah!)"*; or a patient bus driver allows us to load up and we don't have to keep circling the block to make way for MARTA; or we decide, after an intentional delay, to wait "one more minute" before leaving, and we see another of our families, hands waving, racing toward us! And, with a grateful sigh, we're on our way!

We arrive at about noontime in Milledgeville, a lovely, historic community southeast of Atlanta. Here we are always warmly greeted at the Milledgeville Presbyterian Church, where each month a delicious hot meal awaits (as well as special treats for the children), lovingly prepared and served by church members. Not only do we enjoy a delightful lunchtime together, but everyone has a chance to relax and to be refreshed before driving the short distance to Hardwick for the visit. The friendly spirit and the many thoughtful gestures typify the genuine hospitality we experience each time.

Bill Morgan, pastor of the church, shared a letter with the Open Door that he had received last fall. It was from a woman in the Hardwick prison whose mother travels with us. She expressed her gratitude by writing, "Every month you so kindly and friendly feed my family that comes from Atlanta to visit me. The Thanksgiving dinner with all the trimmings was the only dinner I'm sure my mother had. I want to say 'thank you,' not just for my family, but for all those that are fed at your church each month." (In the letter, she had enclosed a small religious tract with a message about how, many times, people wait for, or expect, others to do certain things, and that sometimes "nobody does anything.") The letter continued: "I send this tract to you because you choose to be a 'do-body' . . . you're a doer of the Word, and I praise God for you."

How grateful we are for these Christian friends in Milledgeville who open their doors to us with such a welcome and in a caring way!

In preparing this article, I realized that the portion of our trip I would find difficult to relate would be the visit that families, or friends, and inmates enjoy together. The meaning of this time, however, is partially reflected in the joy expressed by the mother sharing a picture of her son receiving his diploma; and her pride in his hours spent helping other inmates to read. She writes: "The trip to Hardwick means a great deal to me, for it is a time of fellowship with our loved ones; a time to show them that through it all we care, we're concerned, and we love them." And she encourages us: "Keep on keeping on!"

It is reflected in . . . Murphy recalling the touching scene when, as she and her carload of anxious and excited children approached the place where they would visit their mother, the children suddenly spotted her in the prison yard. No sooner had she stopped her car than the children, in Murphy's words, "hit the ground running . . . calling '*mama, mama!*'"

It is reflected in . . . the slow, heavy steps of a grandmother with slippered feet, who walks laboriously through the gate at the Rivers Building, a grandchild on her left and her right, but with a smile on her face and a faithful spirit in her heart.

It is reflected in . . . the letter we received, which says:

> The Open Door Community Southern Prison Ministry has been and it still is an answer to both me and my family's prayer. My husband has been in Hardwick, Ga., for over three years now, and in those first two years me and my daughters went through so much to get to him. Such as three automobile accidents and approximately ten breakdowns, and that within itself was enough to want to give up. Only I knew I couldn't because Hardwick was and still is holding my other half. Even when I didn't drive I would car-pool with families of other inmates. And that too hasn't been very successful. So I start riding the bus but that didn't work too well either because it only gave me about 45 minutes max to share with him. And if I was a few minutes late I would miss the last bus to Atlanta. I did these things to try to save money, because it is hard to maintain a family, home, and car off a salary barely above minimum wage. One evening on our way back from Hardwick, it was raining very hard and getting dark fast. And I couldn't drive no more than 30 miles per hour, and there were times when I had to pull over because I couldn't see. Anyway while driving Interstate-20 West going 30 or less this young man slid right into me. My car went down into a ditch, but with the help of the good Lord I was able to get it out before it completely stopped. After that night things started going from bad to worse. I lost my job a few days later. And I knew that I couldn't see my husband because it was hard enough getting to him with little money. I felt it was impossible to get to him with no money. But through my husband the Lord showed me different. He wrote and told me that he had heard about this church that helps families of inmates with transportation to Hardwick from Atlanta free and he gave me a

number to find out more about it. So I did, only to find out that our prayer had been answered. And I just want to say thank you Jesus! Thank you Open Door Community and May God Bless Each and Everyone of You.

❖ ❖ ❖

I can vividly recall organizing and planning for my own first trip to Hardwick shortly after I had begun working at the Open Door. Murphy, who had already made numerous trips to Hardwick, and on whom I was relying for initial "orientation," became very ill the day before our scheduled visit and was unable to go. I well remember how Murphy, in spite of her illness, pulled herself up in bed, outlined the trip's procedures, drew maps, gave last-minute tips, and, most of all, encouragement.

On that initial trip I was greeted at the church in Milledgeville by Jane Tipton, who at that time was coordinating the noon meal, and whose husband, Clyde, led us in our blessing as we sang "Amazing Grace." As we joined hand to hand in a wide circle, I thought of the bonds this circle represented—bonds not only between friends, new and old, but within these families, sources of strength and encouragement in difficult circumstances.

I thought of families who would enter the prison buildings, allowed only the required picture identification and no gifts for their loved ones but themselves. I was reminded of God's gift to people everywhere and in all circumstances—the gift of Jesus, who gave freely of himself so that we might all know the eternal gifts of God's forgiveness and love. Such gifts bring healing and restoration to the broken places. Jesus not only joins us in our joys and sufferings, but joins us to his resurrection victory and to the hope and promise of God's amazing grace.

Resurrection Women, *by Murphy Davis*

A P R I L   1 9 9 6

After all these years, it is still amazing that the biblical story tells us that the first witnesses to the resurrection of the Executed One were, by all accounts, women. It was an inauspicious beginning, to say the least.

In first-century Palestine the testimony of a woman was worth nothing: not legally admissible in court and certainly not to be counted on in matters of importance. So Jesus, who loved irony and cherished standing cultural assumptions on their heads, chose the women to bear the news.

They were, after all, according to the Gospel stories, his most faithful friends. They were the ones who did not flee. They were able to hear the constant admonition, "Do not be afraid." They were the last at the cross, the first at the tomb. They continued, through it all, to do what needed to be done: to care for his physical needs, to listen with careful attention to all he said, to recognize him when everyone else was confused, to act out (as the menfolk stood baffled) what Jesus taught of discipleship. These women, especially according to Mark's Gospel, were examples of true apostolic leadership.

In these women, legally and socially unreliable, Jesus placed his trust, and to them he revealed the amazing truth of his triumph over death. They were charged, as witnesses to this truth, with the privilege and task of running to bear the news. And thus they became the first preachers of the gospel.

It would seem that our social, political, and legal context is much changed. And yes, in a technical sense, it is. It has been some decades since a woman's legal testimony was inadmissible in court. The more intransigent problem is that our society, like most societies in the modern world, continues to balk at accepting the truth of women's lives. Technically, what women say is accepted. But in a deeper sense, what women tell of life experience is simply unacceptable. For one cannot hear the truth of women's experience (or the experience of any oppressed group) without also looking at a system of domination. In any such system, the experience of the dominated will include stories of the violence which functions socially and politically to enforce the domination. The truth of women's experience necessarily includes the reality of rape, physical and sexual abuse, incest, and other forms of physical and emotional violence. This does not mean that every woman has experienced physical abuse. But every woman in a sexist society is subject to a threatened violence that enforces and reinforces the institutions and interweaving systems of gender domination. The more deeply one's identity as a woman is caught in the meshing systems of race and class oppression, the more likely is the experience of violent domination. In other words, sexism in its harshest form is understood in the experience of poor women of color: poor women who are also Black, Hispanic, or Native American.

I believe that to understand the nature and function of oppression in our (or any) society, we must look at the lives and hear the experience of those in prison. Inside the walls and systems of prisons we practice our social and political biases in their most basic and brutal forms. In a racist society, racism inside prison walls is simple, straightforward, and violent. In a classist society, the poor fill our prisons because their behavior is more likely in the first place to be labeled criminal, and they are less likely to be able to defend themselves against such charges. The poor do the time.

In a sexist society, gender domination in prison is stark. Because the assumptions of sexism are based on devaluing the lives and experience of women, women in prison live under an ongoing threat of danger and exploitation at the hands of their keepers. Rape and sexual exploitation are basic tools. As common as prison rape is, it is tolerated and at points even condoned because it functions to enforce the values of the social and political system. If we take prison rape too seriously we would have to raise basic questions about the entire system. This becomes so complicated that we find it more efficient to maintain a blind eye and a deaf ear.

That blind eye and deaf ear were maintained for many years at the Georgia state women's prison (called the "Georgia Correctional Institution"). Guards and other prison staff regularly practiced sexual and physical abuse against many women in the prison at Hardwick. While, in many cases, the women made reports, nothing was done to remove the staff offenders or to stop their abuse. Finally, in 1992, nearly two hundred women came forward to tell their stories of the exploitation, abuse, and even torture they suffered behind the prison walls. Some fifty staff members were implicated. Of those, fifteen were indicted and a few others quit or were demoted, fired, suspended, or transferred. Only one lieutenant actually came to trial, with more than twenty women ready to testify to his abuse.

The trial took place in Baldwin County, Georgia—a county whose political and economic base sits squarely on the enormous state prison system. How could these women hope that a jury of this guard's peers, dependent on the same system that supported him, would hear their stories with an unbiased ear? In addition, the women were poor and had been convicted and condemned for criminal behavior. In a justice system composed of and controlled by good ol' boys, the women's testimony was discredited because they were "Bad Poor Women." While the lieutenant lost his job, he was acquitted of any wrongdoing or criminal behavior. The prison staff members who had offered to corroborate the testimony of the prisoners were never called.

This guard was, has been, and is a violent and abusive man. Everybody knew it; everybody knows it. But our system winks at such truths because we know with perfect clarity that we're not going to mess with the system. The lieutenant is a necessary cog: one of the "almost poor" put and kept in place to hold down the "really poor." He is a man of color allowed to do what he did to secure the system of gender power. Yes, he had power, but it was beans in comparison to the white guys at the top of the heap: those never formally accused in court or reprimanded in their professional capacity; those who were able to hear the stories, yawn, and go about their business.

But the hope of the resurrection gives the oppressed the courage to fight for their liberation, and I have seen that courage with my own eyes. Resurrection is practiced any time and in any place that oppressed people stand up and stand together to tell the unedited truth of their lives. I have been a privileged witness in accompanying some of the women in the Georgia prison system over months and years as this massive sexual and mental health abuse and exploitation has been revealed as routine. The truth of resurrection is that, for however brief a time, women came together to tell the truth of their lives. One by one, they stood and spoke it, told it, in all its raw ugliness and with all the unimaginable pain. As they did this, they stood together, backing each other because they knew what they said was the truth, comforting each other because giving birth to these ugly truths in the public eye was more than excruciating, and hoping against everything they had known as fact in their bitter and almost hopeless, barren lives. They hoped that their truth might be believed, and the structures of their suffering addressed and mitigated.

To call the legal action a gamble is almost laughable since the stakes in this game were so high, and the chance for real redress almost nil. Probably most of them knew it. Who among them had ever savored the sweet taste of victory? Indeed, while some of the worst offenders were removed, the system based on exploitation and degradation has changed very little. The case in federal court continues, but these are not good days to be seeking justice, humane treatment, and simple human decency for people in prison.

A bittersweet truth about resurrection is that we are rarely given the privilege, or luxury, of sitting in front of the empty tomb to bask in the glorious light of the Risen One. "Run," says the angel. "Run and tell it! Run with all your might, powered by the glorious truth of the vision! Run with the exuberance and joy of your grief suddenly and unexpectedly healed! Run, carrying this unbelievable news! Run, knowing that nothing else in the world matters anymore! This truth is the Truth that will overshadow everything else and set the course for all of life! Run!"

But that angel didn't say, "When you get there, they won't believe you. When you tell them, they will laugh. When you testify to the Great Truth, they will belittle you and your Truth. They will call it 'an idle tale.' Or maybe they will just be too busy to hear you." Maybe later, somebody else, an "almost unreliable witness," will run to the tomb to check it out. You can be sure of this, though: even if the truth is eventually accepted, it will have lost some of its power because, again and again, the full story will have been forgotten and neglected. The truth brokers will build a power base and co-opt the story to meet the needs of one more system of wealth and privilege.

Often, however, the story of resurrection is lost entirely. Fault with the story's bearers is easily found and documented, and the substance of the claim disproven. "Just a story," we mumble, and toss it into the circular file. What did she say? What did she say? Oh, nothing. She's crazy.

Like the resurrection to life and liberation, to solidarity and human dignity, that the women in prison sought and fought for (and though much has been lost, the struggle continues), so the story of the Liberator's resurrection was told by women and discredited. It is amazing that four remarkable accounts got through, containing almost more detail than we can tolerate. The story of resurrection doesn't usually survive. We rarely tell it, and we rarely hear it. We don't like to be laughed at or easily dismissed. We do not fancy being pushed aside as the lunatic fringe.

How amazing God's grace is, then, that resurrection happens again and again to remind us of the hope we have for life and liberation. I know it's true. I've been privileged to see it, and I want to run with all my might to tell you.

Hating Our Children: The Execution of Chris Burger as Metaphor, *by Murphy Davis*

JULY 1994

Though she was an experienced teacher, it was her first month of teaching in a new middle school. When I saw her, I asked how it was going. Well, there was lots to get used to and all. Then she spoke of the adolescent boys who were causing discipline problems in some of her classes. She sighed wearily: "I guess building more prisons is about the only thing we can do. Don't you agree?"

I tried, I really, really tried to keep my mouth from falling completely open or from fainting dead in the driveway in front of the school. Finally I caught my breath and controlled my voice enough to say, in a carefully measured tone, "No, I really don't agree. I think it would be a much better idea to pay you a decent wage, limit your class size to fifteen, and buy books and materials for the school library." This time it was her mouth that flew open. "Well, my goodness," she exclaimed, "I'd never thought of that."

And maybe that is the problem. We're not thinking. The hack politicians fill our ears with garbage about how punitive we need to be, and we don't think. We go along. And our children are going down the tubes.

Nobody short of Ebenezer Scrooge would come out and admit to hating children. It doesn't take much to make even the hard-hearted misty-eyed with stories of sick, injured, neglected, or violated, suffering children. Most of us think of ourselves as people who love children. But at the same time we get excited about stories of individual children and what we might do to help, we are actively, or at least by our silence, participating in the creation of public policy that is nothing short of hateful toward children.

On December 7, 1993, Christopher Burger was executed by electrocution by the state of Georgia. I first met Chris in 1980 or 1981, within the first couple of years of his having been sentenced to die. Chris was seventeen at the time of the crime that landed him on death row, and when I first met him he was a skinny, frightened kid trying to figure out how to grow up. I saw him off and on over the next thirteen or fourteen years, and, indeed, watched him grow up.

What I learned of Chris's life was a horror story. Severe abuse, neglect, abandonment, cruel and capricious punishment, and having been moved from place to place, family member to family member, left him a shaken, confused, disoriented child. Finally he joined the Army to try to find a direction. What he found was more chaos, drugs, and an endless amount of trouble. He was taught more of the ways of violence; he was trained to fight and kill his enemies. The downward spiral of chaos and violence resulted in a tragic death at the bottom of a muddy pond for a young man named Roger Honeycutt, and jail and a sentence of death for young Chris. His life had never really started when the state of Georgia declared it to be over.

Over the next fifteen years, it would be safe to say that the state of Georgia spent some three million to five million dollars disposing of Chris Burger. Through his early childhood of abuse and neglect, there were never any resources. But when he finally stepped over the line, the most enormous resources imaginable were marshaled to get rid of him.

It is an adequate metaphor, I'm afraid, for how we are dealing with our children. We are bombarded on a regular basis with the dreary facts: America's children are in trouble, and in Georgia what we see is an exaggeration of a national norm. Georgia's children are the poorest and sickest in the nation. They go to schools that are consistently rated at the bottom. They are more likely to die at birth or in the first year of life than children in El Salvador. Those in Atlanta are more likely to be exposed to or victimized by violence than children in any other city in the country. And, to solve our problems, we lock up everybody—women, men, and children—at one of the highest rates in the world.

We have heard and tolerated a language of hatred and alienation for so long that we have begun to believe that we are powerless to call on the forces of goodness and kindness. We are afraid of our children, and our minds, spirits, and imaginations have been paralyzed by the fear.

Common sense might tell us that hungry children need to be fed, sick children need to be cared for, homeless children need to be housed, and troubled children need a helping hand. Instead, we participate in and tolerate public discourse that says homeless people "choose a homeless lifestyle"; that there really is no health care crisis; that thirteen-year-old children should be tried as adults and put into adult prisons; and that troubled youths will be "scared straight" by putting them into boot camps where adults will scream and humiliate them into submission by barking orders morning, noon, and night. Finally, if the kids are just too bad, we can electrocute, gas, lethally inject, shoot, or hang them. Since

1973, 125 seventeen-year-olds have been sentenced to death in the United States. Nine of them have been executed. Our lawmakers and courts want more.

When we talk about our biological children, we can be so clear about what we want for them: a good home, a safe environment, a lively faith in the God of love and in the dignity of the human spirit, decent schools, trusted adults and stable peers for their friends, a passion for justice, access to art, music, recreation, enough to eat, adequate health care. . . . Why do we not want these things for all of our children? Is there not some way to think of all children in our town or city, for instance, as "our" children? My children will grow up and be adults in the same world as your children; shouldn't it matter to me what kind of person your child is growing up to become? Shouldn't it matter to me that they be nurtured now to learn to live together in peace and with justice? An African proverb tells us, "It takes a whole village to raise a child." Surely it takes all of us working together to build a society that will nurture all of our children.

We need to pay close attention to the execution of Chris Burger, because this expression of public policy says more than our pious language about what we are willing to do with our children. When they become a problem, we want to sweep them under the rug, to flush them, to lock 'em up and throw away the key—to kill them.

It is typical of the way we have settled for back-end solutions. Instead of doing things that make sense in taking care of children from conception to adulthood, we leave them on their own and wait until critical problems emerge. Then we use the most expensive responses because we didn't do what needed to be done at the beginning. Rather than universal prenatal care, we continue to spend hundreds of thousands of dollars on treating premature, critically ill, and low-birth-weight babies. Instead of intervening to rescue children who are being abused and neglected today, we wait until they become antisocial and violent and spend tremendous resources on imprisonment or execution.

What if some of the millions of dollars spent on killing Chris Burger had been available to Roger Honeycutt's family? (Most crime victim's families are poor and desperately need economic help to deal with their crises.) What if some portion of those resources had been allocated to intervene on behalf of the Chris Burgers who are today being abused and hurt and who, tomorrow, might strike out in violence and confusion?

In Finland last fall, a court fined a man one hundred dollars for pulling his stepchild's hair. In this country, children are beaten, raped, and killed in large numbers, and we seem to be unable to respond. And as much as we know about the suffering, we continue to tolerate the lies, racism, sexism, and class divisiveness that have become trademarks of our political discourse. It is nothing less than tragic. When racism or any rhetoric or policy of hatred is allowed to go on, everyone is hurt, but children suffer first and most severely. Why are we not insulted? Why are we not raising the roof about the destruction of our children and the world they will inherit?

Jesus said, "Suffer the children to come unto me, for of such are the reign of heaven." We will participate in the reign of God only when we can begin to think of all the children as ours.

Becoming Blind Beggars, *by Murphy Davis*

A U G U S T   1 9 8 9

> *They came to Jericho, and as Jesus was leaving with his disciples and a large crowd, a blind beggar named Bartimaeus son of Timaeus was sitting by the road. When he heard that it was Jesus of Nazareth, he began to shout, "Jesus! Son of David! Have mercy on me!"*
>
> *Many of the people scolded him and told him to be quiet. But he shouted even more loudly, "Son of David, have mercy on me!"*
>
> *Jesus stopped and said, "Call him."*
>
> *So they called the blind man. "Cheer up!" they said. "Get up, he is calling you."*
>
> *So he threw off his cloak, jumped up, and came to Jesus. "What do you want me to do for you?" Jesus asked him.*
>
> *"Teacher," the blind man answered, "I want to see again."*
>
> *"Go," Jesus told him, "your faith has made you well."*
>
> *At once he was able to see and followed Jesus on the road.*
>
> —Mark 10:46–52

I'd like to tell you about a man named Roosevelt Green—a convicted murderer and my good friend—who died in Georgia's electric chair on January 9, 1985. Roosevelt was one of the Blind Bartimaeuses in my life, and when he was killed by his captors, he was probably one of the most self-aware, politically astute human beings I have ever known.

At ten minutes after midnight on that cold winter's night, he walked calmly into the execution chamber and made the following statement: "The night I was arrested and taken into the Monroe County Jail, one of the jailers said to me, 'Boy, the lives of two niggers still ain't enough to make up for one white life.'

"I didn't believe him on that night," said Roosevelt. "I thought he was wrong. Tonight I know he was right. He spoke for this society, which is racist from top to bottom. I will die before you tonight because I am Black—and because I was associated with another Black man who killed a white woman. But my life will not be enough to satisfy you. You will kill me and still be hungry for revenge.

"The one thing you cannot do is to make me hate you. I will not hate you even though you kill me. I forgive you, for you are blind. I will die with peace in my heart."

It was not always so with Roosevelt. He was born in Minter, Alabama, and grew up expecting nothing but stoop labor in the cotton fields or driving pulpwood: life was brutal and violent. Even what little seemed his due was stolen by the greed and racism of Alabama plantation life. So ending up on death row was not such an illogical twist for Roosevelt Green.

When I first knew him he was bursting with rage and bitterness (and I would say it was not without some justification). He was a sitting duck for white guards who could taunt him and watch him run wild, and so it became a cell-block sport. His life became an endless round of fights, weeks in the hole, attacks, beatings, mace, stun guns. Many were the visits when he came out in leg irons and waist chains and his hands cuffed behind his back. At other times he was not allowed to come out at all.

But Roosevelt was not still. He formed deep and lasting friendships with a number of people in the free world (or as another friend on the row often said, "out there in minimum security"). And he nurtured a profound and beautiful friendship with a strong, bright man named Billy Mitchell, who has since also been executed.

Together with his friends, Roosevelt sought the life of mercy. He and Billy would for hours on end meditate and contemplate life and then write to friends on the outside—and contemplate again.

I shall never forget the day that Roosevelt said to me, "You see, I've got it figured out now. One of the ways this system keeps itself going is by depending on me to respond in certain violent ways. So you know what I can do? I can *not* respond."

What a moment of healing and liberation! Amazing grace!

Somehow this man managed to take a step back, to observe his own broken life, to confess his sin, and then to freely choose another way to live.

Now Roosevelt was not an angel, and maybe his life wasn't exactly straightened out. But he was breaking a cycle of violence, bitterness, and mercilessness by refusing to hold up his end of the process any longer. He was being healed by God's patient and loving mercy.

The state of Georgia told us they executed a monster that night—a subhuman. The Klan gathered outside the prison in full regalia, screaming, "Kill the nigger!" A bar in Macon threw a Roosevelt Green party with free drinks at the time of death and happy hour thereafter.

The truth is that they killed a human being: a child of God, a seeker of mercy, who had found real healing and new life because he had learned that the anguished cry for mercy is the beginning of new life. He had gained new depths of hope for the human family in spite of his own cruel death. There was no happy ending to this story, but we celebrate new life and good news where we find it.

Roosevelt was one of the blind beggars who have taught me the journey of faith. Blind, begging Bartimaeus was, like Roosevelt Green and like most of the people who hung around with Jesus, an outcast. A beggar with no pride, no claim to dignity, because he was dependent on the mercy, the alms of others.

Perhaps it was because he had so little to lose that he so rudely pursued our Lord. "Son of David!" he shrieked. "Have mercy on me!" It was an embarrassment. There was a big crowd, and Jesus was in demand and very busy. And so, Mark tells us, the people scolded Bartimaeus and told him to be quiet (be polite!).

But his rudeness was irrepressible, and he shouted even more loudly, "Have mercy on me!"

And Jesus heard that cry. Jesus, of course, listened to that cry. It would not surprise you to know, too, that Jesus responded to that cry with mercy, with healing love. "Oh, you want to see? You cry out, in scorn of the consequences, for mercy? Brother, you are healed because your faith has made you well." Jesus didn't say that he would make Bartimaeus well, but rather the faith that had led Bartimaeus to cry out so persistently for mercy—that faith is what healed him. Bartimaeus saw, and Bartimaeus followed Jesus.

The cry of the poor—the cry of the blind beggars—is always strident, always rude, always at an inopportune moment. It is never convenient, never appropriate to the standards of etiquette.

But it is to the shameless beggars that Jesus says, "Your faith has made you well." You, shrieking from the side of the road; you, bleeding, unclean woman sneaking up on me in the crowds; you, hookers and tramps, criminal tax collectors, and smelly fisherfolk; you, demon-possessed women and lepers with decayed flesh, and sick and dying children; you who cry out for mercy: your faith has made you well.

We who follow Jesus in the crowd are mandated to hear this cry. For in the cry for mercy of the blind beggars we hear the cry of the Suffering Vagrant, Jesus the Christ.

In the cry for mercy of the condemned we come to know the suffering of Jesus, who was condemned and executed as a common criminal. In the cry for mercy of the broken victims, the forgotten ones, we meditate on the suffering of the Christ as one scorned and misunderstood, known as an undesirable, run out of town, threatened, and pursued. In the cry of the poor we hear a prophetic word that calls us to change: to give up our selfishness and greed; to give up our righteous front; to learn our own deep need for the ever-flowing mercy of a loving God. That word calls us to give up our Pharisaical prayer, "I thank you God that I am not like them," and to turn toward the real prayer of the humble tax collector, "O God, have mercy on me, a sinner."

And so we must listen and learn; we must be taught to plead for mercy. For the only way to come to God is as a beggar, which is why God comes to us as a beggar to show us the way. We are blind, but most of us don't know it. We are in need, but we consume at a frantic pace to try to cover it up. We know that Jesus walks with a bad crowd, and we're embarrassed to be seen with him.

But those who have no need of mercy, find no need to share mercy. Those who have no awareness of their own blindness do not cry, "I want to see again." Those who live comfortably and in security need not ever beg for daily bread or relief from oppression. Those who are never condemned and who live carefully enough to avoid criticism know nothing of the agonizing ache among those for whom mercy means life over death.

To follow Jesus we must listen for the cry of the poor, the blind beggars. But for an upper-class church to hear the cry of the poor requires discipline. The poor in our day are not, like Lazarus at the door of Dives, right under our noses. The poor are, by specific design, out of our sight and hearing. And evidenced by the new Underground Atlanta and downtown Atlanta's status as a vagrant-free zone, the hope is that you will not have to see, hear, touch, smell, or otherwise encounter anyone you wouldn't run into in the most antiseptic suburban mall. Anyone perceived to be a derelict in Underground is arrested and charged with criminal trespass. And though "the fun's back in town," the fun is not for everybody when some have to live from hour to hour struggling with the real issues of survival: food, shelter, and safe passage.

Begging, of course, is illegal in the city of Atlanta. It's called panhandling. And if you go to municipal court on Decatur Street on Monday morning you will see people going to jail for doing what Bartimaeus did. In our city, Bartimaeus would have been arrested before he could have gotten a hearing from Jesus.

But if we hear the Blind Bartimaeuses, we know that when we cry out to God, "Have mercy on me," our lives are transformed. When we live dependent on God's mercy, then our hearts can be set on God's amazing grace. When we live dependent on God's mercy, then planted in our hearts can be the fervent hope, the daily struggle for the day that justice will roll down like waters and righteousness like a river that never runs dry.

And Jesus will gather the blind beggars, the bleeding women, the halt, the lame, the leper, the lost, and the least and say to them, "Come unto me; your faith has made you well."

Innocent and on Death Row, *by Murphy Davis*

A U G U S T   1 9 9 2

Judge Lamar was a brilliant and highly respected judge in Milledgeville, Georgia, in the early nineteenth century and the father of U.S. Supreme Court Justice Lucius Quintus Cincinnatus Lamar. When a Methodist minister was charged before him with the rape-murder of the minister's sister-in-law, Judge Lamar sentenced him to hang. The man was duly executed. Some years later, Judge Lamar received the news that a man hanged in Mississippi for another crime had just confessed from the gallows to the murder for which the minister had been executed. The devastated judge locked his office, walked to his home, kissed his wife and children (including L. Q. C. Lamar, who was then a young child), and put a bullet through his head.

Murder is tragedy. Execution deepens the tragedy. Execution of the innocent simply boggles the mind. We would like to think it doesn't happen. Many who advocate the death penalty concede that the execution of the innocent is/would be repugnant, but surely our modern system of jurisprudence rules out the possibility. Wrong. We are still human, and as *Sesame Street* teaches us (in something of an updated, secularized version of Calvin's doctrine of total depravity), "Everybody makes mistakes." Everybody and every system.

Marquis de Lafayette, hero of the American and French Revolutions, said in 1830, "Til the infallibility of human judgements shall have been proved to me, I shall demand the abolition of the death penalty." Capital punishment was abolished in Great Britain in the 1960s; the decision was greatly influenced by the execution of Timothy Evans, who was widely believed to be innocent. A study in 1986 by Hugo Bedau and Michael Radelet produced evidence of 349 cases in the United States in which people were wrongly convicted of offenses punishable by death. Of these, twenty-three prisoners were executed.

In Georgia between 1978 and 1987, Earl Charles, Jerry Banks, and Henry Drake, after years on death row, all walked out of prison with convincing evidence that each had been wrongly convicted. Under Georgia law, a person charged with a capital felony is entitled to a lawyer only for trial and one perfunctory appeal. After that time, the prisoner is dependent on volunteer counsel. Charles, Banks, and Drake were all fortunate enough to find competent, committed attorneys who worked for free and who paid expenses out of their own pockets for long years. In each case, these volunteer attorneys were ridiculed by members of the court system and, at times, they even received threats to their own and their families' personal safety.

In November 1991, Gary X. Nelson walked out of the Chatham County Jail in Savannah, Georgia, a free man. Gary spent thirteen years on Georgia's death row for a crime he did not commit. His case is yet another reminder of how easily a mistake can be made and how hard it is to undo a mistake after the fact. Gary was arrested in Savannah in 1978 for the rape and murder of six-year-old Valerie Armstrong. As he entered the Chatham County Jail, he passed Earl Charles in the hall. Earl, another young African American man from Savannah, was being released that day after three and a half years under death sentence for a crime he did not commit. Out went Earl; in came Gary. Almost two years later, Gary stood trial for the murder. His attorney, appointed by the court, was, to put it mildly, incompetent. He did not want to defend Gary and did it poorly. After the jury convicted Gary and the time came for them to sentence him to life or death, the attorney offered an eight-sentence argument in which he explained that a life sentence was worse than death because Gary would have to live with the memory of Valerie Armstrong. The jury voted for death. In 1984, the attorney was disbarred. Gary stayed on death row. We know now that during Gary Nelson's trial the prosecution concealed evidence that could have proven his innocence, and two police officers and a Georgia Bureau of Investigations microanalyst lied in their testimony.

In 1981, Emmet Bondurant, one of Atlanta's prominent criminal attorneys, volunteered to take Gary's case pro bono. Bondurant, Edward Krugman, Suzanne Forbis, and James Kimmel, along with other staff of the Bondurant, Mixon, and Elmore law firm, soon were convinced of his innocence. It took them ten years to prove it to the satisfaction of the court. Over that period, Bondurant's firm spent four hundred thousand to five hundred thousand dollars on expenses (transcripts, expert witnesses, travel, etc.) and legal time. Gary X. Nelson is alive and well. He has a job and an apartment and lives now (as he did in prison) a quiet, disciplined life. He is a Muslim and centers his life in his faith. He enjoys visits with his family but is well aware that much has changed since he went to jail thirteen years ago. Who can count the cost of endless years on death row with the constant threat of death by electrocution? What does that experience take away from a human being that can never be repaid? For years Gary's legal identity was *The People v. Gary X. Nelson*. What can we "the People" say now? "We're sorry! It was just an honest mistake!" What can we give Gary X. Nelson to repay our crime against him?

In ancient Israel, the law said that if anyone lied against a criminal defendant in court that person would then receive the penalty reserved for the crime. Should we then consider executing former District Attorney Andrew ("Bubsey") Ryan? the two Savannah police officers? the GBI microanalyst? And what about the victim—Valerie Armstrong? Is it not reasonable to assume that if the Savannah and Chatham County law-enforcement authorities sought the conviction of Gary Nelson, knowing he was not the murderer, they made an implicit decision not to investigate who had murdered this child? In other words, to send Gary Nelson to death row was to say, "We care more about appearing to have gotten somebody than we do about stopping the murderer of Valerie Armstrong."

Gary Nelson got off death row. But the odds were more than likely that he would have been executed. How often does a private lawyer with the skills and commitment of an Emmet Bondurant volunteer to take a "hopeless" death-penalty case? How many lawyers and law firms have half a million dollars' worth of time that they are willing to give for an indigent African American man condemned to die?

The death penalty raises hundreds of moral, ethical, practical, and religious problems. It is part of a criminal-control system that is leading us farther away from, rather than toward, a safe and just society.

I met a post-office employee in 1977 who looked hard at the button on my jacket ("Why Do We Kill People Who Kill People to Show That Killing People Is Wrong?"). He said, "I only have one reason to oppose the death penalty." He went on to tell me of a man in the small Georgia town where he had grown up who was wrongly convicted and sentenced to die. The prisoner was later exonerated and, like Gary X. Nelson, released. "But the risk of making a mistake like that," said the man behind the counter, "is too much of a risk to take." The man in the post office was right. Everybody makes mistakes. When the life of a human being is at stake, it's too much of a risk.

What about the Victims? *by Murphy Davis*

OCTOBER 1988

"But what about the victims?!" is a question that comes often to those of us who oppose the death penalty. The tone of the question varies, but whether searching or hostile in tone, the question has always grieved me because of the implied assumption that to oppose further violence is to be against those hurt by crime and violence.

This is a very personal issue for us at the Open Door. Our life makes it impossible to cut sharp lines between the victims and perpetrators of crime. We live every day with those who suffer because of violent crime and those who suffer because of the violent punishment of crime. The pressing question, it seems to me, is how can we live in a way that brings healing to the broken victims and that creates fewer victims?

Jay Frazier remembers painfully the 1975 murder of his brother Lenny. He continues to grieve as well for his cousin Ron, who spent seven years on death row and who now serves a life sentence for the murder. "It was a bad thing," says Jay. "But killing Ron—or even hating him—wouldn't bring my brother back."

Al Smith, a member of our family for two years, was murdered at Samaritan House downtown. Jesse Goodwin ("Goatman"), who ate breakfast with us nearly every morning, was beaten to death in a used-car lot on Edgewood Avenue. Our friend Greg Jordan was doused with gasoline and burned to death behind a labor pool on Ponce de Leon. Ed corresponds regularly with Greg's murderer. A dear friend and soup-kitchen volunteer struggles daily with the horrible memory of her daughter's brutal murder in Florida. And just this month, Mary Frances, a regular in our soup kitchen, was murdered in an alleyway, her body mutilated. Often we are sad witnesses to the aftermath of assaults, beatings, rape, and robbery on the streets. Our homeless friends—women and men, young and old—are very vulnerable and often victimized. Surely we are capable of building a society that is not so violent—one that does not create so many victims. Yes, we ask, what about the victims?

But when caring for the victims makes us bitter, hard, and filled with revenge, something is wrong. We need to learn to distinguish between a normal emotional response to being a victim and the posture that we take as a body politic. Anyone who has been victimized or who has spent time talking with victims of violent crime knows that revenge is a very natural response in the grief process: "Oh, what I would do if I could get my hands on him/her!" On the other hand, any pastor, counselor, or psychologist knows that the victim, to find healing and become a survivor, needs to step beyond a fixation on revenge. In one way or another, each person must make peace with what has happened, pick up the pieces of life, and go on. No one can dictate for another person how or when this happens—it sometimes takes a very long time. But experience confirms the biblical understanding of a connection between forgiveness and health. Revenge eventually devours us, destroys relationships, and turns our hearts to stone.

I have, on occasion, heard prosecutors say to juries, "If you care at all about the family and friends of this murder victim, you will send the murderer straight to the electric chair." Cruelty is the only word to describe it. It is not only cruel to the one accused of murder. But if there is anything a crime victim does not need, it is someone encouraging them to make their vengeful feelings a virtue for public display or a weapon to destroy someone else.

When John Eldon Smith was executed in 1983, the Aikens family—brothers of the murder victim—was constantly dragged into the public eye. Their hatred for Smith and their desire for his death seemed to make the TV cameras whir. On the morning of the execution, the media set up in the living room of the home of one brother. Every move and sound was recorded as the family watched reports of the execution on television, right through the gleeful clapping when death was announced. But the minute the execution was done, the media circus was over. How much the Aikens hated Smith was no longer hot news. The TV cameras folded, and the Aikens were left alone. Their brother and sister-in-law were still dead, but the case was no longer newsworthy. Who cares now?

Do we really need to use people this way to satisfy our corporate fascination with violence? Or could we learn how to care for the victims' pain day by day and to reach out to them with healing love? Victims of violent crime do, in fact, need to know that the one who hurt them has been found and restrained; they need an assurance that he or she cannot cause further harm. We dare not ignore this need. Victims most often need economic help—especially if a breadwinner has been killed or disabled. Counseling, time off work, medical or funeral expenses are all needs that often go unaddressed even while the revenge rhetoric fills the air. But no one—individually or corporately—should encourage a victim to believe that the pain will be lessened or the grief assuaged by seeking revenge or further violence. Vindictive responses most often widen the circle of tragedy, creating more victims and exacerbating every wound.

What about victims who will not seek revenge? Sometimes the system does not treat them so kindly. Angie Anderson's eighty-six-year-old mother was murdered in her St. Petersburg, Florida, home in 1984. Her plea to the prosecutor, to avoid seeking the death penalty for the young man convicted of the crime, was ignored. When Anderson pleaded with the jury not to compound her own grief by imposing a death sentence, the prosecutor stated mockingly in open court, "She obviously did not love her mother." When Frank Patton's wife, Becky, was murdered in San Antonio, Texas, he refused the expected thirst for revenge. His pastor, Louis Zbinden, said, "It may be difficult for the cynics of the world to understand, but Frank is a Christian. He understands that if he allows himself to become obsessed by hatred for these men, then it will only lead to bitterness in himself." Patton did not want his wife's murderers to go free: he wanted them behind bars. "It's just that he held to an idea that was temporarily out of fashion—that violence can't be stopped with more violence," Zbinden said. The prosecutor didn't care. Seeing it as a textbook death-penalty case, he vowed to do everything in his power to see the murderers executed.

Is our law-enforcement system able to "care" more readily for victims filled with revenge than those who seek a less violent way? Whose interests are being served? Dan Van Ness authored *Crime and Its Victims: What We Can Do* from his own experience as a lawyer, as a victim, and as a Christian. He locates the root of our problem with justice in our legal definition of who is the victim. In contrast to our predecessors, who understood that the individuals and groups were the victims, today we identify the state as the victim. The disregard for the needs of victims is no accident, then, since they are not part of the legal understanding of crime; legally, the individuals harmed are not the real "victims."

It would make sense, then, that the state would cooperate with the desires of victims only when those desires are in line with the perceptions of the prosecutors and other decision makers. Frankly, the "needs" of victims are sometimes confused with the political interests of district attorneys. Revenge is a popular emotion these days and can often be used by those who present themselves as "tough on crime." It's worth noting that more death sentences are sought in the months preceding elections than at any other time.

Such a political charade has nothing to do with caring for victims. Marie Deans, whose mother-in-law was murdered, has said: "The violence of murder is abhorrent, but the long sequence of trials and appeals that ultimately lead to another killing is not a solution but a process of carrying on violence. And while it goes on, the family lives a day-to-day existence focused on the death of their loved one. It is as if the body was being kept in the front parlor, preserved and waiting to be buried. The catharsis of mourning is delayed while the tension and pain continue to build. It is no wonder that the loved ones believe only the death of the murderer will release them from their living nightmare."

Finally, clarity about the racial and class implications of how we speak of victims is crucial. Which victims do we care about? Those most often victimized by crime—by property crime and violent crime—are those most victimized by everything else: the poor and minorities. Victims of crime are more often men than women, more often poor than middle and upper class, more often unemployed than employed, more often urban than rural, more often young black men than anyone else. The most harshly punished are those who have harmed a "valued" member of society. Even the U.S. Supreme Court has not disputed the clear evidence that we more often give death sentences to those who kill white people—especially if the accused is Black.

And what about the alarming growth in the numbers of women and children who are the victims of violence? Let's keep it straight. Random violence is, indeed, a serious problem. But as my friend Marie Fortune points out, the most dangerous place for a woman to be is in a relationship with a man. The most violent place for an American child to be is in a home. The greatest violence in our society is at the center of our life—in our homes, our families, among our friends, lovers, and acquaintances. This indicates a deep sickness that will not heal with one more cheap political trick or another round of divisive rhetoric.

"What about the victims?" has at times become a code phrase to evoke racial and class fears in a great huff of righteous indignation. The question becomes a whip, not so much a search for an answer as a signal for a response. (We know who's out to get us!) Such hysteria drove the violent institution of lynching (primarily in the Deep South), which for decades brought terror and violent death to the Black community in the name of "protecting" southern white women. Finally, black and white churchwomen banded as the Association of

Southern Women for the Prevention of Lynching, and the white women, those seen as the victims, sounded the cry, "Not in our name!"

When the moral tone is set by political opportunists, the language of love and reconciliation sounds silly. It is always easier and more popular to have a quick fix and to settle for revenge and fear. But this does not help us become more compassionate and helpful to the wounded. If we're going to care for victims we must live with contradictions. In spite of a natural flow of feelings, "getting even" will never heal anybody.

Neither will we have a less violent society until we can genuinely confront and change the structures of race, gender, and class that are crushing life and hope from all. Such change will happen with the growth of the Beloved Community, not by piling up more vindictive legislation and building more prisons.

What is crime? And who is hurt by it? Why are we such a violent society? And what does it take to become less violent? Why are we so afraid? And what about the victims?!

God of the Undeserving, *by Ed Loring*

J U N E   1 9 9 0

Today, Larry Lonchar sits on Death Row.
He does not want to live. He wants to die.
The state says he deserves to die.

Larry has committed three terrible, terrible murders.
Mr. Lonchar wants to believe in God but cannot.
He cannot say, "I believe. Help Thou my unbelief."
His heart and mind are tortured by unbelief,
By the fear of nothingness,
By the hell of death by electrocution.

Perhaps by the standards of justice here in the asphalt wilderness and red-clay molehills of Georgia, Larry Lonchar deserves to die.

Many even render the scriptures—the Holy Bible—as a support for death by electrocution. "An eye for an eye and a tooth for a tooth," they say.

Yes, many folk in this state and more and more folk in this country are calling for death as a means to life,

are calling for violence as a way to peace,
are calling for racial superiority as a route to brotherhood
  and sisterhood,
are calling for prisons and jails as the journey to freedom and
  security.

So maybe Larry Lonchar does, on the basis of laws of the state of Georgia and the will of the people, deserve to die.

But, I come to you today, in the name of the one who created the heavens and the earth, who took the raging waters and the terrifying winds, who stood on the edge of chaos and the abyss, who walked through the valley of the shadow of death—and feared no evil—who was before the sun was in the sky by day and before the moon was in the sky by night. This God said,

"Let there be light."
And there was light.

Mighty mountains rose up on the flat plains.
Rivers jumped into their channels.
Angels began to sing on high.

And this God, I'm talking about the Great God Almighty—
Jehovah—
Yahweh—

This, our Creator and Redeemer, filled the land with love, drenched the waters with mercies, filled our bodies and spirits with the image of God.

And then said, "I come on behalf of those who are undeserving."

The government may help the deserving poor, the model prisoner, the "A+" student; but the church stands with the undeserving poor.

The business community may help those who have potential to achieve; but the Body of Christ bends over the Body of the Broken Ones lying in the ditch, passed out in the gutter.

The greatest heresy of today is the false platitude mouthed over and over and over again in this city and often in the church:

God Helps Those Who Help Themselves.

NO!

God helps those who cannot, and even will not help themselves,
The undeserving,
The murderer,
The homeless and the stranger within the gates,
The aged and the widow and widower,
The children and the orphan and fatherless,
The drug addict,
White folk!!!

"I came not to call the righteous, but the lost;
Those who are well have no need of a physician, but those who are
sick," says Jesus our Shepherd.

It is we who call on the name of the Lord in our helplessness.
Then God hears and responds.

When is prayer real in our lives?
When we have to pray,
When we are hungry for food we don't deserve,
When we are thirsty for a living water to drink that is not
*   our own,*

Then we kneel down,
We groan and lament,
We knock on the door,
We seek,
We ask.

And God hears us.
The Shepherd comes to us,
Responds to us,
Changes us,
And leads us—
Closer to the Promised Land,
To the New Jerusalem,
To the Beloved Community
With Jesus Christ our Savior.

Dr. King once said that if we get what we deserve—an eye for an eye and a tooth for a tooth—we will be a blind and toothless society.

Well, you know what we got sitting up in high places and on high thrones?

People with lots of fine (if false) teeth,
But, oh my Lord,

> *They are blind, blind as a bat flying around in Underground
> Atlanta!*

Where does the insidious falsehood and anti-God, anti-church statement
come from?

God Helps Those Who Help Themselves

Many Christians believe it comes from the Bible! But such a statement
could not come from Holy Scripture because the story of God's revelation is exactly the opposite: God loves us and dies for us and rises for us and lives in us
precisely because we cannot do it for ourselves.

Sarah and Abraham were old and barren. The seed of God's covenant promise did not fertilize the egg of hope until Isaac's parents could no longer help
themselves. Why do you think Sarah laughed?

Slaves were way down in Egyptland lamenting and crying and groaning
and, when God saw that they could not help themselves, she lifted up Moses-
the-murderer to lead them to liberation. Why did Jesus respond to the grief and
agony of Mary and Martha? Because Lazarus was beyond help and hope. He was
dead.

Yes, the great heresy of the American churches is the belief, preaching, and
practice that God helps those who help themselves. Could it be that the God of
the Bible and the God of the mainline churches are in fact different Gods?

A fundamental purpose of the incarnation was to reveal and demonstrate
that the God of the Bible is the God of the oppressed, the weak, and the undeserving. Why was Jesus born in a barn? He had to be for God to be God!

God helps those who help themselves! This fundamental lie about our God,
but a fundamental tenet of American culture, comes from *Poor Richard's Almanac*—the aim of which was to make Poor Richard rich. Benjamin Franklin
believed the Puritan work ethic was good for the American way of life. All the
mystery and mysticism, love and justice, church and community based on the
primitive Hebrews and their God needed, according to Ben Franklin, to be done
away with. What better way to separate the ethics of Puritanism and the spirituality of scripture than to teach Americans that hard work, wealth, and success
are the results of helping yourself and then of receiving the blessing from a God
who doesn't care that much anyway?

The basis of all Christian ethics is love. The test of Christian love is the capacity to help others by charity and the establishment of liberation for all who
cannot help themselves.

> *Love your enemy.*
> *Bless those who curse you.*
> *Feed, clothe, visit the least:*

> *Larry Lonchar and the 2,557 others on death row in America,*
> *Peggy Coyle and the 11,317 homeless women and men, boys and girls in Atlanta,*
> *Rich folk, some who know and many who do not know, that their wealth is disease,*
> *You and I who suffer and grieve precisely at the point of our helplessness.*

So let us tell the truth about our God and stop the myth that would put the God of the Bible to death. Let us build Christian community—the church— whereby we can glorify and celebrate the God who welcomes the prisoner and makes a home for the homeless. Let us struggle to influence a culture that day by day is more violent and aggressive toward the old, the poor, the children, gays and lesbians, women, and the mentally ill, so we may know the salvation and integrity, the joy and hope of following our God, who helps those who cannot, and even will not, help themselves.

Death-Row Visitation: A Listening Post and a Seeing Site, *by Ed Loring*

JUNE 2000

I was in prison and you visited me.

—Jesus the Jew[3]

The morning is crisp and clear. Redbuds shiver and dogwoods dance along the interstate as the eighteen-wheelers define the meaning of American life (or is it death?). The teamsters are carrying promises and goods at the fastest speed possible while consumers wait at the mall doors for the unlocking of hope and dreams stuffed into the toes of the latest-style running shoes. Consumers consumed—a nonjudicial death penalty for those who give their allegiance to the American Way of Life (or is it death?).

---

3. Literal visitation of Jews in Georgia prisons is most difficult. Of the 42,837 adult state prisoners in Georgia, only 29 are Jews. (The estimated Jewish population in Georgia, as of 1999, was 87,500, or 1.1 percent of the state total.—ed.) How might we live out our baptismal vows more faithfully? Proclaim liberty to the captives?

The only resistance work over the next hour, as we drive to Jackson State Prison, is to pray when the truckers, with Confederate flags glued to their grilles and hearts, flip the middle finger at us or honk like demented beasts arising from a turbulent sea. ("If you put and end to oppression, to *every gesture of contempt*, . . . then the darkness around you will turn to the brightness of noon" [Isa. 58:10].) Murphy reaches across my lap where the Word sits and shakes open to Ezekiel 34 and pulls her dark glasses from the glove compartment. We are on the way to visit several of our brothers on death row.

I

We want to do what Jesus does: reduce the distance. We want to incarnate the Word into our lives and flesh. So, responding to the mandate to "visit the prisoner," we prepare to enter another world at the Georgia Diagnostic and Classification Prison. Here death row is incorporated among some 1,500 diagnostic prisoners waiting to adjust to the Georgia prison system and then travel to one of our forty-one prisons. Here Death is resident and life is an alien. Many prisoners and some staff struggle to choose life, to resist the awful oppression and despair of violence, hatred, and the technological efficiency that defines the inner life of a prison machine. Even if the beast does not devour the whole person, all of us who enter are wounded and weakened. Yet we go, knowing that God's love, promise, and presence are relentless in the bowels of this institution, whose mission statement is to bind and kill. Jesus proclaims: "Liberty to the captives!" and he is executed. Between the bars and deep within a few prisoners' eyes, tokens of resurrection are passed to us like the bread at Eucharist or breakfast grits.

Murphy returns her dark glasses to the glove compartment. We leave our Bibles in the car, for we are only allowed to take "state Bibles" into the visiting area. We lock the car and head up the hill. Standing below a tall tower, we give the guard our names and tell him our aim and purpose: to make a pastoral visit to friends under the sentence of death. He informs us that count is not yet complete. We stand and wait under the Georgia state flag, which whistles Dixie in the wind. Twenty minutes tick away, and the count is complete. We enter and walk toward the visiting area.

II

The visiting area is neither the prisoner's world (the cell block is) nor the visitor's. Nevertheless, it is a most significant "meeting ground."

We do "enter the world" of the prison staff, trustees, and prisoners being visited. We who go into the prison "leave our world behind," but we do not enter the primary space of the prisoner's prison life.

Yet much about this space tilts toward the world of the prisoner. We are searched and often hounded by the guards and by their rules and machines as we enter, not the belly, but the jaws of the beast. Female visitors are more humiliated than men in this clearance process. This is the most male institution on earth, even more so than the dressing room of a pro football team or the Army barracks after a battle. Of the two thousand people inside the beast, only a few are women—and these are staff, guards, and visitors.

Our visits had to be approved twenty-four hours earlier by the chaplain's office. After clearing two metal detectors and, if we cannot clear the machine, a strip search, we wait while the prisoner is brought by a "transit guard" to the visitors' area. This takes from fifteen minutes to one hour. All of this time counts as "visitation time." The clock begins running at a stated time and the visits end at a stated time, no matter when the visits actually begin. One some occasions, our visits are disrupted so that we have no more than thirty minutes together. At other times, a second prisoner is never brought to the visiting area, and we are left without explanation.

III

One of the most joyful and graceful experiences in death-row visitation are the contact visits. *We are thankful.* We are under the surveillance of cameras and guards, and we are locked in the visitation area; however, the guards remain outside the visitation space. We are afforded time and place for private conversation, prayer, and Bible study.

Pastoral visitors and lawyers are not allowed to purchase anything from the vending machines unless the prisoner is under death watch and his death is only a few hours away. This is the most difficult part of our time together. Justice is important; supper is essential. Without breaking bread (cheese crackers) and sharing soft drinks together we do not have the material sharing of food that is the fundament of Christian community. On the weekends, family visitors are able to purchase from the vending machines, and tokens of the Beloved Community are more visible. A growing number of death-row prisoners are Catholics. A priest or deacon from outside the prison serves them the Eucharist every week in their cell block, in the belly of the beast. We rejoice even as we yearn for a shared meal with our beloved friends and, for the most part, fellow baptized disciples.

In addition to bans on food, ministers and lawyers cannot bring their children to visit. In 1980, the warden at Jackson instituted the "Hannah Rule"— we've called it that after our daughter, who was an infant at the time—which disallowed the practice. There is no exception when the death watch is in force. Children re-create and redefine space; they are as necessary for hospitality as bread and wine. The presence of children scares the ubiquitous acolytes of death.

The prisoner who leaves his cell block behind and journeys to the "meeting place" under the strong arm of the escort guard has a more difficult journey than we do as visitors. He is strip-searched, including body cavities, both on the way up and the way down. Some of our friends have experienced torn anal tissues as a consequence. When there is tension between prisoners and the guard pulling escort duty, some inmates refuse to come for the visit. The humiliation and harassment are simply too much to bear.

The meeting room or visitation area is transformed nonetheless when we are finally together, locked in and watched, but free at last, if only for a short moment. Here, for a flash, we from the "free world" and those in prison, who are under the state's—but not God's—sentence of death, are neither prisoner nor free but one in heart and mind (Gal. 3:26–28). We extend to one another our welcome and friendship; the beast flees into the sea, and we are brothers and sisters by the blood of the Lamb. For a moment, Babel is silenced. We speak truth in love to one another.

Then, suddenly, the guard hits the steel bars and calls, "Visitation is over." The emperor takes off his clothes again, and we begin our descent to the parking lot. Nevertheless, the history of the world has changed, and a chink in the prison wall has appeared to those with eyes to see. A tiny child's step, a puny, planted mustard seed has tilted the universe: Liberty to captives is at hand. Resistance to the death penalty has grown a little leaf; angels sing, and the reign of God flashes.

Speak a Word to the Discouraged, *by Murphy Davis*

A P R I L   1 9 8 8

Editor's note: This article adapts a commencement address delivered at Associated Mennonite Biblical Seminaries in Elkhart, Indiana.

> *The Desert will rejoice*
> *and flowers will bloom in the wastelands.*
> *The desert will sing and shout for joy;*
> *It will be as beautiful as the*
> *Lebanon Mountains*
> *and as fertile as the fields of*
> *Carmel and Sharon.*
> *Everyone will see the Lord's splendor,*
> *see God's greatness and power.*

Give strength to hands that are tired
and to knees that tremble with weakness.
Tell everyone who is discouraged,
"Be strong and don't be afraid!
God is coming to your rescue. . . ."

—Isaiah 35:1–4

What an honor it is to be able to speak to you, the graduating seminarians of 1987, with your friends and family, your faculty, and your community. I am grateful for a relationship that has continued over the past several years between the Open Door Community and the Mennonites of northern Indiana. It would be hard to say how important it is that many of you, your friends, and family members have visited us, lived and worked with us, and stood with us, resisting the powerful forces of death that crush human life and dignity and make the lives of the poor hell on earth. Thank you.

The thirty-fifth chapter of Isaiah speaks to us of beauty—of flowers blooming in the wasteland, streams of water on parched earth. "The desert," Isaiah tells us, "will sing and shout for joy." What beauty is represented here for us; and what an image of rightness, the Reign of Justice. For Justice and Beauty are, in the scriptures and in life, deeply intertwined.

Our good friend Will Campbell is a Mississippi-born, self-described steeple-dropout Baptist preacher who now does a little farming in the hills of Tennessee and writes good stories. Seven or eight years ago, Will was invited to Florida State University for what he expected to be a "general discussion" of the death penalty. (The story is well chronicled in his latest book, *Forty Acres and a Goat*, but I heard it first the morning after from friends in Tallahassee who were there.)

When he got to Tallahassee, Will discovered that this "general discussion" was in fact a formal debate on the death penalty and televised, to boot! His horror grew when he learned that his opponent was an internationally known professor, philosopher, theologian, and author.

The professor presented a long and scholarly position paper—quoting a lot from Hobbes—saying why the death penalty was such a nifty idea. And then the TV camera turned on Brother Will. The moderator announced solemnly, "Mr. Campbell will now present his position in opposition to the death penalty." Will claims he was seized with a sudden deep empathy for the people whose plight they were there to discuss. He moved on wobbly legs to the microphone. He gripped the podium, looked out at the audience, and finally drawled: "I just think it's tacky." And he sat down.

After the cheering audience quieted a bit, the shaken moderator proceeded, in the finest academic form, with an attempt at exegesis (and at salvaging the debate!) on the word *tacky*. Quoting now from *Forty Acres and a Goat*:

"Tacky is an old Southern word, and it means uncouth, ugly, lack of class."

"Yessir, I know what it means" [said Will]. "I try not to use words if I don't have some vague notion of what they mean. . . . My worthy opponent chose to pitch this discussion on a philosophical level. . . . I wouldn't have done it that way myself. I'm a bootleg country preacher from the hills of Tennessee, by way of Mississippi. Don't know much about philosophy. But in my limited exposure to the subject, I do seem to recall that there was something called aesthetics. And if your synonyms are correct, if a thing is ugly, well, ugly means there's no beauty in it, there's no truth in it. And if there is no truth in it, there is no good in it. Not for the victim of the crime. Certainly not for the one being executed. Not for the executioner, the jury, the judge, the state. For no one. And we were enjoined by a well-known Jewish prophet to love them all."

The world will be saved by beauty, says Dostoevsky. Isaiah seems to agree as he weaves his words into the biblical vision of justice and salvation.

> Flowers bloom in the desert
> Springs water the parched earth
> The lowly are lifted up and called
>   by name
> The blind see
> The captives are set free
> The lame dance and leap for joy
> Healing comes for the broken victims
>
> Tiny fragile flowers of Hope
> bloom in the wasteland
> of death and despair.

Archbishop Oscar Romero, the great pastor of El Salvador, described his pastoral mission as feeding the hope of the poor. "My aim," he said, "is to encourage a hope that I honestly glimpse. My work has always been to support the hope of my people. If there is even a spark of hope, it is my duty to nourish it, and I believe that every person of goodwill must likewise nourish it." This is beauty.

There is, on the other hand, a prosecutor in eastern North Carolina named Joe Freeman Britt. His circuit includes Robeson County, one of the poorest counties in the South. Britt has become famous around the United States for his ability to win death sentences, and it has won him the title, "The Deadliest D.A." Joe Freeman Britt has made a statement that, I think, helps us to think clearly. "There is," he says, "within every person a tiny flicker that says we should preserve life. It is the prosecutor's job to extinguish the flame." Now that is what we call tacky!

Compare, if you will, the beauty of Romero's pastoral mission of feeding hope. Mr. Britt's description of his own task is gross and crass, but it only exaggerates the social and political forces of our day that would extinguish hope. For every time the cry of condemnation and alienation rises from the people, the flowers wither, the darkness rises, the hope fades—

> "I am not my sister's/brother's keeper!"
> cry the people.
> And hope fades.

> "People stand in soup lines because it's
> the easy way out,"
> pontificates Ed Meese.
> And hope cringes.

> "We will never trust the Russians,"
> cries Ronald Reagan.
> "Give me a Star Wars budget!"
> And hope rolls toward the grave.

> We try and try to shut our eyes to the violence
> against women and children in the American home.
> And the darkness encroaches
> and hope sneaks out the back door.

> And our hands grow tired
> and our knees tremble with weakness,
> and we become so discouraged.

The irony about hope—and encouragement—is that when we struggle to keep hope alive in someone else we keep it alive in ourselves.

> And hope grows and flourishes
> like unlikely flowers in the wasteland.

My friend Alpha Otis Stephens was executed in December 1984. Alpha grew up poor and black in Macon, Georgia. He was regularly and severely beaten by an alcoholic father until his mother, fearing for his life, dressed him, packed him a lunch, and put him out. Alpha became a six-year-old homeless wanderer.

It would not surprise you to learn that Alpha became a violent man. He learned to pass along what life had dished out. And, finally, he became a murderer. He took the life of one Mr. Henry Asbill—a human being, a child of God. And for that crime he went to death row and lived there for ten years. And finally, for that crime, he was killed—in our name.

But that is not all! In the case of Alpha O. Daniel Stephens, God used another prisoner—Charlie—to move Alpha toward hope and redemption. Alpha described it like this:

> Yeah. I changed. The thing that made me change the most was what Charlie did. When I came to Jackson [prison] I was violent. Goodgawda'mighty, I was violent! Most everybody jus' lef' me alone. 'Cept Charlie. I stayed in my cell all the time. He started comin' sittin' in front of my cell. Jus' sittin'. Lookin'. At me. Finally I say, "What you starin' at?!"
>
> "You," he say. "Jus' tryin' to figure how can anybody be so mean. You crazy or jus' ain't got no sense?"
>
> I didn't say nothin'. He didn't go 'way. He didn't never go 'way. Seem like he jus' work so hard to make me be his friend. So finally I jus' give up. Me an' him was always friends after that. That changed me. Man, I jus' couldn't be mean aroun' ol' Charlie.
>
> Everybody in prison called me Daniel. But Charlie, he called me "Brother Alpha."

Brother Alpha is dead now. But if I have nothing else to say to you, may I just be a witness to the beauty of hope reborn—of life restored. The beauty of State Prisoner #D-9164 being called Brother Alpha. The beauty of the word of life spoken to one discouraged to death—of life-giving water on the parched earth of a human soul.

Surely you have seen it! Surely you know the vision of flowers in a wasteland.

You—graduating senior seminarians—are being sent out by your friends, your teachers, your families. After some years spent here in reflection, study, prayer, and work, you are being sent into places where you will be needed very much. You are very beautiful because you are full of life and hope. And you hold in your hands and your hearts a great power. This is good because you are very needed.

There is much ugliness in this world of ours: Apartheid has just won a victory. Its grip is not diminished but, lately, it has been strengthened here.

Lies and doublespeak and excessive talk are not only tolerated but have become a source of pride in all levels of government.

A president who has thumbed his nose at the laws of the United States government and every law of human decency has not even slipped in the popularity polls—God help us!

The poor? The poor are being crushed. From the borders of Nicaragua to the homelands of South Africa. From the hamlets of El Salvador to the farms of the United States. From the squalid streets of Los Angeles to the bulging, overstuffed, rat-infested jails of Louisiana. From the teeming projects of Chicago to the migrant camps of Naples, Florida. By policy in the boardroom and interrogation in the back room. By threats and homelessness, hunger and exclusion. By endless imprisonment and racism that kills. By military games and disease without health care. By state execution and death sentences on the streets. By sexism that violates us all and abuse that bruises the souls and bodies of children. By labor pools that extract slave labor and blood banks that suck the life-flow from those who have no other way to get ten dollars.

The poor are being crushed. In our midst. In our name. Their flesh and their blood is the grist for our endless greed, our insatiable hunger to blame somebody, to use somebody, to sacrifice somebody, because we do not want to be who God has called us to be. Because we do not want to claim our kinship with one another. Because we do not want to pay the price of building a beautiful world where justice and mercy can reign. Because it is expensive, and unpopular, and hard, and uncomfortable, and you can get hurt. The poor are being crushed.

"Inasmuch," says Jesus . . . (oh, how we wish he wouldn't say it!).

"Inasmuch," says Jesus . . . (oh, maybe he meant something else!).

"Inasmuch," says Jesus, "as you have done it to one of the least of these my sisters and brothers, you have done it unto me."

Jesus is being crushed. Jesus needs you—your life, your hope, your body, your body presented as a living sacrifice. Jesus needs your prayer, your attention, your love.

Go. Go and find Jesus.

Speak the word: "Be strong. Don't be afraid. God is coming to your rescue."

And the flowers will bloom even in the desert of this land. The flowers will bloom even in the wasteland of your own loneliness and confusion. The tender, living, fragile, beautiful flowers will bloom. See them. Love them. Thank God for them.

Go!

Alternatives to the Death Penalty, *by Ed Loring*

S E P T E M B E R   1 9 8 8

On August 7, 1988, retired Supreme Court Justice Louis F. Powell Jr., standing before eleven thousand U.S. lawyers, called for an end to the death penalty. "Perhaps," Mr. Powell said, "the time has come for the Congress, as it is free to do, to take another look at a system that no other democracy deems necessary." This is the voice of a conservative calling for the reform of a system that does not work.

Today, 2,048 people are under the sentence of death. On average in Georgia, ten years elapse between sentencing a person to death and their electrocution. Mr. Powell sees the system as "imposed haphazardly," and he recalled many chaotic late-night decisions on appeal, just hours before a person was to die. Noting that the murder rate in the United States is four times higher than in Canada, which has no death penalty, Mr. Powell suggested that the use of handguns is the source of the "soaring murder rate."

The good news in Mr. Powell's speech is that it indicates a shift in the times. Increasingly, people are becoming disenchanted and tired of the death penalty and the pain and furor around executions. Government leaders, prison administrators, and prison guards, as well as district attorneys and defense lawyers, are beginning to oppose the death penalty for reasons of good government, including the drain on fiscal resources, time, and staff energies, not to mention simple human fairness. Death-row prisoners are predominantly poor, a disproportionate number are of racial minorities, and they endure a dehumanizing wait of eight to fourteen years for appeals and death. These facts lead increasing numbers of people to cite the unfairness of the death penalty, which has a structure so complex that a fair and impartial outcome is rare.

Another bright ray in the dawning, not to be overemphasized, but nonetheless important, is that two national leaders are opposed to the death penalty. Reverend Jesse Jackson has helped underline the point that in the United States the death penalty is a civil rights issue. At the Democratic Convention in Atlanta this year, the mantle of moral and political leadership was finally placed on Jesse's shoulders—not only for the Black community, but for a significant portion of those who struggle for peace and justice. An anti–death penalty agenda among activists for social justice is emerging as part of the party's platform.

Presidential candidate Michael S. Dukakis is also opposed to the death penalty: a political liability in this election year, many pundits believe. However, the climate is such that he has not qualified his position. As head of the Democratic Party, he stands for millions as a symbol of cultural values and political position. This is especially significant given Mr. Powell's call for the U.S. Congress to do something about the death penalty and its drawbacks.

The signs of the times are that a new political and cultural context for fighting the death penalty is emerging. Historical change toward justice becomes a "mighty act" when what is right (the death penalty is wrong!) gets tied to the self-interest of a class or a system. Frustration over excessive expenditures, diversion of time and energy from fundamental concerns of criminal justice, the economy, local needs, and the haphazard and unfair nature of the system are now providing an opportunity for new analysis, new coalitions, and an end to the death penalty in the United States.

PROBLEMS IN THE ANTI–DEATH PENALTY MOVEMENT

I have been part of the national anti–death penalty movement since 1976, when the U.S. Supreme Court upheld Governor Jimmy Carter's death law as a model for the nation (*Gregg v. Georgia*). From the beginning, we have had two serious problems which have not been faced, nor have proposals been made to overcome the hurdles. The move to end the death penalty, among those finding pragmatic reasons to do so, gives occasion to face our problems and to propose new alternatives.

First, the public perception of anti–death penalty advocates is that we are unconcerned with victims and that we wish to mollycoddle prisoners. Most common is the charge that we would have murderers go free (and district attorneys have used this charge to great advantage against us). This attitude is further embedded in people's minds by the destructive myth that the only alternative to a death sentence in Georgia is seven years in prison and a free walk. In actuality the average time for homicide in Georgia is fourteen years, and, for former death-row prisoners, that time is even longer. But we, as a movement, have not responded creatively or concretely to these images, and the movement has been damaged by our inability to address our reputation among the majority.

If the first problem is located on the outside, the second stumbling block is in the movement's center. Because the death penalty has been so popular over the past fifteen years (75 percent of the American people have been in favor), and resistance to it among civil rights groups, peace and justice organizations, and other progressive forces and individuals has been a low priority, we have had one goal: to abolish it. The price for this unity among people with varying values and political means has been an agreement that we would not offer an alternative to the death penalty. In order to avoid conflict, we have become politically ineffective and subject to the deepening myth that we are anarchists who would immediately set all prisoners free. The time is at hand when we must develop legislative alternatives to the death penalty and begin to build coalitions between moralists and pragmatists, who together can end the death penalty in the United

States. We must, with grace and patience, face inner conflicts and step forward with a sentencing proposal for first-degree murder.

TOWARD AN ALTERNATIVE TO THE DEATH PENALTY

As noted, members of the anti–death penalty movement have come from many places to join forces. The foundation is a belief that the death penalty is wrong. I come to this human value by way of the Judeo-Christian faith, and thus want to lift up two biblical norms basic to a consideration of an alternative.

First, the Bible is a book about the struggle and ultimate victory of life over death. Biblically informed people and traditions oppose death in all of its dehumanizing manifestations. A verse of Holy Scripture to which I attempt to submit my life and values is this: "I am now giving you the choice between life and death, between God's blessing and God's curse, and I call heaven and earth to witness the choice you make. Choose life" (Deut. 30:19). Any alternative to the death penalty needs to be about human life in its deepest and most sacred dimension.

Second, I turn to 1 Corinthians 13:8: "Love never gives up." The community of faith always holds the hope of repentance and a new life. This conversion is demonstrated by the fruits born in relationships and behavior. This hope for conversion sets people of biblical faith against the death penalty and against the closed sentence of no parole. A refusal to consider parole is, like death itself, a hopeless and faithless position. However, prison without parole is always a valid option for those who have not demonstrated a change of character and behavior that warrants release.

The two biblical norms of commitment to life and the never-ending hope for forgiveness, reconciliation, and new life must relate to political necessities. Security of the state (that is, controlling violence against citizens) and the possibilities of major changes within the criminal justice system are the two points we have to address to the satisfaction of a majority of state representatives and senators. Because of the developing concerns with government money, judicial overload, and fairness of application of the death penalty, we can now begin to work for new coalitions between progressives and mainline political interests. The formula for such a coalition must be an alternative to the death penalty, which is, on the one hand, long-term, and on the other hand guarantees parole consideration at some predetermined point.

I suggest that the prison term for first-degree murder be for life. In addition, after twenty-one years (that is, a life sentence by parole-board calculations), a prisoner will be considered for parole on the basis of his or her prison record and the resources available within the community (e.g., a place to live, friendships and associates, work, etc.). Of course, the word "considered" is as important as the word "parole" in my suggestion.

We at the Open Door and Southern Prison Ministry now are attempting to begin a conversation with you, our readers. We would like to hear responses and ideas from politicians, death-row prisoners, prison guards and administrators, househusbands, college students, homeless folk, anti–death penalty advocates, and those who now favor the death penalty. Please write to us and help us chart the way for a workable alternative.

CONCLUSION: IN THE MEANTIME

As we wrestle to discern the signs of the times and to discover new possibilities for an end to our foe—the death penalty—we must remain on the front line of the battle and never ease up in our fight for peace and justice, for reconciliation and new life. So as we wait for the concrete ways to work faithfully and lovingly in this world, which belongs to our God, let us act.

First, we must pray for peace and the end of a system of violence and oppression. Also, we must live a life of resistance to the cultural values which choose death on so many levels of personal and national life. We need to write letters every week. First, get related personally to a death-row prisoner by mail. Second, let us write to our representatives and newspaper editors, especially concerning the cost and judicial chaos of the death penalty. Discover the role of your local district attorney. He or she is the ultimate contact in death penalty cases; no one else in Georgia can initiate a death penalty trial. Does your D.A. work for life or death? What alternatives to the death penalty would she or he give serious consideration? At the terrible, terrible times of execution, please come to a vigil. We now have three scheduled across the state—in Atlanta, at the state Capitol; in Jackson, on the prison grounds; and in Americus, at the Sumter County Courthouse—and hope for several others this fall. So, let us pray; let us live lives filled with hope and peace; let us act in favor of life as we build a movement with a concrete, plausible alternative to the death penalty.

Part IV

THE SACRAMENTS
OF HOSPITALITY

We are an experiment with truth. We "make the road by walking."

—Murphy Davis

Liturgy and Life, Sacrament and Struggle,
by Murphy Davis

NOVEMBER 1996

Liturgy is a word that comes from the Greek, meaning "the work of the people." When we come together on Sunday, we make liturgy: we make work together. We say often that what we do here at the Open Door—all of the meals that we serve, all of the showers and clean clothes that we offer, all of the prison visits, all of the small acts of charity that respond to the suffering of our friends, as well as the advocacy—all of our work that we do, comes from the worship that we share. We worship together every day. We gather at least a couple of times each day to pray and reflect on scripture and to share our concerns. But the time we gather with each other on Sunday afternoon is a very particular time, a time set apart to sing, to pray, to listen, to reflect on scripture, and to celebrate the sacrament together. Every Sunday we celebrate the Eucharist—the Lord's Supper—Communion—around a table that is always in the middle of our circle, which brings us bread and juice that become for us the broken body and spilled blood of Jesus Christ. From time to time we also have the privilege of celebrating baptism. On a somewhat regular basis we celebrate what we also believe to be a sacrament: foot washing.

We celebrate these sacraments and our liturgy together in a context of two thousand years of experience and tradition in the church of Jesus Christ. Over these two thousand years, the disciples of Jesus have tried to live out the liturgy, to form it, and to come together around worship in different ways, at different times in history. The liturgy is the way, through the tradition and the sharing of worship with Christians around the world, that we mark our time. We divide the liturgy into a cycle and order, so that we have ways of remembering and celebrating the drama of our faith.

Soon we will begin the cycle again with Advent. Then we celebrate Christmas and Christmastide, Epiphany, Lent, Easter, Eastertide, and Pentecost. By celebrating this cycle we affirm that there is a holy quality to time. Time is not just something that passes on a calendar, where we mark the days and turn the months. When we share time in the midst of a community of faith, we come to know the regular seasons and cycles that bring us the stories of faith. Through these stories, and through remembering this drama, we call ourselves again and again to lives of faithfulness.

The liturgy—the work of the people—is something we make together. It doesn't just come from a book. It doesn't just come from a tradition of two thousand years. It's not something that someone else gives and that we repeat. We understand ourselves at the Open Door to be in the tradition of liberation theology, so that the enterprise of doing theology together is dynamic. The term used in liberation theology is the practice of *action-reflection*. God gives us work to do. From that work we do together, we shape our theological reflection. From our theological reflection we refine our work; we change the ways that we work together. And from new ways that we work, we reflect theologically in new ways, and so the process of action-reflection always builds on itself and is dynamic. We never have a theology that is written down, with a period at the end of the sentence, that is true for us once and for all. We are an experiment with truth. We "make the road by walking." We are working every day to "work out our salvation with fear and trembling" and to try to understand how God is present here and now in concrete ways.

The same can be said about our worship life, which is also based on an action-reflection model. Worship brings us together out of great diversity. We come into this circle out of many traditions: Roman Catholics, Mennonites, Baptists, Pentecostals, Presbyterians, Lutherans, and Methodists. We bring our traditions together, and we share our life together, and our life interacts with our worship. Our worship form is never canned, finished, or set, but it is a process of living together and of finding a way to worship our God in these historical circumstances. That is not to say that we ignore the Tradition. It is not to say that the Tradition is not important to us, but we try not to take a tradition and paste it on top of our life—to tie up the loose ends of our life with customs from another place and time.

When faith moves through a particular community and settles into our souls, it issues in a new kind of liturgy, something that we hope is always fresh. So the crucial questions around which we gather are where and when and how and with whom do we experience the faith. What place does the struggle for justice, for the New Heaven and the New Earth, have in our life? Our hope is that part of the answer lies in our worship: how we worship, where we worship, with whom we worship. If we do not have that kind of dynamic process, then our worship can become cold, static, and inauthentic.

I don't mean to disparage the Tradition—the great songs and hymns of the church, the liturgies, the prayers. But the Tradition always has to be brought into the present with integrity, with authenticity, for it to mean something for the worshiping community as it finds a place in the larger Christian community.

To relive the Tradition is to guide it toward lively interaction with the experience of God among us now. So we receive the Tradition as a gift, and it can be a powerful instrument for teaching and spiritual formation, as much as it can become a weapon in the hands of people more concerned with preserving power, authority, and privilege.

We want to receive the Tradition and to help it interact with our life and work and calling. The songs we sing, the way we pray, and the way we reflect on scripture are shaped by the here and now of our lives together. What this means at the Open Door is that we have particularized our liturgy and our liturgical life to reflect, deepen, and nourish our struggle with and on behalf of the homeless poor, women and men in prison and jails, the condemned, those on death row. But then neither would we want our liturgy to be seen as normative in any other community of faith.

The question for our liturgy and life is: How are biblical truths and the structure of life, the structure of worship, and the structure of theology related? Over the years we have developed particular forms of liturgical celebration out of our life and work.

In 1985, as we approached Holy Week and Easter, we became aware that March 31 was Palm Sunday; and on that day—the last day of March—all the night shelters for homeless men, women, and children in Atlanta would close. So it was a gift of the Holy Spirit that we would initiate Holy Week with the Homeless. For eleven years now we have gone onto the streets during Holy Week to remember the Passion of Jesus Christ, as we walk the Via Dolorosa of the homeless poor. In 1989, as we anticipated the coming of winter and the inevitability of suffering and death among the homeless, the Holy Spirit again gave us a new liturgy, from the ancient texts of Israel. That year we first marked Sukkoth—the Festival of Booths, or the Festival of Shelters—in which the people of God are called into the city square to remember the Israelites' time of homeless wandering, as a way to remember that God always calls us to open our homes to the homeless poor.

There is a more recent liturgy that we begin to celebrate in a few weeks, in Advent: ChristKwanza. It is a time when we bring into our community, shaped by European tradition, some of the traditions and the forms of worship in Africa. We remember our calling as a people of diversity and celebrate those traditions together.

Week to week we share a more regular cycle of liturgy. Our work emanates from our worship. Our worship and our liturgy reflect our work. We bring our work into the context of worship for consecration and discernment in prayer. This is the rhythm, and the shape, of our life together.

The central question for any liberation theology is: How do we create an alternative community, and how do we nurture the vision and the resources for an alternative way of life? The crucial questions include: How do we live together?

How do we worship together? How do we struggle together to follow Jesus? With liturgy and life, we also raise the questions of sacrament and struggle.

The sacraments have been an area of great debate throughout church history. Through the time of church councils and the shaping of church tradition, there were points at which people were willing to kill each other over the sacraments and how they were defined. The Roman Catholic tradition celebrates seven sacraments. Most Protestant traditions celebrate two. Here at the Open Door we celebrate three, because we believe that foot washing is a sacrament and is commanded by Jesus with the added promise that if we do this we will be happy, as Jesus says in the thirteenth chapter of John.

Traditionally, a sacrament has been defined as an outward and visible symbol of an inward and sacred grace—something material that teaches us about something sacred, something ordinary that teaches us about something holy. Sacrament is in essence a way of nurturing a vision, a way of feeding a sacramental vision. Seeing the holy in the ordinary, seeing the sacred in the material, is a transcendent way of seeing, believing that what we see under our noses is not the whole story. Seeing things as they are is not the way things have to be.

It's a radical notion that we sing about in "We Have Another World in View." Sacrament brings that other world into our presence. So if we lift the edge a tiny bit, we understand the sacredness that moves through all of life. Sacramental vision leads us to another way of seeing: seeing the holy in the mundane. We're reminded by the prophet that, without a vision, the people perish. If we believe that what we see in the material world is all there is, then despair is a likely option. When we look to the Gospels, we find that, in all of Jesus' miracles and teachings, he uncovers the miracle in the ordinary.

Annie Dillard writes about line drawings in children's books, drawings that at first appear to be a mass of intertwined and intersecting lines. But the directions say, "Look into the lines and find the tree. Look into the lines and find the cat. Look and find the bucket." Then, with your crayon, color in the bucket mixed in all of those lines. Annie Dillard says that nature is like that.

I think that's a good image for sacrament as well. When we look at bread and grape juice, we see ordinary food. But in the sacramental vision, we understand that this is a holy feast that we share. When we look at water, we see only the ordinary water that quenches our thirst. But when we understand the power of water and the outpouring of God's Spirit, then we understand how the cleansing of baptism changes our life. We understand that it is a holy work when we invite our homeless friends to share food and drink and showers. There is holiness, there is sacrament, in sharing elements that become holy. It is the same vision that we receive when we look into the eyes and the face of a stranger and see the presence of God. When we look into suffering people's lives, we understand the Passion of Jesus Christ.

We need sacrament because we have before us a deep mystery; we do not have words to describe the mystery of the presence of God in our lives. We have sacrament to act out the drama. We have sacrament to give us understanding. In sharing the bread and juice, we remember the story: the sacrament of liberation, forgiveness, and healing. In sharing our own lives and stories, we come to understand the truths of our lives and how our experiences become holy as we share life with one another.

We come to the Eucharist each week as the center of our lives. We come into this circle because we understand that it nourishes us; it makes us whole. Table companionship has been the starting point of every ministry at the Open Door. Everything we do starts with dinner, whether in our prison ministry, or our soup kitchen, or any ministry that we share.

As we come to Eucharist, I read a story from Luke's Gospel that is not normally read as a Eucharist passage. But I believe it communicates some of the truths of Eucharist. The incident takes place when Jesus was moving around Galilee, preaching and teaching and healing. He had healed many people of their diseases and demon possessions, and he was in active conflict already with the government. Jesus had sent his disciples off, and they returned to tell Jesus everything that they had done.

> Jesus took them with him, and they went off by themselves to a town called Bethsaida. When the crowds heard about it, as usual, they followed him. He welcomed them, spoke to them about the reign of God, and healed those who needed it. When the sun was beginning to set, the twelve disciples came to Jesus and said, "Send the people away so that they can go to the villages and farms around here and find food and lodging because this is a lonely place." But Jesus said, "You yourselves give them something to eat." They answered, "But all we have is five loaves and two fish. Do you want us to go and buy food for this whole crowd?" There were about 5,000 men there [we can assume there were 15,000 to 20,000 people, if the women and children were counted]. Jesus said to his disciples, "Make the people sit down in groups of about fifty each." After they had done so, Jesus took the five loaves and two fish, looked up to heaven, and thanked God for them. Then he broke them, and gave them to his disciples to distribute to the people. They all ate and had enough, and the disciples took up twelve baskets of what was left over. (Luke 9:10–17)

This story is presented as one of the miracle stories. It seems to indicate supernatural power that Jesus had to take a little bread and a couple of fish, and to serve between five thousand and twenty thousand people. It *is* a miracle. It's amazing. We don't know how it was done. We don't know how Jesus took a little food—with the disciples saying, "This is all we've got. It's not much. We can't feed everybody with this"—but Jesus took that little, broke it, and gave thanks for what they had.

The interesting thing is that the text never says that all the people ate from the five loaves and two fish. It says there was plenty. There was enough. There was so much more than necessary that the disciples took up twelve baskets of leftover food. That seems amazing, because they started with only five loaves and two fish, which would not have filled twelve baskets, or even one.

The miracle is that Jesus took what little there was and gave thanks. And giving thanks, he began to share it. I wonder if the real meaning of this story is that in the crowd, here and there, some people had pieces of bread tucked in their pockets. And somebody had another fish under his cloak. And somebody else had a satchel with two pieces of bread. Nobody brought the food out at first because, can't you imagine that feeling? "Look at all these people. I've got a piece of bread, but I'm not pulling it out of my pocket, because if I pull it out, somebody might want some of it. And then there won't be enough for me."

But there was enough when Jesus took the little available to him and his family, gave thanks, and looked up to heaven, broke the bread, and started passing it out. Can you imagine that a pocket opened here, and a satchel opened over there, and somebody pulled a string of fish from over his shoulder, and they started passing the food around? Is it possible that sharing was empowered in the simple act of giving thanks? Is it possible that, when one person gave thanks and began to share, the anxiety of scarcity was healed? I like to think that this was the way it happened.

Jesus was being a good Jewish boy when he gave thanks. There is a traditional Jewish blessing called the *barakah,* said before every meal, every sharing of food. We say these words when we celebrate the Passover Seder every spring: "Blessed are you, O LORD our God, ruler of the universe, who brings forth bread from the earth." Jesus would never have considered eating, or giving out food, without giving thanks. Rather than showing us a miracle, I think Jesus was showing us how to live. Rather than impressing people already impressed with his power and magic tricks, Jesus showed what to do when people get hungry. Rather than overwhelming us with his greatness, he tried to overwhelm us with the greatness of sharing so that everybody has enough. In this story, Jesus says that if we give thanks for what we have, it will increase and produce abundance.

Eucharist, the word for this sacrament we share, means the giving of thanks. Gratitude is the basis of this table. Gratitude is the basis of the life of faith. It is what our friend Horace Tribble, who visits and prays with us every week, calls "an attitude of gratitude." That is the basis and heart of the life of faith. Giving thanks reminds us of the holiness of every meal shared in love. There is enough for everyone.

There was enough on that day in that lonely place for Jesus to feed the multitude. I don't think that he produced all that bread and fish, but he taught people how to share. Whether a child brought forth the loaves and fishes, or the disciples had them in their pockets, something started when Jesus gave thanks. All it takes is saying "thank you" for what we have. What little we have is enough.

Gratitude is key. Gratitude makes us real. Gratitude helps us build solidarity and community. Gratitude is at the heart, and struggle is at the center. It takes a vision—a vision nurtured by gratitude—to see abundance in the bread when it seems so little; to see the presence of God in the stranger and outsider. In that vision, struggle is a given. When you know there is enough food but that people are still hungry, it produces struggle. When you know that there is enough shelter for everyone, but that people live in the yard and get rained on, there is struggle. Without this vision, we shall surely perish in the struggle to go from the way things are to the way things can be.

We struggle to release the bread in the crowd, and we struggle to release the Christ in the bread. We struggle to release God in the stranger and to press the vision even when everyone else seems blind. When Jesus said the bread and body were broken, he knew what he was talking about, but he gave thanks. He released the sharing. The deed took him to the cross, to the instrument of torture and execution, to the worst that the world could offer. But even there death had already been overcome. In the cross, Jesus wanted us to see the power of life. In the instrument of despair, Jesus wanted us to see the means of hope. In the executed criminal, Jesus wanted us to see the Lord of Life.

We come to the table for nourishment. We are fed here. Here is where our life becomes a banquet. Our life becomes a sacrament when we share this bread and this cup. The sacrament helps us to grow in love, to know the meal of liberation and the healing of fear. The meal invites us to freedom and makes us part of the community of liberation, the God movement, the Beloved Community. It is ours to give thanks, to share the bread and cup, broken and poured out for us, in love, in struggle, in hope.

A Gift of Earthen Vessels, *by Murphy Davis*

AUGUST 1985

There are days, to tell the truth, that you just have to wonder if living in community is worth it. Like marriage and family life, community is a great idea, but the reality requires more blood, sweat, and tears than anybody told you about ahead of time. And sometimes you just wonder.

You stir a soup pot, and there seem to be more hungry people at the door. You open the shower line, but more hot, sweaty, dirty bodies appear the minute you've finished. You visit prisoners, but for every visit there are five more unaddressed needs. You sit down to pray, but the cacophony of thoughts and feelings won't lie still long enough to get through a simple "Lord have mercy on me, a sinner." You work to stop the death penalty, and the state sets another execution date.

We live together out of a commitment to the love that Christ gives us to share as a body, but sometimes it seems the best we can do is fail each other. Sometimes we wonder: is it worth it? Wouldn't it be better, or easier, to give up? To go back to a more traditional life style—one not so weird or isolated or cut off from mainstream culture?

A few weeks ago a little cardboard box came in the mail from St. John's University in Collegeville, Minnesota. Inside were a simple pottery bowl and cup. They were crafted as a eucharistic set by Richard Bresnahan, who was trained as a master potter in Japan, and sent through our friend Frank Cordaro of the Catholic Worker family. The message said that an identical cup and bowl had been sent to every Catholic Worker house in the country. (We are very honored to be included and considered a "Presbyterian Catholic Worker.") Frank wrote:

> These Eucharistic sets are a gift to you from the Potter and our community. We wish to thank you for your special ministry to the poor and your ongoing struggle for justice for a world where it will be "easier to be good." These Earthen vessels were formed after the simple soup bowls and water glasses that are the common utensils in the hospitality houses. We hope they serve to remind you of the links between your work with the poor and the work of the potters here at St. John's.

Richard the potter added:

> It is with great hope that the love and care taken by so many to create a piece of earth for everyday use, is enjoyed by those who inherit the earth.

A gift of simple earthen vessels. The vessels are to hold the body and blood of Jesus Christ. They sit on the little table at the center of our worshiping circle each Sunday night, and we pass them to each other even as our brother Jesus passed them to us. We gather around the table because we know something (perhaps not enough, but at least something) about our own weakness and failings and fragility. We know that if we serve the poor, it is not because we are good or loving or smart. It is because of the mercy of Jesus Christ, who lives among us and teaches us to forgive each other.

The earthen vessels are very fragile, and so are we. Their only strength comes from the fire of the kiln, and so it is with our strength. The vessels come to us as a gift and a reminder: we are not alone. God has not abandoned us. God comes to us each day through the Spirit and through our homeless and imprisoned friends. God comes to us through the scripture, through the sacraments, and through prayer. God comes to us through an amazingly wide circle of friends who support our work and support us through gifts and shared work, money, letters, and words of encouragement.

We must often remind ourselves: when things seem the most bleak and desperate, we are saved not by our own plans or work, but by God's good grace. When the confused and hurt disciples walked down the road from Jerusalem to Emmaus, they had lost their sense of purpose and direction. The stranger who joined them on the road eloquently illuminated the scriptures, but still they were confused. It was only when the stranger was welcomed into their home, gave thanks, and broke the bread that they recognized him. And they jumped out of their seats: "Didn't our hearts burn within us?"

When our hearts burn within us we usually figure it was the soup. But regularly we are reminded that in the ongoing work, in what at times seems pure drudgery—the grimy, sweaty business of cleaning pots and cooking and driving a rattling car to the prison—we look up only to discover that Jesus was with us all along.

We come together out of love: love of the poor, love of God, love of each other. But our love is shallow. It is never enough. We find ourselves too easily becoming judgmental and haughty and bitter. We turn our backs on each other, on God, and on the cry of our sisters and brothers who suffer, and we must cry out again and again to God: "Take away my heart of stone and give me a heart of flesh."

The simple earthen vessels remind us of many truths. They remind us that we ourselves are simple earthen vessels, created for the simple purpose of holding life and love that come from God. They remind us of the deep connection between the soup bowls and teacups of our kitchen tables and the pottery bowl and cup of our eucharistic table. They remind us that community is a fragile gift from God to be held gently with hearts full of gratitude.

Stranger at the Table, *by Hannah Loring-Davis*

Editor's note: The following adapts sermons preached at Guilford College Friends Meeting and at the annual retreat for the Catholic Workers of Southern California.

It is truly a gift to be invited to share a simple reflection on my life and on my walk toward discipleship. To share this with others who are on the journey fills me with a powerful sense of the Spirit of God.

Over the past three and a half years, while I have been away at college, one of my major struggles has been to learn how to become my own person, separate from my parents and my home, without becoming removed from what they have taught me, and from the gift of life that they have shared with me. It's a hard thing.

I have realized over the past few years that I am called into a life similar in a lot of ways to what my parents do. I am an activist—I have learned this passion and way of life from family and friends, mentors and teachers. But the tricky part of this for me is that I have to break into a social and vocational circle where I am known as Ed and Murphy's daughter. Granted, it's nice to have a little leg up, riding on a good reputation that I haven't had to create for myself. But who doesn't want to be known as their own person? In many ways, I guess it's just a matter of time, part of growing up.

I go to a small Quaker college in North Carolina. During my time at Guilford, I have become more and more interested in Quaker tradition, especially given their emphasis on peace and nonviolence. Quakers don't tend to do a lot of preaching—they wait for divine inspiration, "the Quaker call," to bring words or song out of silence. You might guess that being the child of two Presbyterian ministers admittedly makes feeling "the Quaker call" a little difficult. We Calvinists just like to hear ourselves talk—whether God is calling us to do so or not. But I tried and tried not to be my parents' child as I prepared for this day. However, especially when it comes to the use of the English language, I am my father's child—and I have not been able to escape the Protestant homiletical tradition of a reflection with too much to say and not enough time in which to say it. Last night, on our way to the car after dinner, my dad wrapped his arm around me and said, "Now, Hannah, I sure hope you have three points to make tomorrow." And how else, I ask, would I prepare? Even the lectures I got as a child had three points, often they were titled, and they usually had a quiz at the end.

The first seventeen years of my life, I lived at the Open Door Community.

As a child, I was known as the community troublemaker and, depending on whom you ask, I still am.

Every afternoon I would come home from school, peel off my polyester Catholic school uniform, and jump into the rattiest pair of shorts I could find. After running around the house, terrorizing the thirty other folks who lived there, we would all gather for dinner. The tradition was, and still is, that before we sat down to eat there was a time to reflect on the day, to get volunteers to do dishes, to make announcements, and to lift up prayer concerns. For years, the five minutes that this ritual took seemed like hours—my tummy was so empty, and in my four-year-old head I saw no reason for this foolishness, going on and on like that.

But after I made it through what seemed like an hourlong supper circle, we would sit down and eat—my favorite part of the day. It was not until the last years of my life at home that I began to realize what a profound effect that eating and sharing time at table had had on me. For it was around those tables that I gathered with many people whom I loved and with whom I shared my life. The table was where I had heard many stories—stories of life and death, abuse, pain and liberative healing, alcoholism, and drug abuse, and the stories of sobriety and faith, struggle and strength. Around those tables I realized how different I was from the people I went to school with, and that I was in school made me different from so many of the people with whom I ate.

Coming to understand what was happening every day at dinner was challenging. No longer was dinner just filling my empty belly with food, but it became a much more political act. I realized that there is soulful transformation when bread is broken in the company of strangers. This transformation has come with the realization that it is the sharing of experience that leads to deeper understanding.

In her song "Overlap," Ani DiFranco, a contemporary folksinger, writes: "I know there is strength in the differences between us, I know there is comfort where we overlap." It is truly in the strength created by distances and the comfort within overlapping places that transformation occurs; with the embrace of difference, learning and teaching occurs. That we may be students and teachers at the same time is a life-giving event.

At my dinner table, I began to understand what Christine Pohl was talking about when she said, "Shared meals are central to sustaining the life of a community and to expressing welcome to strangers." At the dinner table at the Open Door, I am the stranger. As a full-time student, I am living a life of educated privilege and at the same time eating with people broken by the domination system that formal and especially private education perpetuates. Thus, as I welcome strangers to the table, I am, in turn, welcomed by the stranger.

At these tables we can begin to understand the dialectical nature of being both shepherd and sheep. As we welcome folks to our table we incarnate God's words in Ezekiel 34: "As shepherds seek out their flocks when they are among their scattered sheep, so I will seek out my sheep. . . . I will feed them on the mountains of Israel, by the watercourses and in all the inhabited parts of the land."

As we welcome the stranger to table, we—both as stranger and host—are called out of the scattered flock to the "good pastures" that God has promised. In taking on the role of shepherd, we too are guided by those we welcome into our lives and to our tables.

One such life-giving experience taught me the connection between the supper table and the communion table. My mother was sick with cancer; I was in the tenth grade. She was in the hospital for the second time, and I was really scared. After our Sunday evening worship, a large group of us went to the hospital and gathered in a fluorescent room, a hellhole they called the visiting room. I felt a little uncomfortable—this was *my* space, with *my* mom, a place that we had spent many hours in tears as well as laughter—and here were people that I lived with and trusted and loved, and who brought me courage and comfort. But with us were a number of people that I didn't know at all.

One of the ministers in the community performed a short eucharistic service. Bread was broken and passed, followed by the cup. And there was a miracle of healing. No, my mom didn't jump up and walk out of the hospital, but, over time, she healed. And I was transformed—the act of passing the bread to the man next to me, a man whose name I did not know, made me uncomfortable until I realized the significance of this sacrament. He passed the bread to my mother and, in that simple act, brought her a healing that a doctor would not have delivered with ten doses of chemotherapy.

I realized later that I had welcomed this man, with great reluctance, into space that was very sacred to me. These visiting-room chairs had held me for many hours and days. Although my welcome was reluctant, by bringing this man into my space I was led to the "good pasture"—a pasture of healing, and a pasture of replenished hope. In the midst of this small miracle came a renewed sense of grace and strength for the uphill journey toward healing.

I liken this experience to that of the disciples on the road to Emmaus. Luke's account says: "As they came near the village to which they were going, Jesus walked ahead, appearing to go farther. But they urged, 'Stay with us, because it is almost evening and the day is now nearly over.' So Jesus went in to stay with them. While at the table with them, Jesus took bread, blessed and broke it, and gave it to them. Then their eyes were opened, and they recognized Jesus, who then vanished from their sight."

Just as the scales fell from the disciples' eyes, the experience at the hospital taught me a new way to see. We are all shaped, deep within our souls, by this shared experience of miraculous grace that happens most often at the table, in the company of strangers.

Let us renew our commitment to each other. Let us lock arms and stand strong again. Let us go into the world and find people with whom to share our food. For as we welcome the stranger, our lives are transformed; each time we do this we welcome the image and incarnation of God into our lives again. If we are all created in the image of God, then we welcome Divinity to our table.

If there is one thing that I am sure of, it is that my life has been created and shaped at the dinner table. This occurred not because I felt happy or satisfied or comfortable, but because, by sharing my conversation with people whose mere presence pushed me to think in new and deeper ways, everyone at the table was transformed and made new.

And what a simple act it is.

A Death in the Family:
Reflections on Romans 6:1–11
and Matthew 10:24–39, *by Stan Saunders*

S E P T E M B E R   1 9 9 6

Editor's note: On July 23, 1996, Stan Saunders and his wife, Brenda Smith, had their seven-month-old son, Carson, baptized during the Open Door Sunday worship. Ed Loring, Murphy Davis, and Chuck Campbell, a professor at Columbia Theological Seminary, participated in the baptism. What follows is the sermon Stan preached at that service.

You've probably heard by now that we are planning to have Carson baptized today, and if you've seen any baptisms lately, especially baptisms of babies, you may be thinking that this will be a pleasant experience, a chance to look at a cute, little baby—the very image of sweetness and purity. You're probably thinking that someone will splash a little water on him, and as a worst case he might cry a bit, and then he will be "saved"—as if by magic—and we can all relax and have a nice supper. If this is your basic sense of things, you're probably not alone, since most of us have witnessed baptisms like this somewhere along the way.

"A Death in the Family" also appeared in Stanley P. Saunders and Charles L. Campbell, *The Word on the Street: Performing the Scriptures in the Urban Context* (Grand Rapids, Mich.: Eerdmans, 2000), 41–47.

Not long after I moved to Atlanta, I happened to watch a baptism on TV. It was the TV broadcast of a local church service, and the pastor—a kindly looking, older, white-haired man—took this cute little baby in a pretty white gown, said a few words and poured a little water on her head, and then held her up for everyone to see. The people in the church on TV "oooohed" and "aaaahed" and smiled and seemed to think it was all just the nicest thing. Watching this event on TV gave me a kind of critical distance, leading me to the observation that baptism has become, at least in the mainline churches, a benign rite, at best a cheap, sugarcoated salvation spectacle, designed mostly to make us feel warm and happy.

When we baptize we are telling a story. And it seems to me that the basic story line most observers would get by watching this ritual in many churches is that pastors are old, babies are cute—even cuter next to old pastors—and that something magical and nice happens when the two of them get together. I do not mean to disparage this image altogether, and I have to admit that I very much enjoy watching babies being baptized, but I do think there is something wrong with this picture. It has do with what's usually missing. Whatever else we might think is going on during a baptism, there should be no way to avoid the conclusion that while baptism is about new life and celebration, it is also about a death in the family. And I worry that when we baptize without making the reality of this death painfully clear, we are telling a version of the gospel story that has no cross in it. And that just isn't the gospel. So, in case you are tempted to watch what happens here today and merely smile, I need to tell you what will really be going on here.

In a few minutes we are going to put my son Carson to death. And soon after that we hope to raise him again. In fact, if all goes according to plan, these events will happen so quickly that you might think the death didn't really take place. But don't be fooled. Carson Paul Smith-Saunders is going to die today. Brenda and I have come to believe that this is necessary because we no longer trust our capacities, as sinners living in a broken and distorted world, to raise him up in a way that befits the dignity and beauty he possessed at the moment of his birth, and to preserve his life from the powers of violence and death. We are convinced that his ongoing participation in this world will only corrupt and finally destroy him. So, we've decided to give him back to God.

For us, his death today is real, not just a symbol or an abstraction. This reality is tempered only by the hope we hold for what this death means. He will cease to exist under the powers of this world, and will be transformed and transferred to a completely new and different kind of existence, with different powers and possibilities for life, with new eyes to see the world, and most important, with a new family and a new Lord. To use Paul's words, today Carson will be united with Christ in a death like his, he will be buried with him, and he will be crucified with Christ so that the body of sin might be destroyed. And when he is raised up again today, his primary family will no longer be Brenda and myself, or the Smiths and the Saunders, but now it will be all of those who live "in Jesus Christ," especially the family that is the Open Door Community. I want to make very clear what we think this means, first by talking about what Paul and the early Christians meant when they talked about baptism.

In the early chapters of Romans, Paul contrasts the story of Christ with the story of Adam. Adam is the representative character for the typically human story. His story is about disobedience, the fall from grace and the loss of paradise. Adam's life, and the lives of children, including all of us, is a story of frustration and toil and violence and death. Paul uses the words *sin* and *death* to describe the most important powers in Adam's life, and also in our lives. Because the term *sin* quickly entered the realm of religious language, which usually causes our ears to become heavy and our eyes to glaze over, it needs some fresh unpacking. When Paul talks about sin as a power, he is not thinking, as we usually do, of individual acts that break some law or taboo somewhere. For Paul, sin is the whole fabric of life lived in denial of the reality of a loving and merciful God. Sin is where all of us live, whatever we happen to be doing at the moment—good or bad—when we go about life as if the God of Jesus Christ did not exist.

At the beginning of Romans, Paul suggests that sin is not the cause of our alienation from God, but its symptom. When we choose to turn away from God, and become worshipers of the idols of this world, we inevitably enter a world where sin reigns over us. Sin is thus a powerful stain that covers everything we do and prevents us from seeing clearly and acting rightly. When sin is the dominant reality in our lives, we will necessarily conform our lives to its power—whether by giving in to its patterns and assumptions, for example by practicing the politics of self-interest and domination, or by denying its reality by engaging in pretense and deception. This means that for Paul, sin is not so much about the choices we make to do this or not do that, but about an even more basic loss of freedom and power to make good choices at all. Sin is the loss of freedom and power to become who we were meant to be. And when we have turned away from God and refused to trust God's graciousness, we can no more avoid sin and its consequences than we can avoid breathing in the air. The story of Adam, then, is the story of life frustrated and held captive by the alien power that Paul calls sin.

We all have our own personal versions of the story of Adam. These versions involve all of the events that have made us who we are—the families we were born into, our losses, our accomplishments in this world. Whatever we bring with us today—our skin color, our gender, our family histories, our stories of abuse and pain, our stories of life on the street, our bad self-esteem, our arrogance and pride, our ambitions and our insecurities—all of these together make up our particular stories in Adam. But the good news Jesus and Paul want to share with us is that we no longer need to live under the power of sin and be defined by our old stories.

According to Paul, there is only one way out of Adam's story of sin and death. We have to learn how to die as Jesus did. Baptism is a training in dying—dying especially to sin and the old self—so that new life can come into being.

Now you might say that Carson doesn't have much of an Adam story yet, but the reality is that his stories of sin and death have been in the planning stage for some time now, just waiting to swing into place at the right moments. The powers of this world have been ready and waiting for Carson to come along, just as they were ready for all of us.

As we all know, in this culture, our humanness is determined by how closely we stand in proximity to the standard that is usually held up as the norm for what it means to be human—white maleness. What do people see when they look at Carson? A boy. A white boy. These factors determine who he is, how he will be treated, what expectations we have for him, and how he will relate to other people. In real and powerful ways these definitions of humanity and his participation in them will determine what Carson's life means and what his options are.

Today, when Carson dies with Christ, all of these pieces of his identity, and all of our fleshly hopes and dreams for him, die, too, for baptism means the complete obliteration of this reality and these marks of identity. From this day forward his identity is in Christ, and Christ alone. This is the good news of the gospel. It's precisely what Jesus has in mind when he calls his disciples to give up their lives in order to save them. But, as the mission discourse (Matthew 10) makes clear, there are very real dangers attached to the call to follow Jesus in his mission. Think about how strange Carson's baptism today will make him, and how hard his life will be, after he has been raised from the dead today.

We fully expect that his dying and new life in Christ will eventually make him the butt of jokes and ridicule, like the disciple of Jesus, like Jesus himself, who was called Beelzebub—the king of the garbage pile—by his enemies. We expect that he will find it difficult sometimes to understand and get along with his playmates and peers, who may speak a much different language and have different codes of interaction than he has learned in the community of faith. He will have to struggle throughout most of his life to find ways to shape an identity that is not tied up with his being white and male, and if he succeeds it will make his relationships with women and men and with people of all colors more complex and difficult. He will need to learn to get along with others, and get out of trouble, without turning to dominance and intimidation. And we worry that learning these baptismal arts will make him vulnerable. We hope that he will not suffer because he has not learned to use violence to defend himself.

Carson's death today also has important and potentially painful consequences for Brenda and myself. In the first place, we know that if he's going to grow up in the Open Door Community, all of our plans to have him support us in our old age are hopelessly doomed. We also sense that we are not very well equipped to teach him all the things he will need to learn. We know that he will need to work with others of his kind—those who have made the transition from sin and death to life in Christ—to build economic relationships around sharing, gratitude, and dependence on God, rather than exploitation and self-interest; but we know that we are often not very good models or teachers for him in this regard. We know that as a disciple of Jesus he will sometimes have to struggle against his own family, even Brenda and myself, because we have been raised in this world and are too often consumed by the insecurities and addictions of the American middle class. That will cause us pain. Most important, we will have to learn how to love him without possessing him, or seeking to make him in our image, or making him a slave to our own needs, for he will no longer belong to us. We worry about how we can teach him to discern and trust in a God who promises to love and take care of us, when we so often struggle to trust God ourselves. How can we give him up to death, when we fear our own deaths so powerfully?

Of course we wouldn't be here doing this today if it were not for our own baptisms and the hope that God has nourished in us through the years for a new creation. And we wouldn't be *here* today were it not for the hope that we see at work in you all at the Open Door Community. Just as surely as we know that this baptism today marks the death of Carson Paul Smith-Saunders, we also trust that it marks the beginning of a new life, the life of Carson Paul, disciple of the crucified and raised Messiah of Israel and friend of the Open Door Community.

New and different ways of looking at and being in the world can only be sustained in the midst of other people who have also died to this world and whose stories and practices reflect—individually and corporately—their new reality. Carson will receive today a new identity in God, but that new being will only come into its fullness in the midst of a community that also lives in Christ.

I believe that baptism is the doorway into a new social order. Specifically, baptism entails the formation of a new people whose newness and togetherness render all "prior stratifications and classifications" and divisions, all prior stories and social arrangements, null and void. Paul talks about this most clearly in Galatians 3, where he says that as many of us as have been baptized into Christ have clothed ourselves with Christ. "There is no longer Jew or Greek, there is no longer slave or free, there is no longer male and female; for all of us are one in Christ Jesus." Now, the unfortunate fact is that it's not very easy to learn this baptismal reality in most churches today.

And that's where the Open Door Community comes into the picture. Today Carson joins the church universal, but he also joins the church particular—in this case the family that is the Open Door Community. We could have had Carson baptized in most any church in the city, but by having him baptized here today, we are intentionally committing him, as well as ourselves, to the peculiar ministry and disciplines of this community. We believe that there are some things he and we can learn only here in the midst of this chaotic, broken, and grace-filled family. And so we are joining our family with yours; and we are entrusting him to you. We hope and trust that you will love him and play with him and share your life with him as fully as you can. But we also have some other things in mind. Specifically, we are trusting you to treat him not as a person of privilege but as another brother and child of God. We hope that you will teach him how to negotiate the streets of the city with compassion, and wisdom, and faith. We want you to help us teach him to respect the dignity of all peoples, including his own God-given dignity, and how to suffer for the sake of others in the name of Jesus Christ. Please, teach him how to stand up and acknowledge the God who is re-creating a fallen world. Teach him how to lend his intelligence, his influence, his hands and voice and body to the mass of humanity that has no hands and no influence. And teach him the arts of mercy and forgiveness and how to hold on to hope in the midst of adversity and suffering.

And while we're teaching him all these things, let's not forget to learn from him—about how to play, how to look at the world through new eyes, and how to give forth perfect praise to God.

There is a death in our family today. But thanks be to God who raises us up every day to live in Christ.

Lent: Forty Days of Detox (Mark 8:27–38),
by Chuck Campbell

MARCH   2001

"Get behind me, Satan!" Jesus' words to Peter seem rather harsh and extreme. Jesus here is not a nice, polite southerner. And he certainly wouldn't receive very good marks for the pastoral care he gives to this friend who feels anxious about Jesus' impending death. What is Jesus doing? You just don't go around calling somebody "Satan," especially a friend, a disciple, who has just confessed you to be the Messiah. You just don't call somebody "Satan," particularly someone who wants to save your life and to help you be a *successful* Messiah. Jesus' behavior seems rather bizarre.

In fact, the whole text seems bizarre. Entering this text is like entering a house of mirrors, where all the shapes become distorted, and things are not what they seem, and illusion and reality get confused. In this text, Peter becomes Satan. Here the Messiah—the one expected to crush Israel's enemies and to reestablish Israel's power—is the one who will be rejected and who will suffer and be executed. In this text, death is life and life is death; we save our lives by losing them, and we lose our lives when we try to save them. Here the cross—the most brutal means of execution imaginable—is the way of power. In this house of mirrors we enter a world in which everything seems off balance. Truth and illusion do battle, and it's hard to tell one from the other.

That's what happens when Jesus comes face to face with Satan. A battle ensues between truth and illusion. Satan, you see, is the spirit—the driving force—of what we call "The System" at the Open Door, and what Walter Wink calls "The Domination System." Satan works by capturing our spirits and by shaping our imaginations—by "stealing our souls," to borrow an image from a recent article in *Hospitality.*[1] Satan works by the power of illusion, luring us to believe that the System's way is the way of life, when it is really the way of death. That's what Satan tries to do to Jesus in the wilderness; he tries to lure Jesus to the way of the System, rather than to the way of the cross. In our text, Jesus faces the same kind of temptation in his encounter with Peter. So Jesus has to battle the power of Satan's illusions. He has to battle at the level of the imagination. He has to help Peter and the disciples and the crowd and the church see the world differently. He has to try to free imaginations that have been captured by Satan's house of mirrors—by the illusions of the System.

We know those illusions, don't we?—the illusions of the System. They sound something like this: "Real life comes from gaining power *over* others"—men *over* women, whites *over* Blacks. "Real life comes from feeling *superior* to others"—insiders superior to outsiders, heterosexuals superior to homosexuals. "Fullness of life comes from possessing *more* than others"—so folks consume and accumulate until some have more than they could ever use, while others live on the streets with nothing. "Real life comes from *winning*"—so "We're number one!" becomes the rallying cry of our culture. "Victorious living involves *violently defeating* our enemies," whether killing them with weapons or putting them in prison.

These are the illusions of the System. And this is the spirituality of the System—*over, superior, more, win, violence, defeat.* This System seeks to steal our souls; it wants to become the air we breathe, until we cannot imagine alternatives. On his journey to the cross, which begins in our text, Jesus time and again seeks to expose these illusions. He seeks to help his disciples and us see the world differently so that we might live in it differently. Not surprisingly, the story before the story we read this evening concerns Jesus healing a blind man. Jesus is

---

1. See "The Soul Stealers" in Part Three (ed.).

trying to open our eyes. He is taking our imaginations through detox so we might see the world in a new way and live as new people.

This is what Jesus seeks to do in his encounter with Peter. Peter's imagination has become captive to the System. To be sure, Peter's intentions are good. At the political level, Peter has recognized the significance of Jesus' ministry, and he has confessed him to be the Messiah. He wants Jesus to succeed. But Peter's imagination is captive to the System's understanding of power. He can only envision power *over* others; he can only imagine the Messiah as a military leader who will win victory through violence and domination. He simply cannot imagine an alternative.

Peter's intentions are good. At the personal level, Peter wants Jesus to live, not to be executed. Who can blame him? But Peter has no conception that the way of the System is the way of death. Peter cannot imagine a death larger and broader and deeper than physical death. He cannot comprehend that when we become captive to the System, we become little more than walking dead people.

So Jesus tries to help Peter see. The way of the System is in fact the way of death. Resisting the System—even if it means crucifixion—is the way of life. But Peter cannot imagine that alternative. It's tragic, really. Peter thinks he is offering Jesus life, but he asks Jesus to take the way of death. Peter is a lot like a friend offering a drink to an alcoholic: "Here, take a drink. It will ease the pain; you'll feel better, more alive." But when alcoholics are in recovery they know that those promises are illusions: the drink is not the way of life, but the path to certain death. So Jesus responds, like the recovering alcoholic may have to respond when tempted by a drink: "Get behind me, Satan!"

Those words no longer sound so extreme. Peter has become an embodiment of the System. And such sharp words are necessary. The illusions of the world have to be named boldly and dramatically because they are so subtle and pervasive. The Christian short story writer Flannery O'Connor was asked why she wrote strange stories with such bizarre characters. She responded something like this: "When you're writing for people who are blind, you have to draw big pictures." Or, to put it another way, when you're speaking to people whose imaginations have been captured by the System, you have to speak boldly. As Ed Loring discovered the other day, the word for "prophet" originally meant "shouter." And that is appropriate. In the face of Satan's illusions, we are called to become shouters. We are called to be like the little child in the story of "The Emperor's New Clothes." When everyone else goes along with the illusion in order to appear good and obedient and wise, the little child cries out before the emperor, "He's naked!" The spell is broken; illusions are shattered. And the people are set free in laughter.

In the face of Satan, in the face of principalities and powers, Jesus speaks boldly: "Get behind me, Satan!" There is no other way. In fact, Jesus' words are an act of love. Jesus demonstrates his love for Peter and for us by speaking directly and boldly—by jolting us out of our captivity to the System, by awakening our imaginations to the alternative way of God.

This story has caused me to rethink the season of Lent. Often we understand Lent as a quiet, introspective, private time. But that is not the picture we get in the lectionary. Last week, we read the story of Jesus' temptation in the wilderness. Lent begins with the conflict between Jesus and Satan. This week, the struggle with Satan continues, as the spirit of the System again tests Jesus in the person of Peter. Lent, the lectionary seems to be saying, involves this ongoing conflict with Satan. During Lent we remember and celebrate Jesus' life-and-death struggle with the System and its illusions. We remember and celebrate the ways in which Jesus exposes the powers of the world and helps us see them for what they are—not the way of life, but the way of death. During this season, we remember and celebrate how Jesus frees us from the power of death, so that we might follow him on the way of life—even to the cross.

That is why Lent traditionally ended with the wrenching and dynamic sacrament of baptism. For in that sacrament we ritually enact our dying to the old world and our rebirth into the new. In the early church, those baptisms required people to renounce Satan and all his works. They included exorcisms, through which the church cast out the demonic power of the System, which steals people's souls. Baptism was the culmination of Lent, during which the imaginations of believers went through detox.

❖ ❖ ❖

Lent is not a quiet time, but a time of heightened conflict. It is, in fact, a time of detoxification. During Lent we examine ourselves and our communities; we look honestly at our own captivity to the System. We explore how our lives and communities have been shaped by the spirit of the System—that spirit of *over, more, win, defeat, violence.* During Lent we seek to discern where Jesus is saying "Get behind me, Satan!" And that discernment can be as painful and wrenching as detox.

Lent is also a time to take up practices that reshape our imaginations in the way of Jesus. Lent is not just about our heads or our spirits, but about our bodies. To be sure, the way we think often shapes how we live. But the opposite is also true. The way we live shapes how we think—how we come to see the world. During Lent we take up and reaffirm the practices through which the Holy Spirit frees us from the illusions of the System—practices that embody an alternative to the ways of the System. We take up afresh practices in which we stand *with* others, not *over* others. We renew practices in which we *share,* rather than grab for more. We engage in practices in which we *serve* others, rather than trying to defeat them. And we live out practices in which *reconciliation* and *shalom* replace violence against strangers and enemies.

In this sense, the Open Door is a Lenten community. For these are the practices that shape our life together: the Hardwick trip, the breakfast, the showers, the soup kitchen, the death-row visitation. These practices help form an alternative imagination. At the center of all these practices is this table, where, as the Christian educator Michael Warren has reminded us, the shouts of "we're number one!" are transformed into the celebration that "we are one!" Lent is a time to reclaim these practices and to recommit ourselves to them. For these practices challenge the illusions of Satan. They detoxify our imaginations. They help us, in the words of the song we often sing on Wednesday mornings, "shake the devil off." Through these practices, the Holy Spirit is at work to reclaim our souls and to set us free from the spirit of the System.

Shaped by these practices, we're ready to take up the cross and to carry it into the streets. We're ready to take up Jesus' *political* resistance to the System. We're able to name and expose the illusions of the System in the public arena. This is what we've been doing through the Grady Coalition. And this is what we will be doing during Holy Week through our twenty-four-hour street vigils and our public worship at Grady Memorial Hospital and the jail and City Hall and the Capitol. We will be seeking to follow the way of Jesus and to expose the illusions of the System. We will be taking up the role of that little child who shouted, "He's naked!" in the face of the emperor. We will be proclaiming that the kingdoms of this world already have become the kingdom of the Lamb.

We're in a life-and-death struggle with the spirit of Satan, who would steal our souls. We're taking our imaginations through detox. And we're trying to expose the illusions of the System. To be sure, it may not seem like we're doing much. It may seem like no one is listening and no one really cares. The illusions of the System are powerful and pervasive. The story of Jesus is more realistic than the story of "The Emperor's New Clothes." In Jesus' story, everyone doesn't see the emperor's nakedness immediately and begin to laugh. Rather, the crowds turn on the one who shouts, "He's naked!" They respond with angry cries of "Crucify him! Crucify him!" They prefer their captivity to the freedom Jesus offers.

But in the face of those cries, Jesus gives us an odd promise that, to the System, makes no sense: "Those who lose their life for my sake, and for the sake of the gospel, will save it." Salvation belongs to the Lamb who was slain. Trusting that promise, we can continue the struggle of Lent. Trusting that promise, we come to the table to be nurtured for that journey.

How Happy You Will Be! *by Elizabeth Dede*

M A R C H   1 9 8 9

In the church year, we are now in the middle of the penitential season known as Lent. It is a time of inner reflection, of repentance and change. Often when we repent, we reflect on mandates, because we become aware of the laws and commandments that we have broken as sinful people. Thus, as we go through Lent, we often give things up and take on disciplines in order to conform our lives to the will of God.

Indeed, mandates are an integral part of Lent. During this season there is even a day called Maundy Thursday—the Thursday of Holy Week. *Maundy* is the Middle English word that means "mandate." Traditionally, on that Thursday, many churches celebrate the Lord's Supper, remembering that on the night he was betrayed, before he was handed over to be killed by the state, Jesus shared a meal with his followers, and gave them the mandate to continue to share that bread and cup in his memory.

The Gospel according to John gives a different account of Jesus' last Thursday with his followers. In addition to the meal that he shared, Jesus also bent down and washed his disciples' dirty feet. When he was finished, he gave his followers the mandate to do the same—a mandate that we rarely follow. So during this season of Lent, I think it is important to reflect on foot washing and to put it into practice.

At the Open Door we often practice foot washing at our community retreats. For me, it has become a sacrament every bit as important as baptism and the Lord's Supper. And unlike the Lord's Supper and baptism, I have several specific memories of foot washing.

I remember how awkward I felt the first time I practiced foot washing. It was the middle of February, my feet were cold, and I thought it was pretty ridiculous to perform this ritual that no church I had ever attended practiced. But then I was a staid and sedate Lutheran. When it was over I was completely surprised to find that foot washing had become for me a holy ritual with as much, or more, meaning than the Lord's Supper.

Then there was the time when Gabriel Cole Vodicka, a little baby at the time, plopped himself down by the tub of water, and, smiling and giggling, splashed himself from head to toe. We wondered if he felt like Peter: "Lord, do not wash only my feet, then! Wash my hands and head, too!"

Once Rob Johnson preached a mini-sermon on foot washing and coined a phrase that floated around the community for a time. "Foot washing," he said, was a "novelty of niceness." It is something new and different for the leader to bend down and serve. And while it may not be necessary to wash each other's feet, it is a "niceness" to have your feet soaked in warm water and rubbed dry with a towel. After the sermon, we went through our days looking for "novelties of niceness" to perform for each other.

Perhaps the strongest impression I have of foot washing is the unsophisticated, uninhibited sense of joy I always experience. Somebody struggles with stifling the giggles as their feet get tickled, but the laughter always wins, and the room fills with happiness.

However, foot washing is not just a laughing matter, and I have often thought about its sacramental qualities. As there is more to the Lord's Supper than a piece of bread and a cup of juice, so there is more to this mandate to wash each other's feet than soap and water. Foot washing is, as are the traditional sacraments, a means of grace instituted by Jesus. Jesus says to his followers, "I have set an example for you, so that you will do just what I have done for you. I am telling you the truth: no slave is greater than their master, and no messenger is greater than the one who sent them. Now that you know this truth, how happy you will be if you put it into practice!"

What was it that Jesus did for his followers? It was a fairly amazing, yet simple, act. Jesus, the Lord and Teacher, the master of the slaves, the sender of the messengers, stooped and washed the dirtiest part of his students, his slaves, his messengers. Then he instructed them to do the same for each other, and to learn the truth: that he had sent them to serve the lowly, not those who typically are served. Jesus promises happiness to his followers if they put into practice the truth he has just taught. So there is grace—a fitness, a blessing, a mercy granted—in the simple act of servanthood.

Here we are in Lent with a mandate to serve—not the rich and the powerful (who typically have servants)—but the poor and the oppressed (who typically are servants). How will we know that we are following Jesus' mandate? Jesus tells us clearly through the gracious gift of joy: "How happy you will be if you put it into practice!"

Traditionally, Lent is a time of sadness and mourning. The hymns we sing are somber, telling of Jesus' suffering and death for us. Often we practice a discipline of giving something up for Lent so that, in some small way, through deprivation, we can experience the suffering of Jesus.

Perhaps this Lent we should focus more on Jesus' mandate to practice the truth and to find happiness. Perhaps we should spend this season of Lent reflecting on our daily activities and the happiness in our lives. Is there joy in what we do, or are we merely occupying our time so we can be numb to the dread that fills our days? Do we go to work because it makes us happy, or are we trapped by the need to make money so that we can buy a new car, or a newer, bigger house, or a television, or a computer, or anything else that fills our lives with a false sense of happiness—false because it masks the pain and struggle of our world, false because it is self-serving, false because the desired object might break, or crash with economic failure. Most important, are we serving the poor and the oppressed? That is where we will find happiness, according to Jesus' mandate.

To those of us on top, it seems strange that Jesus would suggest a life of servanthood as the source of happiness. There is much suffering, much pain, and it is felt keenly by the poor, because they cannot buy their way off the street or out of prison; the poor cannot comfort themselves with material goods to forget their struggle. Those who live in service to the poor must know and feel the suffering and pain, too. How can there be happiness where there is suffering and pain?

In the January/February 1989 issue of *The Other Side,* an interview with Elizabeth O'Connor touches precisely on this question. In answer to a question about vocation, O'Connor says, "I have been listening to Bill Moyers interviewing Joe Campbell on PBS about the power of myth. Campbell says that we need to be in touch with our bliss. Of course he's right. Our vocation, if it is truly a call for us, is bliss. But because we carry the opposites in us, the way of finding out our vocation in life is to be in touch with our pain. Our pain will put us in touch with our bliss and with what will heal us."

There is much pain in the world—war, starvation, race hatred, homelessness, poverty, prison, broken relationships, death—and in those places of pain we find the people Jesus calls us to serve; when we serve in those places, we know not only our own pain, but we know the happiness that Jesus promises.

Elizabeth O'Connor gives as an example of a person who found bliss in his vocation the inventor Thomas Edison. When asked, "What do you fear?" Edison answered, "I fear only one thing. I fear the dark." Through this fear, Edison became the inventor of the electric lightbulb and gave us light in the dark.

Unlike Edison, I fear many things, but I have a particular fear of separation and loneliness. That pain is one reason that I have a vocation to visit in prison. In some small way, I feel the great pain that my friends in prison know as they are locked away from family and friends. The loneliness of their lives, shut away from the world, makes my heart hurt, because I fear the same loneliness. Sometimes seeing the daffodils bloom in the field at Dayspring Farm makes me cry. They are so beautiful, and the thought of never seeing them again is too painful. Yet my friends on death row live with that pain every day.

I remember planning a visit to my friend Jack on death row and looking forward to it with dread. I was afraid of being locked inside for so many hours. I didn't want to wait for the guard in the tower to notice me and to unlock the big, heavy iron gate. I didn't want to sign in. I didn't want to go through the metal detector. I didn't want to give up my keys and license. I didn't want to wait for two more big, heavy iron gates to be opened. I didn't want to go. I had nightmares. I dreamed that, after I had visited Jack, I got into the car, but I couldn't get off the prison grounds. I kept driving around, but there was no way out. On the free side of the fence, friends kept walking by, but they were all wearing prisoners' uniforms, and nobody would look at me or help me. I was alone and separated from everybody I love. Perhaps Jack sensed my dread, because a few days before the scheduled visit I received an invitation to a picnic from him. That lightened my heart, I visited Jack, and we imagined our picnic and laughed and talked, and I was in touch with my bliss that day. Certainly, Jack's life on death row is no picnic, but he has taught me and given me much joy, even in the midst of pain and suffering. I'm sure that is the kind of happiness Jesus promises if we follow the mandate he gave on the last Thursday of his life.

As we fast and pray and confess and repent this Lent, let us remember Jesus' mandate that we wash each other's feet. Let us look for the places of pain where we can serve and find our bliss. Let us help the tired, sore, and dirty among us know the promise of happiness as we soak them, tickle them, rub them, and make them clean again. "How happy you will be!"

O Sacred Head, Now Wounded, *by Elizabeth Dede*

FEBRUARY 1988

> *O sacred head, now wounded,*
> *With grief and shame weighed down,*
> *Now scornfully surrounded*
> *With thorns, thine only crown;*
> *O sacred head, what glory,*
> *What bliss till now was thine!*
> *Yet, though despised and gory,*
> *I joy to call thee mine.*

Not too long ago, for our evening's entertainment, Tim, Dietrich, and I got together to sing. We enjoyed being with each other, the three-part harmony was fun, and the attempt at music brought joy to our hearts. For some reason, though, I kept breaking down at the third line of "O Sacred Head, Now Wounded"—I couldn't seem to make it to the glory and the bliss. The musical line was too difficult for my unpracticed ear.

Perhaps my inability is indicative, though, of the violence, the grief and shame, that surround us at the Open Door. More often we see despised and gory heads than blissful ones.

❖ ❖ ❖

Last summer, a young, strong man barged into the orderliness of our Wednesday-morning shower line, and, ahead of twenty-three people who waited patiently outside, he shoved into the shower room and proceeded to take a shower. After considerable struggle, we managed to persuade him to put his clothes on and leave. We normally don't provide showers in such a chaotic manner, and, because of the gross disturbance, we asked him to stay away from our house for several weeks. With much verbal abuse ringing in our ears, we restored some order and continued the showers.

The next morning, as we opened the door for the Thursday soup kitchen, there he was again, barging, shoving, and shouting his way to the front of the line. With his bare-midriff T-shirt, muscles rippling in his abdomen, biceps bulging, and loud voice roaring, he was not a person we relished confronting. Again, we asked him to leave because we have a peaceful home and do not allow that kind of violent presence in the house or yard. Finally, after much blustering and threatening on both sides (he offering to kill us, we promising to call the police), he left.

But the next morning, as we were loading the van to bring the grits, oranges, eggs, and coffee to the Butler Street Church, he was back again. Forcefully, he demanded an egg. Again, we reminded him that he was not welcome. By this time, we were worn down. We asked him to go away for a year. Not daunted by this new development, he sauntered down to the sidewalk and bellowed, "Now I'm on public property. Just try to make me leave." What glory, what bliss he seemed to be enjoying. This time we did call the police, but by the time they arrived, he had walked off. We never saw him again.

❖ ❖ ❖

Last summer, I began to visit my friend on death row. Once we talked about enduring all kinds of hardship. He told me of encouraging words his father had spoken: "You may have a broken heart, but you don't have a broken neck; hold your head up." When the world despises you, the weight of that grief weighs your head down. Sometimes the semblance of glory and bliss helps the broken heart. It makes you appear more honorable, less shameful.

❖ ❖ ❖

Recently, as I rode to Jackson, Georgia, to visit my friend, Dietrich told me this story:

> I went out for a walk last night, and I saw a big, strong
> man, with his back to me, standing in the shadows of the alley.

As I passed by, he quietly called out, "Hey! Come help me get dressed." I stopped and told him to come out into the light. He did, and I recognized him as the one who had given us so much trouble last summer. But now he wasn't flaunting his bulging muscles, or loudly threatening me. Instead, with his head hung down, he quietly asked me to help him get dressed. It became apparent that he had been beaten and stripped. Blood flowed from a gash on his head. I told him to wait while I went inside to get some peroxide and bandages.

When I came back and cleaned his wound and bandaged his head, he kept asking, "Why are you helping me? Why are you helping me? Don't you know who I am? Why are you helping me?" I told him that I was helping him because he needed help and because he had asked for help. And I told him that I recognized him as the one who had caused us so much trouble and been so threatening back in the summer.

I helped him pull up his pants and zip up his jacket and put on his coat. Then I put the blood-soaked cap back on his head. He told me about the shame of this beating—how the man who had done it to him must be down at the liquor store, flaunting his strength and glorying in the weakness of the beaten. He told me of the grief of living in a cat hole in the frigid winter, with no family or friends to turn to. And then he walked off into the darkness.

❖ ❖ ❖

When my friend came into the visiting room, I could see that he had been beaten badly. Both eyes were blackened and swollen, his nose and cheeks were puffy, his forehead was bandaged. Though my friend struggles every day to live in peace with his fellow prisoners, he had suffered a seemingly unprovoked attack. His face was beaten, his nose and cheek cracked. The back of his head had been split on a steel door, his back lacerated by wire.

As we sat and talked, my friend told me of some of his grief. He was in physical pain, and he felt pain for the man who had beaten him, who was now being threatened with violence from other prisoners. My friend worried about the pain of separation from his friends if prison officials decided that he should be moved to a different cell block. Finally, he told me of the grief of his mother's death. After a long illness, she had died on New Year's Day. My friend could not attend her funeral.

Even in all this adversity, my friend's spirit was in good health. He told me that he rarely experiences joy, that he never prays for it. But he knows peace and always asks God to give him a peaceful heart.

❖ ❖ ❖

Another verse of "O Sacred Head" goes like this:

> What language shall I borrow
> To thank thee, dearest friend,
> For this thy dying sorrow,
> Thy pity without end?
> Oh, make me thine forever,
> And, should I fainting be,
> Lord, let me never, never
> Outlive my love for thee.

I suspect that I would not be able to sing the third line of this verse either, "Oh, make me thine forever." I am fainting.

❖ ❖ ❖

Words fail me. I do not know what language to borrow. When will the violence end? If the sacred head was wounded two thousand years ago because of our sins, why do we continue to see beaten heads, weighed down with grief and shame?

Have we outlived love? Never. Never. Love never gives up. Why is a young, strong man living on the streets without a home when we slip on the ice and snow and the radio reports it is nine degrees? Where is our love for our sisters and brothers? Where is our love for Jesus? Why are people condemned to die when we all know that Jesus has already died to atone for our sins? Where is our love for Jesus?

During Lent we participate in a penitential season when we remember Jesus' suffering and death. As we remember the Passion story, we must remember our own part in that bitter passion. When we have not given a home to a homeless sister or brother, we have caused Jesus to be homeless. When we have passed by an injured person, we have passed by Jesus. When we have not fed the hungry, we have let Jesus go away hungry. When we have not visited the prisoner, we have missed the opportunity to be with Jesus. When the state has executed people in our names, we have executed Jesus. As we reflect during this penitential season on our part in Jesus' suffering and death, we must come to repentance—a turning away from our old selves. It is not enough to feel sorry for the times when we have ignored, injured, or killed Jesus; we must realize that we have done these things, and then we must change.

At the end of the Passion season, we experience not only death, but resurrection. That resurrection gives us the strength to change. When we have come through repentance, we must feed the hungry, give homes to the homeless, care for the sick and injured, visit those in prison, and bring life to those condemned to death; otherwise, the resurrection has no meaning. We may as well leave Jesus dead and buried if we are not willing to respond to the living Christ among us. Even now, may the risen Jesus fill us with love and peace so that we all can know our sin, act in a new way, and hold up our heads in resurrection glory and bliss.

Easter Comes Even When We're
Shut Outside in the Storm, *by Murphy Davis*

MARCH / APRIL 1986

For the past ten years our lives have been lived in increasing solidarity with women and men in prison. For the past six years our love and solidarity with homeless people has grown.

Part of the cost of discipleship is to know the painful tension that exists between faithfulness and failure. Even as we try to set our sights on Easter morning, our vision is often blocked by the darkness of Golgotha, and the pain of displacement often seems more prominent than the hope of resurrection. The road to Jerusalem mocks our attempts to proclaim the resurrection: that it is time for the blind to see, for the lame to walk, for the prisoners to be released, for the homeless poor to be recognized as citizens of the Kingdom of God.

As we serve, we struggle to say, "Our little crumbs of service are not enough. What the poor and downtrodden need is not our piecemeal charity, but justice." Not that we will close the soup kitchen or shower line or shelters. Not that we will stop visiting in the prisons and jails, or stop writing letters. Indeed, the lines at the door are longer each month. The number of prisoners grows faster than we can count. And so we will pray for the grace to continue in service. But this is not an answer. An answer would only come in the form of justice. Wholeness. Enough for all God's children.

There is no need for homelessness, or hunger, or the quick tendency to cage other people. There is sickening overabundance in the world for the privileged class. The world's rich struggle constantly with being overweight while billions starve. Medical technology steams ahead with organ transplants and the creation of artificial organs while the simplest health care is largely unavailable to the poor. Black infant mortality in the United States rises. The cries of the poor go largely unheard. And so we cannot satisfy ourselves with words alone. Talk is cheap and often changes little. We must struggle to find the way to embody, to incarnate, the misery of the poor in the public arena.

Last year, Palm Sunday—the beginning of Holy Week—happened to fall on March 31, the last night for ten out of thirty of the city's winter night shelters. It has been our hope that the city and church shelters would stay open past April 1. The critical need for shelter and hospitality is hardly a seasonal reality.

So we decided as a liturgical act of solidarity to join our homeless sisters and brothers and to take our Holy Week worship to the streets. From the Sunday night of Palm Sunday to the early morning of Easter we would live on the streets in twos, fours, eights. Each night as we gathered for worship we would welcome those who had been out for twenty-four hours and send others out to wander the streets and shadows of the city.

I was in the first group. We gathered for worship on the evening of Palm Sunday, and then we left to walk downtown. Norman Heinrichs-Gale, John Pickens, and I set out with Richard Schaper (one of the pastors of the Lutheran Church of the Redeemer). We left bursting with energy. I thought I knew something about the streets. I though it wouldn't be so bad. It was supposed to be only about fifty degrees that night, certainly warm enough to be out.

What I learned by 7:00 P.M. Monday has forever changed my feelings, thoughts, and sense of urgency about homelessness.

The entire night was an experience of being moved. "You can't stay here!" "You have to leave!" "Move on!" Bus stations, hospital waiting rooms, even heating grates outside buildings: "*Move on.*" Security guards seemed to be everywhere. The rules were all the same. You can't sit here. You can't stay there. "You have to go!"

The only sleep I got all night was at the Trailways bus station. For fifteen minutes I drifted off. But then my shoulder was shaken. This guard was apologetic: "I'm sorry. You can't sleep here. You'll have to leave. Don't you have any place to stay?" I went to waken Norman, who was sleeping soundly several chairs down from me. He jumped up without realizing that his legs had gone to sleep because of his odd position in the chair. He reeled around, trying to keep his balance, and finally we managed to leave.

We found a place to slip into a park and could have stayed all night. But it was too cold to sleep. A fifty-degree night is not warm. It was not life-threatening, but when your only bed is the ground or the concrete, it's too cold to sleep. And so we kept moving, wandering with no real place to go. The early-evening spring in our steps slowed. By midnight it was a labored shuffle. How long 'til morning? How long?

We knew that 6 A.M. would bring the opening doors of the city's day-labor center. There we sat in plastic chairs and slept, but no one made us move on. It was very crowded and noisy, but sleep came easily for thirty minutes or so.

Eight o'clock brought the blessed opening of the "grits line" at Butler Street Church. We at the Open Door had been preparing this breakfast for a long time by then, but never did I realize how wonderful a bowl of hot grits, an egg, orange slices, and a steaming cup of hot coffee could look. Finally I felt warm inside.

We headed for Central City Park. All I wanted was to lie down and sleep in the sunshine. It was still chilly and windy, but I fell asleep on the grass.

I woke to find that my male companions were a short distance away, so that I appeared to be alone. Two young men nearby started to hassle me. Groggy and disoriented by this time, I nearly exploded with anger. I was angry that I felt so bad. I was mad at these guys for hassling me. I was angry because I felt vulnerable. I was furious with a society that assumes women to be objects for male sport. I got up in a huff and stalked off, muttering under my breath.

We hit all the soup kitchens on Peachtree that day. Even after I was satisfied, I kept eating and kept drinking coffee because it was more pleasant to sit down in a friendly space than to stay on the move. We saw many friends at St. Luke's and Redeemer. "Hey!" said one guy who occasionally comes to our soup kitchen. "Hey, did you get put out of 910?"

We talked about what we were doing, why we were on the streets, why Holy Week was an important time for us to share with our homeless friends. Our explanations were met with a mixture of interest and curiosity. To many it seemed strange that anyone would be on the streets for any reason but a cruel twist of fate.

The rest of the day was a blur: we moved around, always looking for a place to sit down and rest, a place to use a bathroom, a spot to warm ourselves in the sun. Time became very heavy. My feet and legs ached. The day was very long.

As the sun set it got cold again. I was afraid the 7:30 P.M. worship service in the courtyard of Central Presbyterian Church would never come.

But finally we gathered, a little knot of folk, singing, reading scripture, standing very close to keep warm, praying for our homeless friends with a newfound fervor.

John, Norman, Richard, and I got in the cars with those returning home. Four others left the circle and disappeared into the night.

And so it went through the week. We gathered for our Holy Week liturgy on the streets for six nights, at Central Presbyterian (home to a large night shelter, now closed for the spring), St. Luke's Episcopal (soup kitchen), Central City Park, First Methodist Church (women's day shelter), City Hall, and Plaza Park. Always we were outside, whatever the weather. Each night a group would come into our circle and another group would leave.

On Good Friday we learned something new about being outsiders. As we gathered on the steps of City Hall for our liturgy, storm clouds hung in the sky. We hoped we would not get wet. We were joined by friends from Columbia Seminary and St. Jude's Catholic Parish.

Perhaps, we thought, we'd start a bit early to finish before the rain. Rob Johnson began a prayer to open our worship. He recalled that the curtain in the Temple was torn in two as Jesus died. The wind picked up. Suddenly a siren blared through the city, and we realized in horror that it was a tornado warning. The rain and wind ripped through our little circle like a freight train. It seemed almost to lift the children off the ground. Without a word we all ran toward the building. Lights shone within, and as we began to knock frantically and then to pound on the doors we saw three guards sitting at a desk in the center hall. As the wind tore at us we clung to each other and held the frightened children close. In a matter of minutes we were soaked to the skin. For what seemed like forever the guards sat passively and stared at us. They did not move from the desk.

Some of us began looking for a ditch, but there was nothing. There we were, in front of glass doors as the sirens wailed and the wind threatened to sweep us away. The guards talked to each other. After what seemed an eternity, one of them picked up a phone. A man in a tie appeared from an upstairs office. He pressed his weight to open the door against the wind. We could come in, he said, and stand between the two sets of doors 'til the storm passed.

We re-formed our circle. As we dripped on the floor we began our liturgy, "The Family of the Crucified" (adapted from a liturgy written by the American Christians for the Abolition of Torture).

"We have come together . . . to walk with Christ down the Via Dolorosa, to enter into his sufferings. Christ is in agony today in the sufferings of his people and in the pain of those who suffer as he did—homeless, despised, arrested, tortured, mocked, abused, and finally, executed by the state.

"As we ask Christ to let us enter into solidarity with him we sense his response: 'Enter into the sufferings of those who suffer and are oppressed in your world today. I suffer continuously in them. . . .'"

There we stood: on the marble floor of the entrance to Atlanta's City Hall. There we stood: conscious that we had chosen for a short time to go to the streets, to give up the privileges of sitting comfortably inside for worship; conscious that God had given us the gift of an experience of vulnerability. There we stood: at the foot of the cross, awaiting the dawn of God's new day, perhaps a day when all the safe, warm spaces are not locked and protected by security guards.

Holy Week on the streets helped us long for Easter. The winds of Good Friday stirred our passion to extend the safe, warm space and to welcome those locked out in the storm.

Easter morning burst forth in the grimy, desolate parking lot beside the municipal market on Butler Street. Multicolored helium balloons and bright flowers covered the fences and walls, and music filled the air. We gathered to sing, dance, preach, pray, and shout with 350 of our homeless sisters and brothers: "Jesus Christ is risen from the grave. He ain't dead! Freedom is real! Oppression will be overcome! Love is stronger than death! All of the doors are gonna swing wide and the children of the earth are gonna come inside and feast together."

And feast together we did! Three hundred fifty of us shared a huge breakfast, there in that grimy parking lot that had become beautiful: we shared steak and eggs, grits and coffee and buns, and it was glorious! Lord! How this city needs Easter! Lord! How the human race needs Easter!

And Easter comes! Again and again. Even when we're shut outside in the storm: Easter comes! Even when we wander the streets, lost and alone: Easter comes! Even when we get lost in our resentment and bitterness: Easter comes!

Jesus Christ wouldn't stay in the grave. Easter has come. Hallelujah!

Easter Foolishness, *by Elizabeth Dede*

A P R I L   1 9 8 7

The message about Christ's death on the cross is nonsense to those becoming lost; but for us being saved it is God's power. The scripture says, "I will destroy the wisdom of the wise and set aside the understanding of the scholars." So then, where does that leave the wise? Or the scholars? Or the skillful debaters of this world? God has shown that this world's wisdom is foolishness!

God in her wisdom made it impossible for people to know her by their own wisdom. Instead, by means of the so-called foolish message we preach, God decided to save those who believe. We proclaim the crucified Christ, who is the power of God and the wisdom of God. What seems to be God's foolishness is wiser than human wisdom, and what seems to be God's weakness is stronger than human strength.

❖ ❖ ❖

A sense of the ridiculous, of the absurd, is a healthy thing, and necessary, as we have come to know. Therefore, between the seasons of Epiphany and Lent, here at the Open Door, we observe the holiday called Mardi Gras on the Tuesday before Ash Wednesday. Mardi Gras is a day when we behave foolishly and celebrate. This year clowns came to entertain us; we ate turkey gumbo; everybody dressed in a silly way with costumes provided by the clothes closet. (I disguised myself as a tree, dyed my hair green with food coloring, and now, almost two weeks later, I still display the tint of ridiculousness.) We paraded around the house, banging pots and pans; Joe Bottoms, wearing lovely curtains, led us in the boogie contest. Even as Mardi Gras allows us to celebrate wildly before we enter the penitential season of Lent, when we fast, abstain, and consider our sinful human nature and the passion of Jesus, Mardi Gras also allows us to leap ahead to the joys of Easter, one of the most ridiculous, foolish, absurd days imaginable. It is good to reflect at Easter on foolishness and nonsense because on Easter God's "foolishness" is shown to be God's ultimate wisdom, and God's "weakness" is displayed finally as God's strength.

Much in our lives seems foolish. Our community is formed of two partners, one novice, ten resident volunteers, one child, and eighteen formerly homeless people. We all live together in a big, old house. Those of us on staff receive fifty-dollar-per-month stipends and survive on donations of food, clothes, and money. Most of us who are partners, novices, or resident volunteers come from privileged backgrounds, and many of us have permanently or temporarily set aside careers as scholars. Our daily work consists of cooking grits and eggs, making coffee, cooking soup, serving food, helping people find clothes, and calling out names for spaces in the shelter. Certainly, our disappointed professors, friends, and families will call this ridiculous.

During Holy Week, the Open Door Community keeps a twenty-four-hour presence on the streets in solidarity with our homeless sisters and brothers. Throughout the year, several of us go out once a month to spend twenty-four hours with our friends on the streets. We are taken in the police wagon to the city night shelter; sometimes we sleep outside in the park or on the steps of the Fulton County Health Department; we eat at the grits line at Butler Street; we sit in the labor pools; we watch the bent and broken struggle into Grady Hospital; we eat at the soup kitchens; we observe the proceedings at municipal court, and grow sad when friends are sentenced for public urination because no public toilets are available, or for criminal trespass when there is no place to go. Indeed, this time on the streets often seems like so much nonsense.

I remember one cold, rainy night in August when we huddled close to the doors of the Fulton County Health Department, hoping that the pouring rain wouldn't blow in on us, shivering from the cold, not sleeping from discomfort and fear, and praying for the morning to come quickly so that we could get inside. How ludicrous, I thought, that we sit in these foul conditions across from a hospital and in front of a health department, when the healthy, human thing would be to sleep in a bed in a warm, dry home. What a weakness in society that our friends John, Preacher, and Pork Chop spend most nights in the summer on those stoops because nobody cares enough to help provide them with homes! And most people who sleep in beds in warm, dry homes would laugh derisively at the ridiculous suggestion that they spend a night on the steps of the Fulton County Health Department and so begin, maybe, to understand this weakness.

Right now we are struggling for a park, the Al Smith Park, in downtown Atlanta. Plaza Park, where many of our homeless friends live, will soon be closed as part of the development of Underground Atlanta. We want a new park with toilets, water fountains, and shelter so that our sisters and brothers on the streets can continue to find sanctuary in downtown Atlanta. It is foolishness that a city which will host the Democratic National Convention, a sign of our country's liberty and justice, will not host its own children, will not provide even the most meager home afforded by a park with toilets and water fountains. How non-sensical that we must struggle for a park when justice requires warm, dry, safe homes for all of God's children!

As we struggle for this park, we march down Peachtree Street every Tuesday during the noon rush hour. We bang on an old soup pot, ring a bell, carry signs, and pass out leaflets about the park campaign and about our solidarity marches. When ignored as though we were invisible, when people shove their hands in their pockets to avoid taking a leaflet, when greeted with blank stares, when people laugh and shout, "Get a job!" we feel foolish. And I suppose we are a ridiculous band of fools, making music with unlikely instruments, and wondering if this is what it means to sing the Lord's song in a strange land.

Yet it is a great privilege to do these foolish, weak things. As I reflect on the nonsense of our lives, I am given resurrection joy, even when, in the cold light of reason, all of our efforts seem defeated and ridiculous. It is a wonderful gift that God gives, to share in her weakness and foolishness. What a seeming weakness that God came to us as a helpless baby who couldn't find room at the Hilton, but was born in a barn instead! How foolish that God's own son should die for the sins of humanity! Yet God is strong and wise, because that same weak baby who grew up strong and met a humiliating death also overcame death by rising again on Easter—such amazing strength and wisdom to overcome death!

We know the Jesus for whom there is no room in Plaza Park. We know the Jesus who dies in humiliation when there is no public toilet, no home with a bed, no meaningful work. We know that Jesus because he comes to us in the homeless poor.

So our foolishness and weakness become wisdom and strength as we gain the hope and promise of the resurrection. We will continue to do ridiculous things with the knowledge that we'll have victory—we will have clothes and food even as God is victorious on Easter, as a foolish, weak death on the cross is overcome by the mighty rising from the grave.

God rejoices with us on Easter morning at the foolish sight of five hundred people, gathered in an ugly parking lot decorated with ludicrous balloons, at a ridiculously early hour of the morning, singing, dancing, eating, and celebrating the taste of the victorious banquet that is ours.

The Festival of Shelters:
Power for the Peace and Justice Struggle, *by Ed Loring*

A U G U S T   1 9 9 2

Once upon a time there was a rather large hippopotamus in a rather large room. In order to enter the room you had to agree never to mention the hippopotamus. You could feel it, sidle up to it, smell it, but never, never call it by name or in any manner speak of it.

As time went by the hippopotamus grew larger and larger, and more and more people came into the room. Space shrank and attention to the hippo grew, but no one would dare speak up. Oh, occasionally the children would play with the hippopotamus when the elders were not looking, or a guest from a far country would be astounded and, after a couple of scotch and waters would ask an impertinent question like, "Did you see . . . ?" before being hushed and slyly taken from the room.

Sometimes a long-haired prophet from the wilderness would enter, uninvited, and yell, "Look at that hippopotamus! Hey, man, look at the size of that thing. If you don't get that hippo out of here it's going to crush you."

Oooh, would the citizens be angry!

"The no-good bum, she ought to get a job."

"She's just wacko, a paranoid schizophrenic," others agreed.

Others didn't grasp the significance of it all, because the hippo had been no-named for so long that they had missed its presence. The prophet, saddened and ashamed, grieved for her people.

One evening during a torrential rainstorm the never-named hippopotamus went wild. He began devouring the children, stomping the grown-ups to death, crushing the furniture. Finally, amid the groans and shrieking of the wounded, he began to strangle. Rings and credit cards, car keys and beepers had stuck in his throat. Like blind Samson pushing at the Philistine columns, the choking hippo tore into the walls and the house came crashing down.

WHY THE FESTIVAL OF SHELTERS?

The American way of life has absorbed and domesticated the particularity of a biblical and Christian witness. This is most clearly observed around Christmas, Easter, and when the state of Georgia crucifies a death-row brother. For those of us in the family of faith and household of hope, it does not have to be that way. We can refuse and resist. We can find other public expressions of our inward faith.

The biblical themes of birth in a barn, of God's claiming the flesh and social experience of the marginalized, are a basic Christmas narrative. So is the political exposition. Herod, like all political powers, is afraid of this startling birth. He cannot control the astrologers from the East. He signs death warrants for the children, and violence and death mar God's entry into human flesh. Christmas brings a revolution in the air; it is a most political and spiritual story. Enter Santa Claus, a Coke-sipping, old, benevolent, American, white male god. When I was a child, Santa had powers of judgment. He kept an eye on children and knew who was naughty and who was nice. But ashes and switches don't help the economy, so Santa has become the incarnation of the spirit of consumerism: Buy, Buy, Buy. Christmas is a sad time for many, because stores and businesses make it or go bankrupt during this season. There is, then, still an ultimacy, a crisis of faith, connected with the final day of the fiscal year. Christmas crucifies the Christ!

Holy Week and Easter are the most important liturgical witnesses to the proclamation of biblical truth. Easter is the highest festival. It is the foundation of all Christian theology, congregational life, and engagement in the world for peace and justice. The biblical themes are awesome: betrayal, persecution, the use of political power to silence prophetic voices, the death penalty, crucifixion, God's passion and suffering and *death, death, death*. Then, lo and behold: the fidelity and courage of women, descent into hell, and resurrection, *life, life, life*.

Not long ago, after an Easter worship, Murphy and I went out to dinner with Bill and Trudy Green. The tables in the dining hall were decorated with Easter bunnies and American flags. Men and women were dressed in beautiful clothes proclaiming spring's wardrobe, and the children squealed and played, anticipating the afternoon's Easter-egg hunt. This room was filled with Christians, but many men were conspicuously absent, as they had been from worship. The National Collegiate Athletic Association basketball tournament was in its final stage. Easter, like Christmas, is an important American holiday. But the cultural expressions distort and hide the biblical testimony of a God and people of faith who are called to new life and the pursuit of love and justice. Santa Claus and the Easter bunny are accomplishing in the United States what Herod and Pilate could never do in Palestine: the domestication of the people of God.

Over the years, we at the Open Door Community have sought liturgical expressions for our faith and a way of life that point to the character of our God, rather than to the Dow Jones average. We have resurrected an Old Testament festival which is very fitting for compassionate people: the Festival of Shelters. Through the observance of this festival we are empowered each fall to make a public and specifically biblical witness in the heart of our city. We hope that you in the Atlanta area will join us this September. We ask you who live far away to plan and celebrate your own Festival of Shelters in your city square.

WHAT IS THE FESTIVAL OF SHELTERS?

A Harvest Festival

The Festival of Shelters is a harvest festival like our own Thanksgiving, and it is a festival of redemption. It combines earth care and human liberation. The festival is a time of eating delicious foods and enjoying the sensual depths of our good bodies, and it is a time to remember God and the poor, and to step forward on the jagged journey for justice.

As a harvest jubilation, creation, food, and rest are signalized. *Creation:* In the beginning . . . God . . . created the heaven and the earth! And God saw that it was good! And God was very pleased. And God rested. The very intention of creation is goodness. Look at it. Creation is a call to celebration. Creation is doxology. Thank you for my wonderful tingling, jingle-jangle flesh and this good, good earth.

Food: there is enough! There are no food shortages! The harvest is gathered and there is enough for everyone. There is no flaw in creation; there is no surplus population. Even in days of famine the people of God found food and confessed their loyalty to the Giver of Harvest. The Festival of Shelters is a liturgical witness to the political analysis that hunger has nothing to do with food shortage. Hunger is a result of public policy and personal fear and greed. Neither God nor the earth is responsible for hunger. Both share the glory of this Thanksgiving merrymaking.

But then, as now, hunger and poverty stalked the land. Hunger is a perennial Harpy. Thus the social policy of the Bible demands that the right of gleaning the fields be instituted and protected (Lev. 19:9–10). Harvest festivals are spirit-filled precisely as they are inclusive of hungry people and protectors of barren lands. The gleaning laws are of special importance to us in the United States, for implicit in them is the wastefulness and generosity of our loving Creator. Gleaning prohibits maximizing profits—a business principle always at odds with the health of the human family. Efficiency is sacrificed for love of neighbor and stranger. Harvesters must slow down their work to make certain the gatherers at the edge have time to pick up the crumbs. Today that might mean the drivers of garbage trucks would wait until hungry people finished going through the dumpster before upending the steel coffins holding the corpses of our corpulence.

The Festival of Shelters, rooted in memory, and inclusive of everyone in the community, is a fete with poor and hungry humans whose very existence indicts us because creation is good and there is enough for everyone.

Rest: woefully needed in our land is rest. We drive, push, produce, achieve, make it, come, survive, win, but we cannot rest. Why? Workaholism is idolatry. Rest, that Sabbath which is the completion of the harvest and even creation itself, is the mark of trust and fidelity rooted in a biblical way of life. Neither

Christmas nor Easter, Thanksgiving nor any single Saturday or Sunday, offers us rest. We have forgotten who we are; we are forgetting what it means to be human.

The Festival of Shelters is a time for our bodies, souls, and spirits to rest. It is also a time for the land to rest. The Bible always holds together our bodies of clay and the clay itself. As people and earth rest, we are to remember the Creator of earth and flesh and the human struggle with the earth, the dirt, the weeds; the pain in the farm worker's back; the exploitation of the poor; the loss of the family farm; the pollution of the earth by fertilizer and machine. By this gala occasion God roots our lives in the land in praise and the struggle for justice. Ecology and journey for justice are one piece in the same tapestry, and this Thanksgiving commemoration makes the relationship manifest.

A Festival of Redemption

The Festival of Shelters is an occasion to remember the forty years of wilderness wanderings on the jagged journey to freedom in the land flowing with milk and honey. In the wilderness, that place that each of us knows so well, the people of God lived in shelters, booths of branches, or they were simply houseless and homeless, dependent entirely on their God. Homelessness is a memory of the people of God, a wilderness memory. The wilderness, which we all know so well, is a place of hunger and grumbling, and miracle! For lo and behold—there is manna by morning and quail by night. And enough for everyone to have all they need.

Today, however, housing and food are the products of our hands, acquired through rent payments, mortgage payments, grocery bills, utility bills, property taxes. We have to work long and hard for room and board. Almost hard enough to make us believe we deserve something better.

The powerful insight of scripture—the biblical meaning woven into the fabric of the Festival of Shelters—is this: a harvest/creation festival is a redemption/liberation festival. Harvest bounty and wilderness wanderings are forever conjoined for people of faith. It is as though our American Thanksgiving were a time of national recommitment to justice for and restitution to Native Americans for their land and to African Americans for their labor.

But why the shelters? Why booths of branches? Why days and nights outside my home? As we read in Deuteronomy 8, a house is a place of forgetfulness. The wilderness, the streets, jails and prisons, hospitals and cat holes are the places of memory. So Yahweh commanded the people to leave their own yards and the harvest fields to remember their redemption as they celebrated their harvest.

The greatest threats to the Christian faith are forgetting about God and idolizing the self. The Bible recognizes, yet we have failed to see, that the threat of idolatry is the consequence of a good harvest. Abundance leads us into believing that we have willed our accomplishments and that our success is the product of our own efforts. The surplus food we have in the United States is because of our superior technology and our inherent righteousness. Our jobs and professional expertise are due to our initiative and pragmatism. We are not homeless because we are superior to the poor, and we are good managers. And although addiction and mental illness afflict the middle class and well-to-do, we are mature enough and moral enough to maintain ourselves, whereas our lazy and immoral fellow citizens are not. Even our health is an idol of our own hands. We jog at 5:30 A.M. and eat sprouts twice a day! Cancer and AIDS, like unemployment and homelessness, are marks of failure and the lack of motivation or morals. So with the harvest of wealth and health it is natural enough for people to forget their God and to come to believe such confessions of faith as:

> "I did it!!"
> "God helps those who help themselves."
> (Jesus only came for the sick and unrighteous.)
> "Pull yourself up by your own bootstraps."
> "The homeless are that way because they wanna be!"
> "The people in the soup kitchen line are too lazy to work.
>   They are just freeloaders."

So the God of Creation, the Lord of the Harvest says come and celebrate success by remembering me: leave your houses and practice homelessness because

> "I am the Lord thy God who brought you out of the Land of Egypt, out of the house of bondage."
> While we were slaves and prisoners, white middle-class worshipers of mammon, racists, and sexists . . .
> While as African Americans we were imprisoned and chained by white lies and personal fear and sloth . . .
> "I," says the Lord your God, "came to you and lifted you up and out of the pit.
> "While you lived in tents, booths, and tabernacles in the wilderness
>> "I cared for you.
>> "I fed you.
> "Now, you who have homes, jobs, land, food, and drink
>> "Beware!

"I give you the Festival of Shelters with the harvest. As you celebrate the goodness of life, remember your redemption."

And we who have the basic necessities of life remember our redemption by living in servanthood with the poor. We stand in political, social, and congregational solidarity with the homeless and the prisoner.

THE FESTIVAL OF SHELTERS FOR TODAY

Beware! There is a hippopotamus loose in the land. We need people to name the hippo. We need lovers of the Lord who can remember redemption and share the harvest with the hungry. We need white men who are prepared to fail and to be fired from their jobs, who can reenvision the Christian life and give voice to grief and courage in both our churches and society.

We need African American men who will stand up and lead us in our justice struggle.

We need white women who can grant us courage and give us wisdom in this sexist society that blames victims for their wilderness wanderings.

We need Black women to show us the way, to demonstrate the faith, to be bearers of God's justice in this land of oppression and greed.

We need each other to reconnect the harvest of earth with the liberation struggle on earth.

So I plead with you today from the streets of Atlanta and the prisons of Georgia, from the soup-kitchen lines and death-row cells, from labor pools and church-basement shelters:

Remember the Lord thy God
Who gave you your houses,
Cars, MARTA cards, all the
Food you need, good clothes and
Even much of what you want
And in the joy of Thanksgiving
Celebrate the Festival of Shelters

Remember your redemption
Serve the poor
Kill Santa Claus
Chase the Easter bunny back into his hole
Name the hippopotamus
and embrace
the cross of Christ
for your naked self

for your wounded neighbor
for the oppressed and poor
for your sister and brother
yea, even for Jesus Christ.
Amen.

Fragile, Do Not Drop, *by John Cole Vodicka*

NOVEMBER 1994

Shortly after midnight, the wind began whipping through Woodruff Park in downtown Atlanta. The night suddenly turned colder, and my bones told me I needed more cover. I crawled into a fairly large cardboard box to shield myself from the weather and even perhaps to get some sleep.

As I lay in my box, looking through the opening at the city lights all about me, Asher pulled his box in front of mine. He, too, settled in for the rest of the night. The backside of Asher's box now blocked my view of the high-rises. I noticed that on his box, a packing box normally used by moving companies, were written these instructions: "This End Up." "Fragile." And "Do Not Drop." I stared at these words for a few minutes. I thought, "How wonderful. Asher has found cardboard shelter this night, shelter that comes with instructions to all who pass by: 'This end up. Fragile. Do not drop.' He is safe. This human package is safe for this night."

And how ironic. These words on the box, "This End Up," "Fragile," and "Do Not Drop," were never meant for Asher's or any other human being's welfare. These words were meant for material goods that are to be moved from one household to another. Goods we consider precious and irreplaceable—expensive china, priceless kitchenware, glass and porcelain fixtures and ornaments—material goods we can't bear to have damaged or destroyed. Yet now this box of Asher's, and my own, and no doubt hundreds of boxes throughout Atlanta that night, were being used as overnight huts and homes by countless numbers of homeless folk, fragile and broken folk who cry out for justice, whose presence begs us to recognize them as human beings who need our attention and care.

"This end up." "Fragile." "Do not drop." I stared at these words on Asher's cardboard home, thinking that perhaps if God could slap this same label on each and every one of us—homeless and housed, rich and poor, prisoner and free, young and old, man and woman, white folk and persons of color—we could learn to live together in ways that truly allowed all of us to share in the tree of life.

We all struggle in life to stay right-side up. We fall down. We take tumbles. We fail one another. We backslide. The bottom falls out. We are fragile people. We break or live broken lives. We need mending all the time. Sometimes, when we feel that we're on track again, we are dropped suddenly into the pit of despair. We look around for someone to recognize our humanity but are met only with resistance and oppression.

The homeless in Atlanta—fragile and broken, every one of them—are treated with disdain by the powers and principalities. At best they are invisible or a nuisance that is barely tolerated. I see this most clearly when I spend a night on the streets with members of the Open Door Community. At worst, the city's homeless are looked upon as an expendable segment, which can be harassed, beaten, or banished, whenever the need to do so arises at City Hall. Instead of treating our homeless sisters and brothers as fragile human beings to be handled with care, to be nurtured and empowered—to be housed—we allow those who set and enforce policy to run roughshod over the lives of broken, already hurting people. The system treats the homeless poor callously and with contempt.

How strange, I thought, as I lay in my box that night on the cold concrete that envelops Woodruff Park. How awful, I silently screamed while looking at the words neatly printed on the box my friend Asher now slept in: "This end up. Fragile. Do not drop." How awful that in this consumer-mad society we can demand that great care be taken of our material goods and prized possessions, yet at the same time ignore the cries of the wounded poor, the homeless, the prisoner, the outcast, and the lonely.

The good news is that God is not pleased. God is on the streets with Atlanta's homeless and in the prison cells of Georgia. She feels the hurt and neglect and oppression that are daily heaped on the backs of our homeless and prisoner friends. God knows that fragile people need to be embraced, not humiliated and shunned. God tells us that one day the poor shall inherit the earth. God knows, yes she does, which end is up.

Advent, *by Murphy Davis*

Advent is almost here. In the rare and delicious moments I have taken lately to think ahead, I've thought of Advent and how this wonderful liturgical season will never be the same for me after the celebration of Advent in 1983.

The season is a celebration of all the best and most joyous themes: peace, joy, hope, love, light. If you can manage to overlook the tacky glare of the American consumer Christmas, the season is one of joyful anticipation: hope for the coming of God; the birth of a tiny babe who came and yet comes as the Liberator, who calls us out of our slavery and into the glorious light of God's freedom.

At the end of the first week of Advent in 1983, we were gifted with a visit from Jürgen Moltmann, a well-known German theologian who had spent the fall term teaching at Emory University. We had invited him for supper, and on the cold, rainy Saturday in December, he sloshed into our house, bringing immediate warmth with his wonderful, contagious laughter and endless questions about our work and the plight of the poor in the United States. We ate supper and spent the evening in animated conversation. We had a great time and invited him to come back for worship the next night.

Sunday night he bustled in with a bottle of *Liebfraumilch* tucked under his arm. We gathered for worship and excitedly waited to hear what he would say to us—this world-renowned theologian, author of many scholarly books (some of them very thick!).

Jürgen Moltmann told, very simply, the story of his coming to faith. When World War II ended, he was a seventeen-year-old soldier in the German army and was taken to a prisoner-of-war camp in England (or maybe Scotland). As the days and weeks went by, he and others learned what they had not known: of the slaughter and death in Nazi Germany before and during the war. With this knowledge, despair seemed the only real option. All of this happened while he had been a soldier in the German army. The world became a very dark and hopeless place. In the face of such staggering evil, how could there be reason for hope?

Someone came to the prisoner-of-war camp and distributed pocket-sized Bibles (in English!). As he spoke to us years later, Moltmann pulled the same little Bible from his pocket. It fell open with a slight touch to the book of the prophet Isaiah. "I read this," said Moltmann. " 'The people who walked in darkness have seen a great light; those who dwelt in a land of deep darkness, on them has the light shined . . . ,' and I shall never forget it. The world had become only darkness for me. But slowly, gradually, I began to see a very tiny flicker of a light. Advent is the time of remembering.

"You know," he said, "I understood eventually that unless it is dark, you have no need of the light. If you are surrounded by light you will not seek light. But when it is very dark, ah, the light! For those who 'dwell in the land of deep darkness,' light is precious, light is life itself. God comes to us like that: a tiny, flickering flame, a great light in the midst of the deep darkness of our lostness and despair."

It was good to hear this deep and personal sharing in our Advent journey. Little did I know how I would cling for dear life to that reflection, for the events of the remaining weeks of Advent shook my faith in ways that I could hardly have imagined on that night.

On December 15, in the middle of the third week of Advent, my very good friend, whom I had visited for four years, John Eldon Smith, was electrocuted by the state of Georgia—just ten days before Christmas. "Smitty" was a fifty-four-year-old Pennsylvania man, well-loved by his elderly parents, his young grandchildren, a number of close friends, and the other men on death row. His life was snuffed out by two jolts of 2,300 volts of electricity, carefully administered by button-pushing guards who were "just doing their jobs."

The days that followed the killing found our community about the tasks of burial and comforting Smitty's family. It seemed that everywhere around us the electric chair was being celebrated. "Now we would all be safer, for this monstrous, defective bit of subhumanity had been stricken from the face of the earth." (Could they really be talking about that warm-hearted, funny little man I knew so well?) The cry for revenge grew more and more strident.

One week later we made a feeble effort to pick ourselves up to prepare Christmas dinner for our homeless friends. The temperatures in Atlanta suddenly fell to zero and below. It was as cold in Atlanta, for a full week, as anyone could remember. But it was Christmas. And so most of the soup kitchens closed because the volunteers needed a holiday. And most of the night shelters in town were unable to extend the hours of protective shelter because so few volunteers were available.

In that fourth week of Advent, and even as we celebrated the Nativity of our Lord, twenty of our homeless sisters and brothers died in the streets and alleyways of our city. Some twenty bodies were found—frozen stiff in dark corners, abandoned cars, vacant buildings. Other homeless people lost legs, toes, fingers. Some of those who suffered and died that week were known to us by name. Others were not. Day and night we cooked hot food and fixed hot coffee and tea to take out onto the streets. We squeezed as many extra bodies into our dining room and the Druid Hills Presbyterian shelter as the space would bear. But it all seemed a mere drop in the bucket.

Advent of 1983 was a time of death and intense suffering. Nothing—nothing in my background as a white overeducated Christian; nothing in my studies; nothing in my spiritual instruction or pastoral counseling—nothing had prepared me to meet with such utter failure, grief, and suffering.

Up to that point we had spent a number of years in work against the death penalty and organizing on behalf of homeless people. And there, in a period of two weeks, in this most joyful season, we could point to nothing but failure and broken hearts. I could not pray, for I had no idea what to say to a God who would allow such suffering among people I knew and loved. For many months that followed, my body was bone-weary and my heart seemed sore to the touch, and the only thing I knew was utter confusion.

But again and again, Jürgen Moltmann's simple story rang in my ear. "Unless it is dark, you have no need of the light." I knew for sure that it was very, very dark. I also knew that I had never had such a deep longing for the light.

I deeply believe now that God sends us of the First World to share the plight of the world's suffering people precisely to create this longing. When we pad ourselves and protect ourselves from the tragedy that is the common experience of most of the world's people, we live in a world that is artificially lighted like the blinking lights of a Christmas tree: the slightest trauma, and the light goes out. Until that time we are hardly inclined to seek light, because we think we have enough of it.

"Unto us a child is born . . ." Oh, how we long for that child who is the light of the world. When John the Baptist, that rough-and-tumble Advent figure, is in prison, he sends his disciples to ask Jesus, "Are you the one who is to come, or shall we look for another?" Without a pause, Jesus says, "Go and tell John what you have seen and heard: the blind receive their sight, the lame walk, lepers are cleansed, and the deaf hear, the dead are raised up, the poor have good news preached to them."

When we grope in the darkness, we seek light. When we grope through death, we seek resurrection. When our lives are lived in solidarity with the poor and oppressed of the earth, the light shines on us in the promise of good news that comes to the poor; in restored sight and hearing; in the cleansing of disease; in the leaping and dancing of our lame legs.

Expectations diminish. Hope grows. We are not abandoned: God is with us!

Prepare a Road: Advent Prayer, *by Elizabeth Dede*

NOVEMBER 1996

Someone is shouting in the desert, "Prepare a road for the Lord; make a straight path for him to travel!"

In the desert of the city, O God, you send the voice to cry out: "Prepare a road for the Lord!" But do we hear? Forgive us, gracious God, when the noise of traffic, of jet airplanes, of honking horns, of construction, of a life gone mad with busyness drown out your call. Tune our ears to hear the cry of the poor. Help us to meet Jesus, and to make a smooth road for him to travel.

Oh, Lord, how shall we meet you? Break down the barriers that keep the rich from the poor, the strong from the weak, whites from Blacks, men from women, straights from gays. Liberate us, O God, come and save us. Help us to bring the Beloved Community so that the city will be a place of rejoicing for all people.

In the wasteland of the prison cell, O God, you send the voice to cry out: "Prepare a road for the Lord!" But do we hear? Forgive us, loving Savior, when the cheers for chain gangs, the clanging gates, the pounding metal doors, the silence of hostility, or the roaring of rage and the shouts of vengeance seek to silence your call for peace and goodwill. Tune our ears to hear the cry of the prisoner.

Oh, Lord, how shall we welcome you when you are locked away? Snap the bars; swing wide the doors; come, O God, and set the prisoners free. Liberate us from fear and hate. Bring justice for the oppressed.

In the desolate places of war, O God, you send the voice to cry out: "Prepare a road for the Lord!" But do we hear? Forgive us, Prince of Peace, when the noise of bombs, the roar of tanks, the wailing of mothers, and the terror of children destroy the beauty of your Peaceful Community. Tune our ears to hear the moans of the wounded ones.

Oh, Lord, we long to greet you, for you are our hope, the delight of our hearts. Give us peace in Bosnia, Chechnya, Nigeria, and all the war-torn places on your earth. Teach us to care for and love each other. Replace the bitterness of greed and prejudice with the sweetness of peace.

In the emptiness of our hearts, O God, you send a voice to cry out, "Prepare a road for the Lord!" But do we hear? Forgive us, Immanuel, God with us, when despair, addiction, sickness, hardness of heart, and doubt cut off the voice that calls within us.

Light a fire in our hearts, O Lord, and melt our hearts of stone. Help us turn toward each other in love and care, and work with each other for justice and liberation.

Then we will turn toward you; we will see you on the road made straight and smooth; we will run to greet you, and the Beloved Community will be here. Amen! Come, Lord Jesus. Come! Amen!

Merry Christmas! *by Marc Worthington*

F E B R U A R Y   1 9 9 2

At this writing the New Year has just begun, and at the time of your reading, Christmas is probably long past. What will February bring? The weather will likely turn colder. The requests for warm coats and caps will likely increase. And the deluge of people offering food, clothing, money, and time will likely diminish as the new seasonal joys of impending credit-card, tax, and heating bills, and the resumption of regular work and school hours, loom over the volunteers and supporters who make the Open Door's offer of hospitality possible.

Christmas as a state, business, and ecclesiastically approved national holiday may well be past, but as a believer of the good news I know that I've got some work to do in making its meaning and effect carry beyond, and ask that you join me in some reflections.

❖ ❖ ❖

"We're glad you are here," I was told by one neighborhood resident as he brought in his donations. Volunteers came from nearby, including one whose jogging path crossed our sidewalk; a Buddhist couple brought warm blankets; a Muslim delivered food. Even the poor themselves who have little to spare saw fit to bring in shoes and other clothing; homeless persons, rather than passing items on to their friends as a gift or for profit, delivered them to our door.

Those words, "We're glad you are here," which greeted me while I answered the phone and door, were of great comfort to a community which knows well the truth of a prophet not being welcome in his or her own land. It's usually fine to help people in need as long as those people stay out of my neighborhood. So while all the assistance that I witnessed was welcome, that which came from those living in the immediate area caught my attention most.

"I wish they'd just go away" was the sentiment, however, of a letter to the editor in *Creative Loafing,* an Atlanta newspaper, a few days later. It was written by a person who decried how difficult it was to go to the drugstore without being panhandled; this person concluded that the only available solution was not to go to the store. I can understand the fear and irritation of that writer. But I confess that I listen more closely to the pain and anguish of our brothers and sisters on the street, whose day jobs through the labor pool pay only a minimum wage that cannot procure decent housing, and to complaints of the poor with illnesses, who wait for weeks for an appointment at the county hospital, then hours at the clinic, then hours more for a prescription—all for sicknesses that too often could have been prevented were decent food, housing, and jobs within reach. I hear also the voices of the people in San Francisco who recently elected a mayor whose campaign platform included the "answer" of shipping the undesirable homeless off to work (or is that concentration?) camps. But I also hear the despair of a single mother, for whom neither low wages nor welfare check open the door to a life in a warm house, free of drive-by shootings, gangs, and drugs that in a flash can take away her life and those of her children. I think I have some sense of what would drive me to drink, or drugs, or to TV, ad infinitum, in such situations. Most of us succumb to depression and hopelessness in less life-threatening scenarios.

Those people who bother us also sustain, challenge, and threaten us. In strict economic terms, the dishwasher, hotel housekeeper, construction day laborer, alcoholic farm worker, and panhandling "bum" who once was in school and who did many of the above and other jobs, ensure everyone's survival and well-being. Try doing without them. But in the deeper Christian notion of what it means to be an act of creation, to be human, they are not the other—they are us, in different guises.

Christmas was in December and is now a glorious birth of God become human, foreshadowing the breaking of God and human being through the suffering of the cross, foreshadowing what is forgiven and reconciled through resurrection. Far too often we do not know what we do. We do not know what we do, or what we say. We know only what we feel, fear, and desire, and that passion can bring both death and life, depending on how many of our other faculties we can or are willing to use to act, rather than to react.

While told we are the salt of the earth, the light of the world, the branches of the tree, there is caution in that salt can lose its flavor, light can be extinguished, and branches can die. Christmas dies, with no Grinch needed to steal it. We can and do accomplish this every day on our own, individually and collectively.

As I offer these thoughts, I know that the birth of the Christ child is an ongoing event, that God is through, among, and with us, and the message was to all, for all time. The incarnation offered hope and a demand for both response and responsibility.

Christ made it clear that his Parent was not the kind of God you wind up on the Sabbath, or, by extrapolation, on Easter, Christmas, or other Holy Days. Neither the burden nor the yoke of this realization seems light. But I guess I've grown tired of avoidance and denial so that in my spiritual journey I will turn to light and life more frequently than ten years ago, knowing that the cross is on the road. Avoiding the drugstore to avoid panhandlers, shipping the homeless to work camps while offices and factories lay off workers, building larger prisons—none of these will cure our illnesses. The real answers have not yet been forged in justice, but whatever form they take, I know they will not come easy or without discomfort.

The Catholic priest Henri Nouwen speaks of prayer as a transparent way of life, in which one sees or rather tries to see beyond one's own experience-and-expectation-shaped view of the moment, in order to see the Christ in the other, and the other in you; to see the connection between and within the living branches of a tree. This is not the effusive love of New Age psychobabble, but a call to action. In this action, concrete steps are required and sustained by dynamic faith. These steps make a mark on the lives of all we know, and those we don't know, and on those we are afraid to touch, be they prisoner or panhandler, "foreigner" or neighbor.

Somewhere during hurried holiday preparation I read of the beginnings of one Catholic Worker house of hospitality. The later-to-be founder is seen offering a pot of soup to homeless persons every day and then hurriedly leaving after delivery of his sacrifice. One day, one of his beneficiaries/victims poured the contents of the pot on top of our hero. When the server queried why this was done, he was told that he had never stopped to talk to anyone, that he had treated the soup eaters like animals. The one who ate with prostitutes and tax collectors exhorts us to break through the veneers and aged and brittle varnishes which color, distort, and make difficult the way of the Paraclete.

It was once and will again be said, "We are living in desperate times." My Christmas prayer, now almost Lenten, is that we steer clear of desperation-driven short-term reactions. Let us instead remember and honor a God who chose to live and die with us, so that by opening a door with words and action we may know the difference between justice and law, truth and deceit, vision and delusion; let us hold close the cross and resurrection; let us not shrink from the inevitable pain which accompanies the joy of birth.

Thanks be to our Creator and to all that makes this life possible. Let us make life, rather than mere existence, possible for everyone. I look forward to greeting many more volunteers and supporters on the phone and at the door who read these words. God bless us one and all. Merry Christmas.

Dayspring: A Message from My Childhood,
by Elizabeth Dede

A U G U S T   1 9 8 8

I am often amazed at the paths God takes through my life, which to me seem unpredictable. While my two older sisters always knew that they would be nurses, I never guessed until my last year of high school that I would study English literature in college. And in college, none of my wildest imaginings about my future included the Open Door. And yet I feel and believe that God has worked through my life and its different experiences. Dayspring Farm is one of the places where I experience God as God has worked through my life in what seem to be disparate events. As I ponder the totality of my life, I find that I have been led to this place and this time and these people in a direct way.

I remember well that last fall a recurring agenda item for the Open Door leadership team was the name of the farm. For a while we thought of naming it "Dorothy Day Farm"—and with good reason. Dorothy Day founded the Catholic Worker, which has helped form our life and work at the Open Door. She put her faith into action by loving the homeless poor of New York, and she put her love into action by feeding the hungry and living with the poor. Dorothy Day also knew that "love in action is a harsh and dreadful thing," so she practiced Sabbath rest and believed that farms should be established so that people from the city could rest. So "Dorothy Day Farm" would have been a good name. But something was missing. The name didn't capture the essence of our farm.

Finally, Murphy suggested the name "Dayspring," and my soul immediately resonated. I knew that was the name for our farm, although at the time I couldn't say why. We weren't even sure where "Dayspring" came from. "Must be the prophet Isaiah," Murphy and I said, when Ed asked about it. We knew "Dayspring" from "Oh Come, Oh Come, Emmanuel":

> Oh come, blest Dayspring, come and cheer
> Our spirits by your advent here;
> Disperse the gloomy clouds of night,
> And death's dark shadows put to flight.
> Rejoice! Rejoice!
> Emmanuel shall come to you, O Israel.

My curiosity whetted, I looked the word up and learned that "Dayspring" comes from Zechariah's prophecy about his son John, in Luke 1. When I read

Zechariah's prophecy I was happily surprised to find a connection to good memories of my days in college. Every day at morning prayer we sang a beautiful setting of Zechariah's prophecy:

> Blessed be God who has visited and redeemed us.
> God has given us salvation
> By the forgiveness of our sins.
> Through the tender mercy of our God,
> The Dayspring from on high has visited us,
> To give light to them that dwell in darkness,
> And in the shadow of death
> To guide our feet into the way of peace.

In my college days, the words had no particular meaning, and I loved them only because the music was so beautiful and I loved to sing. But last November, when we chose "Dayspring" as the name of our farm, those words all of a sudden became meaningful, and I was glad that I had sung them daily for four years because the words came back so readily.

You see, names are important. The name "Dorothy Day" would not have called to mind anything from my past. Names are important. The name "John" freed Zechariah to proclaim his prophecy. You may remember that Zechariah did not believe that he and his elderly wife, Elizabeth, could have a child. Because he doubted the angel's promise that a child named John would be born, Zechariah was struck speechless. For nine months he could not talk. It was only after the baby was born and Zechariah wrote, "His name is John," that the gift of speech returned. Zechariah's first words were the beautiful prophecy about his son John, who would prepare the way of the Lord. John means "God is gracious." Indeed, God has been gracious to us in the gift of Dayspring Farm.

❖ ❖ ❖

My father's name is John. When I was a small child living in Fort Lauderdale, Florida, he preached a sermon on Christmas Day entitled "The Dayspring." God was gracious to me in giving me my father, because while today we have our struggles relating to each other, my dad, John Dede, helped prepare the way of the Lord for me.

In that Christmas Day sermon, my dad talked about *visitation*—a word that for me has come to be jam-packed with meaning. At that time I was probably only three years old. My dad said, "The Dayspring has visited us, poor and humble though we may be." And we were a poor and humble congregation. In the early 1960s, my father had a mission church of Black folk in Fort Lauderdale. On that Christmas Day there were six white people in a church of Black sisters and brothers, whose faces I hardly remember except when I have strange dreams of my early childhood, sitting on my godfather J. Pinckney Davis's knee, learning how to read and sing a hymn like "Oh Come, Oh Come, Emmanuel."

"The opening chapters of the New Testament speak of many visits," my dad preached. "The angel Gabriel visits Mary. Mary visits Elizabeth. The angels visit the shepherds. The shepherds visit the lowly child in the manger. Wise people from the East visit Jerusalem and then Bethlehem and then the child. Mary and Joseph visit the temple with the child. But the supreme visit, the greatest and best visit of all these, is that this child, the Holy God, visits us sinners. The Almighty God visits us creatures of the dust. And we know that this visit is really far more than a mere visit; for Christ came not just to visit and then to leave us. Christ came to abide, to come and live forever with us. The eternal Son of God on Christmas Day becomes our brother and stays with us as our brother."

On Christmas Day we remember that the Dayspring comes to visit us. The word *dayspring* came into the English language from early translations of the Bible. In the 1500s, *dayspring* was used for that point on the horizon at which the sun rises. The sunrise is gradual. So seems our meeting with Jesus, our Dayspring.

We do not and cannot always rejoice in, or even feel, the shining splendor of the morning star. We often do not know that Jesus visits. "Every heart has a bitter sadness all its own," my dad said. How true! Those friends I sat with in church a quarter of a century ago could not sit on the same beach with me in Fort Lauderdale; they could not go into a restaurant with my mother.

"Every heart has a bitter sadness all its own." Dayspring Farm became a part of our community after a particularly sad time. By the time we began to celebrate the Advent of Jesus—our Dayspring—in 1987 with our first retreat at Dayspring Farm, five of our friends on death row had been killed; some enthusiastic and hopeful members of the community had left in sadness and with a sense of breakdown; and Hannah Loring-Davis had survived a very serious accident. During Advent it didn't seem that the Dayspring was about to dawn.

"Every heart has a bitter sadness all its own." The Butler Street Breakfast is full of sad hearts that belong to young Black men who have no work, no home, no meaning in life. The prisons are full of sad hearts that know the emptiness of days locked away from family and friends. Our war-crazed world is full of sad hearts because the peace of the Dayspring is shattered by bombers.

"Every heart has a bitter sadness all its own," my dad said, "and yet the bitter sadness is not all our own. Christ, our Dayspring from on high, knows our bitter sadness, and shares our burdens and problems. We need to be conscious of Christ's presence in our lives and ask for Christ's support. Then we will find relief. We all, therefore, have reason to rejoice with Zechariah in 'the tender mercy of God whereby the Dayspring from on high has visited us, to give light to us who sit in darkness and in the shadow of death, to guide our feet into the way of peace.'"

My father's Christmas sermon ended with those words. I was too young then to question its conclusion. While it is true that we need to be conscious of Christ's presence in our lives, to know that the Dayspring is visiting, I wonder how we can know.

It seems to me that the answer lies in that all-important act that takes place over and over again in the opening chapters of the New Testament: visitation. Our friends in prison sit literally in the shadow of death, but as we visit them the light of the Dayspring shines. My experience of prison visitation is always that I am visited. When I go to the prison, I feel overshadowed by death until I am visited by my friends, who always bring with them the light of Jesus. So in our prison visitation we can be conscious of Christ's support. We can know that Christ shares all our burdens.

The Butler Street Breakfast is another place where we visit and are visited, and I always feel a sense of life after I've served the meal. Again, I believe we go to those that sit in the darkness. They sit in the darkness of a filthy slave-labor pool; they dwell in the shadow of death from skyscrapers downtown; they are consigned to dark church basements for their meals; they wait through the night with no home and no bed; they dwell in the darkness of racism, which is obvious as we serve the breakfast to two hundred people, of whom only two are white. And yet the Dayspring dawns and shines on our lives as we share a meal. As we eat with hungry sisters and brothers, we can experience Christ's presence in our lives and be conscious that he relieves all our needs.

Our lives in community are almost a continual act of visitation, and, as Jürgen Moltmann reminded us, we can always feel Christ's presence in each other. There is no problem or burden so great that we cannot find relief in the gift of life in community. Christ, the Dayspring, visits us, even as we visit each other.

Finally, the Dayspring dawns on our lives at Dayspring Farm. For two weeks in May, I did my morning devotions on the front porch while the sun rose over the hill. Quite literally the Dayspring shone on me, even as Christ's light was allowed to shine in me through prayer and meditation—something that I don't do enough of in the city. As we rest and recreate and meditate and communicate with God, as we worship together, share the Lord's Supper, and wash each other's feet, we remember and experience and are conscious of Christ, the bright Dayspring, shining on us and sharing both the joy and the bitter sadness of our hearts. Truly God has come to the Open Door and set it free. Through God's tender mercy—in the gift of Dayspring Farm, in each other, and in the greatest gift, Jesus—the Dayspring from on high has visited.

Part V

SAINTS AND MARTYRS

Man cannot live on cornbread alone.

—Willie Dee Wimberly

Amazing Grace: Willie Dee Wimberly, December 18, 1918–March 15, 1992, *by Murphy Davis*

M A Y   1 9 9 2

It was, as I recall, a cold gray afternoon in early 1983. I was on house duty and came into the living room to find an Atlanta police officer standing beside an elderly black man, who sat with his hands folded and his hat on his lap. His ebony face was serene, and he bowed his head in greeting as I approached.

The officer handed me a letter and explained that he had been sent by a municipal court judge. Mr. Willie Dee Wimberly, the judge wrote, had come before her in court on a charge of criminal trespass. It was her determination that there had been no criminal trespass; the issue was, instead, Mr. Wimberly's homelessness. Could we, the judge asked, take him at the Open Door?

We did in fact have a bed, Willie Dee Wimberly decided to stay, and from that day he became a part of the Open Door family.

Willie Dee's story unfolded in bits and pieces. One way or another he ended up in Atlanta (there was a fragment of a story about walking and riding a bicycle from Milledgeville). What we do know is that for thirteen years he lived in a makeshift lean-to on what is now a prime piece of real estate in Buckhead. After he had been there for some years, a restaurant was built on the front part of the lot. For several years they peacefully coexisted. But when the restaurant owners decided to expand, they called the police and had Willie Dee Wimberly arrested and charged with criminal trespass.

We heard that in court Mr. Willie Dee claimed squatter's rights to the property, and they said he might have had a legal point. It's funny to think of the stir it would have caused if he had been able to pursue the legal battle and claim his little piece of Buckhead.

Instead Willie Dee Wimberly created a new home for himself, and surely there is no way to tell the story of the Open Door apart from the story of Willie Dee.

Willie Dee often stood midway down the main hall in our house. It was his post. He tipped his ever-present hat and bowed in greeting to all who came and went. He was blessing. And still is. Receiving his smile or taking time to shake his hand and talk awhile was always one of the best gifts I can think of.

His frame of reference was not yours or mine. My only guess is that somewhere along the line "reality" became too painful, and so Mr. Willie Dee moved into another reality. Wherever it was, his reality was deeply spiritual and deeply rooted in the dignity and survival of African American people.

The first hint of this came not long after Willie Dee came to us. Someone reported smelling smoke outside his room. The day before, we had invited Paul Turner, an older white man, to move into the same room with Willie. What we finally discovered was that Willie Dee was rolling up newspaper, lighting it, and moving to every corner of the room to burn out the evil spirits. He wasn't so sure about living close to white folks! He soon became the only person in the house with a personal smoke detector installed over his bed.

His sense of place was rock solid. In 1985, Willie Dee ended up in Grady Hospital with a kidney infection. When we took him he was too weak to protest. But as soon as he was slightly better he began his efforts to leave the hospital and to come home. The nurses responded by taking his street clothes away. When Ed and I visited, we found him sitting on the side of his bed in a short hospital gown and his hat. He was ready to go, and he returned joyfully as soon as they checked him out and returned his pants.

When Willie Dee went to Grady again (unwillingly, of course) in February of this year, the news was hard. Cancer had spread so far that there was nothing to do but to bring him home and help him die. Hospice Atlanta came to guide our care. But, as usual, it was Mr. Wimberly who helped and gifted us. He died with the grace and dignity with which he had lived. He was in charge; his certainty about what was coming next kept us laughing and crying, but always grateful.

What a miracle was this little man, thrown out of Buckhead like a piece of human garbage, given to us by God as one of the most golden and precious gifts any of us will ever know.

On the Monday before he died, Eddie, Zig, Paul W., and I were in his room as he perched on the edge of his bed, wearing a large pair of dark glasses. He interrupted our busyness and said decisively, "Now we gonna sing a song—together. 'Amazing Grace.'" And with a clear voice he led us through. As the song hung in the air he nodded his head solemnly and said, "Thaaat's right. Amazin' Grace."

And so it was.

Grace Us with Your Presence, *by Elizabeth Dede*

M A Y   1 9 9 2

Willie Dee Wimberly and I were about as different as two people can be. I'm a big, strong, young, overly educated white woman. Willie Dee was a tiny, ancient, very Black man with little formal education. However, it is possible that I learned more of lasting value from Willie Dee Wimberly than from any other person in my life. He taught us at the Open Door Community about hospitality, joy, humor, unearned love, grace, persistence, blessing, and simply being. Perhaps the biggest sadness I feel is that Willie Dee Wimberly was truly one of a kind, never to be replaced by anyone—and he defies description, so it is difficult to share him with others who didn't know him.

To put it simply, Willie Dee lived on a different plane of reality. In front of the library down the street from us there is a beautiful, huge, old oak tree. One day I was going to return a book when I came upon Willie Dee, standing at the base of that tree, looking up, and chatting away with it. The thing you can't understand is that I don't believe Willie Dee was crazy: he and that tree really could communicate. We, on this other plane, don't have the ears to hear, or the language to speak.

Sometimes life at the Open Door seems heavy and too sad for words. For me it has been particularly so since Willie Dee died, because he was a person who truly radiated joy and brought comedy (in its life-affirming sense) everywhere. All Willie Dee had to do was to walk into a room, with his hand raised in the traditional Willie Dee blessing, and a smile would break out on every face. Even now, when I am filled with sadness because I miss Willie Dee, I still find myself smiling when a familiar image of him comes to mind.

Funny stories abound about Willie Dee. Many of them center around cornbread, because Willie Dee loved it, and sometimes ate it for breakfast, lunch, and dinner. He was a stubborn old man, and when he didn't want to do something, there was no persuading him. On occasion, Willie Dee would decide that he did not want to eat meals with the whole family, as is expected of members of the Open Door Community, and no amount of cajoling, threatening, or persuasion could get him to budge from his room. Nevertheless, we always tried.

One day Phillip Williams was on house duty, and, at lunchtime, Willie Dee didn't join us. Phillip went back to Willie Dee's room to see if he could roust him. Willie Dee very cordially said, "Thank you, but I'm not hungry today." To which Phillip replied, "Oh, come on, Mr. Willie Dee, we have some of your favorite cornbread for lunch today." Willie Dee looked at him wisely, nodded his head, and said, "Man cannot live on cornbread alone." Phillip realized that Willie Dee would not be joining us for lunch that day.

Even when he was very sick and couldn't get out of bed, Willie Dee still had his sense of humor and his way with words. One afternoon on a visit, I wanted him to drink something. I started telling him about how 7-Up is my favorite drink, hoping I could convince him to have some. Willie Dee said to me, "Ms. Elizabeth, you're just gonna have to get you another customer." I guess I did sound like an ad campaign for 7-Up.

Willie Dee was a peculiar dresser. He was most famous for hats and sunglasses. He had an amazing collection of hats, ranging from paper bags to Sherlock Holmes caps, and you never knew what pair of sunshades you'd see him in next. One Sunday at worship, Willie Dee was the last to receive the bread and cup at Communion, so he returned them to the table. Standing there in a knitted ski cap (it was probably summertime), with dark sunglasses that were too huge for his little face, he raised his hand in benediction, and said, "Very well! Very well!" The presiding pastor couldn't have dismissed us with any better blessing.

Willie Dee's biggest gift to me is his teaching about unearned love, a lesson that I will never completely learn. Although, intellectually, I don't believe it, I've always lived as though I could work hard enough and do everything well enough to make people love me. Willie Dee didn't fit into that sort of works-righteousness lifestyle. The only time his name appeared on the Open Door work-rotation chart was every Saturday, when he was listed for his day off. Even on the Saturday the week after he died, Willie Dee still had a day off listed. That is not to say that Willie Dee was lazy. He worked: Willie Dee kept a vigil in the hallway during soup kitchen and showers, and he always cleared the tables and wiped them after lunch and dinner. But his work didn't appear on the rotation chart; Willie Dee didn't fit into its categories. When I first moved to the community six years ago, I heard some grumbling about "that old man who didn't do his fair share of work," but that didn't last long. Willie Dee was loved by everyone because of who he was. Our love for him didn't depend on the good work he could do. Willie Dee proved to me that unconditional love does exist.

Before Communion, Lutherans sing, "Grace our table with your presence, and give us a foretaste of the feast to come." I've sung that thousands of times, but I never understood how presence could grace until I met Willie Dee Wimberly. I believe that in Willie Dee I know what that Welcome Table is going to be: big, strong, young, overly educated white women will sit down with tiny, ancient, very Black men with little formal education and sing "Amazing Grace," eat cornbread, and laugh together about the latest story the tree told.

His Name Is Ralph, *by Murphy Davis*

F E B R U A R Y   1 9 9 0

I was speaking to a group of friends at Roswell Presbyterian Church not long ago when someone said, "Tell us one of your Open Door success stories." My mind immediately went to my friend and brother Ralph Dukes, and I gave them a thumbnail sketch of Ralph's life in our community. It was fun to do that, and I reflected as I drove home on the gift of Ralph's life among us.

When we first met him we knew him only by his street name, "Deadeye." He had lost an eye in a fight in the early 1970s, and the cruel frankness of street life bestowed the name. He was one of our first guests when we opened the Clifton night shelter in 1979. Back then we brought folks in at widely varying levels of sobriety. Ralph was a regular around Ray Lee's Blue Lantern Lounge on Ponce de Leon, and his level of sobriety was usually pretty low. But Ralph was a peaceful person and we liked him from the start. When we began to require sobriety in the shelter, we didn't see him for a while.

But then we moved into Ralph's stomping grounds—Ponce de Leon. We saw him often but not often sober.

One day in March 1983, all of us who were partners were away from the house. We returned to find that Mary Himburg, one of our first resident volunteers, had brought Ralph to live in the house. "You invited *who* in?" I remember bellowing. One by one, each of us assured her, "He'll be drunk and out of here in less than a week."

It embarrasses me to remember it: we—who so loudly proclaim that no one is beyond hope! Though I always liked Ralph, I didn't think there was much chance of his laying aside the bottle. But that was nearly seven years ago. Now Ralph himself is a partner in the community; he has never touched a drop of alcohol since the day he came through the door. When he left the streets he left the cruel street name behind. His name is Ralph.

Ralph Edwin Dukes Jr. was born in Decatur five days before Pearl Harbor, on December 2, 1941. He lived with his parents and brother in the farm home of his grandparents. Much of East Lake, McCoy Park, and Oakhurst Park was his grandaddy's cow pasture. His daddy was a butcher, who, as Ralph said, "worked to drink." He drank himself into a peaceful stupor every evening. When Ralph was in tenth grade at Decatur High School, his daddy disappeared and was not heard from until a letter came three years later from Texas, with the news of his death. They learned that he had been sent by the court to an alcohol rehabilitation hospital in San Antonio. He successfully completed the program and remained to work in the hospital. By the time of his death he had become the superintendent.

But the legacy of alcoholism had passed on. Ralph graduated from Decatur High in 1960 and went to work for his uncle, Henry Erwin, who owned a metal-fabricating plant in Tucker. He learned to weld and worked there until 1969, when he went back to Decatur High to teach welding and electronics. This was Ralph's favorite job, and he would have loved to stay, but the budget was cut and his job eliminated.

From then on there was fierce competition between Ralph's work and his drinking habits. "I didn't take my first drink," he said, "'til I was twenty-one. But then I tried to make up for lost time." He held a series of welding jobs and remembers sitting in his Clarkston apartment one night saying to himself, "Ralph, you got a choice: You gonna either drink liquor or you gonna work." The liquor won out, and Ralph began to live on the streets. For eight years he lived on Ponce de Leon (literally on Ponce). He survived by collecting cans, pan-handling, and cleaning up Ray Lee's Blue Lantern Lounge and the Ponce Pub. "Just like my daddy," he says, "I worked to drink."

He almost made it out once before. One night he met Steve Duke, a gui-tarist, at Ray Lee's, and Steve said to him, "Look, why don't you get yourself straightened out?" Steve helped him get into Rockdale House. For eight months Ralph was sober, helped cook for the house, and went to AA meetings. But at the end, Ponce drew him back like a big, bad magnet. He got off the bus and immediately ran into a couple of his drinking buddies. "Before I knew it I was at the Druid liquor store buying me a half-pint. Eight months of sobriety and just like that, it was over. Back on the treadmill to oblivion."

Eight years on the street took their toll. Ralph wanted to quit drinking, but he couldn't do it on the streets. "But once I got a roof over my head and a bed that was mine for as long as I needed it, I could do it. As they say in AA, I was sick and tired of being sick and tired. I'm thankful I came out of it in one piece. The piece is a little frayed, but it's one piece."

Ralph Dukes left the streets and became a sober, hardworking member of the Open Door family. When we celebrated his birthday that first year, he stood up and said, "I thank you for celebrating my birthday. I don't remember any of my birthdays for the last twenty years because I've been drunk. If Mary Him-burg hadn't brought me in here I might be dead. Thank you."

Ralph is up every morning at 4:00. He makes pot after pot of coffee for the house and the Butler Street Breakfast. Then he walks to the corner to pick up the morning papers and is back before most of us are up. By mid-morning he's setting up the dining room for the soup kitchen. His afternoons and many evenings are spent in the clothes closet sorting and sizing hundreds of pairs of pants and socks, shirts and underwear to refresh those who come in for show-ers. In between, he reads five to six books a week. (He misses his buddy Frank McGuire, whose bookstore was Ralph's favorite haunt.)

After eight years outside on Ponce, Ralph has spent most of the last seven years inside. "I stay put," he says. "I need time to do all the things I have to do. If you're not busy doing something, you can expect a ton of trouble."

Ralph became a partner last year and says this has changed his life. "Yes, it's different. I try to be more meticulous—more careful—about everything I do. In order to be a leader you have to set an example. The thing I try to say (non-verbally) is, 'Hey—it's here. You can get it too if you want it.'

"But, you know, you've got to be a special breed of cat to do this work. You've got to dig down somewhere and find out there's somebody besides you in this world. Some's just not as fortunate and we've got to do something to help 'em.

"Besides," says Ralph with his sideways grin, "I enjoy doing it."

Running with the Ball Again, *by Ed Loring*

DECEMBER 1987

Willie London took the long way around to the Open Door, but since he has entered our lives he has become a special friend and a most dependable coworker. I am especially thankful to Willie because he, like Joe Bottoms, works each day in my office with me.

When Willie was very young, he moved to Athens, Georgia. He grew up there and graduated from Burney Harris High School in that university city. His social experience was "ordinary," he believes, for a Black child in the dark days of segregation and the violent times of the civil rights movement. Willie was an outstanding running back on the high school football team; he enjoyed pressing weights also. Willie, often quiet and pensive here in the house, only laughed and nodded his head when we spoke of lost loves and young manhood glories.

One morning in July 1985, Willie rolled over from his curled position, well-hidden, in an abandoned building in downtown Atlanta. He stretched, yawned, and ran his hand down his leg. Suddenly, he realized he was covered with small shreds of fiberglass. Only the day before, he had worked long hours at a fiberglass factory—a piecemeal, short-term job he had gotten through a local labor pool. Willie got up and sneaked out of his sleeping place, for many among our 8,543 homeless friends do a little jail time when the police catch them scurrying from their cat holes. He headed for the first time to the Open Door Community for a shower and change of clothes. He had heard of the place, but he had never been there. Before long, Willie stood on the front steps of 910. He was told that this day was not a shower day and there was no help for him or his glass-covered body and clothes. The Open Door was shut. Accustomed to hearing "No," too ready, perhaps, to receive rejection, Willie returned to the city streets, itching and aching from the previous day's labor.

Work is a basic hunger of the human heart. Without good work we cannot be good people. God has created us to express a basic dimension of our "imago Dei" through works that lead to nurture, healing, justice, and worshipful play. Unemployment, underemployment, and works that produce injury and harm are social sins, and societies that thrust their members into bad work are visited from time to time by the God of justice.

Willie did more than run with the ball in high school. He worked. He was a dishwasher, busperson, and waiter at the Davis House Restaurant throughout his high school days. His mother, too, knew the travail of labor considered by the majority in our society to be unworthy of coverage under the minimum-wage laws in the 1950s and 1960s. She was a domestic for a white family before being employed by a local motel in Athens.

Willie did run the ball into college and entered Savannah State College in 1966 on a football grant. He began as an art major but later changed to mathematics. A knee injury ended his football playing, but after graduation he was fit for the draft. The Vietnam War was raging.

Something changed for Willie London, or, if not changed, at least became evident during the terrible war years. He saw no battle firsthand, but he began to slide away from himself at times. By 1973 the bottle and not the football had Willie running. He was running hard and perhaps desperately toward a goal line that did not exist.

The downward spiral in an upwardly mobile society is excruciating. A Black man wandering with an alcohol-soluble anchor is a lost man in this white-con-trolled society. In 1975, three years after leaving the Army, Willie was shipped to the VA Hospital for help with nerves and addiction. Then Willie moved back to Athens for jobs on the assembly line and bouts with unemployment, homeless-ness, and alcohol. Finally, in 1979, he was sent by the courts to a halfway house for alcoholics, prisoners, and others coming out of Georgia's institutions.

Out of the halfway house, Willie was running again like a young man with the goal line in view. He was ready to "go for it" and had a sense of purpose and direction. Thirty-two years old in 1980, Willie was now ready to move ahead. But he could find work nowhere. He put in application after application, but everywhere he turned he heard the familiar and death-dealing "No" which had broken him in earlier life. So Willie did what thousands and thousands of poor men and women must do: he reenlisted in the military. This time it was the Navy.

"Blessed are the peacemakers," said the homeless Jesus one day up on a mountaintop. "You shall be called daughters and sons of God," this gentle brother continued. Yes—children of God! Now I have known some peacemakers who disdain those who join the military services, but let me remind you that, as you listen to this tale of sorrow and hope that is the story of Willie London, never, again I say never, judge the poor and oppressed for their choice of the U.S. military—the world's greatest death machine. Three options lie crouched near the door of the poor person's house or cat hole: first, the street—that hell of homelessness; second, the prison—that hell of the houses for the poor; third, the military—that way up and in for the weak and poor. But the price? "Blessed are the poor," says Jesus on the plain, "for theirs is the Kingdom of God." How odd.

In 1981, Willie was running with the ball called life. He felt good. He said "No" to the toothless hag, who from time to time peered out of the liquor bottle and tried to smile at him. Running in 1982 and 1983, Willie saw the ancient lands of Italy, Turkey, England, Belgium, and he did duty in Beirut.

Willie's time was up in April 1984. He did not reenlist but now wistfully reflects, "I probably should have." Willie still held the ball snugly in the crook of his arm when, in 1984, he returned to his civilian life in Athens, Georgia. But again he could find no work. He searched, he hungered, but nothing came from the seeking, knocking, and asking. Finally in October he made the big decision: "I'll go to Atlanta."

"Without a dream the people perish," says the writer of the Proverbs. I, too, have dreamed of carrying the ball through the streets of the Big City where just behind the large walnut door awaits endless opportunity for the one who will only work hard. Willie London, with a dream in his heart of regular work, a house, perhaps a family someday, and, yes, of an ever deepening sobriety which only those who have tasted the mystical haze which is drunkenness can seek; this Black man—slave yet free—came to the city General Sherman once burnt to the ground in the name of human liberation and God's just judgment.

Willie ran to the Falcon Hotel where he slept for $48.57 per week. Willie ran to the labor pool where he made eighteen dollars on a good day of full work. Willie ran and ran and finally ran out. The stumble became a fumble: drunk, so lost, so hungover he remembered nothing, and now everything—even that most precious pink military ID card—was gone.

Willie slept restlessly, when at all, in abandoned buildings, and in the winter months on the floors of friendly Christ-filled churches. Again it was the labor pool, the alcohol, the filth and hopelessness that ate up his human dreams and devoured his shrinking life.

In April 1986, Willie wandered back to the Open Door. Word was that the Druid Hills Presbyterian night shelter was open a month longer than most others. He did not get in at first and retreated to the nearby weed patch. Then one night, Willie got a ticket, and he traded the wet earth for the church floor. On the morning of April 16, 1986, Willie stood in our shower line. Gentle Norman Heinrichs-Gale came up to Willie and asked, "Would you like to live with us?" "Yes," Willie replied.

Eighteen months later Willie, whom I love so deeply, sits beside me as we do an interview for this article. "The Open Door?" I ask. "It's as much of a family as family can be," he says. "I like it because I need it," he concludes.

Willie is running the ball again. He is at home here, and we are at home with Willie. He seldom leaves the house, for the dragon still waits for him behind the concrete wall. Willie works each day, giving us love and hope as he answers the phone and door, or as he sorts the checks and addresses the thank-you letters.

Willie London—Black man wandering in this world, broken and healing— is a sign of joy and hope among those of us who have the holy privilege of sharing life and fighting death among the homeless.

Horace Tribble: An Attitude of Gratitude,
by Murphy Davis

M A Y   1 9 8 9

Horace Tribble is my teacher. Every Tuesday morning like clockwork, Horace appears in our kitchen, and before long he is busily slicing oranges and counting eggs for Wednesday morning's breakfast. Later, with a friendly word for each person, he hands out sandwiches to those who come to eat with us. Many other days, too, Horace joins us to stuff newspapers, to help in the kitchen, to visit with folks in the living room, and generally to pitch in with the life and work here.

I first met Horace Tribble on the picket line at the Empire Linen Company. The workers—most of them black women—had been on strike for several weeks, and the negotiations were wearing on. People were getting tired. With my three-year-old daughter, Hannah, and her friend Christina, I had started taking lunch to the strikers several days a week. One day, as we sat on the wall after lunch, I saw a tall man get off the bus and walk, leaning on his cane, up to the line. I met Horace as he worked his way up the line greeting folks and sharing an encouraging word. Then he sat down quietly. He didn't seem to need to be noticed or thanked. He was simply there to lend his support. His presence was the gift.

And so it is often with Horace. If there is a vigil during an execution, Horace is there. If there's a rally for the homeless, Horace is there. If there's a meeting about neighborhood concerns on South Africa, Horace is there. Friend, brother, encourager.

"It's simple," says Horace. "There're too many people who talk Christianity but don't live it. Why talk the talk if you're not going to walk the walk? We got to live the scriptures. Feeding the hungry, visiting the prisoners, that's reality and I want to be a part of it."

But it seems to me we know Horace best through his prayers. When we come together for our noon worship after the soup kitchen, we often call on Horace to pray. In a clear voice he always begins, "Almighty God, we come to you today with an attitude of gratitude . . ." The familiar greeting tells us who Horace Tribble is. And it teaches us a straightforward lesson about the importance of living a life of gratitude.

Thomas Merton says, "To be grateful is to recognize the life of God in everything God has given us—and God has given us everything. . . . Gratitude, therefore, takes nothing for granted, is never unresponsive. Gratitude is constantly awakening to new wonder and to praise of the goodness of God. The grateful person knows that God is good, not by hearsay but by experience. And that is what makes all the difference" (*Thoughts in Solitude*).

Horace knows the goodness of God because he is grateful for every good gift of God. He is a person who never complains. Often Horace prays, "We thank you, God, for two good eyes to see with; for two good ears to hear with; and two good legs to walk with . . ." Horace has only one leg and walks with some difficulty and pain. But he is grateful to be able to walk.

For Horace Tribble's attitude of gratitude I give thanks. That he is a friend and part of the Open Door family we celebrate.

Two Halves Make One Whole, *by Mark Harper*

NOVEMBER 1987

It was one of those moments which can, on reflection, gently remind us of our need to find ears with which to hear. Or maybe it was simply an occasion to give thanks to God for being blessed—at least for a while—with the ears to hear someone who, as a matter of policy, is rendered voiceless by our society. At the time, however, I remember thinking that either my morning coffee wasn't working yet, or that the vocabulary I had learned elsewhere in life was now leaving me stranded.

I was beginning a Thursday-morning shift of house duty and Jay, a member of the community who had come from the streets, was sitting across from me at the breakfast table. He asked if I could get him "the half." He kind of grinned at my blank response and said, "You know, for the washing machine." What he was asking for slowly sunk in: Thursday is one of the days during the week when Jay washes clothes and towels for our community; he was needing two quarters—a half-dollar—in order to run the machine. I smiled back—a little sheepishly—and went to get "the half."

There are, of course, more painful reminders of the distance between many of us who live and work at the Open Door and those sisters and brothers who either stand in our soup and shower lines or who live here for a time as houseguests. For instance, on any one of the three days a week that we offer hot showers and a clean change of clothes to around thirty-five people, some men and women in line will use an assumed name, and sometimes no name at all. "Write down anything, call me anything," someone once told me. "I just want to stand in that hot water for a while." Maybe he was in trouble with the law; or maybe, on another occasion, he had been involved in a fight at the Open Door, and was asked to stay off the property for a number of months; maybe he thought we had forgotten his face, if not his name. But in a culture that requires a profane number of people to be crushed and stripped of personal worth in order for business to continue, he probably didn't care anymore. His spirit had been stomped out.

I first met my friend Jay in that same shower line. He always signed his name on the list as "Frazier," and when I asked about his first name, he would look up from his cigarette and say, "Frazier . . . just 'Frazier.'" The message was clear: we were coming from different places in this world, emphasized by the fact that, at that moment, I was standing inside the door and he was outside. I was white and in a position of power, while he was a black adult enduring the indignity of having to ask for a shower. I lived in a place where I was loved and made to feel whole; he knew cold streets which break people—and their names—in half. At eight o'clock on a wet February morning, "Frazier" (number fourteen on the shower list) and I were standing only a few feet apart. The wall that separated us, however, seemed to be three thousand miles thick and at least three hundred years old.

A month or so later, Jay Frazier came out of the shower line and moved into our house. He's lived here ever since. And, in the year and a half that we've shared life, the wall that our nation has built between us, grounded in and cemented by the rejection of the biblical promise that all people are "one in union with Christ Jesus" (Gal. 3:28), has been weakened and thankfully made lower. The distance between us has been reduced. Or, as Jay put it, "When there's some love around, things can change—things which a lot of people don't believe ever will. Sometimes, though, you've got to put a plank or two over what you thought were burnt bridges."

Two Easters ago, Jay did just that. When Holy Week arrived in 1986, our community was preparing to spend twenty-four-hour periods on the streets in solidarity with our homeless friends. We were dividing into groups of three to five people and encouraged—but didn't necessarily expect—houseguests who might want to, to go with us. After all, we were going places most of the women and men we live with probably never wanted to see again. But Jay, who had only been living in the house for a few weeks, signed up. My surprise was equaled by his own amazement at the Open Door's peculiar observance of the week leading up to Easter. "Why give up something good," he asked (and continues to ask from time to time), "and put one foot in hell?" Good question, I thought, as Jay and I, along with Alfred and Helen, began a long, cold night feeling the pain of Atlanta's streets.

I'll always be grateful—deeply grateful—to Jay for his willingness to rebuild and to cross burned bridges and to shepherd me through the cancerous belly of a city that for four years had been his home. On the several occasions since that Jay and I have spent together on the streets, I've come to receive this act of reverse hospitality as a profound gift: in recognizing our community's call to know and serve the homeless poor, Jay lovingly has taken it on himself to help us understand the condition and context of those who live daily with both feet in hell. As he openly shares the places from his own broken past, we are reminded of our constant need to share those places of woundedness which, in the sharing, can bond and heal us as a community.

There are other times, too, when Jay reveals his commitment never to forget where he's been, nor the people who walked in the dark places with him. Two mornings a week, he serves coffee with us at the Butler Street Breakfast, a place where he used to eat meals and find a few moments of warmth. But with deep compassion he also serves up a healthy dose of pastoral care to many of the folks he knew in his "street days."

"A lot of people out there—on the streets—are really needing some love, some caring, or at least a handshake to let 'em know that they're still human. And so that's one reason I keep coming down here. Some of 'em will get to expecting you to be here, and you can make someone's whole day if you just show up."

It seems, though, that Jay's special calling to return continually to the streets in service to his sisters and brothers who still suffer can only be understood—and fully celebrated—in light of the fact that he has claimed a measure of ownership in our community. He can serve those who remain in the streets with compassion only because he has sunk roots in a place that gives him the power to do so. As he put it in a recent house meeting, "When I was on the streets, I couldn't really think about helping anyone else, because I had to make it myself. But now that I have a home, and I feel like this is my home, it seems like I'm able to look at what other people are needing again. When I came here, you know, I wasn't expecting to stay. But maybe this old guy I was talking to some time ago was right. He said, 'Have you ever thought that what you're doing here at 910 was what you were put here to do?' I said, 'How you figure that?' He said, 'Well, if you leave you might have some bad luck—you might be going against what God has been trying to tell you to do all along. So I think you should stay on. This place works, you know, because there's love here.' "

And love, as Jay has taught us many times, can be a powerful weapon against wall-builders who would divide and oppress God's children. Love also emerges as the wonderful fruit shared among broken people who have been brought together by God's reconciling spirit. If we are to find the strength and nourishment needed in our struggle to reduce the distance with the poor, we can hope for nothing less.[1]

Calford Davis Barker: May 20, 1927–July 22, 1994, *by Murphy Davis*

SEPTEMBER 1994

Calford Davis Barker came into the Open Door Community on January 18, 1986. John Cole Vodicka was on house duty that day, and he welcomed Carl in as part of the community. It was not an easy transition: Carl had been on the move since he was a teenager and had rarely stayed in one place for very long.

But he worked at it. There were bumps on the path and a detour or two, but Carl struggled on. In May 1989, close to his sixty-second birthday, he became a partner in the community.

Over the years we learned of Carl's life and adventures. We were spared many details, and he seemed to know that there were some memories just as well left undisturbed. They spoke in his silent spaces as his eyes would drift and pain would cover his brow.

Calford Davis Barker was born on May 20, 1927, in Birmingham, Alabama, to Stella Leonard and Jim Bob Barker. When he was three years old his mother died of tuberculosis and, shortly afterward, his father drank himself to death.

---

1. Jay Frazier later became a partner in the Open Door (ed.).

Carl was raised by various loving aunts, uncles, and cousins, but he grew to hate Birmingham. He tasted the bitter gall of racism at an early age. He sometimes told the story of his job as a golf caddy when the rich white man he followed around the fairways would jam a big cigar into Carl's thirteen-year-old mouth and laugh at the n-gg-- boy with a cigar. For the insults he silently endured, his anger was still hot after more than fifty years.

He left Birmingham as soon as he was able and spent the next forty-five to fifty years criss-crossing the country, working every kind of job imaginable. He delivered milk in Bamburg, South Carolina, did gandy work on the railroads, was a political cartoonist for the *Chicago Daily Defender,* picked up garbage, and, in the days before the machine took over, he loaded and unloaded cargo on truck docks, ship docks, and train platforms from Detroit to Miami. He worked with his hands and his strong back, but looked always for ways to work with his mind. A few times he ran from the law, and a few times they caught up with him. He did prison time once with Dr. Sam Shepherd and another time with a man he called Sonny-Boy, who later went to the chair in New York State. (They said he was "Westinghoused.")

Carl often said, "I drank some of everything—even if it had a skull and crossbones on it. I been everywhere, I've seen most everything, I've done everything, and I've had everything but a baby."

All his life he wished he had been a lawyer. His resonant baritone voice would have surely given him command of a courtroom, and his penetrating mind would have been up to the task. But instead, perhaps explained somehow within that perplexing web of fact, circumstance, oppression, and choice, he more often found himself in the defendant's dock.

Remembering it all, sometimes Carl would shake his head sadly and say, "No one is good but the Father; no, not one." Sometimes he would give a look of wonderment as if to say, "How could it have happened that way? How could I have . . . ?" But his years of self-loathing and self-destruction were enough. The punishment needed to end to make way for the healing balm of friendship, family, acceptance, and reconciliation with the past—with whatever it represented and was.

For that, Carl was ready. He stayed put and concentrated on his sobriety and the work of the community. He was never more proud of anything than his eight years of sobriety, and he relished his daily work in the household. When he could no longer work on his feet because of a badly ulcerated, and later amputated, lower left leg, his job became slicing the oranges each day for the next morning's Butler Street Breakfast. After his first stroke, when he could no longer use the knife, he grieved and talked about the oranges that needed to be sliced.

Carl read all his life and especially loved history and biography. He valued intelligence above all, and whenever the last strains of "Happy Birthday" would fade away during a supper celebration, Carl would pause a moment and then demand of the celebrant: "Say something intelligent!" It has become part of the Open Door lore.

What a wide space Carl's death leaves in our home. Never has anyone carried themselves through the halls of this household with greater dignity. We will miss his big voice, his out-of-the-blue remembrances and stories and questions, his interest in listening to guests and "highly intelligent" speakers, and his large heart that regularly remembered and gave thanks for those who had helped him along his way to new life and healing.

But Carl Barker's greatest legacy is in the way he taught us to go to God. Carl often prayed a prayer in our worship services that reminded me of the story Jesus tells in Luke 18 of the Pharisee and the tax collector. The Pharisee raised his arms to God with thanks that he was "not like the others" and listed his many virtues. The tax collector bowed his head in private and pleaded, "O God, have mercy on me, a sinner." The tax collector, said Jesus, teaches us how to pray.

Carl Barker taught us how to pray, and his prayer remains in our hearts:

> O God,
> grant me wisdom to do Thy will.
> Shed Thy good light upon
> my troubled path, that I might not stray
> into the byways of fools.
> And if I stay in a swamp,
> bogged down in the quagmire
> of mine own iniquity,
> O God, be merciful unto me,
> a sinner. Amen.

James Brown Is My Brother, *by Ed Loring*

APRIL 1985

Amid the foothills of the Appalachian Mountains, stretching east into the Piedmont area of the Carolinas, marched the hungry textile mills. The mill owners were hungry and thirsty for profits. The Piedmont had lots of cotton, picked by black hands, and lots of mill laborers—mostly white folk. So from the north came the looms, shuttles, and spools hungry to make cloth and ever higher profits.

My grandfather, an immigrant from Germany, came to Greenville, South Carolina, at the turn of the century and began work in a cotton mill. Some ten miles away in Easley, James Brown's grandfather worked in a cotton mill. My grandfather had a basic German education, married a landowner, invented a machine to measure cloth as it was wound upon the bolt, and slowly and painfully rose to bookkeeper. My mother remembers the fear and suffering the family went through during World War I when people rode by their house and yelled epithets at the German family. Some folks threw rocks, and occasionally a brick went through the window.

James Brown's grandfather did not advance through the mill structure. His son accompanied his father to the houses, stores, churches, all provided by the management. James Brown was born into the economic and cultural poverty of the mill village in which both parents worked.

In 1940, at sixteen, James dropped out of the tenth grade to go to work in the same mill in which his parents labored. Living in a very poor family put pressure on James to become a wage earner. In 1943, James joined the Navy and "learned what I wish I had not learned," he told me, seeing death and destruction in the South Pacific.

Before he left the Navy in 1946, James learned something else that he wishes he had not learned. He learned to drink beer, wine, and whisky, and he was set on a path of loneliness and destruction.

From the Pacific Ocean he returned to Easley, South Carolina—to the mill village and mill work. Pay was very low; work was exceedingly hard; and hope seemed especially dim in the dark and dusty mill.

How does one break out of a life of poverty and the dead-end existence of a South Carolina textile-mill worker? Ten years earlier, unions had been rejected. What was the hope of higher wages? Overtime work, perhaps. Many folk, men and women, husband, wife, and children, would work and work and end the month a little deeper in debt to the company store. If one cannot get out of a situation, what about a drink of hard liquor? That can soften the din of textile machinery and the desolation of a life in poverty. Change, change, for a better life, a new hope, for a new way of life, how do we accomplish it?

One day in 1947, James Brown walked out of the textile mill, never to return. He hoped, as we all hope, for a better life. James began to drive trucks and buses. He traveled across the nation in tractor-trailers and drove Trailways buses between New York City and Washington, D.C., and later over the two Carolinas. There was hope on the horizon and new life in his heart. But there was also the thirst that he had discovered in the war zone. A thirst for ease and comfort, a thirst to forget the poverty and despair of mill-village life: a thirst for alcohol. So James drank his way through many jobs and down many highways. He drank himself through two marriages and lots of friendships and, though the anxiety and pain were dulled for a few days, he found himself sunk deeper into alcoholism.

In 1967, James returned to Easley and got a job through his brother-in-law in the shipping department at Stay-on Manufacturing Company, a factory making baby clothes. He worked there until his mother's death and his dad's move into a mobile home (after retirement from the mill, his father became the custodian of Bushy Creek Baptist Church). Homeless and often drunk, James did not know which way to turn. Hoping just to survive rather than to find a better life, he felt lost.

James Brown turned—like many desperate people in the South, Southwest, and Mexico—to migrant labor. He joined a crew heading to South Georgia to pick sweet potatoes. As he told me, "Oh, they painted a pretty picture of the farm and work, but by the time you got there, you were in debt. They furnished you with wine and cigarettes everyday and wrote it down in the books." Each week everyone was given two dollars in cash and reminded of their debts to the farmer. "You never see a payday in a place like that," James remembered, slowly shaking his head.

After two seasons on the farm, James was told one morning to pack his belongings; in thirty minutes he was to be shipped to Atlanta.

Between 1973 and 1980, James lived on and off the streets of Atlanta. Sometimes he got day work from a labor pool; other times he got yard work and odd jobs from people who would pick him out of the St. Luke's soup-kitchen line. He often slept in the "weed patches" in downtown Atlanta. For a long while, he lived in a dilapidated barn near one of the labor pools. Once in a while James would get a truck-driving job and live in the cab between trips. "The life on the streets was dangerous," he told me. "Sometimes I got drunk to deal with the fear, no home, no place to live. But it was my fault."

One cold night during the winter of 1980, James Brown, bent, chilled, dirty, and hungry, walked through the side door of Clifton Presbyterian Church—a place of sanctuary for God's good friends. He lived with us for six months. At first he was silent and sullen, but slowly he began to talk and relate to those of us in the church. Murphy Davis and James developed a friendship of warmth and sharing.

On another night, a warmer evening, James did not return. Where he went we did not know. What had happened we did not hear. Earlier that day, we later learned, while standing in the line at St. Luke's soup kitchen, a man offered James a job with a carnival, and he took it. For one hundred dollars per week (raised to $120 after a few months), he ran the Ferris wheel or the merry-go-round. With seven other men he lived in the back of a truck. He ate his meals at restaurants and continued to remember his dream of a better life even as he obeyed his thirst for alcohol and its moments of relief.

After two years, James left the carnival and returned to the mean streets of Atlanta. One afternoon I ran into him in front of Peak Load labor pool. I was so happy to see him! "James Brown, I'll be damned," I yelled, feeling like the apostle Thomas when Jesus appeared. James looked more like death than life. Filthy and ragged and a bit shaky, he seemed embarrassed as I jumped up and down with songs of gladness in front of the labor pool. I immediately invited James to come and live with us forever (praying there was an empty bed at the house). He said, "Yes, I'll come," so off we went to 910 Ponce de Leon, where we have lived—sometimes happily, sometimes angrily, but always together—ever since.

James Brown is my brother. He feeds folks every morning at Butler Street CME Church, and he feeds each of us with love and friendship every day at the Open Door. Before a serious stroke a year ago, he often kept Hannah and Christina during common-life meetings. Only once during the last three years has James had a drink. We put him out for the night, and he stayed on the back porch until 6:00 P.M. the next day, when he could reenter. Susan, my older daughter, calls him "Grandpa," and he and Murphy banter back and forth as "Sir James" and "The Lady."

I asked James if he was a person of faith. "No, I'm not a Christian," he said. "I grew up in the church, but I've never been baptized." Then he went on to say that he believed in Jesus Christ and he respected the church. "Well, what do you mean, 'I'm not a Christian'?" I responded. "I'm not good enough," he said. "You've got to be good to be a Christian."

How my heart aches for James. How I wish I could share my life more fully with this man I love so deeply. How I hope for a better life for us all.

Out of the mill village, across the concrete highways, bent over in the sweet-potato field, from the cat holes beneath high hotels, from the jingle-jangle music of merry-go-rounds, off the street with an empty wine bottle in his hand comes this man into our lives. He walks through the door, and he is an ambassador of Jesus Christ. We have learned from his poverty and suffering, from his drunkenness and pain, from his joy and love and work that God loves each of us. And you don't have to be good to be a Christian. Thank you, Lord, for James Brown.

Harold Wind (Orange Man), *by Mark Harper*

JUNE 1990

Editor's note: Mark Harper was a resident volunteer when he wrote this memorial poem about Harold Wind, a deeply loved member of the Open Door who died on June 23, 1986.

Harold's was my first death
there snatched away quick as a wink
lungs lost to a quiet blitzkrieg of
30 years on three packs a day
A mile for a Camel, they used to say
in the end even the distance to the toilet
was too far

Still, how could a shrunken chest
contain a heart so mighty? A muscle to muster the breath
for one more birthday candle
a light as bright as the fluorescent cap you wore
like an orange beacon morning upon morning
cutting through the city's damp sigh attentive
to the errand of mercy

Orange man
light in the darkness of 250 broken bodies
pouring like tired water into the church basement
sleepless, bloody eyes finding a smile and four slices
of an orange at line's end
simple succor for partakers of bitter fruit

Worn-out, finally, you hung up the cap
and taught us about freedom. Even as bony-fingered
death was picking your pocket you
cracked a grin and with language lean shot back
at the thief:
"You gave me six months,
It's been six months.
I'm still here. Ta da!"

And "here" meant family meant more than long lines
of the hungry on the outside

meant counting time as precious on the inside, too
One!
Two!
Three scoops of chocolate!
Blessed are the milkshake makers, soup-kitchen soda jerks
buying time for your withered frame
but all the while being fed by you
a story shared in the kitchen after supper, after the busyness

O Orange man, man of the resurrection
the wind knows no vagrant-free zones
needs no credential but blows where it will
releasing the captives
releasing me

Community Member: Bob Carter, *by Ruth Allison*

N O V E M B E R   1 9 8 8

One of the wonderful things about life in the Open Door Community is the amazing variety of folk who live with us. Some have Ph.D.s while others finished their formal education with the third grade. Most have spent time on the streets and in jail or prison, but some of us were raised with every privilege, and never knew hardship or need. Many have traveled far and wide, and all have interesting tales to tell from their experiences. Although Bob Carter came to live with us only two months ago, he has been a friend of the community for years. He has told us many stories, and we have been able to share wonderful stories from our encounters with him.

I first met Bob within two weeks of moving to the Open Door. It was mid-April of 1987 when another resident volunteer pointed to a distinguished-looking man in our shower line and said, "That is Bob Carter. You might want to see if there is any Hemingway in our bookcase for him. He reads a lot . . . and he speaks fluent Korean." Not too many months after, we heard words of welcome flowing from Bob's mouth in Korean. A delegation of pastors from Korea had come to the Open Door to visit us one afternoon. Bob Carter had been sitting outside on our front steps since lunch, and when they came to the door, he stood and graciously welcomed them in their own language. They were surprised that this homeless man knew and spoke Korean so well, and we were delighted that we could be so hospitable to them through our friend Bob.

I did not see Bob often, for he was very independent, working with considerable skill and experience out of labor pools, reading everything we had to offer on our library shelves, and living the life of a loner. Bob had the very first "Mad Houser" shack built in Atlanta, and he was proud of it, inviting friends to share his quarters and his luck.

Then, when it seemed like forever since we had seen Bob in our soup line, word began drifting back to us that he was ill, holed up in the kudzu two blocks from 910. One day several folks reported that Bob was dead and that he had been taken away. We did some investigation by phone and found that Bob was not in the hospital or the morgue, so Chuck and David, members of the community, went to Bob's shack to see if they could verify the reports. What they found shocked them to the point of tears. Bob was very ill, covered with a strange rash, and unable to move his legs. When they came into his shack, Bob was propped up on one elbow, reading, and he was coherent, although he had hardly eaten in two weeks. A stubborn man, and one tired of the desperation on the streets, Bob refused to go to the hospital.

Chuck and David came home, determined to do something to save the life of our friend Bob. We called an ambulance, but the attendant asked Bob if he wanted to be carried to Grady Hospital; he declined, so they packed up and drove off. A counselor for emergency mental health services told us that we had two options. First, we could keep calling an ambulance until the attendants became annoyed and had Bob arrested for public disturbance. Second, we could wait until Bob's health had deteriorated so badly that he was unconscious and unable to refuse treatment.

Horrified by this farcical approach to public health and the welfare of a human being, we phoned our good friend Dr. Marty Moran and asked for his help. He immediately responded, came to visit Bob, and confirmed our suspicions that Bob was seriously ill and in need of hospitalization. Dr. Moran contacted a friend of his from the Atlanta Police Department, and together they helped us force Bob to seek medical treatment. In the face of such persistence and Dr. Moran's obvious concern, Bob, weakened by his prolonged illness, was no longer able to refuse treatment and was finally taken to Grady, where he spent one week in intensive care and two weeks recovering in bed.

Chuck and David and others visited Bob while he was in the hospital and invited him to become a member of the Open Door. So Bob moved in with us. Since then he has told us many stories about his life before Atlanta—quitting Tulane only twenty-eight hours short of a degree; teaching in a private college in Korea; getting married; managing restaurants; selling his artwork in Jackson Square in New Orleans; working as a powder monkey . . . and somehow managing to continue as a loner, keeping very much to himself in spite of the people around him. It was only after he got mugged here in Atlanta, and the bankroll that he had accumulated to buy into another restaurant was stolen, that Bob began to live on the streets. Three years on the streets nearly destroyed Bob's spirit and his pursuit of life.

During the past few months, if you have called or come by the Open Door, you have probably been greeted graciously by Bob. Now his main job is handling the huge number of requests and donations that come in every day through our front door and over the telephone. It is wonderful to have Bob here, still reading everything he can get his hands on. Our lives have been enriched because we share life with Bob. We hope that he will continue to entertain us with stories about his past and that we will continue to have wonderful stories to tell about our life together.[2]

Breakfast with Curtis, *by Ed Loring*

JULY / AUGUST 1987

Curtis rolled over. His foot was trapped in the kudzu vine like a moth in a spiderweb. "Oh Christ," he prayed in disgust. Slowly, he pulled himself up, dislodged his foot, and began his ascent toward the dumpster behind Hardy's Liquor Store.

Only yesterday afternoon Curtis had been released from the city jail for the seventh time in three years. He had walked and walked until the city-sick, pale darkness had covered his. Hidden, he had crept toward his cat hole. He cursed the night and felt the fear juggle in his abdomen as he clambered downhill to his weed-webbed home. "Crap, what if some dude is in my hole," Curtis mumbled inaudibly. "I've been in hell for ten days." Wet vines flung their arms at him while giant leaves pursed their putrid petals and spit in his face. The angry earth denied her child, throwing rocks in his shins. Suddenly, an invisible tree cracked Curtis between the eyes. Red blood flowed into his wiry mustache. "Jesus Christ!" he confessed, falling to his knees. He was lost.

Today was another day. "One day at a time"—he remembered the line from the fathomless lessons he had forgotten at detox. Finally, he arrived. Leaning his shoulder against the giant green dumpster's side panel, Curtis opened the beggar's version of a drive-in window at Wendy's.

---

2. Bob eventually left the Open Door Community and moved back to the streets, where he later died (ed.).

Not much. Amid the broken glass lay a bottle of vodka with a corner in it. Curtis spilled it. "What the hell? Juice is easier to come by than bread in these godforsaken streets." Curtis wanted to scream, but his voice got stuck deep in his esophagus. He spit. "Oh, god, I hate to eat out of garbage cans," he hoped.

Curtis turned and walked toward the sidewalk. His eyes were swollen, and dried blood stiffened his facial hairs. Bending his head into the position of prayer released the pressure behind his eyes and slackened the throbbing pain inside his skull. The tiny corner of vodka had not helped. Hunger now flared in his belly and began to shout mercilessly, "Feed me! Feed me! Feed me!" The noise became more than Curtis could bear.

"Help me. Help me," he yelped to the voice that was screaming at him for food. He slipped on a crooked cobblestone and stumbled into the street. A drift of cool air bathed his face like a gentle balm. In the instant that his feet spun toward heaven he dreamed of grits and eggs and steaming coffee. The violent cries hushed as a joyous vision of a thankful breakfast table filled the slits of his swollen eye sockets. Someone called, "Curtis, Curtis, you come on now, son. Your breakfast is getting cold. . . . You hear me? Come on, now. Let's eat. You've got a lot to do today."

Almost instantaneously Curtis smashed headlong into the street. Before the driver could raise her right foot for the brake pedal, the MARTA bus crushed his skull flat as a delicious blueberry pancake.

LeBron Walton: Just Surviving,
by Elizabeth Dede with LeBron Walton

FEBRUARY/MARCH 1997

In the winter of 1996, LeBron Walton hobbled into our lives after a night when temperatures dipped into the low teens. Since he had been caught in the rain the day before, his clothes were frozen to his body. The long, bushy beard he wore at that time was white with frost. LeBron couldn't put his shoes on because they were frozen, and his feet were frostbitten.

Now, a year later, LeBron Walton has walked with fierce pride out of our lives. He wanted to work at a paying job, to have money, to "be a man," as our culture defines man.

We miss LeBron, because in the year that we shared we were challenged by his anger toward racism and bigotry. We listened to his social analysis of the abuse of the Black man in American society. He laid it out plain for us. We hope that his future will be a steady, sober, strong, and meaningful life, full of good work, health, food, friends, and a home. We pray that he will have these good gifts, because we want much more than survival for LeBron.

The transformation we witnessed in LeBron Walton's life was a truly amazing gift of God's grace made flesh. The hobbling, frozen, raggedy, bearded, silent man who limped into the Open Door spent a year regaining his health, renewing his sense of self-worth, recovering his sobriety, rediscovering his voice, and realizing the beauty of his face, his hands, his feet, his whole race.

But LeBron, standing straight and proud, stepped out of this transforming space and time, we fear, into nothing. He searched for work and found a job at a chicken-processing plant. For little more than five dollars per hour, LeBron Walton stands all day in one place, repeatedly reaching into a headless chicken to grab its craw, twist, and yank it out. One chicken per second flashes before his eyes. When one hand tires, he switches to the other. After one day, his arms and hands swelled from carpal tunnel syndrome. Rest from the repeated motion is the only cure, but there is no rest at one chicken per second.

A wage of five dollars per hour is not enough for life. You can't have a place to live, food, transportation, and health care on such a meager salary. Our friend Mike Griffin, who directed the major renovation of the old Imperial Hotel, says that affordable, safe, decent housing alone requires a wage of nine dollars per hour.

Before LeBron Walton left the Open Door Community, he sat down one evening to tell about his life. We share his story because it is the cry of the oppressed that God hears. May it move us to work for justice, to demand a life-sustaining minimum wage, to call for the abolition of all abusive, sweat-shop labor practices, to create good and meaningful work for all people, to make home together, and to build the Beloved Community.

❖ ❖ ❖

I was born in 1951 and grew up in Chattanooga, Tennessee, with my father and stepmother. My father was divorced from my mother when I was very young—I don't know the exact age, but I had to be around two or three years old. My mother wasn't taking care of her children like she should have been. My father got a divorce and got custody of all seven of us. We were separated—my sisters and brothers and I. Some of us were sent to Alabama to stay with my father's mother and aunt. And some of us stayed in Chattanooga. We stayed with some aunts on my mother's side.

I gather that my father wasn't sending stuff down to help my grandmother and my aunt, so she said that he had to come and get us. He came and got us with his new wife. Immediately we knew that we didn't like her. You know the stepmother story? She was typical.

My father was still in the Navy at the time. We stayed in an apartment while he was in the Navy doing service in the Korean War. Not all of us were united at the same time, but we stayed with my stepmother, and she abused us. She was tyrannical. She was mad because none of us belonged to her biologically. She couldn't have children, and she took that out on us. She made it a sad situation around the house where we lived. We grew up, and there was no love in the house because she didn't show any love. As young children, you know, you've got to have that. You need that to grow up to a healthy human being. We lacked that love, and it affected me, I know, and a brother of mine, who's been in prison all of his life. He went first to reform school, and then to prison at a very early age for stealing, and stuff like that. In 1976 he was convicted of multiple rapes up in Cook County, Illinois. I guess he's still doing time. I haven't communicated with him since then. We didn't grow up as a family because there wasn't love. My stepmother didn't create an environment for cohesion in the family.

I grew up in a decent neighborhood because my father was able to pay higher rent with the job he had. I never did stay in the projects or in the ghetto. He bought us a home in 1959. It was a decent house.

So I guess I got to blame my stepmother and my family situation again because I remember so many days going to school hungry, dirty, pissy because I didn't know how to take care of myself; I was just a child. My stepmother wouldn't coordinate any efforts with my older sisters for us to get together as a team to prepare ourselves for school. So I went to school ashamed and embarrassed because I was hungry and I had to ask people for a piece of sandwich. She sent us to school maybe with two dry baloney sandwiches but no breakfast, so I'd eat the sandwiches as soon as I'd leave the house. So I'd be hungry in school all day, and I'd be dirty and smelly. I couldn't concentrate on my schooling.

We were so segregated that I wasn't conscious of racism. In the seventh grade I went to an integrated school, and that's when I dropped out. You could just feel the tension in the air. You knew that you weren't welcome there. That was 1967. I just stopped going. I did whatever I could to survive. My father, I guess, was a basically decent man. Seems like he had an attitude against his children because his wife had an attitude against us. He wouldn't stand up for us when he found out she had beat us for nothing. She always did something mean—restricted us to the house—she always did something mean to make life miserable for us, and my father never did stand up for us.

My father had a good job after he got out of the Navy. He worked for Dupont and had one of the better-paying nonskilled jobs in the city for Black people. He worked a swing shift at different hours, so he was rarely at home. He wouldn't take up for us. He just left us there to make it on our own with no concern for us. I guess he figured, "As long as I keep 'em off the streets and put a little food in 'em, then damn 'em."

I remember when we first came up from Alabama, she was talking about adopting us, and I wanted to tell them so bad, "Hell, no! I don't want you as my mother!" She put that intimidation in us; she put fear in us, so I wouldn't speak up. She wasn't a very nice person.

I came to Atlanta in 1986 from Florida. In 1977 a lot of bad things happened to me. First, my father died, and then I got laid off a good job at Dupont. They repossessed my car and everything else, and I was sleeping on the street in my own hometown. That aggravated an ulcer to a point where it perforated my stomach lining, and I had to have an operation. My sisters arranged for me to go and stay in Alabama with my aunt to recuperate. I didn't like it down there because there weren't any jobs, you know. It was right down at Tuscaloosa. The biggest employer down there is the University of Alabama—about thirty-five miles away from where I stayed in Green County. I didn't have no transportation to get out and get work. So I called my brother down in Tampa, Florida, and he came to pick me up. I did a little of this and that down there, but I didn't do no good down there, either. I stayed there six years.

I guess the brightest spot for me in Tampa was when I enrolled in school—an electronics school—really good. I got my GED in the military. I went to college at the community college in Chattanooga while I was working at Dupont. I tried to go to school at an area vocational-technical school for air conditioning and heating and refrigeration. I went there nine months, waiting on the VA to pay me for going to school. They never did send my money. I was scheduled to go up to Nashville to have counseling with them so they could release my money so I could continue with school. I was driving my old raggedy car up there. I just let it go down when I lost my job. I was speeding, and an unmarked police car stopped me. I was driving without insurance, speeding. So I blew my appointment with the VA. They didn't release no money, and I had to drop out of school.

The best job I ever had was the one with Dupont. They had a synthetic-fiber production. My job was to put these undrawn, twisted spools of strands of yarn onto a machine, and we strung it up in an intricate way, and the machine drew and twisted the fiber at a uniform rate, winding it on a spool. That was semi-skilled work because it took time to get that touch. I had to string it up and read a diagram and string it up like that. It was a kind of delicate operation.

I was a military police in the army. I trained security dogs—German shepherds.

Electronics—I have a natural feel for electronics. I'm really proud of myself for the little small achievements I made in the little while that I was at the vo-tech. Considering my background in formal education, especially. Algebra and trigonometry, geometry, calculus. It just lets me know that I can learn what I want if I put some effort into it. I was making *A*s and *B*s in that advanced stuff.

I got a loan, but before I could use it, I broke my leg, and I started drinking again. That was my excuse for dropping out. That was a bad mistake I made—not finishing at that school.

Right before I came to the Open Door I had a little camp set up on the railroad tracks. It was pretty peaceful down there. The day before the freeze came, the police came down there and wrecked our camp. They told us to leave, or they'd lock us up. So I came up here.

It was raining that day, and I came to take a shower, to get some dry clothes on. I had been drinking. I wasn't drunk, or belligerent, or anything like that. I don't do those kind of things unless somebody mess with me. But I couldn't take a shower, or get dry clothes. That night it froze, and I froze with it. My feet froze along with it.

I was laying out there in the yard. The blankets I had over me were frozen around me like a tent. I had to take my shoes off during the night because they were wet, and I figured if I took them off my feet would stay a little warmer. I got up that morning and snow was on the ground. Everything was frozen; my feet were frozen, and my shoes were frozen so hard I couldn't put them back on.

Thank God I was in the yard. I hobbled up to the door, and Ed saw me, and immediately he knew I was in trouble. I took a shower and changed clothes. He asked me to stay for a couple of weeks for my feet to heal. I said, "Thank you."

Mainly now I don't feel so badly about humanity. I've met some very kind, compassionate people here—they care about others and will extend help to others if they can. My mind has cleared up from all the abuse of living on the outside. My body is healthier from eating good food and proper rest and being in a peaceful, inspiring environment. I just feel better generally. I feel like I can go out there and get me a job, stay straight, and try to find some semblance of decent life.

For sure, I'm so glad that I came this way. It was a life-changing experience. It was an attitude-changing experience, because like I said, it just made me realize that there are still decent, compassionate people in this world. I had been out there in those streets, homeless and jobless and doing whatever I could to survive for so long, and being ignored and kicked to the side. That has a way of clouding your view of all people. You become suspicious of all. You hold contempt for all. You categorize all in the same negative blot. That's mainly how most homeless people get treated because of the way they're dressed. They look all unkempt and everything—unclean.

The Open Door categorized me, too, because I had been drinking. I can't blame you. You can't tell how somebody's going to act or react after they've been drinking. Automatically you assume, "Oh, this guy is drunk. He's going to cause all kinds of problems if we let him in the house. We just got to get him out of here." You just categorized me with all the rest of the ones you experienced being drunk and not being able to communicate or follow instructions. So when I was drinking and tried to get a shower and some dry clothes on that day in 1996, you just kicked me on out. The Open Door didn't want to be bothered with what you thought I would do. You know, that just added to it. I said, "Damn. Just total disrespect because of what they assume, because I'm homeless and I come to this place needing some basic help. They assume that I ain't no good; that I'm stupid, or dumb; I ain't never been worth anything in my life."

A year later I started looking for paid employment, and I started making plans to leave the community. I was riding the train going out to see about a job in Dunwoody, and I saw a guy who uses the services here. We got to talking, and he told me, "I know where you can immediately get a job." So I went out there the next day, and they hired me. So I started working.

I work on a type of conveyor line where there are chickens hanging in stirrups by their legs with the feathers off and the head chopped off. After the neck skin is split open, my job is to reach in and take the craw and the windpipe out. We go through about fifty thousand or more in a day. I do about one chicken a second. The chickens are drained by the time they get to me, so there's not a lot of blood.

I be on the site from 7:00 A.M. until 5:30 P.M. That's the longest we can work in a day because they have federal inspectors there, and they shut it down at 5:30 P.M. That's the longest they're willing to work. And when they stop, everything stops. That's about ten hours of work. We get a ten-minute break every hour. We get a thirty-minute break from 9:30 to 10:00, and we break for lunch from 12:30 until 1:00. We're not paid for that hour of break time.

I looked for work at a restaurant, in construction, at an animal hospital. I just couldn't find anything else.

I realize I'm getting old, and my mind is willing, but my body ain't able. I try to work at a pace that I used to work at when I was younger. I try that these days and these old bones and everything just won't take that abuse and stress. I reach up, grab, twist, and pull down. That's the motion. When I wear one hand out I go to the other. Because my left hand is swollen, I had to wear a steel-mesh glove. It was so tight around my fist. After you flex your fist fifty thousand times a day, that's a lot of pressure.

There are a lot of Mexicans working in the plant, and I can't read their age too good. But this young Black guy, he seems to be the youngest one, he's nineteen or twenty. There are some old women who work over there. If they're not actually sixty, they look it. I'm quite sure there are illegal aliens working there, too.

I make $5.25 an hour, with a fifty-cent bonus if I get there on time every day. I get a quarter raise this month. In three weeks I've saved $412. I make about

$140 a week. The first week I didn't work but about seventeen hours. The next week I worked twenty-three hours. Then last week I worked forty-five hours. This week we were scheduled to work 44½ hours, but some trucks didn't come in Thursday and Friday, and we got off early so that knocks the hours down.

You can live very meagerly on that amount. I'm going to find something else. I don't like any of the places I can live. I don't like the neighborhoods. Up the street there are a couple of apartments for one hundred dollars a week. That would give me forty dollars' spending money for transportation—that costs more than I make. And it takes a lot of food to work out there. I eat more out there than I ever ate in my life. And I don't gain no weight because I'm steady burning it off. You must eat. If you don't eat, you can't work. I know some jobs I went to I could make it all day without eating if I had to. You got to replenish that energy.

They aren't doing nothing for the injuries to my hands. I've told them about it, but I haven't pushed it. If I pushed it they might move me to another department, but I'm on probation now. Being injured this early in the game, they could just replace me. Other people have the same injuries, and they just keep on because they need the money. There are seven people at my station. They haven't gave us any brochures on insurance, but they told us we have medical, dental, profit sharing. I guess they'll wait till the probation period is over—ninety days. The attrition rate is so high; they be betting that you won't make it.

My dreams for my future? I don't know. Just surviving.

Thank You, Rob, *by Ed Loring*

J A N U A R Y   1 9 8 7

Editor's note: This article honors Rob Johnson, who, along with his wife, Carolyn, Ed Loring, and Murphy Davis, were the founders of the Open Door Community.

Thank you, Rob, for coming in 1977 to the Atlanta Presbytery Task Force on Evangelical Social Concerns. There we met and as though the breath of the Holy Spirit pushed us toward each other, we reached across a table and grasped each other's hand. Shortly thereafter, we shared Walter Brueggemann's reflection on Exodus 16. Do you remember how thrilled we were by the call to liberation at the hands of the gentle yet fire-filled Yahweh who brought us to a new diet in the wilderness? Yes, we began as brothers preparing for World Food Day with a shared secret in our hearts: food, diet, and menu bring revolution in a wilderness land which seeks and cries for justice and broken bread. (Did we, then, standing by your shiny blue motorcycle in the parking lot, see a twilight flash on our journey's path, revealing that a million bowls of soup and 783,421 bowls of boiling grits were before us?) We began sharing manna.

Thank you, Rob, for joining Clifton Presbyterian Church and for helping to lead that little band of clowns for Christ through waters that swirled about us in a sea that seemingly would not part. Remember how you arose in the eleventh hour of my despair and brought the broken bodies to a healing and reconciliation that today is a source of strength in that faithful and foolish congregation?

Thank you, Rob, for your crisis of faith in 1979 when you, like saints and radicals before you, lay down the academic dream and the professional dream and took up the costly cross of obedience to another way. It was, and is, a way defined by servanthood, life together, covenant relationships, and the biblical politics of life over death. It was, and is, a way defined by justice rooted in charity and mercy, a way demanding us to choose the side of the homeless and the prison. Your tears contained the waters of my own grief as well, and your shaking shoulders were signs of depth and stability for us all. Later that week we passed the pen, signed the covenant, and the Open Door Community was born.

Ah, Rob, my friend and brother, thank you for sharing childbirth. First little tiny Christina broke forth so unexpectedly that we barely caught our breath, and then her life was on the line for days. Remember how we wept and prayed? And Hannah, the opposite: three weeks late, big and fat and another girl. And you and I, all but simultaneously, began this fatherhood adventure. If there has ever been a fruit of our hopes and dreams of life together—I mean something so concrete that Satan's big air-powered sledgehammer could not even chip it— that is Christina's and Hannah's love. Want to see the biblical way in action anyone? Come visit and you shall see . . .

Thank you, Rob, servant of the hungry, friend of prisoner, leader of this small toe of the Body of Jesus Christ. You have told the truth to our friends who live in houses and have rooms in which to read, as month after month you have lovingly edited *Hospitality*. Our paper is well-known and appreciated. It is a voice on behalf of the voiceless; it is a sign of survival and hope; it is an instrument of social change and a call to love and reconciliation among all peoples on behalf of the oppressed and prisoner. You have gifted us with this newspaper. Thank you, Rob.

Thank you, Rob, for your trip to Nicaragua. Thank you for your constant care and call in our lives that we keep our eyes not only on the streets of Atlanta—filled as they are with discarded and unwanted men and women, boys and girls—but on the streets of the cities and villages of our brown and black friends in Central America, too. Hate begets hate; violence brings more violence with an ever deepening bitterness. You remind us that this little country, which after the overthrow of Somoza immediately abolished the savage death penalty, is no more than an extension of the streets of Atlanta. Those forces which cry out to establish a vagrant-free zone or a safeguard zone or whatever they call it this week, are the same forces that bomb the campesinos in Nicaragua and burn the shantytowns of South Africa. Thank you, Rob, for teaching us that we are all one in this world that God loves so much, that God gave us Jesus so that none on the streets and in prisons, in the banks, at City Hall, in the Pentagon, or in the junta in Managua might perish but that we might enjoy life always—together!

And finally, thank you, Rob, for being a source of deep thankfulness and joy which resides down in my bowels. You, my beloved brother, have taught me something of what it means "to drink from our own wells," as Bernard of Clairvaux says. You have given me that daily love and forgiveness and trust which is the foundation, the rock, on which radical Christian community is built. What a source of faith and joy this has been for all of us at the Open Door!

You have stayed with us through the most terrible times our lives have ever known: the rending of the fabric of common life; when friends grew hostile (often not without reason and purpose) and neighbors organized to end or limit our ministries; while others have wished to silence our voices or to change the structures, agenda, dreams, and vocation of God's call for the Open Door. Thank you, Rob. Your long-haul commitment and willingness to bear the brunt of persecutions and rumors have been a source of life and maturity for me. How, through your witness and that of others like you, I want to disarm my own heart and bear the cross of Christ with ever deepening radicality.

And, Rob, my teacher, how I thank you for giving me and all of us the joy of a glad heart and the light feet of angels dancing. You are poet and musician, you are clown and storyteller, you are silly and very funny. In the midst of our hard work and hurting lives we sing and shout and play and party. Thank you for your glee!

Rob, we will miss you.

S. A. Williams: Dereliction and the Death of a Dumpster Diver, *by Ed Loring*

OCTOBER 1999

I: AUGUST 1, 1999

A loud banging assaulted our front door. Agitation mingled with the stifling heat of more than one hundred degrees. I went to the door, pushed wide the heavy green frame by hitting the panic bar. Quentin's face was contorted, his breath heavy and foul, eyes on fire like Ponce's asphalt in the boiling heat. "S. A.'s dead!" he sputtered all over me.

This is the manner of our living. This is the style and fashion of our dying. While in the heart of planning our response to S. A.'s death on the torrid evening of August 16, our newest partner simply rode away from us on a bike. He bumped against stones and holes pedaling down the alley. We have not seen him, nor heard a word about him. We have filed a missing-person's report with the Atlanta Police Department, telephoned hospitals and jails. We have, like beggars shrouded in velvet, pled for information on the streets. Nobody knows the trouble I've seen but Jesus and a few men hanging out at the corner by the green dumpster. This is the manner of our living. This is the style and fashion of our dying. Have you seen him? (At 9 P.M., ten days later, Adolphus found him and brought him home.)

August 1, 1999, Sunday—Eucharist Day—and Angela Howard's birthday. Angela, who moves and serves with the aid of a white cane, was preparing to leave us. She is now, like Hannah before her, in Ghana. So the evening celebration was a "thank you" time, a "happy birthday" time, and a "good-bye" time. For everyone who stays a year at the Open Door Community we must say 723 good-byes. Twenty years ago we believed "hello" and "welcome" and "yes" would be our main words, like Levis are our main pants. Didn't happen. "No," "we are filled," and "good-bye" are the syllables that drip from my lips like the saliva off S. A.'s chin while having a seizure and smacking his head on our driveway.

Quentin, shoulders drooping, eyes wild, turned, went away. I returned to our sanctuary for it was nigh five o'clock. Senator Vincent Fort was preaching on the role of the poor in history and the necessity of knowing American history from sources outside the Domination System. After all, Jesus was executed by the state at the request of respectable people. So I did not mention S. A.'s death even when I spoke the words of institution over the bread and juice. I wanted us to focus on Senator Fort's good-news message, on Angela Howard's "good-bye," and on the broken body of our first-century Jewish peasant servant-leader who wouldn't use guns or hurt flesh, but who sure as hell would love to turn over a computer or two in the stock-market trading centers in Buckhead. I knew there would be plenty of time to face death.

Who can control wildfire? The Dakota Sioux were called "those with burnt thighs" by the pioneers taking their land. They could not, on ponies, outrun the grass fires on the Great Plains. Quentin's fire burnt us bad. Before Angela blew out her twenty-two candles we all knew. The grief and horror would grow in us over the next eighteen days like waters in Noah's time. This is the story we knew by heart before the darkness beat out the dying day.

❖ ❖ ❖

On Saturday night, July 31, S. A. Williams, like all of us, climbed into bed. Unlike 98.2 percent of us, his bed was not inside a house or prison or insane asylum or the belly of a nuclear submarine. He clambered into the dumpster where on occasion he made his peace with God and the police and slept the night away. Because I knew S. A. for fifteen years, I can imagine his dreams that night. Like Lennie in Steinbeck's *Of Mice and Men,* S. A. dreamed of a little house and a room just to himself. Since S. A. nearly froze to death each winter, he likely dreamed of a stove to heat the house, and, though he loved our cheese grits and Dick's surprise soups, he would have a kitchen all his own with a spacious pantry, but not full enough to make him greedy. Or, maybe, as the sweltering night transfigured the Goliath-like steel trash container into a kiln, his muse danced with visions of bubbling grits and boiling soup inside his bony head. But

> What happens to a dream deferred
> Does it dry up
> Like a raisin in the sun?
> Or fester like a sore—
> And then run?
> Does it stink like rotten meat?
> Or crust and sugar over—
> Like syrup sweet?
>
> Maybe it just sags
> Like a heavy load.
>
> Or does it explode?[3]

---

3. Langston Hughes, "Harlem," in *The Collected Poems of Langston Hughes,* ed. Arnold Rampersad and David Roessel (New York: Vintage Books, 1994), 426.

According to custom the welcomed guests must leave the church property early. The wandering fugitives pack their black plastic bags, then slide their cardboard beds into their chest of drawers hidden amid vines and prickly holly bushes. Sunday is a special day. Now they tramp toward various Sunday breakfasts where the congregations celebrate resurrection with delicious scrambled eggs and fat slices of bacon fried crisp—one of S. A.'s favorites.

Someone along the way heard him bounce backward. His hands slipped along the edge: *thud . . . thud* again. Officer Weaver will begin his Sunday sunrise service soon—rounding up those who show themselves after the hideous racket of hide-and-seek between the bushes and sanctuary. And then another figured, too, as I would have, wouldn't you?—S. A. had scaled the dumpster wall so often before. Like Levite and priest, she hurried on to church.

Heat hurts. Bears down hard: cooks, fries, broils, bakes, roasts, toasts, poaches . . . Perchance he had a seizure. He often did. But it was the horrid heat that murdered him. Indexed at 110 degrees by 2 P.M.; he was found at 3 P.M. turned mostly black—the fateful color of us all.

II: 1985–1999

S. A. Williams was a quiet man. He traveled alone, though he had many friends in the yard and along the streets. He was sixty-five years old at death, but he seemed sixty-five when I met him during his fiftieth year. S. A. felt lots of pain, as we all do. Resembling many of us who live in houses, or behind bushes, and even in garbage cans, S. A. was an alcoholic who turned to drink to help him hide his pain and to blow the candle out. More often than booze, he drank coffee. He was always in line when the twenty-gallon 6 A.M. thermos, prepared by Ira, was placed in our front yard. He smoked. Mostly rolled his own. Bummed them if need be.

Oh! S. A. Williams was a stubborn man. He had a thousand seizures in our front yard, on the driveway (his favorite 910 hangout), and in our shared bathroom. Did he take Dilantin? I know not. I doubt it. He writhed like a man in the electric chair just after 2,300 justice-achieving jolts have established that Jesus' death means little (if anything) in Confederate-flag-flying Georgia. We would, again and again and again, like a liturgy in worshipful fashion, call 911. Bitten tongue swollen, eyes aglaze, and gloom covering our yard like mountain mist, he would squirm until the Grady ambulance arrived. Never, not once, did they refuse to come. Revived, but for the glare and stare far off into another yard and another time, S. A. would refuse to go to the hospital. He refused treatment. Every time. He never came to our Harriet Tubman free medical clinic. He simply said "no."

❖ ❖ ❖

Canning is not a calling, not a vocation, not even a job. Canning does not appear on aptitude tests. You cannot do it with dignity or feel self-esteem even when you have plucked the most cans at day labor. Canning is work done by those with no place and with nothing to do, by the poorest of the poor. But there is an art and skill, courage and bodaciousness required. Canning season is that short period between the time a neighbor puts her garbage on the curb and the garbage collectors collect it. With the growing environmental-justice movement, money is offered for aluminum cans. A corps of homeless people—mostly men (although Judy is one of the best canners in our section of the city)—trudge the city streets, going through the trash for cans and other leftovers. It is dangerous work, but canners can make several dollars by nightfall.

S. A. was a canner. Often seen bent over, his head invisible as he peered among the bits and bones, papers and broken toys, S. A. would dive deep and sometimes come up with a trove of cans. Sometimes we would see him walking down Ponce de Leon with a black plastic bag thrown over his left shoulder. The bag bulged with stinking beer or RC-Cola cans smelling yucky like a syrupy sweet. Maybe there is a serpentine congruity in that S. A. found his deathbed at the bottom of a dumpster.

S. A. Williams was a homeless human being. Surely this is still considered an oxymoron in the lexicon of life in America. Quiet, friendly, never a trouble-maker or hostile even when pickled to the gills. He seldom went to jail, even during the homeless roundups by the Marlboro men in blue urban-cowboy clothes. S. A. became a part of our lives. He was present to us who pitch our garbage in the back and put our bodies down in the most comfortable inn in the land: the Open Door Community. S. A. was part of our larger family—the Extended Community, we call it.

We miss S. A., and we grieve. Like the Open Door partner who walked away from his home, there he was. He is no more. S. A. gives to me, even now, the gift of imagination. How will it be for me? I am almost sixty years old. Someday I'll be out by the dumpster emptying the garbage, singing "Glory, Glory, Hallelujah," and angry as hell about something. Then the next day I'll be gone. Should I, in my eighties, fall into the Open Door Community's dumpster while pouring the soured soup inside, before suppertime some twenty-nine folk will be looking for me, and, dead or alive, they will pull me out. I wish we could have given that gift to our dead brother: Mr. S. A. Williams.

III: A SCATTERING CLOSURE

By the sweat of your brow
You shall eat bread

Until you return to the ground,
For out of it you were taken;
You are dust
And to dust you shall return.

—Genesis 3:19

The body hunt was unusually simple. Kazy and Susan did the phone work. The DeKalb County medical examiner was glad to help us claim the body after the state of complete dereliction had been established. Maybe the money we saved the county can be put toward DeKalb's Grady pharmacy fund. Who knows?

After a lengthy discussion within our little household of faith, we decided on cremation and a funeral service in conjunction with our noonday meal for hungry folk. Adolphus asked the St. Vincent de Paul Society to help us with the costs. They often have come to our aid with caskets for our friends who have perished on the streets or who have been immolated for the god of retributive justice. With love and pastoral care, St. Vincent opened wide his hand, a full measure sifted between his thumb and forefinger.

On Friday, August 6, I signed the necessary papers. The National Cremation Society then picked him up from the county morgue. Sometime on Saturday, S. A. Williams was burned to dust and ashes. Steven Beals and Rebecca Rose were gracious every step of the way. Dick Rustay went to the Third World Mennonite shop in our neighborhood—Ten Thousand Villages—and purchased a beautiful Vietnamese vase for S. A., which now sits beside Willie Dee Wimberly's memorial on our mantelpiece. On Wednesday afternoon, after serving 157 folk minus one in the soup kitchen, Dick picked up S. A. and brought him home in a cylindrical box.

On Friday the thirteenth, Joe B. Hinds and Sandra had their letter to the editor published in the local paper, and, on the following Monday, after much work and some negotiation, Joe got a death notice in the newspaper for $39.60. That same morning, August 16, Adolphus left for vacation; that night our partner vanished.

The funeral was set for Wednesday at 11 A.M. in our backyard with a prodigious barbecue and watermelon feast to follow. One hundred fifty of us gathered for worship and remembrance. Murphy and Elizabeth led us in singing C. M. Sherman's favorite hymn, "Pass Me Not, O Gentle Savior." We prayed, wept, and shared stories of S. A., mixed with Ralph reading the Twenty-third Psalm, and Kazy and Eric reading from Romans and Revelation. Our hearts panged when we sang "Wayfaring Stranger" amid the tales of S. A. wandering the streets and alleyways. Dick then led us in the spreading of S. A.'s ashes. Many of us came to Dick from our hands-held circle, filled our cupped hands with S. A. Williams, and held his dust as though he were an injured baby bird. We took him to places where we remembered him—the front yard under the large maple tree, the side yard where S. A. fought so many demons and finally lost, and the back where we stood together, a family forlorn in North America. Our circle broken.

Just two miles from us at North Avenue Presbyterian Church, at exactly the same time, our beloved author Celestine Sibley was being funeralized. Mike Luckovich published a cartoon in the *Atlanta Constitution,* where Ms. Sibley worked. In the cartoon, Celestine Sibley is arriving in heaven, and Saint Peter takes her to a beautiful log cabin in the pristine forest. I wondered. What will Saint Peter have for Mr. S. A. Williams? An air-conditioned dumpster? Or will S. A. and Lennie's dream come true: a small house with a stove and a well-stocked pantry. "In my Father's/Mother's house there are many dwelling places. . . . I go to prepare a place for you." (Gosh, won't it be a day of raging glory when the poor get housing on earth as it is in heaven? No dumpster diving then!)

Thanks to Joe, Kristen, and Murphy, we had enough chicken, potato salad, pork and beans, and watermelon for everyone to have seconds. Big hunks of chicken, too! The congregation had grown to 170 by lunchtime. We set tables all over the backyard and basketball court. We drank gallons of iced tea Ira had brewed to keep us cool in the horrid heat. We laughed and we stumbled in our throats. We said "good-bye" to S. A. For a few moments we were neither Black nor white, housed nor homeless, rich nor poor, hungry nor filled. We were the family of S. A. Williams. We were one. Then we set our feet on the street again.

Part VI

THE THEOLOGY
OF HOSPITALITY

The streets, not the university, are the place to discover the word of God.

—Ed Loring

Invitation to the Body of Christ, *by Murphy Davis*

MARCH 1992

> *There was once a rich man who dressed in the most expensive clothes and lived in great luxury every day. There was also a poor man named Lazarus, covered with sores, who used to be brought to the rich man's table. Even the dogs would come and lick his sores. The poor man died and was carried by the angels to sit beside Abraham at the feast in Heaven. The rich man died and was buried, and in Hades, where he was in great pain, he looked up and saw Abraham, far away, with Lazarus at his side. So he called out, "Father Abraham! Take pity on me, and send Lazarus to dip his finger in some water and cool off my tongue, because I am in great pain in this fire!" But Abraham said, "Remember, my son, that in your lifetime you were given all the good things, while Lazarus got all the bad things. But now he is enjoying himself here, while you are in pain. Besides all that, there is a deep pit lying between us, so that those who want to cross over from here to you cannot do so, nor can anyone cross over to us from where you are." The rich man said, "Then I beg you, father Abraham, send Lazarus to my father's house, where I have five brothers. Let him go and warn them so that they, at least, will not come to this place of pain." Abraham said, "Your brothers have Moses and the prophets to warn them; your brothers should listen to what they say." The rich man answered, "That is not enough, father Abraham! But if someone were to rise from death and go to them, then they would turn from their sins." But Abraham said, "If they will not listen to Moses and the prophets, they will not be convinced even if someone were to rise from death."*

> —Luke 16:19–31

Luke's story is, first of all, about some rich folks: good solid citizens of the community, Dives and Mary Jones.[1] They were rich, yes, but of course it hadn't always been that way. No . . . why, they worked *hard* for what they had—pulled themselves up by their own bootstraps, you might say. Scrimped and saved and then—well, don't you think they deserved to enjoy what they'd made? Yessiree! It was the good life for the Joneses. Life was a party. They bought their clothes at Phipps Plaza, drove good cars, sent their kids to good schools, and threw a lot of dinner parties. They loved gourmet food. Good folks, mind you. Even churchgoing folks. They were looked up to in the community.

But the story is also about some folks who never dared walk up to the Joneses' front door: Lazarus and Gert Phillips were folks you might see occasionally around the back alley behind the Joneses' home, but never for long. They were—well, face it, they were vagrants: smelly and unhealthy looking, and they wore dirty old clothes that didn't fit right to start with. Lazarus and Gert tried to eat out of the Joneses' garbage can—there was always so much good leftover food thrown away. But it was harder than it used to be, what with the neighborhood watch and all. The neighbors were on the lookout and would call the police in a flash if they saw a stranger on their street. And of course the city council had passed some ordinances that made it a lot easier for the police to haul the likes of Lazarus and Gert off to jail—again.

So the long and short of it was that they had to work pretty hard to stay out of sight. They felt like animals, slinking around in the shadows and eating other people's garbage. Lazarus had an ulcerated leg—bad circulation from the years of labor-pool work that kept him on his feet all the time—and Gert had diabetes. But every time they went to Grady they were patched up and sent back to the streets. So the situation got worse.

Finally, one morning, Gert and Lazarus were found frozen to death in the abandoned car that had become their home. Around the same time Dives died in Piedmont Hospital, just three months after Mary died at Northside.

When they all got where they were going, Dives and Mary realized right quick that they were pretty hot and uncomfortable. 'Course comfort was more important than anything, so they were upset when they looked way up and saw Lazarus and Gert sitting around a fine table and enjoying a delicious meal with Mr. Abraham and Miss Sarah.

"Not fair!" they cried, and then they took to hollerin'.

"Mr. Abraham, Miss Sarah! Hey! Remember us? We're good Presbyterians. We went to church and tithed and even helped with the stewardship campaign.

---

1. The name "Dives" comes from the Latin term for *wealth*. The name appears in the Vulgate, a Latin translation of the Bible (ed.).

And hey, look, it's awful hot down here so y'all please send Lazarus and Gert down here with a little drink of water. I'm sure they won't mind. Okay?"

"Wow," said Miss Sarah, "looks like things have really changed, huh? But remember how long y'all enjoyed everything you wanted? You had all the good stuff and ol' Lazarus and Gert were lucky to get your garbage."

"Besides," said Mr. Abraham, "it's a shame, but they can't get to where you are and you can't get over here. You see, somebody put up a security fence—matter of fact, I believe it was you. Yes, you put up a fence to keep Lazarus and Gert and their kind from comin' around you. Now even though you want them to come to you they can't. Nope. The fence can't be crossed from either direction. Sorry folks. You built the fence. You'll have to live with it."

I assumed for most of my life that this story of Dives and Lazarus meant that, if you're rich and you're not kind and helpful to the poor, you'll go to hell and burn forever and never get a drop of water on your tongue. Maybe that's part of what the story is about. But I think this story reminds us that we were created for community. Then we are reminded that when we break community with our neighbors—when we isolate ourselves with our privilege, when we segregate our neighbors, when we create, or settle for, public policy that labels and segregates and divides us—then we create hell on earth.

One of the gifts of scripture is that it paints very clear pictures.

"Do you want to see heaven?" asks Jesus. "Do you want a picture of life abundant? I invite you into the Kingdom of God, the full life, the Reign of God's power and amazing grace.

"Come on, I'll show you what it looks like. I'll draw you a picture." Again and again, Jesus, the prophets, and the psalmists show us a feast, a party, a celebration, a banquet where the blind, the crippled, and the lame come from the highways and the byways; they come from north and south, from east and west, to sit at the overflowing table of the Kingdom of God. They are the misfits and the prodigals, the foreigners and the friendless. They come, perhaps uncertain at first, but soon drawn into the joy of the celebration. They sit together, enjoying newfound sisters and brothers and the abundance of everything they need and more, which is what our Creator wants and intends for every child of God.

But often in this picture, sulking around the edge, just outside the circle of the fun and laughter, is the elder-brother party pooper. He sees life as a system of simple, unbending rules.

"I worked hard and did right so I deserve a lot. . . ."

"My sisters and brothers messed up and ended up homeless or in jail so they deserve what they got."

"If Lazarus and Gert are so poor they obviously weren't as deserving as I am. I studied hard in school and paid off my student loans, and now I have a good salary and it's mine."

"I came early to work in the vineyard and I, by rights, should get a higher wage than those who came late."

But God has an odd sense of humor. God is throwing a party, inviting everybody in, and urging us to do the same. There are no questions at the door about what you earned or deserved—just a welcome.

But the elder brothers—the Dives of the world—are too concerned with grasping their good reputations and their possessions to open their hands and their arms to enjoy . . . to dance . . . to sing . . . and to laugh with their sisters and brothers.

So Dives' and Mary's parties are reserved for other people who look, act, and smell like them. They rush around shopping, and if they see Lazarus and Gert they look quickly away and try not to think about them. But by the time they finally figure out that they're living in hell, it's too late.

Sorry, say Abraham and Sarah, but you were in a position to make the rules, draw the lines, put up the fences, do the city planning, get on the Olympic committee and the neighborhood planning unit. . . . You worked it out to have the best things for yourselves and to keep the poor away from your door. Not in your neighborhood, remember? You set up this segregation. And now you've got to live with it. And yes, I know, it's hell. Segregation is hell, whether for reasons of race or class. It's hell for those who plan it and for those who endure it.

Mr. Dives and Miss Mary are in charge these days. They sit in the mayor's office, on the city council, in the governor's office, on the state legislature, the Congress, the Senate, the Office of the President, and in the court system. Our public policy spouted from their mouths says, "We got ours (and by golly we're gonna keep it and increase it), and if you didn't get yours it must be your own fault (and one way or another you should probably be punished)."

By that kind of logic, your cousin caught in credit-card theft is a *criminal,* but Neal Bush and John Sununu just misspoke.

That attitude is the foundation stone for the willy-nilly violation of basic human rights of a growing number of people in our city and around the world. The segregation of the poor, the deepening racism in individual attitudes and broad public policy, and officially sanctioned violence that stretches from the projects and poor neighborhoods, to the streets, to the execution chambers—all are signs of an official policy that crushes the poor.

Our society deeply hates and despises the poor, especially the African American poor. We express our hatred with a public policy that tears down low-income housing all over the city while homelessness increases two, five, ten times in just a few years. We express our hatred with a public policy that creates the situation and then sits silently and passively even though the fastest-growing group of homeless people in Atlanta consists of children under age six. We express our hatred every time we do not challenge the myth of the lazy poor, despite knowledge that almost half of the people who live in shelters in Atlanta work, but still cannot afford to rent or buy their own home. We express our hatred every time we send people to spend twenty to forty days in jail for public urination, in a city that has no public toilets. We express our hatred when we are passive in the face of business and government leaders who are creating the odious vagrant-free zone in downtown Atlanta.

We express our hatred through our state legislature, which allocates hundreds of millions of dollars for new prison construction while saying that we cannot afford good schools or health care. Such spending goes on, even while we in Georgia lock up a higher percentage of our people than any jurisdiction in the world, including South Africa. Only a blinding hatred and fear would let us increase our prison population in the United States 100 percent during the 1980s. At the same time, crime increased 7 percent. During the Reagan-Bush years, the prison population doubled, and you and I both know what that means in terms of race and class.

We express our hatred every time a public official speaks for us, saying the death penalty is an answer. If we kill a few more poor people and African Americans (called *criminals,* of course), then we will be safer and happier. We never set out to be hateful. And we don't mean to be hateful now. But when greed gets hold of us and the body politic, when the privilege of a few is more important then the well-being of all, then we create a social policy of hatred and segregation. Once we're on this path, it takes a loud wake-up call and a life of discipline in community to move in any other direction.

It was too late for Dives and Mary Jones by the time they figured out the peril of separating themselves from the poor. Abraham points out plenty of opportunities to learn the peril. After all, they had the Bible; they had heard the story of Moses. What kept them from responding? What keeps us from responding? The biblical message seems harsh. Why, in fact, is it called "good news" anyway? We'll find the answer to these questions only if we can join in community.

Jesus invites us to a feast, and there we sit with people who are not like us. At the feast we have to lay aside our political hard line; at the feast we have to want to be forgiven and to forgive. We need to hunger and thirst for God's promised justice. We need to sit at God's table, because we need to depend on the mercy of Jesus Christ, which makes us kinfolk with all these brothers and sisters. That is very different from pulling ourselves up by our own bootstraps.

Jesus has invited us to a party—a magnificent feast, and it's free. If we're not too preoccupied with our social position and property values, we'll go in and enjoy. Our isolation, our hatred, and our fear can melt away like snow under the morning sunshine. The invitation to the Body of Christ—a community of diversity and mercy and love and forgiveness—is ours.

Jesus is throwing a party.

It's time to enjoy.

The Marks of the True Church of Jesus Christ,
by Ed Loring

AUGUST 1989

How does a person or a society know where to find the church of Jesus Christ? Where does the Body of Christ reside? Who belongs? How can we discern false prophets and phony preachers in a world filled with electronic media, cold cash, hot flesh, and a ubiquitous emptiness?

If the gospel has no historical and sociological flesh, then the Word of God is no word at all. If there is no church wherein God is making new history and building a new social order of peace and justice, then preaching, Bible study, and missionary work are in vain and an illusion. (Unless, of course, they benefit the old order of oppression, poverty, and death. Then, to the Evil One, the gospelless church and the churchless gospel would be effective instruments of control for the status quo.)

As people of love and justice, we are embarrassed to raise the question as to the place of the Body of Jesus Christ—the church—because we have such a sorry history of violence, persecution, murder, self-righteousness, and war regarding this question and its faithless answers. We Presbyterians come with special laments for forgiveness, for it was Ulrich Zwingli, and later John Calvin, who (when the Reformed tradition began) drowned believers and sanctioned the burning of fellow Protestants with varying views. Yet as the Christian church in the United States has become embedded in the consumer culture of affluence, comfort, and emptiness, we must, for the sake of God's integrity and the honor of the name of Jesus, ask the old, haunting, and often divisive question: where is the true church of Jesus Christ?

The most traditional answer points to the priesthood. Where a priest is ordained through apostolic succession by the laying on of hands, there is the church. During the Reformation, two marks of the church were formulated among Protestants: first, the Word of God is preached in the church; second, the sacraments of the Lord's Supper and baptism are performed in the church. There was a short flurry of activity as well around the idea of a disciplined life within the congregation. Prohibitions against charging interest on money and owning fellow Christians as slaves, however, turned the investment community against such standards.

Today we must add another mark for the true church of Jesus Christ: diversity among the believers. The church is God's primary vehicle in history to break down the old order of violence and oppression and to build a new social order of freedom, equality, and justice. At the birth of the church on Pentecost, the fundamental mark of the gathered believers was diversity; so must it be today in order to be this same church of New Testament times.

For the church to be the church of Jesus Christ, the membership must reflect the diversity of God's creation and include the victims and helpless ones of the old (present) social order, which crushes some that others might have more than they need. A church is suspect if it lacks integration among various racial groups, for the very purpose of the church is to break down dividing walls between Jews and Gentiles, African Americans and whites, and so on, so that one new community might emerge in the city and throughout the land. We have celebrated the formation of Taiwanese congregations in Atlanta—churches based solely on race and ethnic origin. We know, too, of the purpose and power of the mostly African American congregations in our city. But what is not spoken from the pulpits and in the urban-planning meetings is that we majority white Christians spend most of our time and energy forming Caucasian churches—the Buckhead Presbyterian Church. That we celebrate the Taiwanese church, or, beneath the doublespeak of technocratic investments in Caucasian churches, it really matters not. The presence of Jesus Christ exists amid the diversity of people marching across the stage of history, tearing down dividing walls and building new houses and office space for peace, justice, and unity among God's daughters and sons.

Race and segregation are marks of the false church. So, too, are congregations of only one class. A basic mark of Christian life is an inclusive sharing of economic goods, in which everyone has what they need but none suffer the emptiness, despair, and death of having too much. Poor, middle class, and rich together—learning to strip away the forces of oppression and poverty—constitute the true church. The God of rich people who are not learning through word, deed, and sacrament to share their wealth and to restructure the economy, is a dead God. The concept of a rich church is an oxymoron (like cruel kindness). Test it: where is the true church of Jesus Christ? The true church exists where rich and poor work together in congregational life. African American and white, affluent and poor *together* represent a mark of the true church.

We have fallen short of the glory of God. We have allowed ourselves to be duped by the segregations of our society and the insecurities of our psyches: we have turned that most radical group—the Christian household of faith—into a bulwark of social oppression. If you are in an all-white church, please join another community that refuses to mirror the death of our society's structures. If you are in a church of the rich, join Lazarus, because only as we worship and live with the ones covered with sores may we be healed. God wills it so for each and all of us; a congregational life of servanthood and joy, as we become ever more faithful, heralds a new day coming!

The End of the Reformation, *by Ed Loring*

J A N U A R Y   2 0 0 0

The difference between a historian of ideas or intellectual historian—for example, one who studies Christian thought—and a social historian, who would study the history of the lives of Christians, was unknown to me until I became pastor of Clifton Presbyterian Church in 1975. Subsequently, the distinction became significant. A historian of ideas tells what a thinker thought. The social historian tells about the consequences of those ideas as they hit the street and marketplace. Often ideas and their consequences contradict each other; thus, the point of view of the historian is important. As my friend on death row, Robert Conklin, wrote to me recently, "What you see depends on where you are standing." That is why Jesus concludes his Sermon on the Mount with a test for the truthfulness of ideas: "Be on your guard against false prophets. . . . You will know them by what they do" (Matt. 7:15a, 16a). Both the historians of thought and false prophets can tell about the truth of the mind. The issue is how the idea is put into practice.

Catholics and the Lutherans have just signed a document ending the conflict of the Protestant Reformation. This war within the household of faith and the lands of Christendom began in 1517 when the monk Martin Luther nailed his Ninety-five Theses on the church door in Wittenberg, Germany. (If our homeless friends, sent to jail for sleeping in churchyards or for sitting on the steps at 910 during rush hour, think they have it bad, they should read Luther's story. Luther was, for a time, under the ban of the Holy Roman Empire, meaning a death warrant had been issued.) Both groups of the Body of Christ now agree that the individual believer is saved by grace, not by works. The papers have been signed, the Eucharist celebrated, and, hopefully, Martin Luther and Thomas Aquinas are resting better in heaven.

Omitted from the reports I have read is the disaster that the idea of justification by faith alone has meant for the Christian church and Western civilization since the sixteenth century. Paul's idea and Luther's interpretation of Paul's idea, and Luther's interpretation of Paul's idea as interpreted by a million theologians, and preachers' proclamations of Paul's idea as interpreted by Luther—these efforts have been a major factor in the decline of the West and in making the practice of Christian life indistinguishable from consumer capitalism. "Beware of false prophets. You will recognize them by what they do." Often the time lapse between the idea and recognition of the idea's consequences in the shootout at the local school is long. The proof is in the pudding.

The social significance of justification by faith alone is that it does not matter what you do. The Presbyterian Church's liturgical expression of this evangelical doctrine, as it has filtered through our modern lives, occurs every Sunday. Many church bulletins include a confession of sin to be prayed in unison. First comes a moment of silence for worshipers to confess their private sins, or to read the prayer before praying it. After the confession, the liturgist says: "Hear the good news of the gospel. In Jesus Christ, your sins are forgiven." There is no structure or place for accountability. There is no discipline or action, no sense that the future is different from the past, no means to undo the consequences of sin. It does not matter what I did; I am forgiven, and so are you.

Since the mainline Reformation of Luther's day, the fundamental crisis of the Christian church has been community and accountability. There are no means to counteract the devastating consequences of justification by faith or grace alone. A primary casualty of this theology is Christian life rooted in a common life among believers. The church can no longer afford to offer a community life based on the practice of an ethical vision, because it does not matter what church members do. Many young people, even disciples of Jesus the Jew, who visit the Open Door Community are not interested in Christian theology, because Christian thought produces citizens of consumer capitalism rather than cautious snakes and gentle doves for love and justice.

The social and cultural effects on a society in which it does not matter what you do have been advanced by the secularism of the West, particularly the loss of belief in life after death. As a maker and maintainer of cultural values, life after death was an important belief. Heaven or hell as a "place," and not as an emotional state after getting a raise or purchasing a new product, was rooted in the assumption of an ultimate judgment, based in large measure on "doing the will of Yahweh-Elohim," to adapt a phrase from the teaching of Jesus the poor man. Miriam, Moses, Deborah, Ruth, the prophets, Jesus, and some of Jesus' disciples believed it does not matter what we do. That is why Jesus the resister taught the Sermon on the Mount, which is the prescription for the life of discipleship. At the center of the teaching is the mark among Christians of the common life: forgiveness. The more radical the Christian community, the greater the necessity for forgiveness.

James Cone, the passionate Black theologian, says, "The god of the Ku Klux Klan ain't my God." We are called to carry the cross, not to burn it in some Black man's yard. That is a cross of another color, a means to intimidate former slaves and their ancestors. Why have many Christians worked for a constitutional amendment to outlaw flag burning, but have never introduced an amendment against cross burning? Which side are you on? What would the Black liberation movement in Georgia look like if white Christians' actions toward people of color mattered?

The idea of and belief in judgment after death kept human action, called *works,* significant. Most Protestant theology was able to reduce the one human act necessary for a home in heaven to belief that Jesus was the "Son of God"—

a white American male. Thus Billy Graham and the revivalism movement to Christianize America could threaten with the fires of hell on one hand and, on the other hand, promise that one's actions did not matter. There is no call to justice in Billy Graham's life or thought. He is, however, worth millions.

Heaven and hell died as motives for behavior modification at about the same time that Christmas and ethics became separated. As late as the 1960s, children believed: "You better watch out / You better not cry / You better not pout . . . / Santa Claus is coming to town. . . . / So be good for goodness' sake." In the second half of the twentieth century, Santa Claus replaced God for awhile as, at least, an enforcer of obedience to parents and teachers (Exod. 20:12). Now even that is gone. Unruly or gun-toting kids need their gifts to keep the economy rolling. Many companies win or lose based on Christmas sales. Santa Claus has joined the happy chorus, with a Coke in his hand. It does not matter what we do.

The demands of development and economic expansion keep moving rapidly, with consumption as the single most important economic act. The church keeps shrinking in its encounter with social life and its call for justice. It does not matter what you buy; faith in Yahweh-Elohim's grace alone is what registers.

One of the primary reasons for the sixteenth-century Reformation was the need to charge interest on loans to church members. Usury was a sin in Catholic lands (hence the importance of Jewish bankers). John Calvin, parent of the Presbyterians, was one of the first to say that the Bible and its teaching on interest payments does not matter. We can charge interest within the household of faith (even the poor have to pay), and be justified by faith alone. Dorothy Day, a Catholic practitioner, believed that the Sermon on the Mount is a way of life and not a set of ideas or principles. (A beautiful but irrelevant sermon, Reinhold Niebuhr would say.) Dorothy Day, following the teachings of the Sermon on the Mount, taught that monetary interest is the primary cause of war. She wrote that it *does* matter how one uses money. That is one reason that thousands of us march and face arrest each November at the School of the Americas at Fort Benning, Georgia.

We Christians, for the economy to grow, had to do something about Judgment and the possibility of hell. We had to proclaim the gospel so we could still feel at home among politicians who call for bombs on Iraq, the death penalty, and prisons for social control of the African American male population. And we did!

Theologians of justification by God's grace alone—good works do not count—came up with an idea: universalism. God's love is so undemanding and unconditional that it does not matter what any person or society does. Everybody is going to heaven! As Peter Maurin said around the time of the *Catholic Worker*'s founding, "A newspaper for everybody is a newspaper for nobody." The same thing happened to heaven. A heaven for everybody is a heaven for nobody. Belief in life after death had died. A faith basic to Greco-Roman life and the Judeo-Christian tradition had ended.

One must consider the role of social location in denial of the afterlife, particularly of hell. In the South, technological advance, perhaps more than the demands of consumer capitalism, put hell to death. When writing of truth and reality in a quiet, air-conditioned office, far from the maddening crowd, theologians in the comfort zone could not conceive of the fires of hell. The idea of judgment had to go. This helps explain why afterlife, judgment, and hell still exist in the minds, if not the practice, of many poor people, toiling in factories and tomato fields, or sitting on street corners in the heat and cold, waiting for death.

Fyodor Dostoevsky warned in the 1880s that, if God does not exist, then anything goes. It does not matter what you do. More recently, John Updike has written that if God does not exist, only sex matters. The consequence of justification by faith alone and of its corollary—no judgment after death—has led to Christian atheism: Christians who live as though it does not matter what they do, or what practices sustain the economy. Thus we see rich Christians. We have church members who serve in the military—even in peacetime. Some white church members work to keep white power on the Republican Party agenda. Women are belittled and abused, and are taught to forgive the man without his repentance or therapeutic intervention. Homosexuals are cast out like tax collectors of long ago. The homeless are left without housing, and we love our neighbors mostly in our prayers. But it does not matter. We are saved by God's grace alone. Works do not count.

❖ ❖ ❖

We are thankful. We praise our loving Creator and Redeemer, who yearns for reconciliation and friendliness on earth. We are hopeful now that the Lutherans and Catholics have signed the document bringing an end to the Reformation. We are amazed and joyful because of the good news of the gospel of Jesus Christ our Lord. We, too, know that Yahweh-Elohim and Jesus Christ and the Holy Spirit love and forgive and redeem each of us who believes, repents, and practices the way. As our ardent ancestor Martin Luther put it so well: we are simultaneously saints and sinners. Nonetheless, the doctrine of salvation by God's grace alone, without regard for the works of the disciple or the community, is undoing public life and private virtue. In the social context of individualism, the cultural context of consumer capitalism, and the faith context in which solidarity with the poor and oppressed is lacking, the loving message of salvation by God's grace alone—justification by God's unconditional love—has led church and society to a way of life in which it does not matter what we do. We have become disciples of consumer capitalism. Homelessness is the consequence and the proof of the lie.

The radical left wing of the Reformation had a better center than either the Catholic or the mainline Protestant theologians and practitioners. Most accepted salvation by grace alone, as we certainly do. (Thank you, Jesus!) Yet the center of their understanding was discipleship—the call to "follow Jesus." Discipleship was a way of life, a common and disciplined life, rooted in a Christian community. Discipline was a mark of the church. It mattered what one did; yea, it mattered a lot.

"Be on your guard against false prophets. . . . You will know them by what they do," says Jesus. His way of life mattered. He was executed for it.

The Image of the Enemy, *by Murphy Davis*

S E P T E M B E R   1 9 9 0

Editor's note: This talk was presented in June 1990 at the annual Presbyterian Peace Fellowship Breakfast at the Presbyterian General Assembly in Salt Lake City.

Recently, during a visit to Washington, Mikhail Gorbachev said, "The enemy image is becoming a thing of the past." I want to celebrate Gorbachev's declaration and, at the same time, to work on it a bit, because I think he's talking about a large agenda.

We have spent many years building an incredible nuclear arsenal, resulting in the overwhelming physical presence of weapons that could either by specific intent, or by accident, destroy the earth many times over. Spiritually, the buildup has filled our collective interior life with a generalized fear of "The Enemy."

We know, of course, that it is part of the nature of weapons to make us more afraid. The huge profits, intended for the very rich, from military buildup have meant that our leaders have suggested, nurtured, and exploited our fear. We have been told whom to hate and fear and of the dire consequences of not acting out of that fear to continue to arm ourselves, and to arm neighbors who will carry out our policies of maniacal enmity.

But this impulse has by no means been limited to our international posture. For even as Ronald Reagan encouraged us to hate and fear the communist guerrillas and to arm the right-wing government of El Salvador, George Bush invited us to hate and fear Willie Horton, and to lust for ever increasing use of the death penalty. Ed Meese invited us to hate and fear the poor as he assured us that people who eat in soup kitchens do it because they are lazy and don't want to work. According to Reagan, Bush, and Meese, these are our enemies, objects of our collective fear: Central American peasants, African American criminal-types, the homeless poor, and the list goes on. . . . We must realize, people like Reagan, Bush, and Meese say, that all of these folk want to take something precious from us.

So, according to our leaders, our response should be to build up and maintain the number-one nuclear arsenal, to build more prisons and jails, to execute more prisoners, to get a handgun and another insurance policy, and to let the poor and homeless get what they deserve: nothing.

Another common denominator is that all of these collective enmities create policy that comes down squarely on the necks of the poor and the helpless. Campesinos by the thousands are left dead and maimed by our policies. Hundreds of thousands of men, women, and children, most of them poor, a disproportionate number of them minorities, are locked in steel and concrete cages with what looks like an unending mania to spend millions on prison and jail construction, while at the same time we can't seem to find money for housing. The death penalty sweeps in its vicious, racist grasp the poor, the mentally retarded, the mentally ill, the illiterate, and a disproportionate number of African Americans and Hispanics. It grinds out its violence, purporting fairness, but in fact creating one more violent institution with which to hate and punish the poor.

When we opened Clifton Presbyterian Church as the first free shelter in Atlanta in 1979, we estimated that 1,500 homeless people were on our streets. Now, just over ten years later, there are more like 15,000. How many will there be next year and the next?

Yes, brother Gorbachev, I'm afraid we'll be dealing a long time with this "enemy image" before we make it a thing of the past.

The image is more serious for us than most because we believe, we confess, that peace has been made. We believe that God through Jesus Christ has broken down the dividing wall of hostility. Our leaders build that same wall for political gain and social control. But listen! Anytime the enemy image works, we participate in a system that positions itself squarely against the cross of Jesus Christ. That's why Paul says, "Present your bodies as a living sacrifice," or, as Jim Wallis translates Romans 12:1, "Put your bodies where your doctrines are!" That's the power of acts of conscience. Conscience is a fine thing, but until we act on it, it doesn't make a lot of difference what you believe. As James would say, "Faith without works is as dead as a doornail."

Jesse Jackson was in Atlanta a couple of months ago, and he said we have a problem because our insult level is too high. We need to lower our insult level, he said. I think that's right and a helpful way to think. In the midst of affluence there are people living in grinding poverty, and we're not insulted? While the walls in Berlin are coming down, the walls in the United States between the haves and the have-nots are going up, and we're not insulted? In this day of high-tech medicine, the infant mortality rate in Atlanta, Georgia, is higher than in El Salvador. We ought to be insulted! While we yell and scream about Willie Horton, the most pervasive violence against women and children is in the home. But we'd rather ignore it. Couldn't we get insulted? We have stockpiles of "surplus" food, and we have children who are hungry. This week, thirty-six states are cutting back the Women, Infants, Children program that provides milk, cereal, and staples for pregnant women, infants, and children. But who's insulted enough to stop it? There are stockpiles of construction materials and empty buildings in every city, and yet we have hundreds of thousands of homeless. Why aren't we insulted? What in God's name will it take for us to get insulted?

Elie Wiesel tells the story of a German woman who was honored in Berlin several years ago for her work saving Jews during the war. It is obvious what life-threatening risks she took. She was asked, says Wiesel, "Why did you do it?" Her answer was superb. She said, "Out of self-respect." It was possible, Wiesel goes on, even in those dire circumstances during the war, to save people—to break the system. It was possible to say, "We are affirming our right to believe in human dignity." That possibility also means that those who didn't act to affirm human dignity are guilty. They could have acted. This woman, insulted by what the Nazis were doing to the Jews, put her own life on the line. That separated her from the many others who might have felt bad about it, but who did nothing.

Now let's talk about Presbyterians. We Presbyterians are particularly good at doctrine and right order. We're not as good at Christianity as a way of life (putting our bodies where our doctrines are) and at being disorderly when and where we really ought to be. The weakness this creates is that you can go to church and confess to all the creeds—new ones and old ones—and at the same time you can make bombs, plan wars, hate Willie Horton, oppress your workers, beat your family, and it usually will make no difference to your church membership.

I had a jarring experience of that weakness a few months ago. I sat through a painful death watch (execution watch) with a man and his family. We sat for hour after hour in a narrow steel and concrete room passing the time, hoping for a stay, but basically waiting for Larry's gruesome and violent death. I was pained as I sat there, Presbyterian pastor to these folks—my parishioners—to realize that this man sat on death row because after his confused involvement in a terrible crime, the decision to aggressively seek a death sentence was made by a Presbyterian elder. The courtroom prosecutor, who painstakingly explained to the jury why this man was not worthy of life and who convinced them to kill him, was a Presbyterian elder. Finally, the sentence was handed down and the execution date set by a judge who is a Presbyterian elder.

I don't have any idea how to describe the terrible, destructive, gut-wrenching pain of those hours. And it was so unnecessary! All of that pain could have been replaced by real effort to mend and heal and reconcile a broken situation. But, instead, we pulled in another set of folks, ripped their lives to shreds, and caused them grief and humiliation that most of us can hardly begin to grasp. It was made worse for me by the fact that the system was not anonymous or faceless. It was a fabric of specific decisions made by specific individuals and, at every doggoned turn, there was a Presbyterian face.

I find that a serious problem. The church—our church—ought to be insulted. But I've been told in no uncertain terms that it's rude to call the roll in situations like this; that it's not fair to point to specific individuals. We Presbyterians are certainly known for our fine manners. But I'm more inclined to think that if you ain't calling the roll, you're not serious about liberation and justice. Look at the songs of the civil rights struggle. It's no coincidence that they sang through the Albany, Georgia, campaign, "Ain't gonna let Chief Pritchett turn me 'round . . ." But folks, I'm afraid that while we're deeply pained by a breach of manners, we're not pained enough by oppression and the death-dealing power of oppression in the lives of the poor.

Dear peacemakers, when you take a stand for justice and peace, when you live in solidarity with the poor and oppressed, when you stand up for somebody who's going down the tubes, you'll have wars on your hands, so we might as well be ready for a long fight.

A serious problem about standing up for the poor and oppressed is that soon we find ourselves messing with the interests of the rich and powerful. That can be a real problem since we're an upper-class church. But we wouldn't have these "problems" if they didn't benefit someone. We wouldn't have hundreds of thousands of homeless people if it wasn't to someone's advantage. One in three displaced homemakers wouldn't live in poverty if it didn't help somebody. We wouldn't talk about "acceptable levels of unemployment" if one person's unemployment didn't help somebody else's profit margin. Talk about "acceptable levels of unemployment" with the next unemployed person you meet!

Loving the poor, making peace, seeking justice, breaking down the dividing walls of hostility—these are very charming notions, but they're hell to pay in real life. Dorothy Day often reminds us: Love in dreams is beautiful, but love in action is a harsh and dreadful thing.

Yet what a great cloud of witnesses we have to help us in this struggle. God has an odd sense of humor to choose the worst assortment of murderers, thieves, hookers, crooks, and demoniacs to show the power of God's reconciling, transforming, empowering, upbuilding love. We have Moses the murderer, Jacob the thief, Rahab the whore, Mary Magdalene the demon-possessed, and Paul—violent, abusive Paul, who in our fine system today would never have made it. If you had taken a vote among first-generation Christians, Paul probably would have been labeled the most unredeemable, the one who could never be rehabilitated. But there was no popular vote, because God knows we don't do a very good job of understanding. We keep thinking that we can say who's unredeemable and beyond the pale. So nobody was consulted. God knocked Paul off his path, struck him blind, and sent him into the somewhat reluctant arms of the amazed sisters and brothers of the Damascus church.

Like those members of the Damascus church who claimed Paul as their brother, we don't have to be afraid to say that Willie Horton is our brother, anymore than we should fear claiming the Soviets as our sisters. Our foremothers and forefathers remind us that God can deliver us out of the jaws of fear and set our feet on the wide, promised land of freedom.

When we receive the grace of that freedom, our life and our doctrine become one. When we receive that grace, we walk the way of the Prince of Peace, who walks with us and shepherds us to bring good news to the poor, liberty to the captives, recovery of sight to the blind; to set free the oppressed; and to announce that the time has come when God will save her people.

Walk together, children. Don't get weary. God wills goodness for all children of the earth. God promises justice. God's purposes are for peace. May it be so even among us.

Marginality: Life on the Edge, *by Ed Loring*

JANUARY 1986

Jesus Christ calls us to follow him. He lived on the edge of society, at the edge of the systems of the world. He was a marginal man, and Jesus calls us to be marginal women and men in our lives as we follow him.

The first way that we move to the margin is the call to *live by love.* This love is an active love as harsh and dreadful as the cross of Christ. This love is finally and fully tested and achieved as we love those who are closest to us (the community) and those who are the farthest (our enemies).

The world operates through force and is divided by hate and fear. To live by love is to move out of the airstream of the world, to the margin. On the margin one is called a fool, unrealistic, a judgmental person, self-righteous, sick, lazy, and maladjusted. This is just as the Bible says it would be.

To follow Jesus is to begin to love and to find the basis of our lives in relation to others in love. Active love bears fruit. Marginal love is a sociological reality.

The second dimension of the marginality of discipleship is the call to *be-*

come foreigners in the land of the poor. We who are middle-class, educated white folks can never be naturalized citizens in the land of the poor. But we can come as guests and foreigners who live in voluntary poverty, who join the margin on the economic level. We must, as Dorothy Day suggests, give up "compensations" that come from our citizenship in this world.

The power of poverty in the spiritual life comes through our sacrifice and through growth in the Spirit in that discipline. In our lives on the margin we are also empowered by the experience of the oppressed and of those who suffer as we join them as foreigners, even as strangers, in their land. But in their land is where we are called to be, to find ourselves, to die.

A third aspect of the marginality of discipleship is *language.* We must develop a language on the margin that comes from the Holy Spirit and the scriptures, and, like love, such language puts us on the edge of the world.

1. *The first characteristic of language from the margin is silence.* Unlike the world and the powers, we must find large amounts of time and important places to be silent. Noise is so disruptive and violent that only silence can create the space for the incarnate Word of God, who is love, to be heard.

Thus each disciple needs to find daily periods within the active life to be silent. We need to share silence in our community and, from the outward stance of silence, to let a new inwardness of God's presence in our souls grow.

2. *In addition to silence we must keep our language biblical,* and this means not rushing to a new translation of the Bible every few years. We need standards. But, more important, the Bible has a syntax and a reality that is expressed in language, and we must never forsake the biblical basis for the language of discipleship.

The Bible always roots reality and truth in God and persons. Today's world threatens not so much by secularity as it does by posing a mathematical base for language. The computer needs are shaping our lives, and we are reducing reality to fit mathematical computations.

We always relate to people (image of God), and that means names, not numbers. We always relate to God, and that means ultimate values exist and must be discussed on a daily basis. We cannot, today, simply talk about the budget problems and the poor. We must talk about justice, right, God's will, the good life, and all the issues and values being erased by the latest news and tomorrow's economic forecasts.

To talk about values is to be on the margin in a world that prides itself on being nonideological and yet that says that the only consideration is what works.

But disciples must speak on the relation of ends and means and the ultimate ends of the historical process, which is the coming again of Jesus Christ, who is the judge of the world.

3. *The final aspect of language within the Christian community is that of encouragement.* Paul begins his letters with thanksgiving and joy for his fellow be-

lievers. Paul's writings end with exhortations of peace and friendship—words that encourage and bring hope to lives filled with struggle and defeat, even while the disciples live by hope.

Preaching and Practicing Homemaking, *by Ed Loring*

J U N E   1 9 9 3

　　Charles Thomas lives, along with three other men, on my back porch. I step over him every night, and leave him there because there is no room in the inn. "Sorry. We are full," I silently shout. Charles eats in our soup kitchen, bathes in our baths, dresses from our clothes closet, and often receives leftovers from our supper table. Luke is four years old and not our youngest member. Luke keeps on asking, "Why? Why is Charles outside? Why is Charles not coming in for dinner? Why is . . . ?" The peculiar power named homelessness in America has not yet tamed Luke. I often wonder: "Is Charles Lazarus? Am I Dives?" (Luke 16:19–31).

　　We are living in an exciting period of history! As Christendom cracks apart, new light and sound make their way through holes in the walls. Never before have mainline European American Christians had such an opportunity to hear Jesus speak as we do now. The raggedy poor are in our midst; the cry of Christ is in our ears; the marginalized are at the center of our dreams and imaginations. Rather than purchase another gun or a house a wee bit further outside the Perimeter, why not look to see who is coming to dinner?

　　Of course, there are problems. With the realization that housing is more of a justice struggle than a charity program, many people lost interest in the homeless—the so-called undeserving poor. The growth of Habitat for Humanity and Jimmy Carter's Atlanta Project are examples of the search for hopeful products. Some folk are going so far as to build fences and to employ security guards to keep their homes and churches from the likes of Lazarus. But this is the exciting part. No longer can we address the gospel of Jesus Christ concerning the poor without acknowledging our poverty. The old problem of the relevancy of proclamation is answered. The crumbling of Christendom and hardness of heart toward the homeless is fertile soil for planting gospel seeds. Some will yield, it has been said, thirty-fold, some sixty, some ninety!

　　Let me begin with my conclusion. The church of Jesus Christ is not called to build homes. We are mandated to make homes. Within the various vocations of the Christian life, only martyrdom is more noble and exacting than home-making. The message from the pulpit, the policy from the elders, the action by the people of God are very simple, concrete, and direct. Please listen to our friend Isaiah: "Share your food with the hungry and open your homes to the homeless poor" (Isa. 58:7a). And from Paul: "Share your belongings with your needy fellow Christians, and open your homes to strangers" (Rom. 12:13).

When preaching the gospel concerning homeless men and women, home-less boys and girls, Christians need only to be called to hospitality and welcome. Open our homes or a small room in our church to those on the outside. That is biblical love. From the shared task of homemaking emerges the justice agenda: housing is a human right. But that is for the next century. Today let us live to-gether as the Body of Jesus Christ.

Charles Thomas is missing several teeth, and he has a warrior's grin. The streets are like prisons—hellholes for the biblical love ethic. Agape and nonvio-lence are simply suburban syrup without conventional promises, baptismal vows, and a community of mutual accountability. Please never evangelize a homeless person without making home with them. They could easily get killed. Charles worships with us most Sunday afternoons. He grabs a handful of Jesus' bloody body, and he gulps the bloody grape juice. About 8:30 P.M. he goes back outside to our porch. There is no room for him in the inn.

Christendom is breaking up, and God is, once again, at work among white middle-class folk. Filled with blessings and hope, Yahweh refuses to let us go. The time is at hand for us to overcome two tremendous liabilities which have crippled us for centuries. Both must be addressed as we preach to people who live in houses about making home with those who live on the streets.

First, we are finally at the time when we can admit that Martin Luther was absolutely wrong to call the Epistle of James "a right strawy epistle." James is as essential for faith and practice as is Paul. Justification by faith alone in the Eu-ropean American families of faith has undergirded slavery, racism, capitalism, sexism, war, the tobacco lobby, the growth of suburbia, and psychological sub-stitutes for biblical revelation. Justification by grace is clearly biblical. Alone it is an ideological tool for the defense of power and abuse.

James is correct. This book must be preached and practiced as a corrective to the one-sidedness of Luther's fateful doctrine. Listen: "My sisters and broth-ers, what good is it for someone to say that they have faith if their actions do not prove it? Can that faith save her? Suppose there are brothers and sisters who need clothes and don't have enough to eat. What good is there in your saying to them, 'God bless you! Keep warm and eat well!'—if you don't give them the necessi-ties of life? So it is with faith: if it is alone and includes no actions, then it is dead" (James 2:14–17).

We need more than balance, more than a dialectic between faith and works.

We need to preach and practice faith and works, lifting James up and settling Luther down. A new theology of works, seen as essential to justification by faith, will enable us to become homemakers with the homeless.

A second Lutheran legacy that continues to weaken the European American mainline Christian witness, and that causes homelessness among baptized believers, is the inherent classism of Luther's decision to side with the princes during the Peasants' War of 1524 and 1525. Undergirded by the erroneous emphasis on justification by faith alone, Luther chose the wrong side of the conflict. "Which side are you on?" is a question every Christian must face every day. The gospel is clear, while church history is cloudy. We must make reparations for the ways Luther's momentous decision has shaped our faith and practice. Jesus, like the peasants, was slaughtered by princes. We are called by Christ to side with the oppressed against the oppressor. We cannot have faith and not practice it too.

To bring a street person into home or church is to honor both justification by faith and the good works of charity and justice. To make home with the strange beings is to undo—little by little—the history of white folks since 1525, who time after time have been on the wrong side. Ask any Native American, African American, labor-pool worker, homeless person, Sandinista, blues or rock-and-roll singer.

The cracks in Christendom are letting fresh air flow through. We are being called to an old way of life in a new day. Rather than transforming culture into our image of Christ, we may live with him in the flesh and agony of the poor. Only Lazarus could heal Dives, but by his death the gap was too wide to bring them together.

While Charles lies snoring on my back porch in the early-morning hour, another friend sits studying his Bible. His commentary is his life. His faith is that Moses and Jesus are liberators. His hope is that he will be led by the Holy Ghost to a house and a good job. His reality is that he is despised and rejected by most of us. He is dying a slow and incredibly painful death. He has no gas chamber or oven to face, only the endless wandering with nowhere to go, until his body breaks and he is dead.

I note three biblical resources for preaching and practicing homemaking among the housed and the houseless. First is the Cain and Abel story (Gen. 4:1–16). A central theme of the European American experience is loneliness. Though we came to these wondrous shores for religious freedom and economic opportunity, the cost has been too much for us to bear. White folks are, like Cain, marked. We bear in our souls and spirits a curse that has to be transformed into the graceful blessing that it may yet become: "You will be a homeless wanderer on the earth" (Gen. 4:12b). Cain, the betrayer of his brother, had to leave God's presence, his home, and to live in a land called "Wandering" or "Nod," which is east of Eden. The power of connection through imagination is redemptive here. We are the homeless ones. We, white and rich like Dives, yearn for community and connectedness. Like Cain, we fear the land on which we so hungrily walk. As we are empowered to claim our homelessness, our loneliness, our aimless wanderings—looking for a pulpit without the agony of sermon preparation—we can connect with the Lazarus outside our doors and on our city sidewalks. In these days, to claim Cain is to renounce Dives.

Second, none of us will find home on earth. If we are homemakers, we must be careful that home is not our idol. One cause of homelessness among baptized believers is the belief that home is a this-worldly possibility. But Jesus tells us: "There are many rooms in my Parent's house, and I am going to prepare a place for you. I would not tell you this if it were not so. And after I go and prepare a place for you, I will come back and take you to myself, so that you will be where I am. You know the way that leads to the place where I am going" (John 14:2–4).

Last fall, while driving on the famous U.S. Highway 61 toward the King Biscuit Blues Festival, Nibs Stroupe and I talked about the theological and political significance of life after death. Nibs taught me that a fundamental meaning of this doctrine is that we cannot find home on earth. This is a most helpful insight for preaching and the practice of homemaking. We are wanderers on the earth seeking home, experiencing a foretaste as we become homemakers with the homeless. Yet home always eludes us while on earth, east of Eden. We strive for home, for Jesus is our homemaker. How, asks Thomas, can we get home? Replies Jesus, "I am the way, the truth, and the life" (John 14:5b–6a). I am the home.

Paul's Letter to Philemon is the third biblical resource for sermon preparation on homemaking between rich and poor, African American and European American, housed and homeless. Like Jesus, this letter, too, has been neglected. Not because of the battles about norms and hermeneutics, but because of the terrible way the Bible meets us where we are. Cain reveals that we are homeless wanderers. Luke teaches that homemaking is possible only as we invite Lazarus into our houses. Jesus tells us that our home is ultimately in heaven. Jesus is the homeless, in their flesh. Philemon reveals the center of our political and sociological identity, and then proceeds with a biblical love ethic. We, North American mainline white Christian folk, are slaveholders. That is, we say "yes." We say "no." We are the oppressors. In Atlanta, which is 65 percent African American, with a Black mayor, city council president, and majority of the city council, the white business community, led by Presbyterians, Methodists, and Episcopalians, determines public policy. Votes count, resources decide. This letter is peculiarly addressed to us as we watch Christendom crack. The Bible understands us as slaveholders. We must open our hearts to this revelation.

Paul gives us a biblical ethic. While the slaves are still slaves, the poor still poor, the oppressed yet oppressed, Blacks still black, gays still homosexuals, we are to bring them into our homes. Paul does not assert that Philemon is to free Onesimus. Rather, he is to make home with him. Philemon is to practice hospitality; he is to welcome the slave inside as a brother—a member of the family. This is a radical love ethic rooted in covenantal promise and baptismal vows that create a common life. This is no home-building for the working poor every Saturday morning (house slaves, as Malcolm X would say), good though that is. This ethic describes a life together rooted in the redemptive power of Jesus Christ. Now we are clothed, so to speak, with the life of Christ himself. So there is no difference between Jews and Gentiles, European Americans and African Americans, between slaves and free, men and women; we are all one in union with Christ Jesus (Gal. 3:27b–28).

Ironically, the very scriptures used by pro-slavery Christians in eighteenth- and nineteenth-century America are resources for us today as we discover the radicality of life together and homemaking in the body of Christ. The church, although it cannot wait for the end of slavery, poverty, or oppression, might wish it. We must this very day open our homes to the homeless poor. Out of a life together shall emerge a renewed church and a political agenda that will include housing as a human right and constitutional guarantee.

Without taking the poor, the wanderer, the slave, and Lazarus into our homes and churches to practice the vocation of homemaking, the white main-line Protestant church is doomed to die a dismal death. Soon the chasm will be too wide for Lazarus to cross. Which side are you on? Oh, which side are you on?

Walking by Faith, *by Elizabeth Dede*

SEPTEMBER 1990

God's Word seems more appropriate to me today than it has at other times, perhaps because in the Bible I find people battling with fear, and daily I experience a lot of fear. So Jesus' words, "Courage! It is I. Don't be afraid!" (Matt. 14:27), are especially meaningful and significant in our frightening world.

It is easy to find stories of fear, because fear, rather than faith, often seems to control us. I think all of us feel fear about developments in the Middle East, as the deployment of U.S. troops pushes us closer to another war. Is Saddam Hussein of Iraq a madman—a Hitler—who plans to take over the world? And will the United States respond with its usual show of force? Will it respond as it did in Hiroshima and Nagasaki, seeing that as the simplest solution to the world's problems with Iraq? Our fear leads us to see no way out, and it causes us to trust in the destructive power of tanks, guns, and missiles.

But we don't have to look so far to find fear controlling people's lives. I believe that fear dictates Atlanta's policy toward homeless people. We all admit that homelessness in Atlanta long ago reached crisis proportions, similar to the Middle East, and that definite action is required. Similar to our response in the Middle East, one course of action is a show of strength: we can allay our fears by stomping homeless people out of existence. So the city enforces the vagrant-free zone, and at lunchtime in Woodruff Park you see the police in full force. No homeless person will stretch out on a bench while ten officers are around, apparently instructed to threaten anyone who doesn't look part of the lunch-break business crowd. That policy, which can only instill fear about homeless people, causes neighborhood people to act in similar fashion. That is the only way I can explain a letter that the Open Door recently received. It reads, in part:

> Earlier this year, some winos moved into a vacant area behind my house. At first, I didn't worry about it, since they never bothered us, and I felt pretty safe with my three dogs in the backyard. However, as the months went by, I began to notice the amount of trash that was piling up in the area, not to mention the amount of human excrement out in the open. I began to worry, but did not know what to do. I called the police a couple of times, but was told that since they were on state property, there was nothing they could do. (I didn't want the people arrested, I simply wanted them to go elsewhere.)
>
> Finally, after becoming more and more frustrated, my next-door neighbor and I cut down a lot of the brush that they were using as cover, and took away the cushions and plastic that they were using as their bed. I have to admit, I felt sad when I saw the first man come back to his home to find it ransacked.

Again, the fear that we are taught to feel toward homeless people leaves us without any options except to push them away. I wonder, for instance, if the writer ever thought to talk with the homeless people who were trashing the area. In a personal encounter she could have suggested and requested that they clean up the space. Perhaps that would have brought a resolution with less sadness.

We all have fears, so we needn't feel superior to President Bush, to the city government, or to our neighbor. We also find ourselves in good company. It was fear that Jesus met in his disciples as he walked across the water toward their boat: "It's a ghost!" they said, and they screamed with fear. And it was fear of a strong wind that caused Peter, who at first was able to walk on the water, to sink.

We know, too, that the Israelites were scared to death when the Egyptians began coming after them at the Red Sea. In Zora Neale Hurston's retelling of the story of Moses, called *Moses, Man of the Mountain*, she captures that fear in a human way:

> Women screamed in open-mouthed terror and whimpered in fear. Men cursed, cried out and milled about in great whorls. Some tried to run away to the woods to hide, others just stood or squatted on the ground in dumb fear. When they saw Moses come among them they crowded about him. Some clung to him while others screamed at him. He shook them off roughly and kept marching towards the rear.
>
> As the chariots drew near the panic grew in Israel. They committed every kind of folly and showed their inside weakness. Then Moses showed his power again. He turned his back on the Egyptian horde and spoke to his people. Spoke to them in their own dialect as one of them.
>
> Stand still, every last one of you and stop that screaming and yelling. You haven't got a thing to be scared of. That ain't nobody but Pharaoh and his army and we done beat them too many times before. Don't get so excited about nothing! God is going to fight for you just as God's been doing all along. Stand still and see the salvation which God is going to show you today. See those Egyptians there? Take a good look at 'em, because those Egyptians that you are looking at today, you're never going to see them no more as long as you live. And nobody else won't be seeing them either.

I believe we can say that fear gets in God's way: it causes Peter to sink; it makes the Israelites forget that they are God's chosen people; it makes the city government forget that the poor are blessed by God.

Clarence Jordan says in *The Substance of Faith* that we cannot have faith until we understand fear:

> *Why, then, is it so difficult to have faith? Why is faith so scarce? I think the clue to this is simply fear. Faith and fear, like the light and darkness, are incompatible. Fear is the polio of the soul which prevents our walking by faith. . . .*

Fear is very active and it's a very good thing and it works in us and tries its best to keep us alive and it fights with all it's got against this archenemy, death.

We cannot have faith until we understand this aspect of fear—that fear will be overactive in us so long as it sees, anywhere on the horizon, the specter of death. The clue, then, to the triumphant faith of the early Christians lies in the power of the resurrection. They did not go everywhere preaching the ethics of Jesus. They went everywhere preaching that this Jesus whom you slew, God has raised from the dead. Death had lost its sting, the grave had lost its victory. . . .

The life, the crucifixion, and the resurrection of Jesus is one package. I think the weakness of liberalism today is that it accepts the life of Jesus, but shuns the inevitable consequence of the Jesus Life, which is crucifixion, and it thereby denies the power of the resurrection. When we are given assurance that this Jesus and the kind of life that he lived can overcome [fear], then we are freed from our fear. Then we can give ourselves to this God and say, "Let all that we have go, even this mortal life also."

But the stories of that assurance are hard to come by. It is easy to tell stories of fear, but those of faith—of the light shining in the darkness—seem rare in our lives of sophistication, which mostly deny the Jesus Life. So it is important to tell stories of faith, to recognize them in our lives, and to act as faithful, rather than fearful, people.

For us at the Open Door Community, one of those faithful people is Billy Neal Moore, who is on death row. He often writes for *Hospitality,* telling stories from his life filled with faith in the saving power of God. A few issues back, he wrote:

I face the struggle against the state that has spent millions of dollars in their efforts to kill me. There isn't a day that passes when the forces of death are not before me. I know combat soldiers face battle in worse situations for two or three years; but it's nearly sixteen years now that I have struggled in hope that the same God in whom you believe will move in my behalf and spare me.

It is amazing testimony to the power of faith that a man can sit in the darkness of death for sixteen years and still let the light of faith shine through his life.

Now we have the news that the state has an execution warrant for Billy, and the darkness deepens. But on the day I heard the news, I received a letter from Billy, which ended: "Tell Jack I said everything shall be okay simply because God is in control of my life."

We desperately need to note that life of faith in our world full of fear. It is a life full of courage, possibility, and hope. Billy knows death like none of us knows death, yet he has looked on Jesus with the eyes of faith. He has heard the words: "Courage! It is I. Don't be afraid!" Billy has answered Jesus' call to follow him. He has taken the risk of faith, stepped out of the boat into the sea, and has not drowned.

The promise is food for us, too. We need to take the dark places of fear in our lives and turn them to the light of faith in Jesus. There are reasons to have faith. The Israelites were led through the Red Sea, out of slavery into the Promised Land. Pharaoh's army drowned. Jesus is alive! Death has lost its sting! Have courage! God is on our side.

"Something There Is That Doesn't Love a Wall,"
by Elizabeth Dede

M A Y   1 9 9 3

When I was in high school, one of my English teachers required us to memorize one thousand lines of poetry. Being a somewhat lazy scholar, I decided to commit several of Robert Frost's poems to memory, because most of them had a regular rhyme scheme and meter. If I got the pattern down, I found it easy to fit the words in and to remember the whole poem. Consequently, I can recite one thousand lines of Robert Frost. At the time it was a chore, but I have since grown to love the poems. I suppose my favorite is "Mending Wall," which, incidentally, was more difficult to learn because it didn't fit the pattern of the other poems.

In high school I knew little about walls and fences and barriers, although they were there; I can look back and see how they surrounded me. Since those days, I've had some experience of walls, and there is an essential truth in Frost's beautiful opening line, "Something there is that doesn't love a wall."

We've seen it at Dayspring Farm, where an old stone wall, much like the one Frost wrote about, began to tumble. Now it's been wonderfully rebuilt by our good friend Bill Shane from New Hope House, but the heavy rains rush down the hill against it, and already I can see the need for spring mending time. Something wants that wall to fall into a pile of rocks.

It's not that walls are necessarily a bad thing. I rather like having the walls of my room. Living with thirty other people would be impossible for me if I couldn't escape to the solitude of my own space, defined by its four walls.

Something, though, doesn't love that kind of wall either. At 910, we are always in the process of plastering holes and cracks where a long, hard life has begun to wear those walls away. On a recent trip to South Florida to help my sister rebuild from Hurricane Andrew, I was astounded to see many of the walls from my childhood blown down. I didn't recognize the house I grew up in; many of my friends were left homeless; and the old neighborhood is a pile of rubble, with houses and walls collapsed. We love those walls that defined our homes, our churches, our schools, our stores, our workplaces, but something there is that doesn't love a wall.

In the poem, the speaker tells of going out in the springtime to meet her neighbor and to rebuild the wall that separates their property. The heaving of the ground from heavy freezes has caused even boulders to spill. So with the wall between them, they walk down the line and put the stones back together. The neighbor has a favorite saying which he learned from his father (and probably his father learned it from his father, and so on), "Good fences make good neighbors." He likes it so much that he says it a couple of times.

For the seven years that I've lived at the Open Door, we've had an ongoing struggle to be good neighbors. During my first summer at 910, the neighbors in back of us began to complain of the noise and smell and sight of so many homeless people in the backyard. We agreed to put up a high wood fence to separate us. It is a beautiful fence and well constructed. And it works. The people who live in back don't see us, smell us, or hear us anymore. Good fences make good neighbors, I suppose, although I'm not sure you can call a person with whom you have no contact your neighbor.

In the poem, the speaker says of her neighbor that he won't go behind his father's saying. He doesn't seem interested in the history: did a cow several generations ago get into the neighbor's garden? was there a feud over property lines? When the history and meaning is forgotten, the fence really becomes nothing but a dividing wall between the two neighbors. You almost get the sense that the only time they have anything to do with each other is at spring mending time, when they rebuild the wall that divides them.

While the fence at 910 is a good one, it does keep us from being neighbors because of the barrier between us. They don't know what happens in our lives, and we don't know what happens in theirs. I doubt they know that on the morning of Sunday, November 15, 1992, a man died in their neighbor's yard. And I don't know what happened to them that day. Was a child born in their family? Did an old grandfather die in his bed?

On that fence, that dividing wall, there is now a memorial plaque to Robert Vernon Ford, who died on that Sunday morning in our backyard. That dividing wall is an appropriate place for a memorial to Bobby, because we must remember that the barriers that divide human beings from each other—race, class, sex, age, and so on—cause death.

Bobby Ford was fifty-four years old when he died, and he left behind a large number of friends. I don't know much about Bobby Ford; there were barriers between us. He lived outside; I live inside. He was an older Black man; I'm a younger white woman. I come from the privileged race and class—the oppressor; he was oppressed. I do know of his joyful, friendly presence that always reached across those barriers with a laugh, a grin, and a greeting. "Hello, Elizabeth!" he'd call from the benches in the backyard. "How're you doing today?" Sometimes I wished he'd be quiet, but Bobby was always present with a friendly word.

I cannot imagine what his life was like. Fifty-four is a dignified age, when a person should be able to look forward to slowing down for retirement. Instead Bobby was trapped in the rush of our filthy, rotten system. Two days before he died, he told me of another part-time job he'd found: some nowhere job, paying minimum wage. How could Bobby hope to get off the streets? About the only comfort a part-time, minimum-wage job offers is enough money to buy a bottle of vodka to drink away the miseries with your friends. It was cold and rainy in November. How can a fifty-four-year-old man keep any shred of dignity, much less a good and cheerful humor, when he has no home to go to day and night after day and night, stretching into the years? No wonder his heart broke on November 15.

So with Bobby's friends and family we gathered at the fence on the evening of November 22 to remember him and to hang the plaque. After we sang, told stories, prayed, and read God's Word, we moved close to the fence to watch as the plaque with Bobby's name, his birth and death, was hung behind the bench where he spent many days and nights, and where he finally died.

Now spring mending time is here, but in a different way from Robert Frost's poem. Because of the resurrection, we can go behind the old saying; we don't have to rebuild the walls that separate us. The reconciliation, however, isn't easy or cheap. After all, breaking down the dividing walls cost Jesus his life. And while we were distracted by the barriers, Bobby Ford lost his life, too.

We have a price to pay to keep the walls down. The cow might accidentally come into the garden, so we'll have to walk her back to the neighbors and replant the lettuce. There might be confusion over who owns what part of the property. From time to time we might have to smell a bad odor. We will have to become invested in each other's lives. I'll know what happened to you on November 15, and you'll know what happened to me. And we will weep and gnash our teeth in frustration when Bobby Ford's friends go off and get drunk again. But we will love her and forgive him and help them to stay sober, because the walls that divided us are just a pile of rocks now.

The Gospel Truth and a Worldly Lie, *by Ed Loring*

NOVEMBER 1990

One afternoon this summer a big Greyhound bus loped along the interstate highway between Washington, D.C., and Silver Spring, Maryland. The bus was filled with modern nomads—those who shower, shave, eat, watch TV, and sleep in one town and are employed in another—in a hurry. Somewhere along the way a passenger got up and clambered to the back of the bus, where he entered the restroom. A few minutes passed before the passenger returned to his seat midway up the aisle. He whispered a word to the unknown resident alien beside him with a smile and shook his head. The fellow passenger passed the word along and, in a few minutes, those who had hardly shared a sound were whispering to each other—sharing news and telling a story. Finally the person sitting directly behind the bus driver jumped up, leaned onto the driver's shoulder, and proclaimed in an urgent whisper: "There is a bomb on the bus!"

The bus driver swerved immediately to the highway's shoulder and slammed on the brakes. "Everybody out! Everybody out!" he cried as the bus slid to a halt. Quickly the highway patrol was summoned, who, after a cursory examination, sent for dogs who can smell what humans cannot see.

In the meantime, the passengers were frantic. Most of us have grown up in the shadow of the bomb, and it is easy to imagine the fear of being blown to bits. "Oh, God, no! Help me! Please help me! I'll never get home."

How foolish they felt when they learned that there was no bomb. The explanation, perhaps not scientific in its methodology, goes like this: when the rider went to the restroom, he discovered a homeless stowaway crouched in the corner. He beheld an unemployed wilderness wanderer, a sojourner amid the urban deserts and jungles of modern America. Returning to his seat, he winked at the woman next to him and incorrectly said, "There is a bum in the back of the bus." She laughed, stretched her necklaced neck across the aisle, and repeated, "There is a bum in the back of the bus," to the nameless traveler beside her. Bad news travels faster than a Greyhound bus on an interstate highway, and without ideology or conspiracy, the first false fact was transmogrified into devastating fear: "There is a bomb on the bus." (I remember the African American man named Willie Horton, whose name was transformed to signify every white racist fear that flows through the valleys and streams of our land.)

The story made national news. Having picked up the initial police reports, the media flocked to the bus in hopes of excitement. Perhaps a little carnage would benefit the evening TV ratings. Everyone laughed later when the dogs assured the police, passengers, driver, and media that there was no bomb on the bus. "Only a bum, only a bum, not a bomb, on the bus," I was told by National Public Radio as I hacked at the kudzu strangling our trees at Dayspring.

What the riders, the driver, the media, and the vast majority of the American people have not learned is that there wasn't a bum in the back of the bus. It is a worldly lie of devastating proportions, violence, dehumanization—yes, a crucifying of our God, a sacrilege as terrible as "goddamn"—to name a human being, created in the likeness of God, redeemed by the blood of our Lord Jesus, a bum. Yet that is what we believe and how we feel toward the homeless poor in our nation today. There was no bum in the back of the bus, 'cause Yahweh don't make no bums! Rather it is in the flesh of the poor that we meet, hear, touch, love, and serve our Lord Jesus. The poor are our means to life and wholeness.

Now another, even stranger, dimension to this little news clip must be added. The truth is that there was a bomb on the bus. We, who are ready to toss bombs at Iraq in the Middle East for oil, experience bums as bombs in our land. We are afraid. We fear the poor, and most especially, but not exclusively, the African American poor, as bombs about to explode on us. The poor are, to quote Mr. Joe Beasley of Antioch Baptist Church, North, "the new n-gg-rs in our cities and states." The bums are bombs, and thus the rumors were truth on the Greyhound bus. How odd!

The Bible declares: "The poor shall always be with you; therefore I command you: You shall open wide your hand to sisters and brothers, to the needy and to the poor, in the land" (Deut. 15:11). But what have we done by making Jesus' representatives into bums and bums into bombs?

We have turned the neighborhoods into war zones. We purchase ever bigger breeds of dogs and security systems that blurt bell-like screams when shadows dance in our yards. We construct higher fences topped with barbed wire and we beg the mayor to raise property taxes to pay meaner police to enforce meaner laws. What have we done? We have built more prisons and doubled the prison population in the United States in one short decade. We join associations to stop the bum-bombs from entering our neighborhoods; we turn against those who feed, shelter, and help the dying Christ. "Get them out of my sight! Off my porch! From my sidewalk!" How little different is the cry today from the hostile chant of the crowd choosing between Jesus and the thief: "Crucify him! Crucify him!"

And so they said:

"Hey, Mr. Bus Driver,
There is a bomb on the bus!"
"Yes, Mr. Bus Driver."

And this bus is the U.S. of A.
This bus is the Church of Jesus Christ
The Synagogue of Yahweh
The Mosque of Allah

This bus is Atlanta, Georgia,
Peachtree, Ponce de Leon, and Pryor Streets.

If we don't defuse
The bus with justice

If we don't turn the bus around
put the wheels on the King's Highway

If we don't stop telling lies
and calling Jesus' best friends:

> bums
> whores
> lazy bastards
> punks
> niggers
> animals
> crazies
> winos
> rats

If we don't repent
Change this city into Beloved Community

If we don't find Jesus Christ
in the back of the bus
in the soup-kitchen lines

Then . . .

The Bomb is going to blow up
And we
in our pitiful rags and riches

our college degrees and fabulous
careers
our houses, cars, and bank accounts

Will be dead.

or

We can rid the land of lovelessness and fear
Where no one is a bum or bomb
Where everyone has enough
Where justice is our security
and we love one another.

"Ain't no bums
ain't no bombs
on this bus," says Jesus.

"Follow me."

Martin and Rodney: Kings among Captors,
by Ed Loring

JUNE 1992

Racism is not a matter of the heart; prejudice is. Racism is not flesh and blood; it is a power and a principality (Ephesians 6) of this final age of European American hegemony in North America. Racism is power and privilege based simply on the color of one's skin. White folk are racists because we live in a system that favors whiteness and crushes blackness. We live in institutions like churches and schools that teach us that Americans cannot be racists in North America, although they can be as prejudiced as anyone else. But African Americans do not have the institutional power—political, social, or economic—to be racist. Whites are racists. Blacks are victims of racism.

Racism is an addiction, as Nibs Stroupe has taught us in his book, *While We Run This Race*. The first response of an addict when confronted with her disease and with love of the high the drug produces is denial. That denial is not a personal lie; it represents the belief system of the addict. Racism blinds white people to the realities of the systems of power and privilege and to the suffering of the oppressed. The gospel of Jesus Christ promises "recovery of sight to the blind" (Luke 4:18b). The white people defending our court system and arguing that the Rodney King case is sad, but not representative of our system, are blind. Racism's sinister fingers gouge out the eyes of the beholder. Jesus Christ calls us to repent, for God's way is at hand. To European Americans, repentance means seeing what we are doing to African Americans and fighting with all our hearts, all our guts, all our power, to abolish the white racism that infiltrates every level of our lives. We must uproot the racist system. Like Blind Bartimaeus we must cry out for the Black Jesus to heal our eyes so we may get on the road to justice, which is the fight for equality among European Americans and people of color.

Racism, though it belongs only to the white world, also has debilitating and blinding consequences for African Americans. Often they respond to the pain and suffering, the oppression and death, by believing that the "white man" is the enemy, the devil. That analysis is more correct psychologically than politically. White racism does twist white folk into a distorted form of God's image, often closer to the devil than to Jesus. But the principalities and powers which rule the hearts, minds, politics, and economics of the American system are the loci of racism. White men could be killed or converted, but without a drastic change in the system—that is, without rooting out racism—the result would be little changed. The way out of racism, both for white racists and for Black victims of racism, is to restructure our society along the lines of equality. Not an equality of opportunity, but an equality of power in economics, politics, and control of institutions that shape human destiny (e.g., schools and banks).

The gospel of Jesus Christ calls us to nonviolence, I believe. But we white folks must be slow to judge others, because our white racism is among the most heinous forms of violence to stalk the earth since God flooded the world. White racism not only condemned Rodney King years before his arrest, not only devoured Dr. King's skull on the balcony of the Lorraine Motel, but it has been behind our social policies toward Native Americans, the bombs on Hiroshima and Nagasaki, the infant mortality rate at Grady Hospital, and the signs at Druid Hills Presbyterian Church prohibiting homeless people from its property. Readers who have recovered any sight (and about 20/200 is the best any of us white folk can claim) have their own lists calling us to conversion and radicalism.

Yet it was only through violence that liberty was won for the African American slave. Every avenue to abolish slavery was attempted prior to 1861. The Christians converted hearts, and the anti-slavery movement grew. People wrote letters to Congress, petitioned their churches, began alternative communities, and started a new political party. But, in the end, it was war violence, already present in the racism of slavery, that secured liberty for the captives. On January 1, 1863, President Abraham Lincoln issued the Emancipation Proclamation, and slavery ended, although the Confederates fought for another fifteen months. To be an advocate of nonviolence and against the war in 1861 was to be functionally pro-slavery. There was one way, and one way alone, that liberty was procured for the slaves in America: violent, death-dealing war. But liberty was, by constitutional guarantee, granted the African Americans and others. Today the only constitutional slavery we have in the United States exists in prison.

Liberty forms only one-half of the pie of freedom in America. The other half is equality. Liberty without equality leads to poverty, dependence, and a new form of extraconstitutional slavery among African Americans. For whites, liberty and a disproportionate share of power over people of color has deepened the racism, violence, greed, and blindness already inherent in the European American way of life.

After the Civil War, a vision of equality existed among the Radical Republicans and former slaves. These leaders, small in number but powerful in vision, knew that liberty must be joined with equality for slavery to cease and for racism to be rooted up and burned. So a covenantal promise was made: *forty acres and a mule.* Land and the means of production would be the basis of equality.[2] Property rights are the sacred rights in the United States, and land and a mule would give access to economic power and a sharing of political might. The American Dream of forty acres and a mule, the dream of equality for all, died. White racism awoke from the slumbers of war and said *no* to equality among whites and Blacks. No land; no mules. You are free to buy your own land. You are free to purchase your own mule. Liberty, "yes"; equality, "no."

Rodney King deserves the equivalent of forty acres and a mule. So does every other African American in the United States. All people of color must find resources with which to demand and claim their fair share within the economic and political system. That is the basis of equality, and equality of actual power, goods, and cultural diversity is the only way to root racism from this wounded and frightened land.

The time has come to change some lyrics and slogans. What about:

> Equal at last!
> Equal at last!
> Thank God Almighty!
> I'm equal at last.

or

> The land of the free,
> and the home of the equal!

---

2. See Walter Brueggemann, *The Land,* Overtures to Biblical Theology (Philadelphia: Fortress Press, 1977).

White folks, listen. There is only one way to undo the racism that binds us to violence and death. We must fight the powers and principalities over us and within us. The battle is for actual equality of power among all of us in American society.

God calls us to have such a vision. The earth cries out against us, and Abel's blood is on our hands. But the cross of Christ empowers us to march together. Follow the Black Jesus who will give sight to the blind, freedom to the captives, justice to Rodney King, new life to us all. Our God is in anguish about our white racism. The Holy Spirit promises each of God's children forty acres and a mule (Acts 2 and 4).

Wake up!

The Rent Man, *by Ed Loring*

A U G U S T   1 9 9 3

The blue man told Barry Burnside and me to leave. "Visiting hours are over," mumbled the laconic death-row guard. I hugged Richard Walker good-bye and moved quickly down the long, cold tunnel to the outside world. The free-world time was 3:30 P.M. I was in a bit of a hurry, for I was on my way to Dayspring, the Open Door Community's retreat farm, for a two-and-a-half-day respite. I wanted to be on the other side of Atlanta to avoid the terrible rush-hour traffic that clogs the lanes of I-75 North like pig meat clogs the veins of a two hundred–pound, forty-five-year-old, five-foot-ten-inch man.

When I came out of the prison, I saw two African American women standing beside their car and peering under the opened hood. Clinging to the skirts of one of the women were two little boys, ages five and three. As I approached my car the younger woman turned and asked if I had any jumper cables. "Our battery went dead while we were in there," she lamented, and pointed toward the tons of concertina wire surrounding the entrance to the tunnel.

I said I was not sure but I thought I did. I turned toward the back of the Open Door car to see if our jumper cables were there. Indeed, they were! I opened the back of the station wagon and pulled out the jumper cables. Just before driving our car beside theirs, two fellows pulled up and offered to help the women. So I gave them the jumper cables, and they attached them to their car.

I stood toward the back of their car and waited while the electrical juice from one battery flowed through the cables to another. The little boys came around and peered at me from time to time. Once the older child came close enough for me to clasp his little hand and to ask his name. Shortly thereafter he turned to his mother and, looking at me, said, "He is the rent man." With an embarrassed laugh, his mother shook her head and said, "No he isn't. He is a friend."

Shortly after that encounter the car's engine turned over and started with a loud burst. The men gave me back my jumper cables, and all of us set off in our various directions. Likely we will never see each other again.

I often think of that May afternoon and the little boy's experience of me as the Rent Man. It is so important for those of us who are white to understand what white racism does to the images that others see in us. Probably this little boy did not know that he was at a prison. He did not know that I considered myself a "good" person. I had come as a minister to visit those in need. I had come out of the prison in a hurry to move down the road for my Sabbath rest, but stopped to help his mother. His startling description grasped me quickly and made me realize that, as a white man towering over him at the back of his car, he saw me as many African Americans see me and other white men. He saw me as the boss. He saw me as the landlord. He saw me as the oppressor and the one in control. Through the eyes and out of the mouth of this little boy, I continue to reflect on how I present myself in the world in which I move. I am very blessed that I am often able to move in a world filled with African Americans. I am cursed that, by the image I present through the color of my skin and the history of my gender, many people assume that I am the big boss man. I am a racist.

For this little boy who saw me as the Rent Man I want to commit my life to undoing racism. How I long for the day when he will see me and see only a friend, only the figure of a father, or a brother, or an older man to whom he can turn. How I long for that day. I know that day will not come in my lifetime, but it is a day for which I pray and struggle. I hope, in the words of Dr. Martin Luther King Jr., for the coming of the Beloved Community.

I am deeply thankful for this little boy's intrusion into my life. I will fight with my life not to be the Rent Man.

The Dismal History of the Bible, *by Ed Loring*

J U N E   1 9 8 9

Recently the local newspaper published a story about Robert Funk and his cohorts, who converge every so often at the University of Montana to vote on the authenticity of the sayings of Jesus. These biblical scholars are producing a "colored bible" (no offense to African Americans: the colored Bible stands in opposition to the Black liberation struggle in North America). The colors represent the possible and plausible accuracy of the sayings of Jesus.

Thus, green might represent 85 percent of these grown folks' opinion that Jesus really, really, really said it; yellow might represent that he possibly might have and maybe could have said it. In either case, Dr. Funk, whom I knew during my graduate-student days at Vanderbilt University, and friends are wasting their time and our newspaper's copy space. The only way to "know" the Bible and to test the authenticity of its contents is to live it. The streets, not the university, are the place to discover the word of God.

At the other end of the spectrum are our brothers and sisters in the Southern Baptist Convention. They believe the whole Bible is greener than green! Every word is fully inspired and is as authoritative for science as for doctrine! Yet the Baptists do not take a stand against charging interest on loans to the poor—a precept which fills the pages of the Old Testament. Also, Southern Baptists support the death penalty for homicide (as do the majority of North American Christians), but they do not stone to death rebellious sons and adultery-committing wives. In fact, for the majority of Southern Baptists, the "completely inspired word of God without fault or error" basically means that they are safe members of the Republican Party. The white middle-class American way of life is the real standard-bearer. Dr. Robert Funk and the Southern Baptists end up at about the same place, as defenders of the status quo in a sea of injustice. What about the Bible? What about this Word of God?

The Bible is among the most radical documents of human history. In the Old Testament, it presents the story of liberation from oppression and slavery; in the New Testament, the same story is told in terms of life conquering death. Liberation and life are understood as personal and political struggles. No book is more intimately personal, no book is more concretely political than the Bible. Its politics are revolutionary; its economics are radical; and its message of personal wholeness and health is empowering. The Bible is good news to the poor and liberty to the captives. If you read the Bible in the streets, you can evaluate clearly the ideology of the white, Southern Baptist, flag-waving theologians just as you grasp the impossibility of faithfulness according to Dr. Robert Funk and academic Christians.

Yet the song I sing is not a new song, nor is this a strange land. The Bible is the most oppressed book in the history of Western civilization. Even the American Civil Liberties Union has not been able to help! When we read today that the right wing of the right-wing Likud Party is using scripture to justify killing Palestinian children, we are hearing an old, old story. (Dr. Funk, is that green or yellow?)

Not too many years after Jesus' death, resurrection, and ascension, the Roman Empire accepted Christianity as part of a relationship between the state and the powerful. Since that historical period, the majority opinion has been in favor of power, oppression, and the status quo. That is, while the purpose of the Bible is to structure a liberation society, its actual function has been to justify oppression. God is the God of liberation and the God of life, love, and wholeness. Why has scripture been so abused and molested?

In the South, the Bible was the primary document used to justify not only slavery but, most concretely, African American slavery. Most non-slaveholding Christians in the North agreed. Why? The Bible in the American South and in South Africa today is a primary source for "proving" among believers that Black folk are inferior to white and are destined by God to be the servants of whites. How odd—the radicality of scripture results precisely from turning power upside-down and from saying that liberation is rooted in servanthood. How can such twisted use of the Bible happen? Can't the believers of the Bible read it?

God wills women to be free from slavery and sexism. Yet everyday we hear the voices of death and the rulers of darkness quoting the Bible to justify the inferior pay and the oppression of women. When I teach my daughter the Bible stories every night, I often wonder what she will think the first time she hears the biblical argument for the inferiority of women.

The justification of wealth and the imperialism of our nation proceed with blessings and baptism from pulpit to pew. The most life-giving source of water in our world has become a cesspool—the water of death.

So I plead with you today. As we fight homelessness and the criminal-control system, as we work for justice in the marketplace and mercy in our personal relationships: Let the Word of God be the Word of God. Then, oh then, "justice will flow like a mighty stream and righteousness like a river that never goes dry."

Afterword: The Open Door Community and the Catholic Worker Movement, *by Peter R. Gathje*

At the end of this collection, it is important to remember that this community began within and continues to draw strength from a rich and vibrant tradition within Christianity. This tradition is marked by communities of faith that respond to God's graciousness in two ways: first by living in solidarity with and in service to the poor, and second by working to create justice in accord with God's will for human life. Practices of the Open Door, such as worship, simple living, nonviolent activism on behalf of the poor, hospitality for the homeless, and visitation of prisoners, stand within a Christian tradition that preceded the formation of the Open Door. It is this tradition and those practices which distinguish the Open Door in its journey of Christian discipleship.

A reading of *Hospitality*, and an inquiry into the life of the Open Door, reveals that the Catholic Worker movement has been the central example of this tradition and those practices. The Catholic Worker was begun by Dorothy Day and Peter Maurin in 1933. The story of Dorothy Day's conversion to Catholicism, her search for a way to integrate Christian faith with her already strong commitment to justice, and her providential meeting with Peter Maurin, which led to the creation of the Catholic Worker, has been told not only by Day, but by a multitude of biographers and historians. It is a powerful story which has been deeply formative for members of the Open Door Community. As both Ed Loring and Murphy Davis have testified, their visit to the first Catholic Worker community in New York, and their reading of Dorothy Day's autobiography, *The Long Loneliness*, were precipitating events in the founding of the Open Door. Likewise, other persons and communities, such as Mitch Snyder, the Community for Creative Nonviolence, and the Sojourners Community, which also helped to inspire the formation of the Open Door, had also found in Dorothy Day and the Catholic Worker movement important resources for their own conversions, community building, and work for justice. The rich interweaving of influences shaping the Open Door has the common thread of the Catholic Worker.

Thus, after reading this collection of articles from *Hospitality*, a useful way to summarize and to gain a perspective on the Open Door Community is to see how it expresses central themes and practices within the Catholic Worker movement. In a helpful essay published as an introduction to a new edition of Dorothy Day's book *On Pilgrimage*, Mark and Louise Zwick, themselves Catholic Workers, discuss what might be called ten essential characteristics of the Catholic Worker movement.[1]

The first of those characteristics, *a deep connection with yet critical stance toward the church,* is especially evident in the lives of Dorothy Day and Peter Maurin, and continues as an important aspect of the Catholic Worker movement. As the Zwicks state, "Dorothy Day was not an isolated Catholic, sitting on the edge or margin of mainline Catholicism, or [as] part of a sectarian group that lives content in the discovery of its own little truths that it keeps under a bushel. . . . Her radicalism, her commitment to the poor, to a just social order, to peace— all were rooted in her Catholicism."[2] At the same time, Day and the Catholic Worker movement have been very critical of the institutional church on certain points. At one point in her life, Day wrote, "I loved the Church for Christ made visible. Not for itself, because it was often a scandal to me. Romano Guardini said that the Church is the Cross on which Christ was crucified; one could not separate Christ from his Cross, and one must live in a state of permanent dissatisfaction with the Church."[3]

This tension between love for and criticism of the church is clearly present in the Open Door. Those who began the community were driven by a shared intensity of faith that first helped to reinvigorate a small Presbyterian congregation, and that then led to starting a night shelter. Yet that same intensity of faith eventually led to the formation of a type of Christian community seemingly not possible within the confines of a traditional congregation. The very existence of a community such as the Open Door thus has come to stand as a critical alternative to mainstream Christian life. In the Open Door, and in other intentional Christian communities, members' lives are organized around a community seeking to live faithfully to the gospel. Rival institutional and personal demands such as family, work, education, and politics are minimized. In mainstream Christian lives, the temptation is more easily indulged to put personal and institutional loyalties before faithful response to the gospel as nurtured within Christian community and offered in witness to the world. Even more, mainstream Christianity can come to justify accommodation with the dominant institutional struc-

---

1. See Mark and Louise Zwick, "Dorothy Day and the Catholic Worker Movement," in Dorothy Day, *On Pilgrimage* (Grand Rapids, Mich.: Eerdmans, 1999).

2. Ibid., 18.

3. Ibid., 14.

tures and mores, in effect blessing a status quo that falls far short of God's will for human life. Out of the vision of the gospel the Open Door shares with the Catholic Worker and similar communities, it has often been called to dispute such accommodations. As is evident in this collection, many articles in *Hospitality* have taken to task forms of mainstream Christianity that manifest an addiction to economic and political power, that support the death penalty and other forms of state-sanctioned violence, and that fail to openly confront the injustices which afflict the homeless poor and the imprisoned.

Yet the Open Door, like the Catholic Worker, relies on and interacts with mainstream Christianity on a regular basis. A constant feature of life at the Open Door are the donations that come from mainstream Christian churches (many of which are Presbyterian) and faithful individuals. Further, the many ministries of the community rely heavily on volunteers from mainstream Christian denominations. Over the years the Open Door has also cultivated relationships with seminaries and schools, whose students often come to the Open Door to learn of its life and work, and how those learnings might be applied in other settings. Finally, the ongoing publication of *Hospitality*, invitations to speak in churches and schools, the membership of community members in ministerial organizations such as Concerned Black Clergy, and the ongoing standing of Ed Loring and Murphy Davis as Presbyterian ministers all indicate important and fruitful interactions between the Open Door and the broader church. The Open Door is hardly an isolated sectarian group; rather, it draws upon and contributes to the very church it also lovingly, though sometimes stridently, criticizes.

The second characteristic important to the Catholic Worker and clearly present in the Open Door Community is *personalism*. Personalism has two related qualities. First, it strongly emphasizes respect for human dignity. Second, personalism stresses the importance of personal responsibility. The respect for human dignity draws upon two faith convictions: God's creation of human beings in the image and likeness of God, and God's redemptive activity in Jesus Christ. In that redemptive activity, God sanctifies human life through becoming human, and through Jesus' cross and resurrection the powers of sin and death that destroy human life are themselves defeated. Mindful of this God-given human dignity, Christians are called to reject complicity with any form of personal and institutional life that dehumanizes and degrades oneself or others by making persons objects to be manipulated and used. This means that one does not wait for government, or any other institution, to create justice or to care for others. Instead, one embraces a personal responsibility to struggle for justice and to care for others in whatever way possible.

The words of the Open Door Community as expressed in *Hospitality*, and the actions of the community both in serving the homeless and imprisoned, and in advocating for justice, make clear the community's commitment to personalism. Murphy Davis's continual reference to Jerome Bowden's statement, "Peoples wasn't made to be dogged around, peoples was made to be respected," expresses the commitment to human dignity which is foundational for the Open Door. Further, the community's practice of hospitality, in which homeless persons are welcomed into the house for meals and showers, to use bathroom facilities, and, for some, to enter the community itself, reveals a concern not only to provide needed services, but to develop personal relationships that are mutually transformative. As is evident from the many stories in *Hospitality* which tell of these personal encounters and relationships, the community practices the personalism urged by the Catholic Worker. Further, like the Catholic Worker, the Open Door community finds in Matthew 25 a foundational text for its personal relationships with those in the streets and prisons. It is the faith of the Open Door that one meets Christ in the homeless person and in the person behind bars.

The meeting of Christ in those the community serves and for whom the community seeks justice is sustained through the community's weekly celebration of the presence of Christ in the Eucharist. This third characteristic of the Catholic Worker tradition, the *centrality of the Eucharist and shared prayer,* is also frequently referenced in *Hospitality.* In one example of several from this collection, Murphy Davis, in "Liturgy and Life, Sacrament and Struggle," plainly states the importance the Open Door places on Eucharist and shared prayer:

> When we look at bread and grape juice, we see ordinary food. But in the sacramental vision, we understand that this is a holy feast that we share. When we look at water, we see only the ordinary water that quenches our thirst. But when we understand the power of water and the outpouring of God's Spirit, then we understand how the cleansing of baptism changes our life. We understand that it is a holy work when we invite our homeless friends to share food and drink and showers. There is holiness, there is sacrament, in sharing elements that become holy. It is the same vision that we receive when we look into the eyes and the face of a stranger and see the presence of God. When we look into suffering people's lives, we understand the Passion of Jesus Christ.

Murphy's statement connects the "sacramental vision" with the personalism that seeks to safeguard human dignity as grounded in God as Creator and Redeemer. In each human person there is something of the mystery of God's creative and redemptive work. This dignity is not dependent on human achievement or social status; it is entirely God's doing. To deny this human dignity is to deny God. Or as John writes in the New Testament, "Love, then, consists in this: not that we have loved God but that God has loved us and has sent God's

Son as an offering for our sins. Beloved, if God has loved us so, we must have the same love for one another. No one has ever seen God. Yet if we love one another God dwells in us, and God's love is brought to perfection in us. . . . One who has no love for the brother he has seen cannot love the God he has not seen" (1 John 4:10–12, 20). The sacramental vision sees God in other persons, no matter how sinful or poor or contemptible, and the response to which Christians are called is love, just as Christians continue to experience God's love in Jesus Christ and his sacramental presence.

The fourth characteristic of the Catholic Worker found in the Open Door is *voluntary poverty*. From its beginnings the Open Door has sought to live simply, eschewing a surfeit of goods. The community shares goods, relying on a common purse that depends on donations. By this practice of standing in solidarity with the poor whom they seek to serve, community members hope to be freed from the drive for possessions, and also to learn from their sharing, in some small way, the needs and neediness of the poor. In affirming the gospel call to simplicity of life, the Open Door urges that when we share the goods of this earth there is enough for all in the plenty of God's creation. The problem is that our economic system encourages people to judge human worth by accumulated possessions, and people are goaded to hoard goods in a fearful competitiveness. For the Open Door the results of this system and its values are particularly manifest in the existence of homelessness in the United States. As Ed Loring, in "Entering the World of the Homeless, Hungry and Angry," states, "It is absolutely stupid that in the United States of America there are men and women, boys and girls who sleep outside. It is unconscionable that there is hunger—even a famine—that stalks this land in the midst of good, nutritious, happy food." This famine in the midst of plenty comes from the desire for more and more, which makes people fearful of losing what they have; the fear creates barriers between those who have and those in need. Voluntary poverty disciplines the desire for more, and brings into one's experience the needs of those excluded from the basic goods necessary for human survival and dignity. Reflecting this view, Ed Loring brings together personalism and voluntary poverty when he writes in the same article, "We must involve ourselves with homeless people as the way to respond to homelessness. We must be involved with hungry people as the way to respond to hunger. When you come to know hungry people, fasting is a powerful discipline. When you come to know homeless people, sleeping outside on a piece of cardboard is a wonderful practice. In the quest for solidarity, we can bring hunger and suffering into our flesh." The voluntary poverty of the Open Door thus seeks both to show how those who have much can and ought to live with less, and that, if persons and economic structures were committed to sharing God's bounty, all people would have enough and none would be driven into a life of destitution.

The fifth characteristic the Open Door shares with the Catholic Worker tradition is *clarification of thought*. The Catholic Worker has a long tradition of weekly meetings in which a variety of speakers address the issues of the day and invite discussion rooted in a gospel vision of human life. In addition, Catholic Worker communities almost always put out some type of newspaper or newsletter to share their lives, and to reflect theologically on their experiences. The Open Door continues these practices. The rich texture of the Open Door's life comes, in part, from the many persons invited to speak during the community's times for clarification. Likewise, such speakers find themselves challenged by community members to make connections between theology and experiences from the streets and prisons. The pages of *Hospitality* have often contained the reflections offered in these meetings. Important in this clarification of thought is the integration of theological reflections with social and political analysis and experience. The life of faith is deepened when faith engages all human capacities, including the capacity to reflect critically on life's experiences. Peter Maurin urged that the laborer be an intellectual and that the intellectual be a laborer as a way to integrate dimensions of human life too often separated in modernity. The Open Door's commitment to clarification of thought through regular meetings, and through publication of *Hospitality*, indicates that the community encourages an ongoing devotion to faith informed by thoughtful reflection.

The sixth characteristic of the Catholic Worker is *support of workers*. Within the history of the Catholic Worker movement, Catholic Workers many times have stood on picket lines with workers seeking just wages and safe working conditions. Dorothy Day continually emphasized the dignity of laborers, was a constant critic of child labor, urged a living wage so that workers and their families could live in dignity, and was arrested on several occasions for her participation in strikes. Perhaps the easiest place to see the Open Door's continuation of this tradition is in the community's attention to the injustices associated with labor pools. The Butler Street Breakfast began as a way to offer a meal for those going to work in labor pools. Moreover, many articles in *Hospitality*, including several by Ed Loring in this collection, have detailed how the wages earned by homeless people through labor pools are not enough to move a person from the streets into housing. Loring in particular urges what Dorothy Day (drawing upon several papal encyclicals) called a "living wage." He writes, for example, in "Sobering Up: How to Clean Up the Streets in America," that the "bottom line for setting the amount [of the minimum wage] needs to be determined by the market costs for a decent life. How much money does it take to have access to the necessities of life—housing, food, medical care, and so on—plus surplus for crisis, old age, and leisure?" When that amount is determined, then we can establish a living wage. Our society has no intent, however, of making sure workers have such a wage, since it is to the benefit of those in political and economic power to keep labor insecure. On this point one can also turn to Ed Loring's "Why Homelessness Exists in America: Public Policy and Cheap Labor."[4]

This analysis brings us to the seventh characteristic within the Catholic Worker movement, the *criticisms of capitalism and socialism*. The Catholic Worker finds in both of these economic systems the effort to make persons into things. In capitalism, profit is put before persons. In socialism or communism, the good of the state (which controls economic life) is put before persons. In both systems the system itself has priority over human dignity and human good. It is easy to see in these critiques the personalism which is foundational for the Catholic Worker. In *Hospitality*, it is clear that the Open Door offers a similar critique. The failure of capitalism is evident in the streets and prisons, in which persons are punished for being poor. Drawing upon the biblical standard that a society is to be judged by how it treats "the least of these," the Open Door makes the judgment that this society, so deeply informed by capitalist economics, is a failure. In its public protests and articles that pointed to how Olympic development displaced poor people, and to how commercial development such as Underground Atlanta displaced homeless people, the Open Door has shown that such development benefits only a few and adds to the burden of the poor. Moreover, the Open Door has continually pointed out how the criminal justice system punishes poor people while turning away from corporate criminality. (See, for example, Murphy Davis, "A Bag of Snakes.") For all of its criticisms of the capitalist economic system, the Open Door does not embrace statist socialism that would enforce a strict economic equality. The market may remain, but the market is to be hedged by restrictions that insure it will serve human dignity and not become a god to which humans are sacrificed.

Related to this economic analysis is the eighth characteristic of the Catholic Worker, its *attention to agronomy*. Peter Maurin's program for the Catholic Worker stressed "cult, culture, and cultivation." Maurin believed that the loss of farms and the movement of massive numbers into large urban areas led to many of the ills of modern society. Much like Gandhi, who stressed the need for an economic system that was rural-based and devoted to meeting needs at the local level, Maurin stressed that Catholic Workers needed to begin experimenting with a renewal of agricultural life. In the history of the Catholic Worker, this idea has not met with much success. Though there are a few Catholic Worker farms still in existence, the history shows that many efforts resulted in failure.

The Open Door has never sought to start such a farm. Like some other Catholic Worker houses, however, the Open Door has created its own rural retreat house, which it calls "Dayspring." Perhaps more important here, however,

---

4. This essay appears in *I Hear Hope Banging at My Back Door: Writings from "Hospitality"* (Atlanta: Open Door, 2000), 30–33.

is the Open Door's attention to some of the values Peter Maurin was hoping to preserve by establishing such "agronomic universities." One of those values is the concern for nutritious foods. The Open Door in its preparation and serving of meals is careful to offer food that is not simply filling, but that meets nutritional needs. Further, sodas and sweets like cake and cookies are not part of the meals. The Open Door has sought, through the types of food it serves, to counter some of the health problems associated with being on the streets and in poverty. Another shared value reflecting Maurin's convictions is the Open Door's emphasis on the dignity of manual labor. Both at 910 Ponce de Leon and at Dayspring, all the members of the community join in the work as they are able. Just as the clarification-of-thought meetings urge the unity of intellectual life and labor, so, too, does this communal insistence on the sharing of all tasks.

The ninth characteristic of the Catholic Worker movement is *pacifism*. The Catholic Worker has a noble history of nonviolent resistance to militarism and war. Catholic Workers commit themselves to following the nonviolent Christ, who urged love of enemies and the ministry of reconciliation. In the Open Door, community members also pledge themselves to nonviolence consistent with being disciples of Christ. Like the Catholic Worker, the Open Door has stood against war and has participated in efforts to foster nuclear disarmament, to reduce the resources now used for military purposes, and to protest specific instances of military wrongdoing, such as the School of the Americas. But it is perhaps in the community's resistance to the death penalty that its pacifism is most consistently evident. For the Open Door, Christian peacemaking is premised on the life, death, and resurrection of Christ. Christ's life embodies God's alternative to human life as organized around retribution. In response to sinful humanity's attempts to secure itself through death, God offers in Christ a security based on mutual vulnerability and trusting relationship. In contrast to God's way of life, there stands the politically popular response to violence, which is more violence. The stance of the Open Door, rooted in the gospel, is that the cycle of violence can only be broken by peacemaking that attends to the healing of those harmed by violence, and that seeks to redemptively change those who do violence. Both approaches form part of an overall effort to create a just society. These are the tasks of reconciliation and justice that Murphy Davis refers to in "Dollars and Sense," when she writes, "When Jesus began his ministry he read from the prophet Isaiah: 'God has sent me to proclaim liberty to the captives and recovery of sight to the blind.' Prisons and jails stand as monuments to our refusal to live the good news. Until we open ourselves to the healing word of God's justice, we will choose harsh judgment and a deepening violence, rather than a compassionate response to victims, and healing for those who hurt or offend."

The tenth characteristic of the Catholic Worker is the *importance of the retreat.* Dorothy Day urged Catholic Workers and others to participate in a rather intense retreat on a regular basis. She saw that the work of serving the poor and advocacy for justice could be draining, and carried temptations to self-right-eousness and the sense of being irreplaceable. Times of retreat offered space for renewal in God's Spirit, so that Catholic Workers could remember that grace—God's loving and saving presence in our lives—is what makes the work possible. To keep a generous spirit one needs to be refreshed in God's generosity. To wel-come others, one needs to experience God's welcome.

For the Open Door Community, retreat has often served as a time of re-newal in God's generosity and welcome. It was the recognition of an ongoing need for retreat that brought the community the gift of Dayspring Farm, its most commonly used place of retreat. Community members have found Dayspring a place of respite, both in individual and community retreats. It has, by community members' accounts, been a place to which they can withdraw for needed rest from the demanding work of hospitality. Elizabeth Dede, in "Dayspring: A Message from My Childhood," gives voice to how this place of retreat serves the community. She recalls the lyrics of the Advent hymn "Oh Come, Oh Come, Emmanuel," in which "blest Dayspring" is to

> . . . come and cheer
> Our spirits by your advent here;
> Disperse the gloomy clouds of night,
> And death's dark shadows put to flight.

Elizabeth finds through the retreat offered at Dayspring refreshment in the pow-erful presence of God, who makes the life of the Open Door possible.

> As we rest and recreate and meditate and communicate with God, as we worship together, share the Lord's Supper, and wash each other's feet, we remember and experience and are conscious of Christ, the bright Dayspring, shining on us and sharing both the joy and the bitter sadness of our hearts. Truly God has come to the Open Door and set it free. Through God's tender mercy—in the gift of Dayspring Farm, in each other, and in the greatest gift, Jesus—the Dayspring from on high has visited.

Elizabeth's words not only point to the power of retreat, they also provide an apt summary of how faith in Jesus Christ permeates the Open Door and draws together its shared life and varied works. Much like the Catholic Worker, from which the community has drawn, the Open Door continues to see its life together as part of God's faithful, gracious action to bring human life to salva-tion, to a true human dignity and fulfillment in loving union with God. In this life, the Open Door joins with the Catholic Worker tradition in seeking first the Kingdom of God.

Reading List, Including Works Cited

Bennett, Lerone, Jr. *Before the Mayflower: A History of Black America*. 6th ed. Chicago: Johnson, 1988.

Boff, Leonardo. *The Lord's Prayer: The Prayer of Integral Liberation*. Translated by Theodore Morrow. Maryknoll, N.Y.: Orbis Books, 1983.

Bonhoeffer, Dietrich. *The Cost of Discipleship*. Translated by R. H. Fuller. Rev. ed. New York: Macmillan, 1959.
———. *Life Together*. Translated and with an introduction by John W. Doberstein. New York: Harper & Row, 1976.

Brueggemann, Walter. *The Land*. Overtures to Biblical Theology. Philadelphia: Fortress Press, 1977.

Campbell, Will. *Forty Acres and a Goat: A Memoir*. San Francisco: Perennial Library, 1988.

Davis, Murphy, compiler and editor. *Frances Pauley: Stories of Struggle and Triumph*. Atlanta: Open Door, 1996.

Day, Dorothy. *Dorothy Day, Selected Writings: By Little and by Little*. Edited and with an introduction by Robert Ellsberg. Maryknoll, N.Y.: Orbis Books, 1992.
———. *The Long Loneliness: The Autobiography of Dorothy Day*. 1952. Reprint, Chicago: Thomas More, 1989.
———. *On Pilgrimage*. With an introduction by Mark and Louise Zwick. Grand Rapids, Mich.: Eerdmans, 1999.

Gathje, Peter R. *Christ Comes in the Stranger's Guise: A History of the Open Door Community*. Atlanta: Open Door, 1991.

Hilfiker, David. *Not All of Us Are Saints: A Doctor's Journey with the Poor*. New York: Hill and Wang, 1994.

Hughes, Langston. *The Collected Poems of Langston Hughes.* Edited by Arnold Rampersad and David Roessel. New York: Vintage Books, 1994.

Hurston, Zora Neale. *Moses, Man of the Mountain.* 1939. Reprint, Urbana: University of Illinois Press, 1984.

Jordan, Clarence. *Sermon on the Mount.* Rev. ed. Valley Forge, Pa.: Judson Press, 1970.
———. *The Substance of Faith, and Other Cotton Patch Sermons.* Edited by Dallas Lee. New York: Association Press, 1972.

Loney, Randolph. *A Dream of the Tattered Man: Stories from Georgia's Death Row.* Foreword by Will D. Campbell. Grand Rapids, Mich.: Eerdmans, 2001.

Loring, Ed. *I Hear Hope Banging at My Back Door: Writings from "Hospitality."* Atlanta: Open Door, 2000.

Merton, Thomas. *Thoughts in Solitude.* 1956. New York: Farrar, Straus and Giroux, 1980.

Miller, William. *A Harsh and Dreadful Love: Dorothy Day and the Catholic Worker Movement.* New York: Liveright, 1973.

Myers, Ched, et al. *Say to This Mountain: Mark's Story of Discipleship.* Edited by Karen Lattea. Maryknoll, N.Y.: Orbis Books, 1996.

O'Connor, Flannery. *The Complete Stories.* New York: Noonday Press, 1996.

Pohl, Christine. *Making Room: Recovering Hospitality as a Christian Tradition.* Grand Rapids, Mich.: Eerdmans, 1999.

Prejean, Helen. *Dead Man Walking: An Eyewitness Account of the Death Penalty in the United States.* New York: Vintage Books, 1996.

Saunders, Stanley P., and Charles L. Campbell. *The Word on the Street: Performing the Scriptures in the Urban Context.* Foreword by Walter Brueggemann. Grand Rapids, Mich.: Eerdmans, 2000.

Stone, Clarence N. *Regime Politics: Governing Atlanta, 1946–1988.* Studies in Government and Public Policy. Lawrence: University Press of Kansas, 1989.

Stroupe, Nibs, with Inez Fleming. *While We Run This Race: Confronting the Power of Racism in a Southern Church.* Maryknoll, N.Y.: Orbis Books, 1995.

Taylor, Mark L. *The Executed God: The Way of the Cross in Lockdown America.* Minneapolis: Augsburg Fortress, 2001.

Vanier, Jean. *Community and Growth.* 2d rev. ed. New York: Paulist Press, 1989.

Van Ness, Dave. *Crime and Its Victims.* Downers Grove, Ill.: InterVarsity, 1986.

Wink, Walter. *The Powers That Be: Theology for a New Millennium.* New York: Doubleday, 1998.

Open Door Timeline

1977	Ed Loring, pastor of Clifton Presbyterian Church in Atlanta, and Murphy Davis, director of the Southern Prison Ministry, meet Rob and Carolyn Johnson.
JANUARY 1979	Loring and Davis visit Maryhouse, a Catholic Worker house in New York.
NOVEMBER 1, 1979	Night shelter opens at Clifton Presbyterian Church.
JULY 21, 1980	Ed Loring, Murphy Davis, and Rob and Carolyn Johnson sign covenant forming the Open Door Community.
NOVEMBER 1981	Andrew Young elected to the first of two terms as mayor of Atlanta.
DECEMBER 16, 1981	The Open Door Community opens at 910 Ponce de Leon Avenue, N.E., Atlanta, in an apartment building purchased from the Atlanta Union Mission for $150,000.
JANUARY 1982	First edition of *Hospitality* published. The first editor is Rob Johnson.
JANUARY 30, 1982	Soup kitchen begins at 910. Jubilee Partners help cook and serve.
NOVEMBER 19, 1982	First street action held, funeral procession and service for Jane and John Doe, from Five Points in downtown Atlanta to City Hall, to call for the opening of shelters.
DECEMBER 1982	The Open Door begins serving breakfast to the

	homeless. Within two months the ministry moves to Butler Street CME Church and continues there until 1998.
1985–86	Cofounders Rob and Carolyn Johnson leave the community.
1987	Construction begins on Underground Atlanta, a $142 million entertainment and retail center, following release of the "Central Area Study." The study calls for a "vagrant-free zone" in which homeless persons would be subject to harassment and arrest.
1988	Open Door leadership invites Jay Frazier, Ralph Dukes, Carl Barker, Willie Dee Wimberly, Willie London, and Robert Barrett to become partners.
AUGUST 1988	Atlanta hosts the Democratic National Convention, resulting in the arrest of numerous homeless persons on charges of criminal trespass or public urination.
JUNE 15, 1989	Underground Atlanta opens. Eight Open Door members and friends arrested.
NOVEMBER 1989	Maynard Jackson elected mayor of Atlanta.
JUNE 1990	Eight members of People for Urban Justice—including Open Door partners Ed Loring, Murphy Davis, Elizabeth Dede, and C. M. Sherman—begin occupation of the Imperial Hotel in downtown Atlanta to protest lack of affordable housing. The occupation ends July 3 with protesters' arrest.
SEPTEMBER 18, 1990	Atlanta wins bid to host the 1996 Summer Olympics.
NOVEMBER 1993	Bill Campbell elected to the first of two terms as mayor of Atlanta.
JULY–AUGUST 1996	Atlanta hosts the Summer Olympic Games.
1999	Grady Coalition forms in response to proposed increase in prescription costs at Grady Memorial Hospital. The coalition sponsors street actions and sit-ins to dramatize the need for health care among the poor.
2000–2001	Grady campaign continues.
NOVEMBER 2001	Shirley Franklin elected mayor of Atlanta.

Contributors

RUTH ALLISON was a partner at the Open Door in 1987 and 1988. She continues to work for peace and justice.

CHUCK CAMPBELL is associate professor of homiletics at Columbia Theological Seminary in Decatur, Georgia.

JOHN COLE VODICKA is director of the Prison and Jail Project in Americus, Georgia. He and his wife, Dee, along with their sons, Gabe, Luke, and Sam, are former resident volunteers at the Open Door.

MURPHY DAVIS is a partner at the Open Door and has worked twenty-five years among the homeless poor of Atlanta and on behalf of women, men, and children in prisons, jails, and on death row. She was educated in Brazil at the Colegio Quinze de Novembro, at Mary Baldwin College in Staunton, Virginia, at Columbia Theological Seminary in Decatur, Georgia, and at Emory University in Atlanta.

ELIZABETH DEDE, a fourteen-year resident and partner at the Open Door, now works as a community organizer for the Prison and Jail Project in Americus, Georgia. Since 2000 she has been a regular participant and nonresident partner in the Open Door.

PETER R. GATHJE is Associate Professor of Christian Ethics and Peace Studies at Christian Brothers University in Memphis, Tennessee. He became a friend of the Open Door while working on his Ph.D. at Emory University.

MARK HARPER was a resident volunteer at the Open Door in 1986 and 1987. He met his wife, Susan Grine, while she was a resident volunteer. Mark is now a Presbyterian minister and the father of three children.

ED LORING is a partner at the Open Door and a cofounder of the Grady Coalition, which conducts nonviolent protests to help ensure affordable health care for the homeless and poor in the Atlanta area. He holds a Ph.D. in church history from Vanderbilt University, where he specialized in American religious history, particularly churches and slavery.

HANNAH LORING-DAVIS is the daughter of Murphy Davis and Ed Loring. She was ten days old when her parents helped open the Clifton Presbyterian Church night shelter, and two years old when they moved to Ponce de Leon Avenue to begin the work and life of the Open Door Community. She is a graduate of Guilford College in Greensboro, North Carolina, with an integrative studies major in religion, diversity studies, and peace studies.

STAN SAUNDERS is a professor of New Testament at Columbia Theological Seminary in Decatur, Georgia. He and his wife, Brenda Smith, are good friends of the Open Door.

JOANNE SOLOMON was the volunteer coordinator and Hardwick Trip coordinator for the Open Door from 1985 until 1988. She now lives in Perry, Georgia.

LEBRON WALTON was homeless when he came to live at the Open Door. He had many gifts and skills, including training as a dog-obedience teacher. He trained the community dog, Zechariah, while he lived at the Open Door. LeBron found work at a chicken factory, and even though he quickly developed carpal tunnel syndrome, LeBron continued to work through the pain. He moved out of the Open Door and, sadly, became homeless again.

MARC WORTHINGTON was a resident volunteer at the Open Door in 1991 and 1992. He is an excellent classical guitarist and a fine cook. He and his wife, Sue, are nurses and practice in rural New Mexico.

Index of Names and Subjects

Moses, Sarah, 95
Moyers, Bill, 229
Mulligan, Joe, 40
Muscogee County (Ga.), 30

❖ N ❖

National Association for the Advance-
ment of Colored People (NAACP),
111
National Collegiate Athletic Association
(NCAA), 242
Nazarene Manifesto (Luke 4:16–30), 78
Nelson, Gary X., 180–82
Newark (N.J.), 109
New Deal, 69
New Hope House, 329
Nicaragua, 293–94
Niebuhr, Reinhold, 106, 312
Nineteenth Amendment (U.S. Consti-
tution), 69
nonviolence, practice of, 348
Nouwen, Henri, 40, 255
nuclear weapons, 314

❖ O ❖

Oakhurst Park (Decatur, Ga.), 267
O'Connor, Elizabeth, 229
O'Connor, Flannery, 91, 224
Of Mice and Men (Steinbeck), 296
"Oh Come, Oh Come, Emmanuel"
(hymn), 256, 258, 349
Olympic Games (Atlanta, 1996), 116,
120
Open Door Community: AIDS and,
59; alcoholism and, 290–91; critical
reflection and, 346; discipleship
and, 234; Holy Week and, 64, 207,
235–38, 239–40; Lenten practices
and, 226; living arrangements, 72,
239, 345, 348; Mennonites and,
194; neighbors and, 120, 325,
329–30; nutritious food and, 348;
origins of, 293, 341–42; partners,
156, 269; retreats and, 348–49;

uniqueness of, 221–22, 342–43;
worship and, 206–11
"O Sacred Head, Now Wounded"
(hymn), 230, 233
Other Side, The, 229
Owens, Joe, 35

❖ P ❖

Palm Sunday, 235
"Partridge Festival, The" (O'Connor),
91–92, 93
Passover Seder, 210
Patton, Becky, 184
Patton, Frank, 184
Paul: biblical writings of, 219–20,
319–20, 323–24; character of,
317–18; Reformation and, 310
Payne, Billy, 116
Peak Load labor pool, 281
Peasants' War (1524–26), 322
Pell Grants, 139 n. 1
Pentecost, 308
People v. Gary X. Nelson, 181
Peter, as disciple, 224
Philemon, Letter to, 323–24
Phoenix statue, 114
Pickens, Donna, 17
Pickens, John, 17, 235
Piedmont (Carolinas), 278–79
plasma banks. *See* blood banks
Plaza Park, 110, 115, 119, 236, 240
"Pneumonia grass," 114
Pohl, Christine, 215
Ponce de Leon Avenue, 267–68
"Ponce Pass," 64
Ponce Pub, 268
Pontius Pilate, 242
pony, as word, 94
poor: advocacy for, 317; attitudes to-
ward, 306–7, 315
Poor People's Campaign (1968), 97
Poor Richard's Almanac, 189
Portman, John, 115
Potts, Ed, 36
Powell, Louis F. Jr., 199

U.S. Navy, 270–71, 279, 288
U.S. Supreme Court, 185, 200
usury, practice of, 312

❖ V ❖

"vagrant-free zone," 58, 65, 110, 115, 179, 294, 307, 325
Valentine, Elaine, 119
Vanderbilt University, 339
Van Ness, Dave, 184
Veterans Administration Hospital, 270
Vietnam War, 270
visitation, as word, 257
Voting Rights Act (1965), 69, 96

❖ W ❖

Walker, Richard, 337
Wallis, Jim, 315
Walton, LeBron, 286–92
Warren, Michael, 226
Waters, Muddy, 159
Wayne County (Ga.) Correctional Institution, 155
"We Have Another World in View" (hymn), 208
wealth, disparities in, 122–23
Welfare Reform Act (1996), 123
Wells, Ida B., 48
Wester, Don, 22
While We Run This Race (Stroupe), 334
Wicker, Tom, 42
Wiesel, Elie, 316
Williams, Phillip, 36, 265
Williams, S. A., 295–300
Wimberly, Willie Dee, 35, 38, 263–66, 299
Wind, Harold ("Orange Man"), 35, 282–83
Wink, Walter, 223
"Witness against Executions" (Atlanta, 1977), 41
women: in ancient times, 169–70; Bible and, 340; oppression of, 170–71; violence and, 185

Women, Infants, Children (WIC) program, 316
Woodruff Park (Central City Park), 113–17, 236, 247–48, 325
works, theology of, 311–12
World Food Day, 292
World War I, 279
World War II, 249

❖ Y ❖

Yahweh: deeds of, 77–78; as name of God, 77
Young, Andrew, 109, 111–12, 119

❖ Z ❖

Zbinden, Louis, 184
Zechariah, prophecy of (Luke 1), 256–57
Zwick, Louise, 342
Zwick, Mark, 342
Zwingli, Ulrich, 308

Index of Scripture References

❖ Old Testament ❖